The Geography of Morals

The Geography of Morals

VARIETIES OF MORAL POSSIBILITY

Owen Flanagan

OXFORD
UNIVERSITY PRESS

OXFORD

UNIVERSITY PRESS

Oxford University Press is a department of the University of Oxford. It furthers
the University's objective of excellence in research, scholarship, and education
by publishing worldwide. Oxford is a registered trade mark of Oxford University
Press in the UK and certain other countries.

Published in the United States of America by Oxford University Press
198 Madison Avenue, New York, NY 10016, United States of America.

CIP data is on file at the Library of Congress
ISBN 978-0-19-021215-5

9 8 7 6 5 4 3 2 1
Printed by Sheridan Books, Inc., United States of America

To
P. J. Ivanhoe
Friend and Pioneer

CONTENTS

PART I

Variations

1

On Being "Imprisoned by One's Upbringing"

Ethics and Anthropological Realism

In 1991 I published *Varieties of Moral Personality: Ethics and Psychological Realism*. The aim of *Varieties* was to advance an emerging conversation between philosophers and psychologists by introducing moral philosophers to relevant work from psychology, work on temperament, personality types, different conceptions of the self and identity, moral development, gender and morality, social psychology, and the virtues. The guiding ideas were that there are multiple ways to live good human lives; that morality is fragile, subject to vagaries of temperament, personality, gender, class, culture, economics, and politics; and that moral ideals are typically pictures of what kind of person from among the possibilities one ought to be, where "be" is intended in a deep, existentialist sense. Moral ideals call on one to be a person of a certain kind, not just to act in certain ways.

This book, *The Geography of Morals*, is something of a sequel. To me it is "*Varieties Two.*" It might be subtitled "Ethics and Anthropological Realism" or "Ethics and Historical and Cultural Realism." The aim is to extend the argument for ethical inquiry that absorbs the insights of the human sciences and contributes to the human sciences, by bringing some of the main recent advances in culturally attuned moral psychology into conversation with cross-cultural or comparative philosophy. There are several reasons that compel me to write this book now: First, we live increasingly in multicultural, multiethnic, cosmopolitan worlds. Depending on one's perspective these worlds are grand experiments in tolerant living, worlds in which prejudices break down; or they are fractured, wary, tense ethnic and religious cohousing projects; or they are melting pots where differences are thinned out and homogenized over time; or they are admixtures or collages of the best values, norms, and practices, the sociomoral equivalent of fine fusion cuisine or excellent world music that creates flavors or sounds from multiple fine sources; or on the other side, a blend of the worst of incommensurable value systems and practices, clunky and degenerate. It is good for ethicists to know more about people who are not from the North Atlantic (or its outposts). Or even if they are from the North Atlantic are not from elites or are not from "around here." It matters how members of original displaced communities, or people who were brought here or came here as chattel slaves or indentured workers or political refugees or for economic opportunity, have thought about virtues, values, moral psychology, normative ethics, and good human lives.

Second, most work in empirical moral psychology has been done on WEIRD people (*Western Educated Industrialized Rich Democratic*) and there is every reason to think WEIRD people are unrepresentative, possibly the most unrepresentative group imaginable, less representative than our ancestors when the ice melted at the end of the Pleistocene (Henrich, Heine, and Norenzayan 2010).

Third, the methods of genetics, empirical psychology, evolutionary psychology, and neuroscience are getting lots of attention recently in moral psychology, but it would be a mistake to think that these sciences are superior to the wisdom of the ages in gaining deep knowledge about human nature and the human good. The reasons are principled: First, questions about human nature and the human good require sensitive attention to phenotypic traits, such as cooperation, fairness, compassion, altruism, peace, harmony, and flourishing and how these covary with each other across cultured ecologies. Great thinkers like Plato and Aristotle and, in the case of the present study, like Confucius, Mozi, Mencius, Zhuangzi, Xunzi, Buddha, Seneca, and Śāntideva, were sensitive observers of humans in their own times. They make empirical claims, most are testable; some have been tested. They also make normative claims about what one ought to be like and about what is good, good for individuals and good for groups. Some of these normative claims are similar to ethical claims made in North Atlantic traditions, some are not. The second reason why ethicists and social philosophers need to beware of excessive enthusiasm for genetics and neuroscience is because the human good is not a matter of what is just in the genes or in the head. Many of the great goods in human life are goods that are internal to particular practices and traditions, and emerge in particular relations among particular people at a particular place and time. Ethics is part of human ecology, and thus the sciences and disciplines relevant to ethics are not only sciences like evolutionary psychology, cognitive psychology, and neuroscience but also cultural history, sociology, and anthropology. Reading great philosophers from other traditions helps bring into view or helps keep in view the important fact that the particularities of different moral traditions matter. It also makes us aware of the space of possibility, and allows us to imaginatively envision how we might be if everything including ourselves were different, a bit different, or very different.

Surviving Twentieth-Century Moral Philosophy

In a volume celebrating his life and work on the occasion of his eightieth birthday, Alasdair MacIntyre offers this assessment of the overall state of moral philosophy in the twentieth century:

> For on the view that I have found myself compelled to take, contemporary academic moral philosophy turns out to be seriously defective as a form of rational inquiry. How so? First, the study of moral philosophy has become divorced from the study of morality or rather of moralities and by so doing has distanced itself from practice. We do not expect serious work in the philosophy of physics from students who have never studied physics or on the philosophy of law from students who have never studied law. But there is not even a hint of a suggestion that courses in social and cultural anthropology and in certain areas of sociology and psychology should be a prerequisite for graduate work in moral philosophy. Yet without such courses no adequate sense of the varieties of moral possibility can be acquired. One remains imprisoned by one's upbringing. (MacIntyre 2013)

MacIntyre's lament is that traditional academic ethics is defective in how it conceives the nature of lived moralities, and that, partly for this reason, is not up to the task of assisting in the practical, existentially weighty project of moral critique and self and social improvement. Traditional academic moral philosophy operates with an antiseptic and ecologically unrealistic conception of the participants in moral life. There is little sense inside much of moral philosophy that the 'I's and 'thou's, the 'we's and 'they's, the 'us's and 'them's engaged in moral commerce are occupants of worlds defined in part by gender and race, poverty and war, degradation, subjugation, and hierarchy, Hiroshima, Nagasaki, Rwanda, Somalia, the Nanking massacre, inflation, deflation, rape, cocaine, refugees, childhood leukemia, apartheid, caste, love gained, love lost, birth, and death as well as the long and weighty force fields of particular histories, languages, and traditions. We are born into worlds among Confucians or Methodists or Buddhists or Catholics, as Navaho, Shuar, Piraha, Hopi, Aztec, Ashanti, Akan, Massai, Dinka, Nuer, Yoruba, Sunni, or Shia, and we learn to speak, think, and judge, at least at first, inside these worlds. It matters that people enter the world or develop early on characteristic temperamental styles and personalities—for example, that people differ along dimensions such as introversion and extroversion, adventurousness, novelty seeking, and so on. It matters that contemporary American children's books model as an ideal, as an aspirational good, a certain happy face and happy mood—a "happy-happy-joy-joy-kick-your-heels" face and mood, while East Asian children's books model a face of calm and equanimity (Tsai et al. 2007a; Tsai and Park 2014). It matters, if it is true, that among twentieth-century Arizona Hopi deep male friendship is unheard of (Brandt 1954, 28–29). The concept of deep male friendship is understood by the Hopi men, they have a concept for it; it is just that there are none, and it is not clear that Hopi men think that anything is missing or wrong with their lives. It matters that Chinese people have the concept of "sibling," but that since the one child policy went into effect in 1979, there are fewer and fewer siblings, and consequently that the fabric of family relations has changed. It matters that some Achuar of Ecuador still practice a form of polygamy in which wives make meals only for their own children despite living in a communal house, and that a wife in labor goes off into the jungle by herself (with a machete to cut the umbilical cord) to give birth (Descola 1996). Although Achuar girls are raised to be nurturers of both their own family's garden and eventually their own children, sisterhood is not powerful during childbirth. It matters that certain people in the Himalayan region (also to lesser extents in Brazil, Kenya, Tanzania, and China) practice polyandry, where a girl marries several brothers, that they think this practice is fine, even good, nonexploitive, and that it does not in itself engender jealousy or fraught marital or fraternal relations. It matters that the Australian language of the aboriginal Dyribal classifies together women and fire and dangerous things (Lakoff 1987), and that among Gikuyu people of Central Kenya that women are classified with children, goats, and land (Wambui 2013).[1] How exactly it matters to sociomoral and political life at present in Australia or Kenya requires fine-grained multidisciplinary analysis.

How the latter facts or features of traditions, cultures, subcultures, and individuals ought to matter requires descriptive multidisciplinary analyses plus all sorts of critical fine-grained normative analyses, which requires exploration of the possibility space, both internal to the tradition and external to it. What resources are there internal to cultures that practice genital mutilation to see through them, to work around them, to end them? What resources do increasingly oligarchic and nonegalitarian states like the United States have internal to themselves to become (again or for the first time) egalitarian and democratic (Gilens and Page 2014; Piketty 2014)? And if there are no internal resources for sociomoral change inside a tradition, how do novel moral ideas or, what is different, external sources gain a footing—discovery, innovation, commerce, immigration, intermarriage, or revolution?

Virtues that engender widespread agreement when described abstractly can conceal disagreement and regimens of oppression when one gets down to the nitty-gritty details. Colonialist regimes always recommend certain virtues for those they colonialize. Sometimes these virtues are endorsed symmetrically. The colonialist and the colonized are both to be respectful and law abiding. But if one follows the money and the power one will see that these virtues and values disempower and insult the colonialized (Fanon 1952, 1963; Lear 2008). Whether respect, humility, and turning the other cheek are virtues or vices, modes of empowerment or opiates depends on the overall quality of a moral ecology, as well as why and for whom they are endorsed and whether and how the norms of application vary according to gender, status, ethnicity, and so on.

All actual differences across cultures and across individuals make a difference and not just for the descriptive side of ethics. Goods—moral, aesthetic, epistemic—are often internal to practices and traditions and possibly inter-mixed in unfamiliar ways, for example, in the way that Confucians aestheti-cize and moralize what some Westerners might think are merely matters of etiquette, or the way some Piraha of the Brazilian Amazon think that good people should believe their parents about how one ought to live and be, but not believe what unknown people or sources—for example, Jesus—say about how to be and to live (Everett 2009). Other Amazonian peoples, Achuar again, believe a good person should take ayahuasca to discover and then plan for the social role that he or she sees that they will occupy while tripping on the psychedelic during a ceremony (separate for boys and girls) around the time of puberty. These beliefs, practices, and intertwinings may not be for us, but almost everyone will think that some practices are good, bad, right, or wrong depending on how they are situated in a complex normative web that is partly up to the people who live inside or abide the normative web in question.

Moral Particularities

The standard philosophical picture of moral interaction and exchange is his-torically and ecologically unrealistic because it is transcendentally pretentious, conceiving the philosopher's vocation as identifying what is really good or right independently of history or culture. It is unrealistic in another respect. Persons not only live and evaluate in distinctive force fields of history and culture, which are often different based on sex, gender, age, ethnicity, socio-economic status, different personality types, and so on, but in addition most moral situations are highly particular. The picture of a singleton agent who assesses and judges moral situations alone, one dilemma at a time, is just em-pirically weird. It doesn't matter whether the picture is of a singleton rational assessor or a singleton emotional assessor, where the decision is made on the basis of the best reason or the strongest emotion. Neither is the case; the whole picture is wrong. Persons with deep, rich, complex inner lives are fully em-bodied and embedded in social worlds with long histories. We are conduits of traditions, participants and creators, but not by any means sole authors, of our lives. Moral responsiveness and moral sensitivity involve complex historical habits of the heart and mind, not winner-take-all competitions of reasons or desires in singleton agents. Part of the project is to provide a better picture of moral agents and agency.

Iris Murdoch (1967, 17–18) provides an example commonly discussed by philosophers who wish to emphasize the ubiquity of moral particularity.

A certain Mother in Law 'M' feels that her "son has married beneath him," and thus that the daughter-in-law 'D' is not good enough for her son. Over time M comes to think that her view of D is distorted, unfair, and may involve odd cultural expectations, classism, and a certain Oedipal possessiveness. "M tells herself: 'I am old-fashioned and conventional. I may be prejudiced and narrow-minded. I may be snobbish. I am certainly jealous. Let me look again." "Looking again" is the start of the process of "careful and just *attention*." The process of looking again takes time and effort until "gradually her vision of D alters and D is seen in a new way that changes everything." D is now "not vulgar but refreshingly simple, not undignified but spontaneous, not noisy but gay, not tiresomely juvenile but delightfully youthful, and so on."

The parable presents a complex but familiar kind of problem. An individual with a particular history is in a situation, which that individual sees from a particular cultural and historical perspective, as well as from a particular class, race, gender, and economic position. She is put off by her daughter-in-law. She thinks that her son has made a mistake and that D really is objectively unrefined. The problem is not a dilemma, not an emergency. But whether and how it is resolved, or not, matters greatly to the set of relations, the relational ecology it is embedded in, effects, even transforms.

Here is another example that has similar features: My father was born in 1925. He was shanty, not lace curtain Irish. He was an only child, lost his father as a little boy, was raised by his mother, a Catholic nurse, in a Jewish orphanage where she and my dad lived as housemother and housemate among the Jewish orphans. My father was a lieutenant in Patton's Third Army, won a Silver Star for killing six Germans with his machine gun when his unit was pinned down in battle, went to college on the GI bill, became a successful accountant, and the father of six children. He was a good man, but he suffered anti-black racism, a common enough version of that American disease that continues to affect almost all white people. But my father—I saw this all the time and knew it from conversations with him about civil rights during the 1960s—hated this about himself and judged it wrong. He also understood that it was almost impossible for him to purge his soul of all his prejudices and racial suspicions in his lifetime. What he did, and what I admire greatly, was that he tried never to convey his prejudice to his children, and I never heard him encourage or reinforce any racist comment. He saw that he could work for generational change even if not for complete change in himself in his lifetime. This was a noble and realistic response to the particularities of his predicament.

I've said that many, probably most, moral problems are particular, intertwined with history and culture, and not dilemmas or emergencies. Consider a situation I faced today in my hometown:

> *The Schizophrenic and the Professor.* For a decade I begin most days writing at a local coffee shop. I sit at the end of a couch. I am an elder and my

spot is something like an endowed chair at the shop. There are usually regulars to greet, a bit of chitchat, and then some work to do. There are also homeless people on 9th Street. I know most of them. Today, one fellow K., who is paranoid schizophrenic, came in, sat next to me and started to chant (imagine "Hava Nagila" in Gregorian chant) and bounce on the couch we shared. I hemmed and hawed mentally about whether to ask Keith to stop, and about how to ask if I did. In the cacophony, there was the coffee shop's music and K.'s music, which were not harmonious, and there were feelings of annoyance cross-checked by feelings of sympathy and concern, thoughts about the cold weather, walking the dogs later, picking up laundry at the cleaners, and a hundred other things all inside spans of seconds.

What I will feel, think, and do in the coffee shop today depends on my states of mind, on the particular ways my mental and bodily states interact with the particulars of what K. does, the multifarious features of the surround, and so on. As for what I should do, even if I am committed to a general moral conception that says maximize well-being or do what God would do, I need to be paying attention, picking up on as many particularities of what is going on as possible, to have a chance of doing what is best, of doing what the divine or a sage or a saint would do. And doing this requires perceptual skills, skills at reading other minds, and various virtues, a sense of compassion and justice, and so on.

Here are two other examples that occurred this week and that are of a familiar sort to me:

Ego Flattery. The beautiful woman who runs an artist collective, the Carrack Gallery in downtown Durham, suggested that I become a sponsor of the gallery. She mentioned that my name would be posted, en-plaqued, as a sponsor, a special patron. I immediately wanted to do this, to be that guy, "Owen de' Medici." Then I instantaneously thought that the amount that my beautiful acquaintance asked for, which I now wanted to give with pomp and ceremony, black tie, this beauty in her slinky red dress on my arm, and that I could easily afford, I had not thought of giving to any one or any cause, and that furthermore it could obviously do much greater good if given to the local Durham homeless shelter. It was not a close call in my mind even though I could hide behind the fact that Aristotle said magnanimity is a virtue. I felt bad that I had not thought about giving my money to any worthy cause, and bad that I leaned strongly for reasons I recognized as egoistic (my name engraved on a plaque, a lovely woman as well as many imagined anonymous others admiring me) to give the money to support the optional pleasures of rich white people like myself, and not the necessities of the motherless and fatherless, the unlucky, the drunks, the addicts, and the mentally ill souls who live in the shelter just blocks away. As I write these words I have done nothing about the situation, other than entered the space of self-work where my reasons and desires sit uncomfortably with my values, wanting and working some to be a better version of myself. (Update: I made a $5 monthly pledge to the Carrack, not exactly the kind of magnanimity that enabled the Italian Renaissance.)

The Annoying Colleagues. A friend has talked to me a lot over the past year, including this week over lunch, about her difficulties with two colleagues, x and y. She judges x to be thoughtless, rude, and a bully. She judges y to be a narcissist. She harbors resentment toward x and y. But she is confused about whether her feelings toward x are due to the fact that x is a jerk or to the fact that she thinks x is a jerk based on occasional jerky behavior. Upon reflection she tells me that x is not always thoughtless, rude, and a bully. As for y, she tries to judge the egomania as a disorder, a result of a difficult childhood or as overcompensation for low self-esteem or both, and not as willful, or a matter of reckless disregard for others or the common good. And she admits to having seen, once or twice, y behave as if y cares about some other individuals or a common project, independently of y's narrow self-interest. So she has some behavioral evidence from x and y against her negative global assessments of x and y as a bully and a narcissist, respectively. Furthermore, she thinks—I have encouraged this thought—that her possibly mistaken global assessments of x and y ought not to be so global, making her unable to receive x's and y's perceptions, thoughts, and observations from a neutral open pose. My friend is a good and conscientious person. She is working at loving attention. It is a difficult, ongoing project.[2]

The moral problems of life vary with age and circumstance, but they are mostly like these—matters of tender mercies, love, attention, honesty, conscientiousness, guarding against projection, taming reactive emotions, deflating ego, and self-cultivation.

There are still other points to be made about realism that attention to such moralities of everyday life reveal. What are the major practical moral problems? One might think reading philosophy that they are abortion, euthanasia, genetic and neural enhancement, and what to do when there is a runaway trolley and you control switches that determine how many people are killed by it. These problems are very important when they come up, and it is good to think about them. But they have two characteristics worth noting. First, they are not everyday or regular problems faced by most people; second, they have clear social, political, public policy, and legal dimensions, which is one reason it is wise to discuss them in groups, in seminars, and such. But there is a class of problems, such as the coffee shop problem, that do not have nearly so much of the social, political, public policy aspects, and that occur many times on a daily basis for most everyone. There is being kind to the barista or the bus driver, greeting people in a generous spirit, giving the dogs the exercise they need rather than giving them short shrift because one has so much to do, doing one's job the way it really ought to be done, being honest and present and loving.

This matters because by and large across cultures the meaning and significance of a good human life depends more on one's character, one's virtue, one's being in the intimate worlds of love and work and community than it does on one's views about what to do when there is a runaway trolley or a terrorist with secrets, or whether rich people should get designer drugs that make them even more gifted and talented than they already are. To be sure, issues like whether to have an abortion or to help a loved one to die are monumental when they come up. But when they need to be decided, what matters most besides what social mores and the law allow, which will, for better or worse, figure in whether one will feel confident or not, self-respecting or not with one's decision, are the sensitivities or lack thereof of all the individuals involved. These sensitivities are built over time in everyday ecologies where specific beliefs, emotions, norms, and ideals of decency, goodness, and excellence are practiced or not, encouraged or discouraged.

There is a further disadvantage to the level of grain at which practical ethics speaks: it allows philosophers to focus on, and then lament and fret about what others, rarely oneself, don't do or don't think about, about what public policy blokes and corrupt legislators and politicians have or have not done that should be done. There is little discussion in contemporary practical ethics of changing oneself, the one part of the universe that one has some actual control over. The last and best on that topic by philosophers was written by Stoics, Confucians, and Buddhists over one thousand years ago. To be fair, self-improvement, the therapy of desire, *techniques du soi,* are discussed in synagogues, churches, and mosques, and increasingly among neoliberals from the narcissistic pose of gaining calm and equanimity for oneself between bouts of living one's Type A life in self-help groups and zazen parlors, where one sits on cushions with other frazzled secular souls seeking to feel as one deserves, happy and self-satisfied.

MacIntyre's remarks come with a constructive suggestion. Ethicists ought to pay attention to what evolutionary biology, primatology (also the study of cetaceans), psychology, and neuroscience can teach us about the kinds of animals we are and the possibility space of human morality. And we should also pay attention to literature, history, sociology, anthropology, and philosophical work from and about other traditions. Otherwise, one is not aware of the full range of moral sources, not sensitive to the "varieties of moral possibility," and in danger of being "imprisoned by one's upbringing." Often we don't see the possibilities for becoming better than we are or the possibilities for better ways of achieving our ends. The space of possibilities divides into real and notional possibilities, changes that I could actually make in myself or my world, and changes that are practically or conceptually impossible for me or for people like us. But if I see no possibilities, then effectively there are none. And if I don't see that how I conceive the kind of person I am—a man, a white man, an American white man, an Irish American Catholic white man—is itself a space with dynamic shape, porous boundaries, and various points of leverage, then it fixes me and limits my capacities for change and growth in ways that might seem necessary, but that are not.

Ethics and Human Ecology

Are things better now than when MacIntyre voiced his concern about the failure of ethics to engage with everyday practice and with the disciplines that provide thick description and ecologically attuned explanations of the mores and ethos of the peoples of the earth? Do moral philosophers in the early twenty-first century pay more attention to work in literature, history, sociology, anthropology, and the other human sciences than they did last century?

In some ways, with respect to some of the human sciences—especially the theory of evolution, psychology, cognitive science, and neuroscience—the situation is improved. Ever since Darwin, attention to the evolutionary sources of morality has brought a plausible theoretical grounding to claims about ultimate sources of some moral foundations and sensibilities in natural history. Modern humans are approximately 250,000 years old, and many aspects of our social natures are ancient, selected for, and then maintained in lineages that include much older ancestors among nonhuman and hominid primates. Furthermore, for over 99 percent of our species' existence, until agriculture and animal husbandry coemerged only 12,000 years ago, we lived in groups composed of bands of 20–30; almost never before farming and domestication of animals did communities get larger than 130–150. One strong possibility is that most contemporary humans live in entirely new worlds in bodies and minds designed mostly for very different ones, the worlds for which the original equipment evolved, sometimes in nonhominid ancestors. Meanwhile, psychology, cognitive science, and neuroscience provide some knowledge about local generalizations and proximate causes. In such areas as social and political philosophy, which are continuous with ethics, attention to practice has always been the norm. Social and political philosophers work on such topics as disagreement, incomparability, incommensurability, identity, nationalism, inequality, race, gender, alternative conceptions of rights, justice, and desert, so they have typically kept their ears to the ground. But moral philosophy as an academic subdiscipline, especially in the precincts that are considered most rigorous, still favors and selects for Rubik's Cube–type minds over the sorts of historical and anthropological curiosity and critical political sensibility that are valued across most of the humanities, in many sectors in the human sciences, and in the adjacent territories of social and political philosophy (e.g., in critical race theory and feminist philosophy). If Anglophone philosophical ethics is increasingly attuned to speaking in evolutionary terms about ultimate sources (e.g., family loyalty is explained by kin selection), and also to the cognitive sciences in tracking local patterns (e.g., seminarians at Princeton Theological Seminary are prone to moral indifference if they are rushed), and proximate neural causes (e.g., oxytocin enhances trusting and caring), they are weak in paying attention to the force fields of history and culture.[3]

It is worth reflecting on the fact that in the twentieth century metaethics became the highest status area inside ethics the discipline, where the subject matter of metaethics is at two levels removed from ordinary moral life. The subject matter of metaethics is ethical discourse, language, and texts. The normative ethicist asks about right and wrong; they try to answer Socrates's question: How ought I—one, we—to live? The metaethicist, often motivated by the thought that the normative project is sweet, dear, old-fashioned, and premised on a fantasy that there is something sensible to say about what is good and right, asks instead: What (really) are Plato, Aristotle, Kant, and Mill doing when they speak in favor of a particular normative conception? What does ordinary moral discourse assume about the existence of moral facts or moral objectivity, where 'ordinary' means what is spoken in Bloomsbury or Oxbridge or Sydney by people like ourselves, well-heeled white, mostly male, folk.

On the other side, it is a disgrace of twentieth-century Western moral philosophy that it claimed a principled pretense, based on a misreading of Hume on "demonstration" in ethics, to treat the human sciences as concerned with the merely descriptive, the empirical, and the genealogical. The philosopher is the only one authorized to speak about the normative, the universal, and the transcendental. Philosophers enjoy the pretense of assigning to scientists the underlaborer role of describing and explaining morality, and themselves the role formerly assigned to the priestly castes (now exposed by the philosophers as charlatans) of prescribing, of being fully in charge of the departments of oughts (if, that is, there is anything sensible to say about oughts, which we— the philosophers—will decide in due course). This separation, this preposterous intellectual division of labor—as if it isn't everyone's most important task to figure out how one, I, or we ought to live—leaves even the best philosophers open to the charge that they operate in bad faith. They operate only or mainly with the resources of their own traditions, but claim to speak transcendentally. On this view, Anglophone moral philosophy sings the praises of the moral attitudes of the dominant educated classes, serving mostly as both cover and mental hygiene for people who judge themselves already as nice-enough to actually believe that they are nice-enough, and to conceive themselves as open to becoming even nicer, akin to learning to stretch a bit more in yoga, in some nearby world for people of their color and class. It leaves moral philosophy open to exactly the charge that postmodernism heaped on the discipline at the end of the twentieth century: Eurocentric, white, male, and elitist. This was not, and is not, false.

MacIntyre's own hermeneutic strategy has been to read moral theories as reflective of the culture from which they emerge (see his *Short History of Ethics*, 1966). Thus, he understands "the project of the Enlightenment," the project of grounding normative life in secular reason rather than in religion, cultural history, or political pedigree, as the latest poseur in the attempt to find the universal deep structure of morality, and to justify the morality it endorses, the morality of Enlightenment liberalism under the cover of that which is not contingent.

It wasn't as if twentieth-century ethics took an official stand against being psychologically, sociologically, and anthropologically sensitive and displayed no self-consciousness of its own historicity. But there was, and still is, a view that philosophy, real philosophy—"deep throat"—is distinct from history, including its own. And, of course, there is the view that normative ethics is autonomous and distinct from the human sciences, which merely describe and explain human behavior.

Richard Rorty, Charles Taylor, and Martha Nussbaum are important philosophers who, like MacIntyre, accept the historicity and contingency of the liberal moral philosophical project. Unlike MacIntyre, they endorse liberal morality as their tradition, the one they admire, and wish to advance and improve, each in their own original way, Rorty with an ironist's attitude, Taylor with communitarian convictions, and Nussbaum with a liberalism that attends to the role of luck and love in politics. John Rawls, in the decade after his monumental *A Theory of Justice* (1971) was published, took to emphasizing increasingly in conversation and in public talks that his theory of justice as fairness was not meant (or perhaps it was that it did not succeed) as a theory of justice that any rational person at any time and place would accept or endorse, but rather it was the one, possibly "just one," that people who were antecedently committed to forms of life such as those dominant in North America and Scandinavia would accept or endorse. That is, it would work for people who have already accepted that people were or ought to be "free and equal." Rawls was explicit about this point in *Political Liberalism* (1993).

Thus, it wasn't as if the points about historical and cultural conditioning were lost on the best philosophers of the late twentieth century, especially those working in Continental philosophy. But as philosophers like Rorty changed the subject and started a different conversation, orthogonal to mainstream analytic philosophy, and as MacIntyre and Taylor explored the deep and multifarious communitarian, not only liberal, philosophical sources of North Atlantic philosophies, and as Nussbaum and Amartya Sen did noble anthropologically, economically, and philosophically sophisticated normative ethical and political work, much of ethics continued in the voice of an unreflective ahistorical impartial observer who was authorized to speak about the way we think and the way morality is. But why believe in the first century after the human sciences were born that we knew enough about the history, psychology, sociology, economics, and anthropology of morality, that we know enough about the actual phenomena, to be able to speak about it, what we think about it, or to assume that there is an "it" there, or if there is that we know its shape and contours and function, its role in the larger ecologies of human life? Why think that those licensed to practice in the academic discipline of "philosophy" in the Anglophone world—a discipline with clear Foucauldian structure that literally disciplines reading, thought, imagination, and speech—know how to think and speak about what we think, where "we" invites the thought of being representative, or universal, or perhaps what a fully rational person would think or see in our practices or in morality as such.

MacIntyre's concern is that twentieth-century moral philosophy was disciplinarily narrow, unreflectively culture-bound, and psychologically, sociologically, and anthropologically unrealistic. His positive suggestion is for moral philosophers to be less parochial, to explore the resources of other traditions, other ways of being human, to study history, psychology, sociology, and anthropology. One reason is this: If normative ethics is to be helpful in the project of living well, of flourishing, of finding meaning and purpose, of leaving the world a better place, it ought to help us to be attentive, sensitive, and open to value, not cocky, overconfident, and closed to other ways of thinking and being. Many philosophers behave as if their job is to win arguments, leaving one's opponent defeated, maimed, and breathless. A better idea recommended by Simone Weil and Iris Murdoch among others, a decided minority, is loving attention, listening with openness to others, seeking connection, and discovery. Knowing where to go from here, how to go on, what to do next requires knowing what the possibilities are. But a tradition—liberalism or Confucianism or Buddhism or orthodox Islam, say, or a sect inside a tradition—often functions most efficiently by reducing the space of what is noticed as a possibility or an option. Read some literature, history, anthropology, or sociology and "the varieties of moral possibility" open up. Sometimes, perhaps especially in times of personal crisis, or a crisis in one's tradition, this is what is needed, knowing what others have done, tried, or thought in similar situations either in one's own tradition or elsewhere. How different would philosophy be if it worked as hard to hone patient, loving attention and respectful listening, really hearing the other, trying first and foremost to get the other as he or she is, as it does to hone the skills that barely conceal the cruelty and meanness of the modern verbal warrior? It is not optional for the philosopher even in times of "normal philosophy" to speak about morality without marking which conception he or she is speaking about and why. It is just not acceptable on any conception of honest speech that one gets to speak for a discipline or community or tradition, even for a person other than oneself, without explicitly saying that one is doing so. It is one variety of coercive speech to say that "we" think such and so, when my people and I don't. It marginalizes and silences the other.

A Real Revolution in Ethics?

MacIntyre's diagnosis of the state of play in twentieth-century moral philosophy is not idiosyncratic. In an important paper, "Toward *Fin de Siècle* Ethics: Some Trends," Stephen Darwall, Allan Gibbard, and Peter Railton conclude their comprehensive survey of Anglophone moral philosophy, mostly metaethics, over the previous century with these words:

> In the effervescent discussion of the desirability of moral theory, various camps express agreement that more careful and empirically informed work on the nature or history or function of morality is needed. Perhaps unsurprisingly, very little such work has been done even by some of those who recommend it most firmly. Too many moral philosophers and commentators on moral philosophy—we do not exempt ourselves—have been content to invent their psychology or anthropology from scratch and do their history on the strength of selective readings of texts rather than more comprehensive research into contexts. Change is underway in this regard, especially, perhaps, in the emergence of less ahistorical approaches to the history of philosophy. But any real revolution in ethics stemming from the infusion of a more empirically informed understanding of psychology, anthropology, or history must hurry if it is to arrive in time to be part of *fin de siècle* ethics. (1992, 188–89)

Darwall, Gibbard, and Railton mention work, including my own, that was, at that time, the early 1990s, atypical in being empirically informed and that does not just "invent their psychology and anthropology." And they say that topics like "the role of personality, emotions, identity, and self-concept in deliberation have also begun to receive increasing attention" (189). True.

There have been a variety of good signs since the fin de siècle paper. First, the trend toward psychological realism has continued and many philosophers, some empirically informed, and a few who actually do experiments, bring the resources of economics, biology, psychology, cognitive science, and even cognitive neuroscience to ethics. Meanwhile, many excellent biologists, primatologists, cetacean experts, developmental psychologists, game theorists, cognitive scientists, and cognitive neuroscientists claim plausibly that what they learn about the origins of morality in children, or about strategy in economic games, or the effects of certain neurochemicals on the emotions, is relevant to ethics. This is the naturalistic turn in ethics. Second, there are beginnings, really renewal, of a different but related trend. This is ethics that attends to the historical, anthropological, and sociological—to culture. This is the cross-cultural or anthropological turn. It is starting to take hold.[4] Such work aims to bring deep knowledge of resources inside the dominant culture, as well as resources of other cultural traditions, to bear on how we think about the questions and the answers of metaphysics, epistemology, and ethics.

But here's the rub: The trend toward psychological, sociological, and anthropological realism in ethics accompanied by increasingly sophisticated and thick descriptions of how different peoples ask, intend, and answer Socrates's question about what makes for a good human life, comes recently with a certain lean toward the view that substantive moral criticism and positive individual moral change are weak forces, and relatedly toward the view that the distinction between the descriptive and the normative is a thin and uninteresting one, that people pretty much are as they ought to be, given that the sum of causal forces is as it is. The idea that the values people hold, the virtues they admire and aspire to, and the moral psychology they have is explained by the human sciences is thought in certain quarters to undermine the possibility that we can remake and improve ourselves. Max Weber anticipated this. He worried—well, really, he predicted—that the advances in the human sciences (*Geisteswissenschaften*) would take the wind out of the sails of "spirit," naturalize it, and thereby "disenchant" the world by undermining the view of ourselves as creatures specially graced to detect what is good and to self-orchestrate movement individually and collectively toward what is good.

Two major themes inside the moral psychology of the last century and a half are that many of the key forces that produce moral life are hidden in evolutionarily old equipment and in the taken-for-granted structures of social life that support fitness-enhancing strategies, the game to outscore others in the competition to get more of one's genes into future generations, and that, at the limit, the view that morality really has to do with the search for what is right and good is a cover, a fantasy, possibly among those in the know, a lie. Some read the evidence as support for a view of ethics as a strategic cover for fitness, self-aggrandizement, and the will to power, a view defended in Plato's dialogues by Thrasymachus and Callicles, and floated, if not endorsed, by Friedrich Nietzsche and Michel Foucault.

Two common but unwarranted and unfortunate tendencies in recent work in scientifically inspired reflection on ethics push toward nihilism, skepticism, and irrationalism, toward believing that ethics is just emotional noise, lacking in all cognitive significance, and over which reason has no power.

On one side, there is a strange assembly of evolutionists who are nihilists and think that we evolved to be on average nice-enough (Rosenberg 2011). Q: Nice-enough for what? A: Nice-enough to get by long enough to (maybe) get a mate, reproduce, and thus to maintain some proportion of one's nice-enough genes in the gene pool. Morality consists of strategies to get oneself, one's genes that far. You worry: But some not very nice people succeed at dating and mating, and their genes stay in the pool. For this there is therapy: There are fewer of these not-nice souls than there are nice souls, so relax, you are likely to be relatively safe. For the moral nihilist a statement like "killing innocents is wrong" is not about anything. In *Twilight of the Idols*, Nietzsche writes (whether he is endorsing the view as opposed to channeling it, is always an open question in Nietzsche scholarship): "There are absolutely no moral facts. What moral and religious judgments have in common is the belief in things that are not real. Morality is just an interpretation of certain phenomena or (more accurately) a misinterpretation ([1889, 8.1]; 2005, 182)."

For the nihilist, Hitler wasn't bad, just different, and I (we) don't like the way he was. There is no such thing as bad, good, right, or wrong. Some nihilists think that all moral statements that have the form of declarative sentences—"killing innocents is wrong"—are literally much ado about nothing. They are either empty like sentences about ghosts, phlogiston, the heavenly orbs, or the tooth fairy—fantastical—or they are globally false like the sentences of a physics that assumes the Ptolemaic view of planetary motion. "Look at the sunset" ("The sun doesn't set, you idiot; the earth moves into position so you can see the sun where it is!"). Or like sentences about the tooth fairy. The kids think the tooth fairy comes whenever a tooth is lost. But this is always and everywhere false. There is no tooth fairy. Thinking or saying he does or did come and leave money for a lost tooth is not empty. It is meaningful. It is just false. The sentence "The tooth fairy came!" might be interpreted to mean "I am happy that there is money under my pillow!" and "Hitler is evil" might be understood as "I hate Hitler!" but those glosses just prove the nihilist's or fictionalist's point that there is nothing objective about the tooth fairy or evil.

Another prominent view, and it is related, is that reason is impotent in ethics. Even if, contrary to the nihilist or fictionalist, it is true that "killing innocents is wrong" and true that "one ought not to kill innocents," these truths (true facts, rational truths) will not deter people from killing innocents if doing so pays well enough.[5] Q: How might it pay well enough? A: You might have really messed with me and my people in such a way that I want to crush you like a bug or you might have resources I really want. So revenge or gaining access to your highly desirable resources will typically override even the best moral reasons. Jonathan Haidt, a leading voice in empirical moral psychology who defends a view called "social intuitionism," declares that there is a widespread mistake in the way philosophers conceive the moral project. Reason "evolved not to help us find truth but to help us engage in argument, persuasion, and manipulation in the context of discussions with other people" (2012, 89). He writes that "worship of reason is . . . one of the most long-lived delusions in Western history. . . . The rationalist delusion . . . is not just a claim about human nature. It is also a claim that the rational caste (philosophers and scientists) should have more power, and it usually comes with utopian programs for raising more rational children (88).

Nihilism and skepticism about reason both overreach and rest on several shared mistakes. First, so long as there are reasons (of fitness, prudence, flourishing, well-being, goodness, badness, rightness, wrongness, etc.) that can be given for moral beliefs and norms, for why we favor certain values and virtues over others, then moral statements are given a defensible place inside a form of life and can be understood as both about something, and as true or false, minimally inside that form of life. Second, the disparagement of reason, the charge that belief in the power of thought, reason, and imagination is delusional, is most charitably understood as a mistaken reading of recent work on the power of a host of morally irrelevant features of the world, specifically irrelevant situations (situationism) or of certain fast-acting intuitive and ancient brain systems (intuitionism) on moral response.

The consensus is that irrelevant situations can affect moral response—a generally kind person will be less so if there is an annoying noise in the background. There is also widespread – but possible premature -- agreement that there are in the mind two systems, an evolutionarily old, fast-acting system that delivers quick (and what were at least once upon a time) fitness-enhancing responses ("grab your stuff and run"), and a slower system that comes in handy in waging war, doing algebra, and retirement planning. This dual process model is all the rage (Kahneman 2011). Sometimes the rational system, System 2, tries to get into the morality game, for example, you are a utilitarian and compute that you should push a single innocent onto the tracks in front of the runaway train to save the five darling children who are picnicking on the tracks. But you can't actually push the innocent (in time)—it creeps you out. You fail to do what you believe in, what you are rationally committed to doing, what your utilitarian secular faith demands. The darlings—future Mother Teresas and Nelson Mandelas—die. Ergo, Voilà, QED: All those years of philosophical training are for naught, impotent against the system inside you that evolved among ancestral species and just says "no" to putting your hands on conspecifics to force them into harm's way. System 1 defeats System 2. Gut 1; Reason 0. Game over.

There are several quick points. First, such situations are both extremely rare and ecologically unrealistic. Second, the case is cherry picked. Sometimes, reason overrides powerful gut-wrenching distaste. Most everyone will also hate pulling a switch that causes any death, but the overwhelming majority of North Americans think they should (and would) pull the switch if required to save a larger number of innocents than are "sacrificed." Third, the dichotomy between the two systems is simplistic since they are normally interpenetrative—my situation at the coffee shop involves a schizophrenic who bugs me (System 1), but whom I see as human, worthy of respect (System 2), and to whom I try to respond accordingly. Indeed, Kahneman himself says the two systems are a fiction. They mark a practically useful picture, but do not mark a real distinction in the nervous system, and thus not in the mind either. Fourth, there is no amazing new discovery here, indeed no real discovery at all. The picture of a mind that sometimes fights itself is ancient. Plato writes about it, Buddha and Confucius speak about it. Stoicism is almost entirely about it, and every Christian treatise—from St. Paul's brilliant letters to early Christian communities to Augustine's *Confessions* that deal with temptation—explores its insidious recesses, contours, and resiliency. Śāntideva, the great Indian Mahayana Buddhist, writes a treatise in the eighth century filled with practical tips for working one's way around what one is naturally inclined to want and to do, but which isn't worth wanting or doing all things considered. Fifth, the claim that reason is powerful is not a claim about the reason of singleton agents deciding momentous events by themselves, moral Robinson Crusoes. Reasoning is social and historical, something we do with others, and with the resources of human history and culture.

In any case, knowledge is power. Knowledge of human nature reveals strengths and weaknesses, foibles, and cognitive blind spots. It also provides, so I claim, a better picture of what reason, imagination, and various practices of self-cultivation and social criticism can do to make our ourselves, our lives, and our worlds better. There are no findings in the human sciences that should undermine confidence in the force of critical rationality to identify moral strengths and weaknesses, to plumb the depths of moral psychology, and to honestly explore the genealogy of morals. Nor is there any basis for skepticism about the power of imaginative exploration of the varieties of moral possibility. Some of the varieties of moral possibility have been tried and tested, but perhaps not in our time. Most possibilities are unexplored, not yet conceived, and thus are terra incognita.

Thick description and charitable explanation of diverse moral worlds might make us more tolerant of the varieties of moral personality by helping us see why different people are as they are. There is also the matter of criticism and improvement. Persons in complex social worlds possess, develop, discover, and pass on powers and skills that can serve us to criticize forms of life we live inside of and to improve them. Powers of criticism and imagination are enhanced by seeing that others live in ways we might think are impossible. For example, it is a commonplace that anger is a natural emotion, that it is impossible to eliminate it, and that, in any case, some forms of it, for example, the righteous forms—against Nazis or racists—are good, even required (M. Bell 2013). Stoics and Buddhists deny all of this. If one doesn't know that much, that there exist actual communities that claim to have found ways around what we take to be necessary, one is in a certain sense imprisoned by one's upbringing.

So one aim is to defend critical reason, imagination, and creativity in moral life from the nihilists, skeptics, and those who claim that thinking is impotent against human first nature. Since I do not think there is a distinctive faculty of reason, or imagination, or creativity, I could just say that my aim is to defend thinking and reason-giving, the roles of thought, imagination, reflection, social exchange, and cultural critique in both justifying aspects of moral life and creating conditions for moral change, sometimes moral improvement. At the same time, I aim to provide an up-to-date evaluation of what we can learn from work in the rich vein of empirical moral psychology that is attuned to historical and anthropological differences, both intracultural ones that can be hidden by a dominant ideology, and cross-cultural ones to which we pay little or no attention, and to indicate some of the ways it opens up the resources of new varieties of moral possibility, resources for reflecting on the quality of how we are living and about possibilities for being better.

Three central themes that emerge from cross-cultural work and that frame the project are these: First, the right unit of attention for ethics is the whole person-in-communal relations, not person parts, say genes, or the emotional centers of the brain, or the rational parts of brains, not brains, period, but persons who seek to live well in relations with other persons in particular natural and social ecologies with histories. Second, shared human nature is insufficient for flourishing and vastly underdetermines the possibility space for human lives. Third, expanding inquiry beyond the resources of one's own tradition and upbringing is confidence undermining in a worrisome way only if one has been encouraged to believe that "we" have things more-or-less nailed down and other cultures are in various ways primitive, confused, immature, lost. A more ecologically sensitive and realistic ethical inquiry might help us understand why and how things among a people, a tradition, a group, a subgroup, are as they are, how they might be improved, and how insights and resources of other people and traditions might be for us, not just for them.

2

Moral Psychologies and Moral Ecologies

Normative Animals

Ever since Darwin, science has asked us to accommodate the idea that we humans are animals, specifically mammals, more specifically members of the genus *Homo*. We are not part animal and part nonphysical soul. We are 100 percent animal, with all that entails for our nature and prospects.

Modern *Homo sapiens* is about 250,000 years old and currently the only living species of the genus, whose members extend back between two and three million years. For comparison, the loggerhead turtle is 65 million years old and the hippopotamus is 50 million years old. Anthropologists have identified reliably about a dozen extinct species in the genus *Homo*. Neanderthal (*Homo neanderthalensis*) is a closely related species that roamed Europe as recently as 24,000 years ago and certainly interacted with us before we invented agriculture and domesticated animals 12,000 years ago. New evidence suggests that the diminutive *Homo floresiensis*, which some think may have been an offshoot of *Homo erectus*, lived in the South Pacific as recently as 17,000 years ago. In the autumn of 2015, a new species, *Homo naledi*, was confirmed based on skeletal remains in what looks to be a burial site, at least a body disposal chamber, in a cave in South Africa.

To think in Darwinian terms requires several things. It requires thinking historically, in terms of lineages with long natural histories. It requires thinking of lineages as coevolving with ecologies, often microecologies, high mountain ranges, equatorial forests, different postal codes, a particular street in a particular neighborhood, a family. Sometimes microecologies are discontinuous veins in a shared space coalescing around such features as age, sex, gender, sexual preference, ethnicity, education, or religious affiliation. Strictly speaking, there are no shared ecologies.[1] A family that raised clones would invariably offer a novel ecology for each child. The parents have changed in age and experience, there are the age differences among the sibling clones and the effects of sibling interactions, and of course the world outside is ever changing.

The nonshared features of what might seem to be a single ecology, but isn't, cannot be emphasized enough. We often speak in general terms about, for example, China, how the Chinese are, how they are raised, as if, at a time slice there is a coherent unified way of life and a single ecology named by the words 'China' or 'the Chinese.' This can be useful shorthand, a way of orienting ourselves to a certain geography and demography, a kind of political and economic life, a historical landscape. But it is only that, a handy typology that reduces the noise that would attend thinking realistically about China, which is strictly speaking cognitively impossible. There is no such thing despite the fact that we can say truthfully such things as that China— now marking features of a certain nation-state plus distinctions drawn by the Chinese government—is one of the least ethnically diverse countries in the world along with Australia and Argentina. But there isn't a unified or homogeneous ecology in China or almost anywhere else, at least not at any fine-grained level. Han Chinese constitute 90 percent of the Chinese population, but there are over fifty other, mostly indigenous, Chinese ethnic groups recognized by the Chinese government with their own histories and traditions. The most ethnically diverse countries in the world include New Guinea, India, Mexico, the northern parts of Central America, the western parts of South America, and all of West and Central Africa. In India, there are over two thousand ethnic groups. The US Census Bureau identifies only six ethnicities marked by racial characteristics, but America in fact contains a huge number of mostly exogenous ethnic groups, since the original peoples suffered multifarious degrees and kinds of extermination during colonization. Still, America is middling among the countries of the earth in terms of comparative human ethnic diversity. Nonetheless, the point about differences at every level of ecological grain obtains in countries like America with a common language and centralized government. An Irish Catholic growing up in New York in the 1950s and '60s grew up in a different ecology than his Jewish acquaintances and even than his Italian Catholic friends who attended the same school as he did.

***

Ecologies, microecologies, and micro-microecologies can be conceived as landscapes that receive, channel, and interact with organisms who enter the landscape, and who change and are changed by that very landscape. Here is C. H. Waddington's picture of a simple individual, represented by the ball, about to enter a fairly simple variegated landscape (see Figure 2.1). The probable trajectory of the ball and its probable endpoint are easy to see. Now for realism's sake, imagine a multiplicity of nonsimple individuals, balls with variegated dimples, carrying their own individual and social histories in the pattern of dimples, and entering into a much more complicated and variegated ecology from every direction with different initial spin. Such a picture represents the ecological situation across the earth and also the situation in many

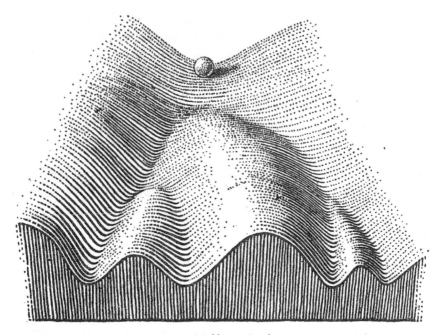

FIGURE 2.1 Waddington Landscape.

multicultural, cosmopolitan locales, places where lucky people come for new opportunities and unlucky people come to escape degradation, poverty, war, and genocide.

Thinking in ecological Darwinian terms requires thinking of species as consisting of particular individuals with distinctive natures, subject to normal variation. It requires thinking of all mammals—and probably all birds, amphibians, and reptiles, too, as sentient, as subjects of experience and thus as psychobiological individuals. And thus it requires thinking of being sentient, possessed of consciousness, as a natural trait, thinking of minds whenever and wherever they exist as fully embodied. It also requires thinking of *Homo sapiens* nonteleologically in two respects. First, nature did not, and does not, have our or any other species' success as its aim. Loggerhead turtles have done well for 65 million years, but are endangered now due to climate change. Neanderthals were short-lived, but, in addition to being less fleet of foot than we are, were possibly kinder, gentler, more heavenly creatures, and it is kind of a shame that they are not still around to model for us what was perhaps a higher standard of virtue. Second, biological evolution does not remotely specify what the prospects, fates, or ends of species members are, in the sense of what-we-are-designed-to-become or will become. A fertilized egg identical to that of Martin Luther King Jr. or Gandhi, or Sojourner Truth or Rosa Parks, or Einstein born at an earlier or later time, and in a different place, is a different person and not, as it were, one of those notable people, although we hope a good and worthy and successful person in their own right. Prospects, fates, ends depend on multiple sources, some in the individuals but most in natural and social ecologies. If some kinds of persons or communities create for themselves well-defined aims and purposes, these ends or aims have coevolved in particular ecologies with antecedent natural and social histories.

For most of human history we lived in small groups, typically 15- to 20-member bands, rarely larger than 150 people. Starting 12,000 years ago, with the inventions of agriculture and the domestication of animals, there was a rapid expansion of the size of social units and thus entirely new ecologies. There are, as I write, 20 cities in the world with over 10 million people and 350 with over 1 million people. There was no direct biological selection for being a farmer or a herder or a city dweller. We got lucky and adapted hunting and gathering skills that were biological adaptations to being eventually pastoralists and, for some, landed gentry and plantation owners. New practices in agriculture, trading, waterworks, and architecture allowed urban development. There was no biological selection for these things, although human psychobiology and natural and social ecologies permit them. Many good ideas are the results of coevolution, where the coevolution is only partly biological.

Consider literacy. Literacy is a common end of persons nowadays but reading and writing are recent inventions, only five thousand years old. There was no selection for literacy. In order to read we utilize brain areas originally selected (not even in our lineage but in ancestors) to track animals (Dehaene 2009). One way to put the matter is that literacy didn't initially matter one iota for fitness. It couldn't have. We were not literate for almost the entire history of our species. Furthermore, literacy does not seem to contribute to fitness, since there is an inverse correlation between fitness—as measured by birthrate, a proxy for inclusive fitness—and literacy. The birthrate is at zero or below in many parts of Europe where literacy is almost universal, and over 5 percent in places like Yemen and Niger, where literacy is low. Nonetheless, literacy seems to be really important for something else: human flourishing.

Finally, evolution allows, but does not require, that we think of the mechanisms that govern social and cultural evolution as operating according to similar mechanisms that operate on genes, for example, the regimen of selection by consequences according to which genes, ideas, norms, and social institutions increase their footprint, but perhaps only for a limited time in a particular place, when they lead to reproductive success or, what is different, to a successful solution to an ecological challenge, or to the flourishing of some population, those in power, the men, the whites, possibly, at the limit, everyone, as well as various serendipities, chance, drift, and randomness (Boyd and Richerson 2005; Richerson and Boyd 2005). One fancy capacity that humans, but not only humans, have is the capacity to create and maintain various kinds of normative order. The normative order uses both the capacities of individuals to acquire reliable dispositions inside themselves—typically conceived as virtues—to do what is judged to be good, right, or expected, as well as public institutions and structures, such as the law and tax codes, to accomplish, regulate, and enforce regimens of order and justice that individuals might not find easy to abide from reliable inner resources. We, but again not only we, are normative animals (de Waal 2006; de Waal et al. 2014; Whitehead and Rendell 2014).

Moral Psychobiology: The Briefer Course

We can now say with the confidence of perfect hindsight that the modern period in experimental moral psychology has two grounding texts. Jean Piaget's 1932 *The Moral Judgment of the Child* (1932) and Hugh Hartshorne and Mark May's *Studies in the Nature of Character* (1929–30). Whereas Piaget's text led to the first paradigm in the history of empirical moral psychology in Lawrence Kohlberg's moral stage theory (1981), Hartshorne and May's findings about the instability of such things as virtues and character, and the lack of predictive power of cognitive stages of moral development, have remained a thorn in the side of every attempt to provide a tame and orderly picture of human moral psychology, a picture that aligns moral thought and talk with the moral emotions and action, moral self-presentation and demeanor with inner feelings, which are as often dark, vengeful, and strategic as they are loving, and behavior, which is often amoral, immoral, selfish, and sinful.

Hartshorne and May discovered what was to become a cause célèbre several times over, first in postwar reflection on how good Christian people could participate in a holocaust (Adorno et al. 1950), then in academic psychology in the late '60s in a turf war between social and personality psychologists (Mischel 1968) about the stability of character and personality, and finally in the last decade of the century in philosophy, when the revival of character and virtue ethics was met with skepticism about the reliability, even the existence, of stable character traits (Doris 2002; Flanagan 1991; Harman 2000). What Hartshorne and May showed was that people are consistent in the moral traits they attribute to themselves, the ones they claim to have—I am honest, reliable, and courteous—but their behavior doesn't match. Hartshorne and May expected to find that there really are honest people and dishonest ones and that, for the honest people, what they say about themselves would correspond to how they act. Instead, they found mixed traits, of variable stability, with a gap between self-description and action, what impolitely we would call hypocrisy (C. B. Miller 2014).

Piaget meanwhile hoped to do for cognitive ontogeny what Darwinism had done for phylogeny, specifically to tell the story of the development in human children of the concepts or practical theories of space, time, number, causation, and morality. Piaget was influenced by a host of evolutionary ideas that were in the air. Besides Darwin's theory, there was still the attraction of Lamarck's idea that learned behaviors could be passed on biologically, and most importantly the idea that ontogeny recapitulates phylogeny – that human individuals are on a fast track to acquire in a lifetime skills that it had taken earlier ancestors a very long time to figure out.

The idea that the human mind might go through clear-cut stages of development took inspiration from the physical and biological sciences. Ordinary water goes through a global state change when it reaches 0°C (32°F) or 100°C (212°F), and changes to ice or boiling water. Butterflies go through four stages from fertilized eggs to caterpillar to cocooned caterpillar to butterfly. Frogs go through three, from fertilized egg to tadpole to frog, or four, if you count prince. Humans change in significant and visible ways, across a variety of dimensions, when they reach puberty, arguably in the same global sort of way water does when it freezes or boils. Piaget thought that a child's development from the fairly helpless not very mobile infant, to a toddler who walks and talks, to a youngster who glides gracefully across the soccer field and can predict when and where the ball and the other players are coming from and going to, shows something like global state changes as least as regards the way bodies in motion behave.

Piaget called his project "genetic epistemology." The aim was to plot the acquisition of various kinds of mostly "know-how" over the life span—knowing how to move through space without bumping into objects or falling off cliffs, having a sense of temporal order, duration, making reliable causal generalizations, and so on—given some fairly strong evidence that infants are not born with the stable structures that represent Peano arithmetic, Euclidean geometry, the laws of thermodynamics, and Newtonian physics fully online, as some might read Kant, the founder of cognitive science, as claiming (Flanagan 1984). The normal assimilation-accommodation process between the child and the world involves preparedness on the part of the newborn, to nurse, for example, and a not perfectly compliant environment. The particular shape of the mother's nipple and breast require the newborn to adjust the idiosyncratic way it purses its lips and opens its mouth. Eventually, normally pretty quickly, the newborn accommodates and assimilates, and comes to latch on to its mother's breast efficiently. As for eyesight, newborns are amazing with faces but have only 20/200 vision at best, approaching 20/20 at about 6 months. The newborn first takes in the world visually from its egocentric perspective. Because it doesn't yet stand or crawl, it doesn't get where things are; it doesn't get perspective, is not competent to judge distances, and so on. But eventually the child crawls, stands, and walks. Each transition in mobility produces new challenges, which the child eventually solves, and the child develops into a cognitively mature being, able to get around the world safely and soundly in all the familiar ways we do. Piaget thought that with respect to space, time, causation, number, and basic logic, children go through four global stages and reach cognitive maturity pretty reliably by their early teens. They have all the know-how that is required to get around and lead successful human lives.[2]

The Moral Judgment of the Child

Piaget called his book on moral development a "preliminary piece of work" (1932, 9). He realized that the moral world did not have the objective features of the physical world of space, time, and causation, but he wondered nonetheless whether it might display a developmental pattern, since logic and number theory displayed such patterns and arguably are not physical or material in the ordinary sense either.

Piaget's experiments involved observing whether the acquisition of moral norms such as govern fair play in marbles or telling the truth to parents showed a similar developmental pattern to that for physical concepts. His answer, using Kant's language of heteronomy and autonomy, was yes. Children, Swiss boys at any rate, are heteronomous moralists at first, yielding to the winds of their own desires unless countervailing forces are imposed by older boys or parents with access to carrots and sticks. Eventually, by twelve or so, they make moral judgments using the language of duty and obligation and see norms as vehicles that are freely chosen to produce various goods of social cooperation.

In 1958 Lawrence Kohlberg finished a doctoral dissertation at the University of Chicago that extended Piaget's work into a theory of six moral stages, which became the dominant model in moral psychology for the next forty years. Again with perfect hindsight, Kohlberg's stages mimic in certain respects a philosophical consensus then emerging about justice reasoning. Kohlberg often claims that his highest stage of moral reasoning is the same as that defended by John Rawls in his monumental *Theory of Justice* (1971),[3] and also that it is the same as that defended by the great German political philosopher Jürgen Habermas (1984), who argued that a just community is one in which every participant has an equal voice, which they use, what he called the "ideal speech community."[4]

Kohlberg proposed six stages in the development of reasoning about justice based on data from verbal responses to dilemmas about competing rights, duties, obligations, contracts, and promises. For most of the paradigm's reign, these holistic orientations or cognitive structures were called "moral stages," implying that they were suited to solving moral problems across all domains of life and of every kind. This turned out to be a big mistake.

Initially (stages 1 and 2), kids offer hedonist reasons for whether, say, it is OK to climb a tree to save a cat when one has promised Mommy that they will not climb the tree. From a young child's point of view, what they ought to do, or think a third party ought to do, depends a lot on what the very specific reward and punishment regimen is for cat-saving versus tree-climbing without permission or with Mommy's forbidding in place. Older children start to be more creative in practical wisdom, so they get that there are various social systems designed to deal with such emergencies (calling 911), and that various norms governing cat well-being and children-safety have rationales beyond their own immediate or future rewards and punishments, and they get that even good faith promises or prohibitions may have unstated exception clauses. Almost all children eventually reach a conventional and gendered understanding of moral considerations at stage 3 ("good boy" and "good girl" stage), where they start to develop a sense of what virtues are called for in various situations, so maybe one gets that Mommy would expect the good girl (one is supposed to be) to run to the next-door neighbor's house and ask the Mommy there what to do. Kohlberg, no fan of virtue ethics, because he thought virtues are culturally circumscribed and relative to situations, called stage 3 the "bag of virtues" stage. Plato and especially Aristotle—Confucius and the Buddha were not in his view—defended moral theories suited to various city-states perhaps, but did not see that true morality demanded universal moral principles. Stage 4 is a social contract stage, so, for example, when faced with a dilemma where a loved one will die unless you steal drugs from the selfish pharmacist who has them and will not sell at an affordable price, one will reason in terms of the right to life, the purpose of markets, ownership, the law, and so on. Stages 3 and 4 are where most everyone settles and are deemed conventional.

A small percentage of people reach Stages 5 and 6. These are the two post-conventional stages where considerations of maximizing utility (stage 5) and doing what is categorically right (stage 6) will replace reasons of hedonism (1 and 2) or being a "good boy" or "good girl" (3) or a conventional law-abiding morality (4).

Kohlberg (1971) argued that the six stages involve both a genealogical and a normative hierarchy, where numerically higher is ethically better, "more adequate," and thus expresses a philosophical hierarchy and progression. Stage 6 is a form of deontological reasoning about matters of justice, represented philosophically by Immanuel Kant, John Rawls, and Jürgen Habermas. Stage 6 is developmentally later than, and morally superior to, all varieties of consequentialist reasoning, represented by Jeremy Bentham, John Stuart Mill, and Peter Singer, which is stage 5. Next on down, come social contract theories at stage 4, Thomas Hobbes, John Locke, and Jean-Jacques Rousseau. Plato and Aristotle are the main exemplars of "bag of virtues" stage 3, but Hindu, Jain, Buddhist, and Confucian ethics, which are also arguably kinds of virtue ethics, would serve as well. Finally, premoral hedonists, individuals like Callicles in Plato's "Gorgias" or Thrasymachus in the *Republic*, who think morality is for losers, an accommodation to the power some others have to keep one from doing what one wants, are stage 1 and/or 2. To be fair, a child of naturally sweet, compliant disposition, who wants to conform to what others want is also at stage 1 or 2. Either picture, the child as scheming opportunist who grows up into the strategic moralist, but is really an amoralist or immoralist, or the child as sweet and innocent and out to please, is premoral.

Trolleyology

Kohlberg did not use trolley problems, a device first introduced by Philippa Foot for thought experiments, and now favored in contemporary experimental moral psychology (Edmonds 2014; Greene 2013; Mikhail 2011). But he easily could have. Like trolleyology, Kohlberg's paradigm asks for verbal responses to hypothetical dilemmas, normally emergencies, in which the subject is asked either what ought to be done, what one ought to do, or, what is different, what they would do. The first asks for a moral judgment about something in the vicinity of what is right, what I think is right, what explicit or implicit social norms say is right, whereas the second asks for a prediction about one's behavior.

Here are the simplest cases. In STANDARD (Figure 2.2) you happen to be at a switch at a railroad crossing, there is a runaway train headed toward five victims, you can SWITCH to the track with one victim. SWITCH? Yes or no? In FOOTBRIDGE (Figure 2.3): Same situation but you can ever so slightly nudge the man on the bridge off it so that he falls onto the tracks. He will die and stop the train from killing the five. PUSH? Yes or no?

FIGURE 2.2 Standard Trolley.

FIGURE 2.3 Footbridge Case.

Contemporary trolleyology is deployed to answer such questions as whether people who say SWITCH in STANDARD and DON'T PUSH in FOOTBRIDGE (in both cases the majority) are:

1. Reasoning as opposed to merely rationalizing after emoting by, for example, checking verbal reports against neural measurements of relative amounts of System 1, HOT, fast, unreflective cognition versus System 2, slower, more deliberate reasoning associated with structures in the prefrontal cortex.

2. Reasoning coherently and consistently across the two cases, as opposed to emoting in one and reasoning in the other, or reasoning using different rules of thumb or heuristics in each case or emoting in different ways in the two cases, say, because one's dynamic unconscious or reptilian brain parts deem one scenario as fear inducing (it runs on the same functional architecture that computes poisonous snakes) and the other as anger inducing (it runs on the same architecture that computes scary father figures), possibly unbeknownst to the subject.

3. Determining, assuming subjects are reasoning in accordance with general principles, which one or ones, the categorical imperative, the principle of utility, the principle that says do what the society expects, judges, or will judge most favorably, thinking about what Mommy or Daddy would say?

4. Determining which answers to the two cases are the right ones, the morally correct ones. Kohlberg thought this was determined partly on philosophical grounds that had to do with which stage was more

logically consistent and equilibrated and partly on grounds of the order in which they unfold, where again Aristotle loses to Locke, Locke to Mill, and Mill to Kant.

Kolhlberg plotted moral development by scoring verbal responses to dilemmas, often ones that are as ecologically rare and unrealistic as trolley problems, and without the benefits of the brain checks. But it is easy to see how he would have thought about and scored various responses to STANDARD and FOOTBRIDGE. A person who reasons consistently at the Kantian-Rawlsian stage 6 would see, or at least could see, the conjunction of SWITCH in STANDARD and DON'T PUSH in FOOTBRIDGE as universalizable according to several versions of Kant's categorical imperative, for example, act always in a way that could be made a universal law. Presumably, one could will without rational contradiction to always save the most so long as it doesn't involve actually killing anyone, as opposed to doing something that results in a death. If a person said SWITCH in STANDARD and PUSH in FOOTBRIDGE, then what stage they are at is to be determined by the kinds of reasons they offer for their judgment. If they say they would SWITCH in STANDARD and PUSH in FOOTBRIDGE because they imagined their mother would approve of those answers, they are at stage 1, 2, or 3. If they give the same answers but claim that these are the right answers according to a utilitarian rule that requires maximizing pleasure and minimizing pain, they are reasoning at stage 5. This is not the highest stage, but it is better than 4, 3, 2, and 1.

Joshua Greene, a contemporary moral psychologist and moral philosopher thinks that there are philosophical considerations that favor utilitarianism as a rational morality over Kantianism, and that such considerations in tandem with brain data that show that many people are just rationalizing after emoting from old brain centers when they say DON'T PUSH in FOOTBRIDGE (Haidt 2001; Greene 2013) secure the judgment that DON'T PUSH is the wrong answer. The right answers are SWITCH and PUSH, and for consequentialist reasons. Deontologists are fooled, and understandably so, by the intuitive force of old brain systems that yelp at the thought of harming innocents, but that are ill-equipped for a world in which there are runaway trolleys, scarce medical resources, soldiers and terrorists with secrets, modern wars to be fought, and necessary sacrifices to be made.

Different Voices

In 1982 Carol Gilligan, a colleague and collaborator of Kohlberg's, published an important and influential book, *In a Different Voice*, in which she argued that women who seem morally sensitive and morally mature do not speak as easily as men in a language of rights, responsibility, duties, and obligations, but rather in a language of care, concern, and compassion. And she argued that Kohlberg's moral stage theory was attuned to mature male moral voices, but not to the equally mature, but misheard, moral language of women. Gilligan's critique from inside the paradigm that it embedded gender bias was one of the main causes of moral stage theory's dethronement as the only theory in town. After Gilligan, a host of related criticisms caused the theory to unravel, except in certain quarters where it continues to be viewed as a credible developmental scheme for plotting something like justice reasoning, and in educational settings where nonegocentric perspective taking is rightly seen as essential to civic morality. Here is an incomplete list of some of the major criticisms that resulted in the paradigm's undoing.

- Moral stage theory embeds bias favoring certain ways of speaking that are gendered. In particular, moral stage theory, especially as a theory that plots development of better and worse ways of moral thinking embeds bias favoring the ways of speaking of white, liberal, well-educated men in the North Atlantic and its outposts, for example, Israel and Oceana.
- Stage theory plots development and maturity based entirely on verbal reports or judgments about what one thinks a third party (Heinz with the dying wife and greedy pharmacist problem or Holly with the cat in the tree and the promise to Mom problem) ought to do in a dilemma. Sentiments, emotions, and action are not studied. If sentiments and emotions are expressed in an answer they are not scored or they are scored down. Indeed, as much as 75 percent of what subjects say is not scored. Why? It doesn't seem to reflect reasoning.
- Moral stage theory uses prompts that are idiosyncratic and unrepresentative in three respects: (1) they are emergencies; (2) they are dilemmas, where there is a forced choice between exactly two options; (3) they involve problems of justice, fairness, duty, obligation, contract, and promise-keeping. Imagine that the child is not asked about whether she should save the cat in the tree given that she promised Mommy that she would not under any circumstances climb the tree, but rather is asked what she should say or not say, do or not do to and for a classmate whose cat has died. It is not clear what resources stage theory has to categorize ways of thinking about everyday kindness and humanity.
- Moral stage theory conceives moral decision-making individualistically. The dilemmas are to be solved by singleton agents. This is ecologically unrealistic. Committees at hospitals decide policies on organ allocation; government agencies deliberate about monetary policy; officers deliberate about costs and benefits

of military operations; and friends talk to friends about tough decisions.

- Morality is not a well-behaved natural kind, but there are better and worse answers to what it is, what falls under the ways of living and being that involve morality. Cross-cultural philosophy reveals that there are no places in the history of the earth where the domain of morality has been conceived to involve only matters of right—obligations, duties, promises, contracts, and such. What is there in morality besides greedy pharmacists, runaway trolleys, and children and parents who are breaking or considering breaking promises to each other? What other kinds of moral problems are there besides emergencies and dilemmas that involve issues of justice, rights, promising, and stealing? There are matters of moral perception, when, whether, and how one sees or fails to see what needs attending to. There is everyday civility, cooperation, and compassion. There is standing up for one's considered convictions, trying to do what is best for each individual kid as their parent or teacher. There is negotiating the intricacies of friendship, respectful interaction with people from different traditions and with different values. There is self-improvement and self-cultivation, and working out the overall contours of a good and meaningful life.

- Moral stage theory is largely silent on the mechanisms and ecological conditions that lead to moral development. Piaget modeled his genetic epistemology on ideas from evolutionary and developmental biology, but mature, Kohlbergian stage theory involves mostly hand-waving about mechanisms. There is allegedly a preset in the mind favoring the maximally inclusive, consistent, equilibrated general-purpose mode of moral cognition one can make one's way to. But there is no plausible story as to why such a preset would exist. The sociomoral world consistently asks the individual to accommodate its complex texture, and voilà, somehow, it does. But the answer to the question of why almost everyone is at stage 3 or 4, the conventional virtue stage or the conventional social contract stage, is because most ecologies encourage, reinforce, and expect people to be conventional. This makes it look like the preset is simply to learn the morality in one's actual world, not to go beyond its boundaries to test for maximal logical consistency or maximal moral sensitivity or attunement.

- Moral stage theory is transparently parochial when set against work in cultural and psychological anthropology. Richard Shweder (1990, 1991) offered evidence from other cultures that reinforced the criticism that Kohlberg's paradigm privileges liberal moral thinking, making reasoning about what is fair and just the main thing morality is about, and missing out on other central domains of ordinary human life and thinking that are alive in other traditions, and even in our own, but obscured by a certain picture that privileges theorizing about right. Ecological realism indicates that most moral problems across cultures involve everyday mercies, benevolence, compassion, and fulfilling communal obligations, often religious ones.

The Virtue Turn

This list of charges involving gender, class, and cultural bias, as well as privileging the theory of right over reflection about what makes for a good human life, might have been met effectively in a gamesmanship sort of way by the response that all these criticisms are descriptive not normative, and thus that such differences show that some types of individuals, women, or some cultures, South Asians, for example, have citizens who are not very morally developed. This move was blocked by the emergence of noteworthy defenses of virtue theory as both a more psychologically realistic model than any principled or rule-based theory of morality, and as normatively superior to principled or rule-based morality (Anscombe 1958; Foot 1978; MacIntyre [1981] 1984a, 1988; Hursthouse 1995; Hursthouse, Lawrence, and Quinn 1999; Annas 1993, 2011).

Defenses of virtue theory also opened up the possibility of non-Western moral philosophies being taken seriously both as credible ways of thinking about goodness, as well as rightness insofar as justice can be conceived as a virtue of individual persons rather than only a political virtue, and as a repository of varieties of moral possibility that we, in the West, had not ever, or not recently, explored for ourselves.

The cross-cultural perspective makes it easy to see how this could happen. Plato conceived the virtues of courage, justice, temperance, and wisdom, as necessary for good character, where good character is constituted by among other things an interactive set of dispositions to perceive, feel, think, judge, and act in the right ways given the situation. Aristotle in the same tradition added generosity, wit, friendliness, magnanimity, and greatness of soul. Aquinas added theological virtues of faith, hope, and charity to the list, while demoting the puffed-up virtues of magnanimity and greatness of soul, which he saw as too closely aligned with wealth and pride. All three philosophers required some sort of practical, rational oversight of the interaction, *phronesis*. This dialectic occurred inside a tradition.[5]

If one crosses to other traditions because of curiosity, trade, war, adventure, invasion, or nowadays by watching films, reading books and magazines, and listening to music, one will see alternative economies of virtue situated in different cultural ecologies. The Confucian list of ideal virtues consists of *li*, following the rites and rituals; *yi*, honesty and rectitude; *zhong* and *xiao*, loyalty and filial piety; and *zhi*, practical wisdom, which may or may not be closely related to Greek *phronesis*. Hindus meanwhile give pride of place to an unfamiliar mandatory virtue, *ahimsa*, nonviolence, and Buddhism calls on us to prize *karuna*, compassion, interpreted as alleviating ill-being, as well as *metta*, lovingkindness, bringing well-being to where there is ill-being, neither of which is the same as Christian *caritas* or *agape*. How such prized traits map or don't between traditions is an interesting and important question. Admiring a virtue from another tradition often expresses more than the admiration for the virtue alone. I may also be admiring the entire surround, the penumbra, the way of worldmaking that makes that virtue possible in the form it is seen and admired.

One move that a defender of global stage theory might make to the virtue turn is that virtue theories are always merely conventional. A virtue theory might be functional in the sense that if people develop the preferred virtues and abide them, the society in which they are embedded will be, at least might be, orderly, harmonious, peaceful, and well functioning. But that is because virtues are designed for order and predictability, not for goodness. That requires postconventional morality, being willing to break the rules when necessary. This criticism won't stick. A smart and effective moral community that has learned the lessons of history will work to create virtuous dispositions in its charges that are sensitive to cruelty, rights' violations, racism, and sexism. Magda Trocmé and Edith Stein were exemplary women who displayed great compassion and equanimity, and zero deference to the Nazis during the Holocaust. Dorothy Day, who with Peter Maurin founded the Catholic Worker Movement in 1933, was indifferent to the charms of money and fancy stuff, deeply compassionate, and willing to pay the price for her socialist and pacifist beliefs. In Vietnam in the 1960s Buddhist monks sometimes sacrificed themselves by self-immolation to protest colonialism and violence and give vivid witness to alternatives, to the superiority of the virtues of compassion and love, to the vices of greed and religious intolerance. One more set of examples: The Stoic and Buddhist ideas that we ought to work to eliminate anger altogether or the Jain idea that we ought to be attentive and attuned at all times to the well-being of every living thing are decidedly not parts of conventional morality, even among Stoics, Buddhists, and Jains. They involve visions of virtues that we do not have but might want to work to have, even if, at the limit, we cannot fully succeed.

The criticism that virtue moralities are utterly conventional—and that can easily be answered—is also commonly raised against role moralities. The objection can be answered on behalf of role morality, too. A role morality need not be conventional in the pejorative sense either. Consider the discussion in classical Chinese philosophy about "rectifying the names." Rectification is normally read as an ethical proposal as well as a linguistic one. One wants to use names like "ruler," "father," and "son" to refer to individuals who satisfy a certain social role plus a normative ideal. A ruler who is self-aggrandizing is not really a ruler; a father and son who are not filial are not really a father and son. Confucius says a father covers for his son and a son for his father (13.18). Mencius gives a different kind of example where a very rich and powerful son takes his father, a murderer, into exile, giving up everything (7A35). The son doesn't cover or conceal the fact that his father has committed a crime, nor does he fight the law, or deny its applicability in his father's case. He accepts the rule of law and its applicability to anyone who chooses to stay rather than go into exile, but he gives up the conventional goods of money and power in order to be a true son, not an ordinary conventional son. Another example of postconventional role morality occurs in Martin Luther King Jr.'s "Letter from Birmingham Jail" (1963). King addresses an audience of fellow clergy who wonder how he, in his role as minister of God, can engage in conscious civil disobedience. He replies that a true minister, one who really satisfies the role of minister, answers to higher standards than a conventional legal or professional code.

Sociobiology

I have said that in the second half of the twentieth century there was one paradigm in moral psychology, Kohlberg's moral stage theory. But there is another way to think about things that claims a second paradigm, which was better suited than cognitive stage theory to the Darwinian spirit of the times. Piaget's genetic epistemology was explicitly modeled on evolutionary thinking. But by the time Piaget's theory sketch for morality was transformed into Kohlberg's moral stage theory the link to evolutionary thinking had receded into the background. Mother Nature has yielded certain adaptations that make humans capable of acquiring morality. The initial settings contain capacities to make functional adjustments to the way sociomoral reality truly is, partly guided by dispositions to seek maximally rationally equilibrated principles.

In 1975 E. O. Wilson published his monumental book *Sociobiology: The New Synthesis*. The last chapter was called "Man: From Sociobiology to Sociology," and it was a powerful provocation to ethics as usually practiced. In rhetoric familiar from hostile corporate takeovers, Wilson asked his fellow evolutionary biologists to consider "the possibility that the time has come for ethics to be removed temporarily from the hands of the philosophers and biologicized" (562).

What does this mean? And why only temporarily? One possibility is that Wilson thought that once philosophers had been chastened they would start to pay attention and utilize the wisdom of the human sciences as opposed to garnering transcendental insights into what is good and right from cushy salons and named professorships in Bloomsbury, Oxbridge, Harvard, and Princeton, and they might be trusted again to assist in the important projects of normative ethics. There are many interpretations—some tame, some not—of what Wilson had in mind by biologizing ethics, and why exactly he recommended it, but here is a not too controversial account. The bulk of *Sociobiology* is taken up with synthesizing the neo-Darwinian theory of inclusive genetic fitness, which says that:

- Fitness is a matter of passing on genes, which can be done by having offspring or, as likely, helping the genes of close relations proliferate.
- Adaptations are dispositions that have been selected for because they tended, when they evolved, to make organisms that possess them fit.
- Many adaptations are terrifically well designed for individual fitness, for example, the postpubescent desire to have sexual intercourse or the disposition to fiercely protect one's offspring.
- Many adaptations—willingness to die for the queen of the colony or, in the human case, to protect one's village—are terrifically well designed for communal success.
- We should infer that the dispositions that appear reliably in human sociomoral life—for example, individual selfishness, altruism toward close kin, reciprocal altruism among unrelated people who interact regularly, but not between strangers—can be explained in terms of genetic selection. These dispositions evolved as adaptations, and they hold "culture on a leash" (1978, 71).
- Whatever ways genes hold "culture on a leash" it matters to moral philosophy because we had better, when we are thinking about new norms and practices, "test their conformity to the unchallengeable starting point" (1975, 562).

Evolutionary explanations could serve both to explain the origins of certain prosocial traits, parent-child love, fidelity to kin, fellow-feeling, and provide explanations for why it is difficult to expand human altruism as widely as almost every great world spiritual and philosophical tradition endorses, why selfishness is so resilient, why women with .7 hip to waist ratio and men with lots of money and .9 hip to waist ratio are desirable, whether hypocrisy is an adaptation, and so on. Human behavioral ecology, evolutionary psychology, evolutionary game theory, and the dual-inheritance theory of biological and cultural evolution are all research programs with clear connections to Wilson's influential work.

Wilson mentions John Rawls's program for political justice as one of the philosophical programs that might benefit from more attention to psychobiological constraints, "the leash" that genes hold culture on, and thus hold morals and politics on. Wilson says this about Rawls:

While few will disagree that justice as fairness is an ideal state for disembodied spirits, the conception is in no way explanatory or predictive with reference to human beings. Consequently, it does not consider the ultimate ecological or genetic consequences of the rigorous prosecution of its conclusions . . . the human genotype and the ecosystem in which it evolved were fashioned out of extreme unfairness. (1975, 562)

Wilson complains elsewhere that behaviorism and Marxism are impractical because they assume much more plasticity in our nature than there is. For Rawls, and Marx as well, enacting and stabilizing a just and egalitarian society won't work, because human nature is "fashioned out of extreme unfairness." Perhaps we can mitigate or rein in these forces, but we can't overcome them in the ways egalitarian normative theories require.

This argument is weak. First, even if it is a fact that our evolutionary past was "fashioned out of extreme unfairness," it doesn't follow either that we can't overcome such tendencies or that we shouldn't try to overcome them. Xunzi, in the fourth century BCE—and long before Kant—used the metaphor of the "crooked wood of humanity," comparing human first nature to bent and gnarled wood and to undisciplined metal that must be radically transformed to be useful, but that can be transformed by feats of human ingenuity, such as occurred over many thousands of years in woodworking and metal working. Second, there are evolutionary thinkers who think that for most of the species history, human evolution did not involve a "war of each against each," but very fair, although hierarchical, relations among small-band hunter-gatherers, and that even as we have left behind that small, tightly knit way of life, we are learning how to extend narrow sympathy and altruism more widely in new social ecologies made up of large numbers of strangers (Boehm 1999, 2012; Fry 2007; Tomasello 2009; Kitcher 2011; de Waal et al. 2014).

Wilson then fires this second arrow straight at the heart of every thinker in the Kant to Rawls lineage, which might also serve as a warning to an entire tradition of philosophers who give pride of place to arguments from strong intuitions: "ethical philosophers intuited the deontological canons of morality by consulting the emotive centers of their own hypothalamic-limbic systems" (1975, 563).

These passages taken together express perfectly a certain feature of the dialectic. Sociobiology, the new synthesis, as well as its descendants and offshoots, aims to provide an "explanatory and predictive" science about what human nature is, or tends to be like, if anything, deep-down-inside-beneath-the-clothes-of culture. Philosophers, who are not sensitive to the evolutionary biology that constrains the possibility space, recommend norms that are psycho-biologically unrealistic, even impossible.[6] To make matters worse, confidence in certain allegedly self-evident truths of morality—such as that economic and social inequality is wrong and that luck ought to be mitigated—that are given transcendental status as deliverances of pure practical reason by philosophers, are in fact emanations from emotional centers shared with long-gone social ancestors designed, and thus suited, only to govern social relations in small kin-related bands, or worse are emanations from some part of the brain shared with reptilian ancestors.

This project of describing and explaining the contours of first psychobiological nature is important, and it is continuous with the project of trying to depict the state of nature in Plato, Hobbes, Locke, Rousseau, and Hume in our tradition, and Mencius, Xunzi, and Han Fei in classical China, to major thinkers in the Hebrew, Islamic, African, and Hindu traditions, all of which are themselves multifaceted, mosaic-like (Carlson and Fox 2014). The neo-Darwinian synthesis provides a promising new methodological idea: The contours of first nature can be revealed by reconstructing what adaptations were selected for (or came along as free riders) in our lineage, possibly in long-gone ancestors, and that now reliably appear in human populations subject to normal phenotypic variation. Biological inquiry along with history, sociology, and anthropology might yield—I'd say it has yielded—an explanatory and predictive account of human nature, both the equipment favorable to the development of morality and the equipment that can be an obstacle to individual virtue, and to social and political harmony, economic equality, and so on. So there is nothing here to complain about.

But then there are complaints that the philosopher, specifically in this case Rawls, "does not consider the ultimate ecological or genetic consequences of the rigorous prosecution of [his] conclusions" (Wilson 1975, 562). On most every view, a just and egalitarian society in which people are more equal and less envious, egoistical, and acquisitive would be better for the environment and our genes, so it is hard to see what that complaint is even about. The crux really comes down to how plastic human nature is. That is something we do not know yet, the experiment is still unfolding. As recently as the turn of the previous century, most scientists and engineers did not think it was possible to fly airplanes as anything more than lightweight gliders, as largish kites. They were wrong. The evidence from cross-cultural philosophy, psychology, and cultural anthropology is that we are extremely creative at remaking ourselves within the constraints of the possibility space, whatever that is. There are multiple locations and levels at which to leverage our psychological, biological, and cultural natures, as well as the ecologies in which they are embedded in ways that help us achieve what is good, better than there is now or than we are now.[7]

Facts and Values

Let's pause and take stock. If my short history of the state of experimental moral psychology and the sociobiology of morals in the later half of the twentieth century is a credible one, then there are new resources to explain characteristic modes of moral judgment in certain ecologies given certain tasks—for example, data on verbal responses to dilemmas, either standard Kohlbergian ones or runaway trolley ones, as well as identification of multifarious adaptations that explain in part why selfishness is powerful, sharing with kin is not so hard whereas sharing with strangers is hard, happily married middle-aged men favor young women, and so on. We now have, we'll suppose, some biological explanations of human nature, of the extraordinary amount of attention given in the Vedas, the Bhagavad Gita, the Old Testament, and Greek tragedy to human war, conflict, genocides, generational grudges, fratricides, matricides, patricides, regicides, sadism, sexual peccadillos of every possible sort, and divine and karmic retribution. Why it is that Plato's sweet shepherd kills the king, takes the queen, and the kingdom the minute he finds the magic ring that renders him invisible, and why is it that Hume's sensible knave is only strategically moral—when he knows for sure he can safely take what is not his, he does? They are displaying a set of dispositions that enhances inclusive genetic fitness, not the dark mark of original sin, the effects of a bad upbringing on a moral blank slate, or bad karma. They are displaying biological adaptations, selected by utterly indifferent natural forces.

One worry that comes up when one accepts the scientific image of persons is that there is no normative place to stand, no normative perspective allowed in such a world. The scientific image says that we are animals who live out our lives in a material world. Some think the image is inherently disenchanting. The world is as it is, going where it is going, what will be will be, and thus a claim to see what is good or bad, better or worse, right or wrong, is just a way of claiming rhetorical high ground for ways of doing things that some group or individual likes or prefers. One is trying to nudge the way things are trending.

According to a standard view of the division of intellectual labor, moral psychology, primatology, evolutionary psychology, economic game theory, neuroeconomics, cultural anthropology, and experimental philosophy are entitled to describe, explain, and predict the aspects of moral life they study, while only the normative disciplines can tell us what we ought to do. On one standard view, philosophers, theologians, and shamans have insight into a world beyond the mundane one. But if there is no world beyond the mundane one, if there are no transcendental sources, then whatever it is that the "ought-ologists" are doing, it is not consulting that world.

One major aim of this project is to defend doing empirical moral psychology and comparative philosophy together on grounds that this intersection is a fertile and underestimated resource for making ourselves, both as individuals and as groups, better, more sensitive, more morally attuned than we are now. A key assumption is that exploration of the multifarious varieties of moral possibility provides material for reason and imagination to notice alternative ways of being and doing, and to sketch scenarios that might be improvements on our practices, values, virtues, and norms. I do in fact think that "oughtology" is legitimate and that everyone, not just the philosophical or priestly castes, should be encouraged to engage in it. I should therefore say something about the challenge that says that a naturalistic picture of reality undercuts the possibility of normative ethics as rational critique, leaving room only for ethical theorizing as disguised propaganda and emotional power plays by various interest groups, for example, priests or philosophers who are employed to maintain and feign transcendental grounding for the extant moral order.

One could give up altogether the projects of providing the reasons for epistemic norms as well as the standards of logic, good reasoning, and justification and, for the same reason, perhaps by explaining all normative speech acts along entirely expressivist lines, as noises people make when trying to get others to think and act as they wish for them to act. Both positivists like A. J. Ayer and poststructuralists like Michel Foucault were for different reasons attracted to a totalizing analysis of sociomoral discourse as hooraying and booing and power plays. This sort of global skepticism is a bad and unnecessary road to go down; we must take a different road.

The roots of the anxiety about the status of reasons and norms in a natural world had a dress rehearsal in Kant's worries about Hume's naturalistic approach to ethics. Perhaps therapeutic relief can be found by revisiting that moment.

Kant thought that moral psychology, sociology, and anthropology, what he called the "empirical side of morals," might tell us what individuals or groups think ought to be done, what they believe is right or wrong, what they think makes a good person, and so on. But all the human scientific facts taken together, including that they are widely and strongly believed, could never justify any of these views.

In the *Groundwork* ([1785] 2002) Kant writes that a "worse service cannot be rendered morality than that an attempt be made to derive it from examples." Trying to derive ethical principles "from the disgusting mishmash" of psychological, sociological, or anthropological observation, from the insights about human nature that abound "in the chit-chat of daily life" and that delight "the multitude" and on which "the empty headed regale themselves" is not the right way to do moral philosophy.

There are reasons of the right kind and the fact that everyone does such and such is not a reason of the right kind. Granny said that much.

What is the right way to do moral philosophy? We need "a completely isolated metaphysics of morals," a pure ethics unmixed with the empirical study of human nature. Once moral philosophy has derived the principles that ought to govern the wills of all rational beings, then and only then should we seek "the extremely rare merit of a truly philosophical popularity."

Kant is right that ethics should seek to provide reasons of the right kind and not, for example, do something silly like try to derive values, virtues, norms, and the like from facts, especially facts like everyone does such and such or that we, around here, are disgusted by the way you are, or think, or look. But requiring a "completely isolated metaphysic of morals" is an overreaction.

Consider this parallel. Humans, like many other animals, are born with inductive tendencies; imagine for simplicity that we are all born with the straight rule of induction up and running: If I observe that A goes with B to m/n%, I infer that the probability that A goes with B is m/n%. (Whenever I go east, there is always water there, so I infer with confidence that there will be water to the east tomorrow). The straight rule as given embeds tendencies to make mistakes based on small and unrepresentative samples. This causes practical trouble. But critters that use the straight rule can use it to sophisticate that very rule. Inductive logic, probability theory, statistics are eventually born. What happened? Nothing supernatural or transcendental, nothing based on a "completely isolated" metaphysics of logic. What happened was that better and better reasoning practices coevolved over long periods of time with successes in engineering, science, and political punditry and so on. If we had derived normative inductive logic and its mates, probability theory and statistics, from actual reasoning practices, the norms would have all the weaknesses of the original straight rule (as well as all the weaknesses that come from not reasoning at all).

Ethics works similarly. One common rationale for favoring a norm or set of norms is that it is suited to modify, suppress, transform, or amplify some characteristic or capacity belonging to our nature—either our animal nature or our nature as socially situated beings. The normative component may try to systematize at some abstract level the ways of feeling, living, and being that we, as moral creatures, should aspire to. The normative component of ethics involves the imaginative deployment of information from any source useful to criticism, self/social examination, formation of new or improved norms, and values; improvements in moral educational practices; training of moral sensibilities, and so on. These sources include psychology, cognitive science, all the human sciences, especially history and anthropology, as well as literature, the arts, and ordinary conversation based on ordinary everyday observations about how individuals, groups, communities, nation-states, the community of persons, or sentient beings are faring. Richard Rorty writes that the formulation of general moral principle has been less useful to the development of liberal institutions than has the gradual "*expansion of the imagination* [through works]"—like those of Engels, Harriet Taylor and J. S. Mill, Harriet Beecher Stowe, Malinowski, Martin Luther King Jr., Alexis de Tocqueville, and Catherine MacKinnon (1991, 207).

With regard to the allegedly insurmountable "is-ought problem," which leaves ethical inquiry to the priestly and philosophical classes who are in touch with moral reality, the key move is one of humility. Norms, virtues, values, best practices are not theorems. Certain practices, values, virtues, and principles are reasonable based on inductive and abductive reasoning. Indeed, anyone who thinks that Hume thought that the fallacy of claiming to demonstratively move from is's to ought's revealed that normative ethics was a nonstarter, hasn't read Hume (Flanagan, Sarkissian, and Wong 2008). After the famous passages in *A Treatise on Human Nature* about is-ought, Hume proceeds for several hundred pages to do normative moral philosophy. He simply never claims to demonstrate anything. Why should he? Demonstration, Aristotle taught us long ago, is for the mathematical sciences, not for ethics.

We are cultured mammals who think, imagine, and explore various parts of possibility space. We are lucky in ethical thinking to be able to use information from all the human sciences, as well as from philosophy and the arts. The arts are a way we have of expressing insights about our nature and about matters of value and worth. The arts are also—indeed at the same time and for the same reasons—ways of knowing, forms of knowledge, natural knowledge. Actually I want to say the same for sacred texts as well—Greek, Roman, and Egyptian mythology, the Talmud, the Bhagavad Gita, the Old and New Testaments, the *Analects* of Confucius, the teachings of Mencius and Buddha, and numerous others. Such works provide many of the deepest insights ever expressed into our natures and our goods.

I close with Dewey's insight that "Moral science is not something with a separate province. It is physical, biological, and historic knowledge placed in a humane context where it will illuminate and guide the activities of men" (1922, 204–5). What is relevant to ethical reflection is everything we know, everything we can bring to ethical conversation that merits attention—data from the human sciences, from history, from literature and the other arts, from playing with possible worlds in imagination, and from everyday commentary on everyday events. One lesson such reflection teaches, it seems to me, is that if ethics is like any science or is part of any science, it is part of human ecology concerned with saying what contributes to the well-being of humans, human groups, and human individuals in particular natural and social environments.

Thinking of normative ethical knowledge as something to be gleaned from thinking about human good relative to particular ecological niches will, it seems to me, make it easier for us to see that there are forces of many kinds, operating at many levels as humans seek their good; that individual human good can compete with the good of human groups and of nonhuman systems; and finally, that only some ethical knowledge is global, much is local, and appropriately so. It might also make it seem less compelling to find ethical agreement where none is needed.

I   Variations

Bibliographical Essay

1. On Being "Imprisoned by One's Upbringing"

In 1969 I read Margaret Mead's *Sex and Temperament in Three Primitive Societies* (1935), which was my first exposure to the idea that some things that are allegedly fixed are not. The first philosophical works I read that took anthropology seriously were Peter Winch's *Idea of a Social Science and Its Relation to Philosophy* (1958) and his *Understanding a Primitive Society* (1964). Winch had been influenced by Wittgenstein, Collingwood, and Simone Weil and took seriously the possibility that alien forms of life needed to be interpreted with loving attention, in their own terms, at least in the first instance, by the standards of sense and rationality that are internal to the form of life.

The anthropological, historical, cultural opening that Winch explored was decidedly side-stream. Analytic philosophy of the twentieth century generally operated with the Enlightenment pretense that the contours of ethics were to be worked out inside the traditions that had yielded the two heavyweight contenders for champion of the world, consequentialism and Kantianism. There were a few exceptions. Two mainstream analytic philosophers, Richard Brandt (*Hopi Ethics*, 1954) and John Ladd (*The Structure of a Moral Code*, 1957) were interested in Hopi and Navajo ethics respectively and wrote sincere but methodologically awkward books based on studies of the anthropological literature and some visits to the American Southwest. Then again both Brandt and Ladd wrote, as the philosophical climate required, with clear caveats that what they were doing was "descriptive ethics," merely anthropological, normatively inconsequential, except perhaps to Hopis and Navahos.

There are nowadays many sources that are working to displace overconfidence in the ethical forms that contemporary North Atlantic philosophy judges to be the finalists in the competition for the right theory, and in overconfidence in the universality of Western ways of thinking. The publication of Richard Nisbett's *The Geography of Thought* (2004) gave pause to the idea of universal cognitive psychology based on some differences between East

45

Asian and North American populations. "The Weirdest People in the World" (2010) by Joe Henrich, Steve Heine, and Ara Norenzayan was a watershed event. For all those psychologists who had joked that we had better hope that North American college sophomores are representative since all psychology is based on studies of them, the WEIRD paper gave an unambiguous answer. This population of Western, educated, industrialized, rich, democratic twenty-year-olds is about the most unrepresentative sample that one could find. Small-band hunter-gatherers, or Amazonian Natives, Inuit seal hunters, or nineteenth-century frontier people would be more representative of the average *Homo sapiens* than North American college sophomores.

As for undermining philosophical hubris: Alasdair MacIntyre's *A Short History of Ethics* (1966), which I read in graduate school in the 1970s, when I also met MacIntyre, was pivotal to my own thinking. It exposed a certain bourgeois pretense in orthodox mainstream ethics (MacIntyre's first book was *Marxism: An Interpretation*, 1953). Ethical theories can be read as much as reflections or reconstructions of dominant moral codes as they can be read as defenses of the atemporal, ahistorical, moral truth. MacIntyre's work showed the influence of Feuerbach, Marx, Engels, Wittgenstein, and Collingwood. By the time he wrote *After Virtue* ([1981] 1984a) and *Whose Justice? Which Rationality?* (1988), MacIntyre was working out views about moral change, moral conflict, and the incomparability and incommensurability of value systems, suggesting that moral change might be Hegelian, involving stark conflict then synthesis, or it might be Kuhnian, involving occasional revolutionary change or displacement of one code by another, or it might be Popperian-Lakatosian, involving competition among interacting moral codes where one code or form of life shows it has better resources to solve a problem or set of problems than its competition and supersedes it. Whether change in moral conceptions produces better or simply different lived conceptions and whether these changed conceptions are coherent and unified ways of thinking and being or helter-skelter kludges, Rube Goldberg devices, accretions of odd, not very well fitted solutions to particular sets of problems that somehow get the job done, is left open. It is one among many consequential questions for those interested in moral progress and whether and how it comes about.

There were several other important moments in twentieth-century philosophy that revealed powerful reason to worry about overconfidence in the Enlightenment project, of conceiving the range of credible moral possibility as a runoff between utilitarianism and Kantianism, both of course in democratic and capitalistic forms, which had independently been declared "winners." I have in mind not just the suppressed, marginalized work in critical theory, work in the tradition of György Lukács, *History and Class Consciousness* ([1923] 1971); Horkheimer and Adorno, *The Dialectic of Enlightenment* ([1947] 1972); and Adorno et al., *The Authoritarian Personality* (1950), but also mainstream work such as Bernard Williams's *Ethics and the Limits of Philosophy* (1985), and

Richard Rorty's *Contingency, Irony, and Solidarity* (1989). Both Williams and Rorty, in different ways, and for somewhat different reasons, suggested that in an antimetaphysical, antifoundationalist age, what Rorty conceived as times of "liberal ironism" in America, cocky confidence in any form of life was unwarranted, odd, possibly in bad faith. The difficulty, of course, is having proper humility in an overall way of worldmaking, and at the same time not suffering immobility when there are clear evils, harms, and injustices being perpetrated.

Action theory in philosophy, hermeneutics in literary interpretation, and *verstehen* in social science were reactions to a crude behaviorism. These movements emphasized the difficulty of understanding even simple actions inside a culture based on the observation that the same behaviors or bodily movements or words on a page might be, indeed often are, different actions or comprise different texts. In a wonderful 1971 lecture, "The Thinking of Thoughts: What Is *Le Penseur* Doing?," Gilbert Ryle invented the helpful idea of a "thick description" to describe the difference between a wink and a blink, scratching an itch and signaling that the coast is clear for the attack. Is Rodin's *Le Penseur* thinking or modeling thinking, in deep thought or posing as if he is thinking? What about Rodin's model for *Le Penseur*, was he really thinking or just pretending to think? Did Rodin recommend that his model really think in order to be a good model, an excellent simulacrum, or did he just ask him to feign thinking, as best he could? And supposing Rodin asked his model to really think, did he specify what he wanted him to think about, and supposing he did ("think about playing with your best childhood friend or what you wish to be when you are older or having great sex or doing the times tables"), how did he know that *le penseur* was doing that? When the natives are dancing are they restless, expressing fear, war preparations, or ecstasy? In *The Interpretation of Cultures*, Clifford Geertz (1973) embraces thick description as the right way to do ethnography. Patient participant observation, thick description, and the like seem to be the right, the respectful ways to understand cultures and cultural groups. They might, if anything can, allow entry into a form of life that is alien and permit experiencing what it is like to be a local, what the world seems like when one embodies "local knowledge."

In addition to anthropological sources, there are also literary and philosophical ways to reveal and express what it is like to be a diminished people, to experience one's self, one's world, one's values in the ways of an oppressed group or people. Frantz Fanon's *Black Skin, White Masks* (1952) and *The Wretched of the Earth* (1963) and Simone de Beauvoir's *The Second Sex* ([1949] 2010) are classics of this genre.

There were a few other books in the 1980s and 1990s that pointed the way toward an anthropologically sensitive ethics. Two stand out in my own formation: David Wong's *Moral Relativity* (1984) is one of the first brave attempts by an analytic philosopher to get inside three forms of life: liberal American, Taoist, and Confucian. Richard Shweder's, *Thinking Through Cultures* (1991) is a deep comparative exploration of moral psychology in India and America, which, like Wong's book, opens up questions of relativism as well as the relation between the surface structure of a morality and its deep structure. Shweder and Le Vine's (eds.) *Culture Theory* (1984) was another early foray into cultural psychology, an inquiry into how subjective experience and social practices interpenetrate, cocreate, and sustain each other.

Finally, Lawrence Blum's *Friendship, Altruism, and Morality* (1980) and many of the papers eventually collected in his *Moral Perception and Particularity* (1994) were important in making me aware of Iris Murdoch and Simone Weil as guides, and to the philosophical importance of both loving attention and moral particularity.

2. Moral Psychologies and Moral Ecologies

I was fortunate as a young man to be involved in three debates about how the moral mind co-evolves with the body and the social environment. The first concerned the effects of sex and gender on morality; the second the relative effects of character versus situations; the third about human animal nature and the ways it shapes moral psychology. I first turned to philosophy to think through whether and how I could make consistent my commitments to both the scientific image of persons as gregarious social mammals and the humanistic image of persons as meaning makers, who seek the true, the good, and the beautiful.

JUSTICE, CARE, AND GENDER

In the 1970s while trying to complete my doctoral dissertation, a philosophical history of B. F. Skinner's radical behaviorism, I took a job at Phillips Academy, a boarding school in Andover, Massachusetts. The headmaster, Ted Sizer, had been dean at Harvard's Graduate School of Education, and introduced me to Lawrence Kohlberg's work, which at the time was all the rage. I set to reading many of Kohlberg's major papers. For philosophers, I strongly recommend "From 'Is to Ought': How to Commit the Naturalistic Fallacy and Get Away with It in Moral Development" (1971) and "The Claim to Adequacy of the Highest Stage of Moral Judgment" (1973), which was published in *Journal of Philosophy*. Jean Piaget's 1932 book *The Moral Judgment of the Child* is a great read, which besides showing the strong influence of Kant in modeling the moral domain, also opens up children's play as an important, underestimated location of moral formation.

In the late 1970s Carol Gilligan started publishing the papers that led eventually to her wildly popular book *In a Different Voice* (1982). The best single collection of philosophical responses to the debate as it unfolded is Eva Feder

Kittay and Diana T. Meyers's *Women and Moral Theory* (1987). Nel Noddings's *Caring: A Feminine Approach to Ethics and Moral Education* (1984) and Sara Ruddick's *Maternal Thinking* (1989) were other founding texts of the broad ethics of care movement, which has contemporary philosophical advocates represented by Eva Feder Kittay's *Love's Labor* (1999) and Michael Slote's *The Ethics of Care and Empathy* (2007). One worry about ethics of care approaches is that they seem sometimes to fall for the temptation of thinking that there is one set of dispositions, the ones in the class comprising love, care, compassion, sympathy, empathy, and fellow-feeling, that can do all or most of the work of morality.

CHARACTERS AND SITUATIONS

The important work of Hartshorne and May eventually yielded a debate in psychology that was over by 1968 about which was stronger—situational influences or character traits, inner or outer forces? That was the year that Walter Mischel published *Personality and Assessment* and answered they both mattered. In 1991 I published *Varieties of Moral Personality*, which provided an updated analysis of the psychological research on situations and traits, personality, and character dispositions. I pointed out that this debate was relevant to the recent revival of virtue and character ethics, but only for the form of virtue theory that almost no one held: that virtues could withstand all situational effects. Gil Harman in "The Nonexistence of Character Traits" (2000) and John Doris in his book *Lack of Character* (2002) took the same research to entail a more extreme view. I personally thought this was much ado about nothing, hyperbole that would be resolved in philosophy in more or less the same way it was in 1968 in psychology. It has been. There are dispositions and there are situations. They interact in complex ways. My still temperate view on the implications of situationism is expressed in "Moral Science? Still Metaphysical After All These Years" (2009). Two excellent essays on comparative philosophy and the situationism debate are Hagop Sarkissian's "Minor Tweaks, Major Payoffs: The Problems and Promise of Situationism in Moral Philosophy" (2010) and Edward Slingerland's "The Situationist Critique and Early Confucian Virtue Ethics" (2011).

SOCIOBIOLOGY

In 1975 E. O. Wilson published his grand *Sociobiology: The New Synthesis*, followed in 1978 by his Pulitzer Prize–winning *On Human Nature*. I have a flash-bulb memory of where I was exactly, at a bookstore in Andover, when I saw the massive 1975 tome. I devoured both books and provided my assessment of the strengths and weaknesses of sociobiology in *The Science of the Mind* (1984; 2nd ed. 1992). Philip Kitcher's *Vaulting Ambition* (1985) is a fine critical assessment by a leading philosopher of biology. The best collection of contemporary reflections on the implications of the neo-Darwinian synthesis and the pros and cons of "biologicizing" ethics is Walter Sinnott-Armstrong's (ed.) *Moral Psychology*, vol. 1, *The Evolution of Morality* (2008).

THE SCIENTIFIC IMAGE AND NORMATIVITY

Wilfrid Sellars's "Philosophy and the Scientific Image of Man" (1963) is the classic source inside philosophy for the distinction between the manifest and the scientific images of persons, and for the idea that the ascendancy of the scientific image has implications for the normative zones of life. If science says there is no such faculty as pure theoretical or practical reason, then what becomes of the search for secure foundations for ethics or epistemology? The debate about whether naturalism deflated, possibly even defeated, claims to find firm, transcendental foundations for our practices, had a focal text in W. V. O. Quine's "Epistemology Naturalized" (1968). There Quine proposed that epistemology be "assimilated to psychology." Some philosophers interpreted Quine's suggestion as a recommendation that normative thinking was now out, done, over, kaput, and met his suggestion with alarm. Hilary Putnam wrote, "The elimination of the normative is attempted mental suicide. . . . Those who raise the slogan '*epistemology naturalized*' . . . generally *disparage* the traditional enterprises of epistemology" (1983, 229). And Jaegwon Kim said, "If justification drops out of epistemology, knowledge itself drops out of epistemology. For our concept of knowledge is inseparably tied to that of justification . . . itself a normative notion" ([1988] 1993, 224–25). I agree that it would be the end of the world as we know it if it were shown that talk of justification of ethical or epistemic norms is simply a quaint, old-fashioned way of speaking. And that in fact all there really are are various power relations that include flamboyant rhetorical maneuvers such as claiming warrant or justification for one's beliefs when there really is no such thing. The good news is that there is excellent work in epistemology that shows how talk of justification has a perfectly legitimate place in a world that lacks transcendental foundations. A few classics are Fred Dretske's *Knowledge and the Flow of Information* (1981), Hilary Kornblith's *Naturalizing Epistemology* (1985), Alvin Goldman's *Epistemology and Cognition* (1986), and Goldman's *Liaisons: Philosophy Meets the Cognitive and Social Sciences* (1992).

PART II

First Nature

3

Classical Chinese Sprouts

Philosophy of Psychology

In 1958, the same year that Lawrence Kohlberg defended his dissertation at the University of Chicago in which he exalted the enlightenment picture of the singleton, impartial, principled reasoner, Elizabeth Anscombe, the Oxford philosopher, penned these provocative words:

> It is not profitable for us at present to do moral philosophy; that should be laid aside at any rate until we have an adequate philosophy of psychology, in which we are conspicuously lacking. (1958, 1)

Anscombe does not say we lack an adequate psychology, although she thought this too. She says we lack "an adequate philosophy of psychology." She offers three connected objections to the Enlightenment picture of moral agency, which help us see what an adequate philosophy of psychology requires. First, the picture of a singleton, rule-governed, principled thinker who solves moral problems by applying a general-purpose moral algorithm is psychologically unrealistic. Most good people in real life do not reason with a general-purpose moral algorithm, either a Kantian categorical imperative or the principle of maximizing overall utility. Second, such reasoners—imagine everyone was Kohlberg stage 5 or 6—would be morally bizarre, speaking a language with no home, solving moral problems in an alienated manner, with abstract rules mediating their relations. No sensible person should want to live in a world in which all moral problems are solved by or justified by impersonal principles. There are reasons of love, friendship, communal solidarity, which are not impersonal. Most moral problems arise in personal and communal relations among individuals with complex shared histories and preexisting commitments of value and affection. They are not problems that can be solved even in principle by any rational person with the right principle. They do not involve any rational person, but rather particular you's and me's, who feel, think, and love.

Anscombe writes, thinking of the Kantian school which tries to secularize the language of duty and obligation that traditionally has its home in obligations to God, that "the concepts of obligation, and duty—*moral* obligation and *moral* duty, that is to say—and of what is *morally* right and wrong, and of the *moral* sense of 'ought,' ought to be jettisoned if this is psychologically possible; because they are survivals, or derivatives from survivals, from an earlier conception of ethics which no longer generally survives, and are only harmful without it." As for the stage 5 utilitarian, she has only this to say: "It is a necessary feature of consequentialism that it is a shallow philosophy" (10).

But, third, it is clear that she has reasons for thinking this: The consequentialist speaks in terms of maximizing pleasure or happiness. But such concepts as pleasure and happiness only find their meaning inside complex forms of life, forms with rich histories and cultural texture, and that are metaphysically and religiously opinionated about the nature of excellent human lives and, typically, how and why excellence has only a contingent relation to pleasure or happiness.

Anscombe thought modern Anglophone moral philosophy was a thin and unappealing gruel. She lamented the loss of richness and texture, what came to be spoken of in terms of "thickness" by Gilbert Ryle, Clifford Geertz, and Bernard Williams, in Kantian and consequentialist ethics and moral psychology, as compared with Aristotle's and Aquinas's thick character ethics and moral psychology. Everything Anscombe says in the essay indicates that she hoped that a return to character or virtue ethics might help provide "the adequate philosophy of psychology, in which we are conspicuously lacking."

We can ask with a half-century's worth of experience: How are we doing in the project of having an adequate philosophy of psychology that is, as it were, adequate in its own right, as a psychology—as an affective, cognitive, social, developmental, and anthropologically sophisticated psychology—and also, at the same time, as a conversation partner for robust ethical reflection? My answer is of the cup-is-half-full sort. Things are better now, and thanks in part to Anscombe's strong hint—perhaps it was a clarion call—for the rehabilitation of virtue theories and the ensuing broadly Aristotle-inspired conversation about virtue and vice, moral emotions, moral character, their contours, their fragility, and their social coloration and cultural situatedness. Even the considerable resources in Kant and Mill that speak of virtues and character have been reclaimed and rehabilitated. And, happily, there has been the increased openness in philosophy to examining the moral philosophies of other traditions.

We are advancing in the project of having an adequate moral psychology, especially if we cut ourselves some slack given that the problems here are very hard. They are very hard, among other reasons, because of the extraordinary difficulty of trying to understand the nature of such complex beings as ourselves by those very same complex beings in multifarious, experimentally uncontrolled, natural and social ecologies. At the moment—ever since the period that gave us diverse works like Hartshorne and May's *Studies in the Nature of Character* (1928–30), Jean Piaget's 1932 book *The Moral Judgment of the Child*, Theodor Adorno et al.'s *The Authoritarian Personality* (1950), Lawrence Kohlberg's (1958) stage theory, and Carol Gilligan's *In a Different Voice* (1982), as well as the emergence of the project to "biologicize" morality in the hands of E. O. Wilson (1975) and a generation of evolutionary psychologists (Barkow, Cosmides, and Tooby, 1992)—moral psychology is an incredibly rich area of research, and this is so in large part because of a tremendous amount of activity at the point where the ethology, biology, psychology, sociology, economics, and anthropology of morals intersect with and interact with philosophical ethics.[1]

One worry about Anscombe's charge to develop an adequate philosophy of psychology before proceeding with moral philosophy, and the impulse to respond to it, is that she seems to presuppose that the empirical, descriptive, and psychological, the human sciences generally, have some relation—in addition to revealing constraints on the possibility space—on normative ethics, on how we ought to be. But, the critic says: Hume taught, and G. E. Moore sealed the deal, that is-ought, facts-values, and the descriptive and the normative are entirely separate realms.

There is this easy reply: First, Hume taught no such thing. He made a purely logical point about deduction, demonstration, and necessity. You cannot deduce that murder is wrong from the fact that everyone hates murder; nor can you deduce that you ought to farm because you both need and want to eat. So what? Both are good ideas and for similar reasons. Second, Moore's argument that because one cannot define 'good,' what is good is not natural, is recognized by most everyone to be fallacious. Moore requires that we provide a reductive definition of 'good.' This cannot be done. But the problem isn't that what is good is not natural or that it is disconnected from the real world. The problem is with requiring reductive definitions in terms of necessary and sufficient conditions. One cannot define 'mammal,' 'chair,' or 'game' reductively either. But all mammals, chairs, and games are natural things and phenomena.

Insofar as Anscombe implores us to reconnect ethics with the human sciences, she is on the right side of philosophy, history, and the human sciences. Surely, our nature, our prospects, and our ends have something to do with how we ought to be. Too many philosophers continue to be resistant to becoming full participants in this fruitful interdisciplinary discussion, isolationist and rearguard, often because of prissy ideas about philosophical purity, as well as continued worries that Hume meant something different from what he meant when he wrote that one cannot derive or demonstrate "ought" from "is," which despite being true does not in any way suggest cutting the descriptive and empirical off from the normative (Flanagan, Sarkissian, and Wong 2008).

Multiple Seeds, Sprouts, and Beginnings

One way to explore the varieties of moral possibility, and at the same time to do better on the "adequate philosophy of psychology" front, is to reflect on such questions as these: What is human nature like, if anything, deep-down-inside-beneath-the-clothes-of-culture? What features of human first nature support moral development and which features hinder it?[2] What do various ecologies demand of persons morally? What, if anything, does morality demand? What sort of equipment is required for mature morality—the capacity to discern the conventional norms and rules in one's social ecology, the ability to reason in terms of some general-purpose moral theory, a set of well-honed moral habits, virtues, or an admixture of all of these?

There are among ancient and extant moral psychologies theories that conceive of original nature as egoistic, others that conceive it as altruistic; others as an admixture, naughty and nice, "the bipolar ape," as Frans de Waal (2005) puts it, part peace-loving, sexy, matriarchal bonobo, part sneaky, aggressive, vengeful, patriarchal chimp. There are theories that conceive us as moral tabulae rasae on which a moral code must be socially imposed and inscribed. Culture must teach from scratch "Thou shalt not kill," "Don't sleep with your siblings," "Don't lie, cheat, steal," "Share your toys," and everything else that it, the wider culture, judges is right or wrong, good or bad.

Some think that some moral dispositions are natural, for example, benevolence or fellow-feeling, which according to Hume would "increase tenfold" even if untutored in a situation of "profuse abundance," whereas other dispositions such as justice will only be invented if there is scarcity, in which case we discover their usefulness as a tool, a bothersome necessity. Others think that morality is a matter of discovery and acceptance by an open and unbiased mind of an independent moral reality. Still others think that this discovery is really rediscovery. We remember or recollect the morality already written on our souls or heart-minds.

In the remainder of this chapter and in the next three, I explore multiple sprout views or modular views of first nature. According to these views, premoral human personality is best described as composed of, or, what is different, as containing a set of relatively distinct dispositions, sprouts, foundations, or modules.

The Sprout Text

Mencius (Mengzi 孟子 391–308 BCE), the great fourth-century BCE Chinese philosopher is the first sprout theorist, claiming first that "human nature is good," which is irrelevant to being a sprout theorist, and second, what is essential to making him a sprout theorist, that there are four distinct sprouts or beginnings in our natures that in normal environments develop into the four most prized Confucian virtues: benevolence (*ren*, 仁), ritual propriety (*li*, 礼), righteousness (*yi*, 义), and wisdom (*zhi*, 智).

Here is a famous text from Mencius, the Jesuits' name for Mengzi, where he states his "four-sprout" view:

> Humans all have hearts that are not unfeeling toward others. Suppose someone suddenly saw a child about to fall into a well: everyone in such a situation would have a feeling of alarm and compassion—not because one sought to get in good with the child's parents, not because one wanted fame among their neighbors and friends, and not because one would dislike the sounds of the child's cries. [F]rom this we can see that if one is without the heart of compassion, one is not a human. If one is without the heart of deference, one is not a human. The heart of compassion is the sprout of benevolence. The heart of disdain (shame/disgust) is the sprout of righteousness. The heart of deference is the sprout of propriety. The heart of approval and disapproval is the sprout of wisdom." (2A6; see also 6A6)

The four sprouts or beginnings consist of dispositions (1) To experience concern, compassion, the impulse to help infants and toddlers in distress, which is extended eventually to one's family, village, nation-state, possibly to all humans, even all sentient beings; (2) To experience shame/disgust at shameful/disgusting actions—for example, lying in one's own excrement—eventually extending the associated feelings to all moral violations; (3) To experience an impulse to defer to humans or nonhuman animals who are larger or more powerful, which is eventually extended to those who are both older and wiser, and embodied by ritual practices (everything from manners to mourning rituals) that attune the heart-mind to receiving, maintaining, and passing on the wisdom of the ages; (4) To experience certain things as right or wrong, fitting or not, fair or not fair, which eventually extends to a mature sense of rightness and wrongness.

The core idea is that what we call character or conceive of as moral personality, even as genuinely unified experientially, or as an interactive set of virtues, norms, and rules, even as a unity of virtues, is, to some significant degree, the emergent product of the growth, regulation, moderation, modification, tuning, and suppression of ancient equipment composed of relatively narrow dedicated processors.

One variety of the multiple sprout view is Mencius's "four sprouts" view; another is the contemporary moral modularity hypothesis, what I'll sometimes call "five modules," which Jonathan Haidt, its foremost advocate, and echoing E. O. Wilson's earlier bravado about sociobiology, recommends as the key ingredient in the "new synthesis in moral psychology" (Haidt 2007).[3]

FIGURE 3.1 The Five Foundational Modules (Graham et al. 2013)

	Harm/ Care	Fairness/ Reciprocity	Ingroup/ Loyalty	Authority/ Respect	Purity/ Sanctity
Adaptive challenge	Protect and care for young, vulnerable, or injured kin	Reap benefits of dyadic cooperation with non-kin	Reap benefits of group cooperation	Negotiate hierarchy, defer selectively	Avoid microbes and parasites
Proper domain (adaptive triggers)	Suffering, distress, or threat to one's kin	Cheating, cooperation, deception	Threat or challenge to group	Signs of dominance and submission	Waste products, diseased people
Actual domain (the set of all triggers)	Baby seals, cartoon characters	Marital fidelity, broken vending machines	Sports teams one roots for	Bosses, respected professionals	Taboo ideas (communism, racism)
Characteristic emotions	Compassion	anger, gratitude, guilt	Group pride, belongingness; rage at traitors	Respect, fear	Disgust
Relevant virtues [and vices]	Caring, kindness, [cruelty]	fairness, justice, honesty, trustworthiness [dishonesty]	Loyalty, patriotism, self-sacrifice [treason, cowardice]	Obedience, deference [disobedience, uppitiness]	Temperance, chastity, piety, cleanliness [lust, intemperance]

For ease as we proceed in the critical comparison of Mencius's four sprout view with the modern five modules view, I set before the reader these two tables, which represent the architecture of the moral mind as conceived by "five modules." I will hold off in-depth discussion of it until the next two chapters.

Across the horizontal in Figure 3.1 are the five modules:

1. Harm/Care
2. Fairness/Reciprocity
3. In-group/Loyalty
4. Authority/Respect
5. Purity/Sanctity

The vertical columns list the four necessary features of each module:

1. They are designed to meet an evolutionary challenge (adaptive challenge).
2. They are naturally triggered by a certain class of situations (proper domain/adaptive triggers).
3. They can be extended beyond adaptive triggers (actual domain).
4. There are certain emotions naturally linked to each module, for example, compassion to children falling into wells as in *Mencius* 2A6 (characteristic emotions).

5. There are virtues and vices associated with each module, for example, caring or *ren* for harm/care on the virtue side; cruelty, sadism on the vice side.

Figure 3.2 provides a set of criteria for module-hood along the vertical axis, as well as the evidence for each. The claim that a bona fide moral module exists requires several kinds of evidence. Each hypothesized module,

1. ought to be associated with automatic affective reactions, for example, taking my toys makes me angry.
2. ought to ground common sense interpersonal judgments, for example, selfish kids and bullies are bad.
3. ought to be culturally widespread, ideally universal, for example, sensitivity to suffering is judged good, humane, normal; indifference to suffering is judged bad, inhumane, abnormal.
4. ought to show signs of innate preparedness by activating a characteristic perceptual-affective-cognitive-conative cycle, for example, you take my things, I am angry, think you bad, and want to hurt you.
5. ought to have a plausible evolutionary explanation, for example, powerful concern for well-being of kin or sexual jealousy.

Mencius is considered to be even more important than Confucius philosophically insofar as he offers explicit arguments for a Confucian way of life, including its ethics. He also differed from the Master in this way: Confucius described the virtuous person as a *ren junzi*—a virtuous gentleperson—where *ren* ascribes virtue generally. A *ren junzi* is a good person, generally speaking. For Mencius, on the other hand, *ren* is the specific virtue of benevolence, one of a team of (at least) four, which together constitute virtue or good character in the wide, general sense. Mencius claims that virtue comes from enhancing or growing four sprouts. Throughout *Mencius*, the book that bears his name, Mencius is both responding to and met in conversations by fellow philosophers who think humans are naturally moral blank slates (Mozi), or that there is a human nature but that it is not good. It is egoistical (Yang Zhu) or neutral (Gaozi) or "bad" in the sense that it is disorderly or undisciplined—not in the sense that it is mean (6A6).[4]

After the famous passage, 2A6, where he posits the four sprouts, Mencius says this: "People having these four sprouts is like their having four limbs." Later at 4A27, he writes that if one grows all four moral sprouts, all four limb buds, "then without realizing it one's feet begin to step in time to them and one's hands dance according to their rhythms." This passage nicely forces a question about the analogy. Do the sprouts of virtue relate to virtue the way the first steps of a toddler relate to adult walking, in which case the relation is smooth, natural, and something most everyone learns, or is the analogy to

FIGURE 3.2 Criteria for Modules and Current Evidence (Graham et al. 2013)

Foundation criteria:	Care/ harm	Fairness/ cheating	Loyalty/ Betrayal	Authority/ subversion	Sanctity/ degradation
Criterion 1: Common in third-party normative judgments	Playground harm: Nucci & Turiel (1978)	Catching cheaters: Dunbar (1996)	The Black Sheep effect: Marques, Yzerbyt, & Leyens (1988)	Disrespect for authority: Shweder, Miller, & Mahapatra, 1987	Food and sex taboos: Haidt, Koller, & Dias (1993)
Criterion 2: Automatic affective evaluations	To cruelty and violence: Luo et al. (2006), Cannon et al. (2011), Graham (2010)	To cheating: Sanfey et al (2003); to unfairness or inequality: Cannon et al. (2011), Graham (2010)	To ingroup betrayals: Cannon et al. (2011), Graham (2010)	To subversion: Cannon et al. (2011), Graham (2010)	To sexual violations: Parkinson et al. 2011; to degradation: Cannon et al. (2011), Graham (2010)
Criterion 3: Culturally widespread	Bowlby (1969)	Fiske (1992)	Herdt (1981)	Fiske (1992)	Douglas (1966)
Criterion 4: Evidence of innate preparedness	NHP: Hrdy (2009); Preston & de Waal (2002); Infants: Hamlin, Wynn, & Bloom (2006)	NHP: Brosnan (2006); Infants: Schmidt & Sommerville (2011); Sloane, Baillargeon, & Premack (2012)	NHP: De Waal (1982); Infants: Kinzler, Dupoux & Spelke (2007); Hamlin et al. (2012)	NHP: Boehm (1999, 2012); Not yet shown in infants	Not yet shown in NHP or infants
Criterion 5: Evolutionary model	Kin selection: Hamilton (1964); Attachment theory: Bowlby (1969)	Reciprocal Altruism: Trivers (1971)	Multi-level selection: D. S. Wilson (2002); Tribalism: Richerson & Boyd (2005)	Rank and dominance: de Waal (1982); Boehm (1999)	Disgust: Rozin, Haidt & McCauley (2008); Behavioral immune system: Schaller & Park (2011)

*NHP = nonhuman primates.

how those first steps relate to doing a waltz or a tango, or for that matter, the twist or the jerk (there really was such a dance), which also require passing through the walking stage, but require more talent, training, and virtuosity, and are less common and culturally specific? These sorts of questions about the distance between the initial settings and the desired settings, the degree of preparedness in the original equipment for the ideal, are important and on my mind throughout.

From these passages we can extract what is arguably the first text known, East or West, to express a version of the moral modularity hypothesis, actually two versions of moral modularity, a descriptive and a normative version.

> *Psychological Four Sprouts*: Human nature contains seeds for four different moral competencies.
> *Normative Four Sprouts*: Moral excellence involves growing all four seeds to maturity.

I'll not worry about differences between seeds, hearts, beginnings, and sprouts, but one could, and it might matter (Slingerland 2015). Furthermore, it is noteworthy that the response of alarm and compassion to the child about to fall into the well in 2A6 is not the response of a baby or toddler to another baby or toddler in distress, it is the response of a competent adult. It is good for a sprout view, although perhaps not absolutely necessary, that newborns show some form of the relevant disposition (see Hoffman 2000).

Contemporary moral foundations theory ("five modules"), makes it a requirement for positing a module that it display signs of innate preparedness (see Figure 3.2). But signs of a modular disposition in a newborn may not be absolutely necessary, so as to allow for sociomoral cases that might be like puberty or sexual coming of age. The adult forms of genital sexuality are not entirely visible in babies, even if one thinks babies are highly sensual, "polymorphously perverse," as Freud thought. We do, nonetheless, rightly think that coming of age sexually is developmentally normal, part of the maturational program, hard to switch off, even as its timing, robustness, and expression is subject to all the usual contingencies of fetal environment, diet, and social mores.

The psychological claim is that human nature contains the sprouts of compassion, shame/disgust, deference, and distinguishing right from wrong, each of which, to speak in an Aristotelian way, has a trajectory, a directionality, a proper function, an *ergon*, a potential, its *telos* that it seeks to actualize. These four spouts mature into the four cardinal Confucian virtues of benevolence (*ren*), righteousness (*yi*), propriety/modesty (*li*), and wisdom (*zhi*), or sometimes more, depending on whether integrity/fidelity/honesty or filial piety are added.[5]

The normative thesis says that growing all four is good, something we ought to do. Not doing so would be like trying to become a person with deficient, missing, or lost limbs. This can be done. Chinese foot binding was straightfor-wardly devoted to limb suppression, limb degradation, and this is one reason it is considered wrong. Some are born without limbs. They can compensate; but this is not considered optimal.

Assuming one grows the seeds properly, one is truly human and a good or decent person. A *junzi* is a gentleperson, one who embodies the mature versions of each sprout. One can fail to be fully human, or at least a fully de-veloped human, if any one of the seeds lies latent or dies (Van Norden 2007). Just as the loss or failure to grow any of the four limbs would lead to difficulty moving through space, loss or failure to grow any of the four Mencian sprouts will lead to difficulty negotiating sociomoral space; one will not acquire the ability to "dance" in the effortless and graceful (*wu-wei*) way that a morally well formed person does.[6]

Mencius's moral sprout view can be summarized as follows: Human nature contains four seeds or hearts or sprouts or beginnings that in a normal en-vironment grow into four distinct virtues, which taken together constitute, or comprise, or are the foundation of good character or virtue generally. The seeds are sympathy or compassion for benevolence (*ren*); shame and disgust for righteousness (*yi*); deference for propriety (*li*); and a sense of true and false, accurate and inaccurate, match and mismatch, approval and disapproval for practical wisdom (*zhi*).

Each sprout is an innate perceptual-affective-cognitive-conative disposi-tion that possesses the potential, the natural trajectory, to grow into one of the four cardinal virtues. If these sprouts are planted in a normal environment they will grow as the four limbs do. If they receive suboptimal nourishment, they will grow some; and if they are not nourished at all, they will not grow (6A8). The best outcome is that the four sprouts blossom into the four cardinal virtues. Barring congenital abnormality or abnormality in social conditions, the best outcome occurs and virtuous agents emerge.[7]

The Aims of Sprouts

So Mencius defends both psychological modularity and normative modular-ity. Although hardly anyone ever asks why it is a good thing that we have four limbs and why they are sized the way they are, it is instructive to consider what one could say if asked. One way to defend Mencian normative modularity for limbs would be to join his view with contemporary Darwinian thinking and claim that:

1. Evolution settled on four limb design (our kind of two arm–two leg design) because it was an adaptation = adaptation[historical];
2. This design is still adaptive = adaptation[current ecology].[8]

3. This four limb design emerges naturally in a species-universal way across normal ecologies; and thus,

4. We ought to grow our arms and legs the way nature designed them to grow.

The "ought" in (4) expresses the bidirectional agent-to-world goodness-of-fit between a universal phenotypic trait and the world (literally, the earth). If Mencius's normative four sprout view were credible, the parallel would run as follows:

1. Evolution settled on four moral sprouts because they were adaptations = adaptation^{historical};

2. They are still adaptive = adaptation$^{\text{current ecology}}$;

3. The sprouts emerge, grow, and are tuned (roughly) the same way across all natural and social ecologies; and thus,

4. We ought to grow the sprouts the way Mother Nature (*Tian* = heaven) designed them to grow.

Neither argument is logically valid for familiar reasons. In each case, we need to add a premise that says:

We ought to allow, not interfere with, even to aid and abet, what nature sets us on course to develop.[9]

This premise, however, is itself an "ought" in need of justification. If the argument seems valid, it is because we supply this premise unconsciously. And if the premise is in fact defensible, it is not just because nature sets us on a certain trajectory, but, at most, that plus realizing the trajectory(ies) suits us, possibly, and worrisomely, only some of us, in current ecologies. "Suits us in current ecologies" is ambiguous between is "still an adaptation," that is, still contributes to fitness as opposed to still contributes to happiness, flourishing, or goodness—each of which is different from the other.

Consider hierarchy. It may be that nature designed humans to defer to older and larger men because the fitness of small-band hunter-gatherers depended disproportionally on male power. In the modern world, it may be in the interest of men, it may "suit us," to keep things this way, but not in the interest of women. Or consider being a carnivore. We were designed as such. But some of us in developed countries and with good incomes can nowadays get proper nutrition without eating meat. If we think that there are good reasons that pertain to the well-being of nonhuman animals not to eat them and do so, then we have a case of an adaptation that we think should not be honored. Furthermore, a vegetarian of the sort I am imagining would be an example of a person who is perfectly fit in the Darwinian sense but who chooses for moral reasons not to respect, as it were, this aspect of their first or given nature. The point is that there is no warrant for developing, even allowing, nature to have its way just because it sets us on a certain trajectory, unless it is also good that it does so.[10]

There is another problem with the "four sprouts" analogue of the four limb argument. It is not sound. Why? Because the second and third premises are false. It is not true that the sprouts, assuming they exist as Mencius describes them, are still adaptive, nor is it the case that the sprouts are grown or tuned in exactly the same way across cultures.

Flourishing and Fitness

I can make these points in a different way. The warrant in the combined Mencius-Darwin view—I admit and intend it as an anachronism—for developing the sprouts to cover what they are designed to cover (what we could call the "adaptive target," which for philosophers of biology is what the trait was "selected for") is because it is fitness enhancing.[11] It is probably the case, at least I will assume that it is so, that some kind of fitness is necessary for flourishing, goodness, and so forth. But fitness is not the same as flourishing, goodness, and their suite, nor is it remotely sufficient for these. And this is one of several reasons why Mencius, were he present, would not accept the full-on fitness-enhancing version of the argument. Many very bad people are very fit. The king with an extensive harem is über fit, but not über good. The person who loves everyone equally may be über good, but not be über fit. This means that arguments for extending a sprout, a module, an initial setting beyond what enhances fitness,[12] requires a different set of reasons than those that pertain to fitness.

In the moral sprout text, Mencius is depending mostly, even if only implicitly, on the readers' or hearers' understanding that there are moral reasons to grow the sprouts in the direction of a realized Confucian *junzi*. This is their natural teleology. When we ask for or offer reasons for extending sprouts in first nature to form good persons of a certain type, we might be presupposing fitness, but we are almost never asking primarily about what makes or might make some individual or population of individuals reproductively successful. We are asking about what will make them good.

Botanical, Agricultural, and Computational Metaphors

Moral modularity in both its classical Chinese, "four sprouts," and contemporary psychological form, "five modules," hypothesizes that moral competence consists of, or is the emergent product, to some significant degree, of a set of autonomous or relatively autonomous sociomoral competences. Whereas botanical metaphors that stress natural untutored growth go well with the view that first human nature is good, and agricultural metaphors that stress cultivation and that picture first nature as a mixed bag of good and bad seeds, are the coins of the realm in ancient Chinese philosophy,[13] social intuitionists vary among themselves in speaking of innate "modules," "first drafts," and "foundations." I use the term "module" throughout, not because I am sure it is ultimately most well suited to describe what advocates of moral foundations theory can sensibly claim, but because its advocates, fully aware of its meaning in orthodox cognitive science, use it.

> We posit that there are a variety of rapid, automatic reactions to patterns in the social world. When we detect such patterns, moral modules fire, and a fully enlightened person has an affectively valenced experience. Not just a feeling of "good!" or "bad!," but an experience with a more specific "flavor" to it, such as "cruel!," "unfair!," "betrayal!," "subversive!," or "sick!" (Graham et al. 2013, 110)[14]

The concept of modularity is useful because it helps direct the mind to a strong and especially interesting interpretation or set of interpretations of the view. This fact alone will be helpful in orienting us. If the concept of innate protomoral modules doesn't work, then we will be clear as to why. For myself, I prefer the messy, botanical and agricultural, living organism metaphors to the crisp, clean, but mechanical, computational ones. But, just to be clear, no modularist believes that the processors are purely mechanical, perfectly predictable, or hardwired. Everyone, classical sprout theorist or contemporary computational neuroscientist alike, agrees that we are dealing with the structure and function of complex dynamical systems that yield morality.[15]

The degree to which a moral psychology is committed to modularity depends on whether it claims that all, most, or only some of moral personality can be explained in terms of the development and interaction of some number of dedicated modules or sprout-like structures, as well as whether it deems itself a useful model or, more than that, a real and accurate picture of the mind and how it works. The strongest view is "modules-all-the-way-up," where I intend the idea that social stimuli activate an intuition, for example, deference, disgust, compassion, and this intuition or gut reaction yields a certain response ballistically. A modules-all-the-way-up system has canalized and vertical architecture.

In a major review of the moral foundations theory, its principal advocates (Graham et al. 2013) write, "Nobody in psychology today argues that the human mind is truly a "blank slate" at birth, but opinions range widely from minimalist positions, which say that there is hardly any writing on the "first draft" of the mind, to maximalist positions such as massive modularity (Sperber 2005; Tooby, Cosmides, and Barrett 2005), which say that the mind is to a great degree organized in advance of experience, including hundreds or thousands of functional modules." They explain: "We are near the maximalist side of the spectrum." But they point out that one could accept the empirical findings of moral foundations theory, and a weaker view, to the effect that there are some, not very well honed, basic dispositional settings in minds.

A weaker view is that moral personality is a joint production of an automatic, ancient, fast-acting, automatic modular system, which many cognitive scientists call System 1, and a more recent system that involves System 2, deliberative reason, what the Greeks called *phronesis* and what classical Chinese thinkers call *zhi*.[16] Such a system has, or might have, bi-directional vertical features, for example, when reason pushes back against some ballistic output, as well as horizontal features as when multiple modules are activated and interpenetrate (I experience compassion and disgust) and I need to think about what to do.

The weakest view is that there are some dispositional sprouts in human nature, which play some role in the development of morality, where the degree of this role is unspecified, but that is understood to have its place in a mix with all the other sources of moral personality in culture, reason, self-conception, temperament, and various nonsprout-like aspects (capacities to absorb entirely new information) of human psychology.

I do not believe that the moral modularity hypothesis is true in the modules-all-the-way-up form. Persons are complex dynamic psychobiological systems embedded in ecologies. Whatever independence or autonomy a subsystem has—imagine a visual processor that computes color or one that computes shape—it was built for the whole system of which it is a part and designed to interact with the rest of the system to produce useful and integrated information. When we play tennis, we do not see "some yellow here" and "some roundness there" and "some motion over there," we see a round-yellow-tennis ball-coming-over-the-net. The autonomy and independence of a processor or subsystem is almost always relative autonomy or independence (Karmiloff-Smith 1992; Elsabbagh and Karmiloff-Smith 2006). That said, the idea that there are sprouts, beginnings, protomoral (or "moralizable") foundations or dispositions, possibly even modules in our nature, seems helpful to some extent.[17]

Multiple sprout views have the potential to serve as analytic tools in terms of which many debates about human moral psychology have a home. If morality consists of one unified moral skill, set of competencies, family of virtues, or a single moral rule or algorithm, then modularity or sprout views will serve as a useful dialectical foil. Either the moral modularity hypothesis is wrong that morality has distinct plural psychological bases or it is right that it does have such sources, but needs to explain how plural foundational sources can yield an experiential or phenomenal unity or, what is different, that it can be steered by, or otherwise controlled by, a unified higher-level cognitive system, by reason or rules or principles or one's considered character, or by what is different still, by social structures entirely outside one's head. Alternatively, if some form of modularity is true, then exploring the nature of each seed, sprout, foundation, or module, its nature, function, and trajectory(ies) across ecologies will yield some additional or more precise knowledge of human moral psychology. And this kind of work will allow more nuanced work on how the various modular competencies interact and intersect, and how they can be guided by higher-level thinking, planning, intending, and so on, if they can. So, for example, one can organize all the work that judges that an empathy/caring/compassion system accounts for much or most of what we call morality. Then one goes to the work in this tradition to see what the evidence looks like, to work by Mencius on compassion, to David Hume and Adam Smith on sympathy and empathy, to Martin Hoffman (2000), Daniel Batson (2011), Carol Gilligan (1982), Nel Noddings (1984), Michael Slote (2007), Eva Feder Kittay and Ellen K. Feder (2002), and Patricia Smith Churchland (2011). If the caring system, upon close examination, ramps up to explain most of moral competence, then perhaps there is no need for multiple modules or modularity at all. If the care system doesn't ramp up, or if, as some think, it can be an enemy of fairness and thus needs to be tempered by other virtues or competences (Batson 2011; Prinz 2011; Bloom 2013a, 2015), then modularity remains a contender. Meanwhile, others, or the same inquirers, can examine theories that posit bases in human nature (perhaps in ancestors as well) for the impulse for justice. Here one studies Hume and Kant, Rawls (1971), Habermas (1984), Kohlberg (1981, 1984), de Waal (2006), and so on, to see what the evidence reveals. Do impulses for justice as fairness have roots in human nature or is "the cautious jealous virtue of justice" an invention due entirely to scarcity, as Hume thought? Can a system designed for care/compassion yield justice or vice versa (P. S. Churchland, 2013)?[18] Then one studies theorists who think humans are naturally attuned to in-group/out-group, to the sacred, and so on, to see what the evidence reveals. Does the evidence support independent sprout-like beginnings or not?

This is roughly the methodology recommended by contemporary advocates of modularity (see Figure 3.2 above), who think the evidence supports modularity fairly well. One might decide eventually, now is too soon, that all the evidence taken together supports moral modularity as a real depiction of the distinct sources of human morality or, simply, that it is practically useful to organize inquiry this way. The first conclusion would be realist, the second pragmatic (Graham et al. 2013). I am mainly interested in the psychological realism question, that is, whether it is true that there are modules—whether the theory that posits modules is correct in the way, say, Copernicus's heliocentric theory is true and not merely useful as Ptolemaic geocentric theory, which is false, was and still is.

Supposing the evidence supports views such as "four sprouts" or "five modules," we then ask whether these are beginnings like the cocoon of the butterfly that is the sprout from which the caterpillar that becomes the butterfly emerges, but that completely dissolves and is no longer represented in the butterfly; or is it like the beginning of the spinal system, which is small and delicate and very soft at first but maintains itself in some highly visible way in the mature vertebrate, or is it like something in between the cocoon and the spine, partly discarded, partly preserved like the oversupply of synaptic connections in the brain that are pruned over time? Or are all these beginnings like dedicated electronic modules in a computer or automobile engine, which either work to do their specific job or not? I now turn to the arguments and evidence for "five modules."

4

Modern Moral Psychology

Twenty-First-Century Moral Modularity

The moral modularity hypothesis that I refer to as "five modules" calls itself "social intuitionism," or "moral foundations theory." Moral foundations theory fleshes out an idea that was anticipated in Mencius and which in its current form is supported by interdisciplinary work in anthropology, cross-cultural psychology, primatology, and economics. Moral foundations theory can be found in the work of Jonathan Haidt and his colleagues (Haidt 2007, 2012; Haidt and Graham 2007; Haidt and Joseph 2004, 2008; Graham et al. 2013). Its roots lie in work by Shweder (1990), Shweder and Haidt (1993), Brown (1991), Fiske (1991, 1992, 2004), Schwartz and Bilsky (1990), and Shweder et al. (1997).

Here again for easy reference are the two figures from earlier. Figure 4.1 displays the five foundations or modules of moral foundations theory. Figure 4.2 displays the criteria for sprout-hood or module-hood, and the evidence for the five hypothesized moral modules.

My focus is on the moral foundations research team led by Jonathan Haidt. Haidt and Joseph (2008) claim that moral foundations theory's five modules map onto the three "ethics" of autonomy, community, and divinity proposed by Shweder (1990; Shweder et al. 1997), as well as onto Fiske's (1991, 1992, 2004) model, which claims that all social relations are outcomes of four psychological schemata that govern communal sharing, authority ranking, equality matching, and market pricing.

That said, I want the reader to think, if possible, of "five modules" as a scientific hypothesis not associated with Jonathan Haidt's complex, multifaceted, and widely discussed research program, which includes his life as a public intellectual and encompasses much more that moral foundations theory. Moral foundations theory is, first and foremost, an architectural hypothesis that posits five modules or foundations and that claims to explain the shape of (all, some, most) actual moral psychologies in terms of these. The positing of the modules is the essential core of moral foundations theory. The reason it will be

FIGURE 4.1 The Five Foundational Modules (Haidt and Joseph 2007)

	Harm/ Care	Fairness/ Reciprocity	Ingroup/ Loyalty	Authority/ Respect	Purity/ Sanctity
Adaptive challenge	Protect and care for young, vulnerable, or injured kin	Reap benefits of dyadic cooperation with non-kin	Reap benefits of group cooperation	Negotiate hierarchy, defer selectively	Avoid microbes and parasites
Proper domain (adaptive triggers)	Suffering, distress, or threat to one's kin	Cheating, cooperation, deception	Threat or challenge to group	Signs of dominance and submission	Waste products, diseased people
Actual domain (the set of all triggers)	Baby seals, cartoon characters	Marital fidelity, broken vending machines	Sports teams one roots for	Bosses, respected professionals	Taboo ideas (communism, racism)
Characteristic emotions	Compassion	anger, gratitude, guilt	Group pride, belongingness; rage at traitors	Respect, fear	Disgust
Relevant virtues [a lid vices]	Caring, kindness, [cruelty]	fairness, justice, honesty, trustworthiness [dishonesty]	Loyalty, patriotism, self-sacrifice [treason, cowardice]	Obedience, deference [disobedience, uppitiness]	Temperance, chastity, piety, cleanliness [lust, intemp erance]

helpful to discuss the core thesis of moral foundations theory separately from Haidt's broader theorizing is because Haidt is associated with four additional, independently controversial views, which are logically and empirically distinct from the core thesis of moral foundations theory. Haidt also thinks that:

- Morality is primarily or mostly produced by System 1, an evolutionary ancient, intuitive system, and that reason, System 2, as traditionally conceived, by philosophers and psychologists as otherwise diverse as Plato, Kant, Piaget, Kohlberg, Peter Singer, and John Rawls, has little power over it (Haidt 2012).
- There is no non-question-begging way to argue for the superiority of one way of configuring, growing, developing the modules over another (personal discussion and correspondence).
- Liberals have a morality that in certain respects more poorly reflects the intuitive system than conservatives, and this is a weakness in liberal morality.
- Liberty/Oppression (rooted in strong distaste for bullies) is a sixth foundation that is especially useful in explaining the distinctive moral psychology of North American libertarians (as I write, Haidt's moral foundations theory colleagues are agnostic on this sixth foundation).[1]

FIGURE 4.2 Criteria for Modules and Current Evidence (Graham et al. 2013)

Foundation criteria:	Care/ harm	Fairness/ cheating	Loyalty/ Betrayal	Authority/ subversion	Sanctity/ degradation
Criterion 1: Common in third-party normative judgments	Playground harm: Nucci & Turiel (1978)	Catching cheaters: Dunbar (1996)	The Black Sheep effect: Marques, Yzerbyt, & Leyens (1988)	Disrespect for authority: Shweder, Miller, & Mahapatra, 1987	Food and sex taboos: Haidt, Koller, & Dias (1993)
Criterion 2: Automatic affective evaluations	To cruelty and violence: Luo et al. (2006), Cannon et al. (2011), Graham (2010)	To cheating: Sanfey et al (2003); to unfairness or inequality: Cannon et al. (2011), Graham (2010)	To ingroup betrayals: Cannon et al. (2011), Graham (2010)	To subversion: Cannon et al. (2011), Graham (2010)	To sexual violations: Parkinson et al 2011; to degradation: Cannon et al. (2011), Graham (2010)
Criterion 3: Culturally widespread	Bowlby (1969)	Fiske (1992)	Herdt (1981)	Fiske (1992)	Douglas (1966)
Criterion 4: Evidence of innate preparedness	NHP: Hrdy (2009); Preston & de Waal (2002); Infants: Hamlin, Wynn, & Bloom (2006)	NHP: Brosnan (2006); Infants: Schmidt & Sommerville (2011); Sloane, Baillargeon, & Premack (2012)	NHP: De Waal (1982); Infants: Kinzler, Dupoux & Spelke (2007); Hamlin et al. (2012)	NHP: Boehm (1999, 2012); Not yet shown in infants	Not yet shown in NHP or infants
Criterion 5: Evolutionary model	Kin selection: Hamilton (1964); Attachment theory: Bowlby (1969)	Reciprocal Altruism: Trivers (1971)	Multi-level selection: D. S. WIlson (2002); Tribalism: Richerson & Boyd (2005)	Rank and dominance: de Waal (1982); Boehm (1999)	Disgust: Rozin, Haidt & McCauley (2008); Behavioral immune system: Schaller & Park (2011)

*NHP = nonhuman primates.

I am mostly focused on the core thesis that there are "five modules" and that they can do most of the work in explaining moral psychology. Although I will have things to say about the other hypotheses, it is the core thesis, not these other claims, that makes for modularity. This is easy to see in Mencius, who believes in modular architecture but is not a skeptic about reason's role or a moral skeptic or a relativist. Nor, of course, is Mencius a modern liberal or a modern conservative, and he is certainly not a libertarian.

Background: Five Modules

"Five modules" advertises itself as a social intuitionist model to convey that the modules consist of dispositions to have rapid-fire reactions, the intuitions, which subserve quick affective-cognitive-action tendencies and that are triggered by specific types of social or environmental situations, akin to Mencius's example of the universal human impulse to save the child falling into the well. If you show a picture of a "hot" student to another student you can make jokes about sexual desire, but not if the picture is of one's own hot sibling and the jokes are about you finding your own sibling desirable. That is disgusting, will induce anger, and so on.

Moral foundations theory draws on interdisciplinary work (Brown 1991; Fiske 1991, 1992, 2004; Schwartz and Bilsky 1990; Shweder and Haidt 1993; Shweder et al. 1997; and de Waal 1991, 1996), and claimed originally that there are three types of social situations or domains of life that people everywhere evaluate in affectively loaded moral terms, zones of life in which moralizing universally occurs:

1. Harm/Care (Care/Harm; Suffering/Compassion)
2. Fairness/Reciprocity
3. Hierarchy/Respect

Evaluative intuitions in these domains are found cross-culturally among humans and in nonhuman primates as well, for example, anger at unfair rewards is found in capuchins and canines and children (Brosnan and de Waal 2003; Brosnan 2006; Bloom 2013b). A fourth and fifth module were then added: an in-group/loyalty foundation that accounts for the universal tendency humans have to create, think, and act in terms of in-groups and out-groups; and a purity/sanctity foundation based on evidence from anthropology of the common role intuitions about what is base, impure, and defiled, on one side, and pure, holy, and sacred, on the other, play in most cultures (Haidt and Joseph 2004). So we add:

4. In-Group/Out-Group (In-Group/Loyalty)
5. Purity/Sanctity (Sanctity/Degradation)

"Five modules" can then be defined this way:

> *Homo sapiens* possess these five innate intuitive psychological modules that are activated in normal social environments by well-defined situation types, and that can be grown/shaped/suppressed/extended/modified in multifarious ways, and which are the basis of all moralities.

The key ideas are that there are (at least) these five intuitive modules and that something in the vicinity of virtues, or special purpose moral skills, are built on them. These five dispositional mechanisms underwrite complex multidirectional syndromes (mind-world-action) that arose originally to meet specific adaptive challenges and that serve now as the foundation of morality, or something in the vicinity. The process of cultivating, sculpting, suppressing the modules, as well as calibrating their relations, yields second nature, the emotional, cognitive, and behavioral responses we make to the complex problem space of sociomoral life. Continuous adjustments of the settings might, in the spirit of industrial strength modularity, be explained completely in terms of social feedback, which is itself mostly or completely explained by the modular settings of those we interact with. Alternatively, one might think that the moral modules broadcast their output to some integrated mental space where they achieve phenomenal unity, in the way that one feels the breeze, hears the birds, sees the mountains, and smells the flowers all at once even though the skin, ears, eyes, and nose compute distinct classes of stimuli. Allowing integration of this sort would be congenial to Aristotelians who think of character as involving a unity of virtues. Or, perhaps the architecture could be a hybrid: some highly vertical systems, some horizontal interpenetration across modules, with a certain amount of top-down control over this output exerted by a general purpose (nonmodular) cognitive system (e.g., System 2 or dorsolateral-prefrontal cortex [DLPFC], what they called reason or thinking in the olden days).

One appealing feature of "five modules" is that it claims to offer a universal psychosocial baseline for comparing and contrasting moral orientations across individuals and cultures, namely, examine how the modules are grown, suppressed, enhanced, and related among themselves.[2] Depending on how exactly "five modules" is framed, in the social intuitionist way or in Mencius's way, it might also be read as embedding a criterion or criteria for judging the adequacy of a type or level of moral competence and performance. Mencius's limb analogy expresses the idea that the four sprouts have as their aim a certain ideal goal state, whereas moral foundations theory is normally agnostic about the proper, mature shape of the modules, although their initial settings provide constraints on the possibility space.

In philosophy, virtues, as special purpose moral skills, are defined as dispositions to perceive, feel, judge, and act in a way that is responsive to tokens of a situation type (Flanagan 1991, 2009). Courage or temperance or benevolence, and so on, are virtues that are appropriately activated by situations that call for them. A kind person sees the old lady standing on the subway and gives her their seat. A decent person feels sympathy for the child who scrapes her knee and goes to help them (this is largely accounted for as a development of module 1). A courageous person sees when the rights of the powerless are being trampled on and stands up for them even at cost to themself (this is largely accounted for as a development of module 2). In the normal life of a virtuous person, declarative rules are not normally consulted, and need not be consulted in cases such as these.[3] The virtuous person, unlike what Aristotle called the "continent person" (whom Kant admired), moves in that *wu-wei* (effortless) manner that Mencius celebrates as suited to our kind of animal. Indeed, Mencius (see 4B19, 6A4–5) makes exactly the same distinction Aristotle makes between the continent person, who does what is right through will power, and the virtuous person (if there are any) who does it because it is their nature, their entire self is attuned to virtuous expression.

Moral foundations theory mirrors Mencius's model insofar as it makes both a descriptive claim that there are five innate sprouts, and a set of normative claims, that we ought to recognize the importance of all five to morality, that doing so will improve moral comprehension across life forms, and that it will lead to tolerance since all, or most, or much of the variation in moralities, in second nature, is variation in the growth/extensions/modifications of shared modules, of a common first nature, which variation is entirely due to cultural variation.

Defenders of "five modules" are sensibly cautious about offering anything as strong as the Mencian limb analogy. They point out that which sprouts develop, and the extent to which different cultures or subcultures build on the modules, depends on environmental and social inputs, as well as culture and history. Privileging some sprouts at the expense of others does not necessarily prevent one from being virtuous, as "cultures vary to the degree to which they build virtues on these five foundations" (Haidt and Graham 2007, 99). Nonetheless, "the available range of human virtues is constrained by the five sets of intuitions that human minds are prepared to have" (Haidt and Graham 2007, 106). American liberal, conservative, and libertarian moral psychologies, as well as Confucian and Buddhist moral psychologies, are all built on the same foundations. Buddhists are influenced to extend compassion (module 1) in ways that Westerners are not; Confucians to extend respect for authority (module 3) in ways Buddhists and Western liberals are not; and Americans to extend "justice as fairness" intuitions (module 2) in ways these others are not. But if moral foundations theory is true, all these forms of life, as well as every other one ever invented or inventable, rest on the same modular foundations.

This last point is important if true. It would mean that "morality" as a psychosocial kind is restricted to the original modules and extensions of the modules.[4] At least, it would entail this if "rests on the same modules" or "is constrained by the five sets of intuitions" is intended to mean that morality just is the shape that the five modules can take and whatever interactions are allowed among them. Imagine a garden in which there are five seeds that grow into five plants or five kinds of plants—watermelon, eggplant, peppers, tomatoes, and basil. If the watermelon gets out first and fast then the basil needs to grow around it. If the tomatoes get tall and are sunward from the eggplant, then the eggplant grows differently than if this were reversed, and so on. The key is that there are no other variables that determine what the garden does or produces than the seeds, the soil, the orientations of the plants and the sun, and the vagaries of the weather. Now if, on the other hand, one is allowed to add a gardener to the situation who can cultivate the different seeds at the right time, prepare the soil according to the needs of each, irrigate in the right ways, and so on, then how the garden grows will be different than if the seeds are left only to their own devices. If we are allowed to add the gardener, we are starting to conceive the system along the lines of a system that is modular at bottom (at root, we might say) but nonmodular on top. If one is allowed to add a consumer for whom the gardener gardens, then the picture gets even more functionally and architecturally complex as a system, and also more normatively complex, since there are now considerations of what is good for the plants, for the gardener, and for the consumer. This better represents the normal situation in most moral ecologies. One consequence of thinking ecologically is that normative properties—flourishing, tasty, good—are not narrow properties of the seed, sprout, or mature fruit alone, but of these plus the system that includes these wider cultivator-consumer relations. Even in such a complex system there are still constraints: the gardener with only the seeds mentioned cannot produce grapefruit, even if the weather is commodious and the consumer begs for it, because he doesn't have grapefruit seeds.

Now, of course, one can start to imagine that there just happen to be accidents that occur and hybrids arise, so that the tomatoes and watermelons meet and form tomato-melons. The farmer singleton or the farmer and consumer pair or the farmer, grocer, consumer triplet like it, want it, and so forth. Then from four original seeds we have more than four plants, etc. The possible relations among the four original seeds, and the (now) five kinds of fruit they yield, and between them and the farmer and the grocer and his customers with their changing preferences, explode exponentially.

According to moral foundations theory, the modules as originally set, or as programmed to mature reliably in a normal environment, constitute the initial settings both in terms of what activates the modules and how high or low the emotional and conative responses are tuned. Extensions of the range of activation of the modules and the tuning up or down of the strength of emotional response, and the actions the intuitions motivate, are accounted for by culture. Moral differences at every level, between individuals, across cultures, subcultures, and so on, might be explained by differences in the initial settings or by the degree to which the five modules are tuned up or down, by the content and scope of situation types to which they are attuned, and by the trump rules governing modular relations when the output differs, when, for example, I feel compassion and disgust toward you at the same time.

What Modularity Is

I should say something more precise about what a module is according to contemporary cognitive science. In *The Modularity of Mind* (1983), the seminal work on modularity, Jerry Fodor lays out the properties that are characteristic of modular systems such as reflexes, face recognition, and the five senses. The five sensory input systems have most or all of the following features: they are domain specific, mandatory, involve limited central access, are fast, informationally encapsulated, produce shallow outputs, operate on fixed neural architecture, are triggered by a restricted class of stimuli (eyes by light, ears by sounds), and demonstrate a characteristic pace and sequencing in ontogeny.

Input systems differ from central systems—think System 2—in that the central systems can draw on any relevant information from any dedicated, special purpose processor, and confirmation is sensitive to the entire belief system. Thought and problem solving are canonical central system processes.[5] Imagine planning what courses to take at the local college over the next several years in order to become an X-ray technician, while working full-time and being a single parent. People with complex lives do this kind of thinking and planning all the time. It is hard to do it well, requires time, patient deliberation, discussion with friends and loved ones, and so on.

On the other hand, consider color perception and taste. Humans can detect several million different hues. And the flavors we can taste are similarly vast. Most flavors that exist have never been tasted by anyone. In both color perception and taste the world abounds with novelty and surprise. But in both cases, the system is modular, or better perhaps, the system has clear modular aspects or features, or is modular in certain respects. The eyes have two kinds of photoreceptor cells on the retina, rods and cones. The cones are differentially activated by medium, short, and long wavelengths, roughly by green, blue, and red light. So yellowish-green light activates L and M cones equally and S cones only a little. Red light, on the other hand, stimulates L cones much more than M cones, and S cones hardly at all. Blue-green light stimulates M cones more than L cones, and S cones a bit more strongly, and is also the peak stimulant for rod cells, which are normally involved in seeing at very low light (night vision) but not so much in daylight. This is only the beginning of course, since the dynamic computations of the cones deliver information from the retina to retinal ganglion cells via the optic nerve to the lateral geniculate nucleus (LGN) in the thalamus and on to V1, the primary visual cortex at the back of the brain, at which point you see the color or colors that are there. If everything goes according to plan, I see the colors that were detected at the retina by the cones. The unique combination of S, M, and L wavelengths received at the retina can be represented as a vector, a unique number that represents the color seen.

Taste works the same way. There are five kinds of taste receptors that detect sweet, sour, bitter, salty, and umami. Each morsel of food activates these five cell types. The information is passed on upstairs and again, if the system works as it is supposed to, I experience what the food "tastes like." Taste is unified in the sense that we grasp a taste all at once, by the mouthful, as it were. Flavors can sometimes be individuated as when we taste the sauce as sweet and sour or as savory and sweet. There was no way of knowing from the phenomenology of taste, even with the familiar phenomenon of flavor detection—that the entire system is, in fact, subserved by dedicated taste buds. Discovering the modular aspects of the taste bud system required third-personal investigation; it cannot be ascertained introspectively. There are numerous possible sensory architectures, including nonmodular ones, that might have produced the phenomenology of taste. Introspection is indecisive about the nature of the taste system.

So it is with the architecture of human moral psychology. The "moral flavors" of life have spread and interpenetrate, and do not reliably occur with such phenomenal distinctness—a dollop of compassion here, a teaspoon of justice there—that they secure the case for or against moral modularity. The fact that we might as moral agents experience dispositions to justice, compassion, and animosity all-at-once, toward a stranger with odd habits, as part of a phenomenological unity, is not decisive as evidence that the felt unity is due to unity at bottom, or is the result of a merger of modular outputs, or whether the system is a unity at bottom with the distinctions in phenomenological texture imposed from "on high" by a cognitive faculty designed or trained to draw the distinctions we think are sensory or perceptual, but in fact are not. These are empirical questions.

A system that is designed to work as the color or taste systems are by reliably passing on information about what is detected at the periphery by dedicated, special purpose processors to me, the organism, is a modular system. A system is a "modules-all-the-way-up" system if it is designed like the color and taste systems to more-or-less reliably pass on the information detected modularly at the periphery to the organism it works for, that contains that periphery, those eyes, that tongue. The "more-or-less reliably" clause is required because there is no interesting cognitive system that is a modules-all-the-way-up system in the sense that the person receives the information exactly as it was computed modularly at the lowest level. A "modules all-the-way-up" system needs to have dedicated processors at bottom and in addition needs to be designed to preserve the information processed or computed at that level all-the-way-up.

However, the experience it produces need not be, indeed typically is not, experienced as having modular texture.

Binding is the name for the process wherein sets of unconscious modular computations achieve experiential unity. When I walk on the beach, I see the beautiful orange sunset. My brain computes large-orange-moving-blob, possibly, size, color, and motion, separately. But I experience a sunset. When I taste the sweet and sour soup and experience it as delicious, perhaps as the best I have ever had, my taste buds are computing the vector of flavors produced by activation of the five kinds of taste buds, but they deliver to me their output as a phenomenological unity, which is what the soup tastes like to me.

One might insist that judging the sunset as involving the sun and as beautiful or the soup as soup and yummy involves some nonmodular features, such as concepts, memory, language, and so on. The fan of strong modularity will perhaps concede that there is some horizontal or top-down involvement from memory and language (one's experience with sunsets and soups), but claim these are weak forces.

One sign that a system has some sort of modular structure is that the deliverances of the special purpose dedicated system are hard to override. You can choose not to go to look at the sunset and you can choose not to order or taste the sweet and sour soup. But if you do go look, you will see orange, and if you taste the soup its flavor will be sweet and sour to you. You can wish the orange look and the sweet and sour taste to go away until you are blue in the face. It won't work. This is cognitive impenetrability. Some think it comes in degrees. If there are moral modules, and if the morality system is modules all-the-way-up, then we might expect it to be unencumbered by central processes in the way, for example, the skeletal reflex system or the pupil contraction and expansion system are or the way color detection and taste systems are. Keep your mind on this point. It is very important.

Reactive Attitudes

If there are moral modules, and if they are like the sensory, perceptual systems, then one immediate difference worth noticing is that they do not produce "shallow" outputs, at least not "shallow" in the sense that the input is just, as it were, received by the mind in the way most sounds or sights are registered. The person who sees the child falling into the well is moved to act; the person who is treated unfairly shows resentment; the contemptuous person reveals her contempt on her face and moves quickly away.[6]

If one were to read the recent philosophical literature for helpful discussions of a quick response system with emotional and conative force and that has something significant to do with sociomoral life, specifically with reactions to the "weal and woe" of oneself and others, one would be pointed to P. F.

Strawson's (1962) work on the reactive attitudes. The reactive attitudes are such states as these:

- Indignation
- Resentment
- Gratitude
- Approbation
- Guilt
- Shame
- Hurt Feelings
- Feelings of Affection and Love
- Forgiveness

Strawson claims that these attitudes are part of human nature and, that they comprise a set of cognitive-affective-conative attitudes toward persons, acts, and motives that help, hinder, harm, support, and obstruct the desires, aims, and plans of individuals and groups. The reactive attitudes are a kind, actually several kinds, of conscious intentional states.

The reactive attitudes have some properties in common with standard modules in cognitive science, but they differ in being strongly affective and perhaps also in being almost always action guiding, almost always yielding or encouraging or being partly constituted by a reaction. Most of what I perceive I do nothing about. I just absorb the information. But when I feel angry or ashamed or you have hurt my feelings, I am inclined to do something about it. Each beginning or sprout of the reactive attitude system might be conceived this way:

1. It is automatic, fast acting, and easily activated.
2. It involves affect (feeling), judgment (thought), and conation, that is, an action tendency.
3. It has features of cognitive impenetrability despite itself being a cognitive state, that is, the affect, associated thought, and action tendency triplet are hard to turn off or keep from being activated; the action can be stopped but only with considerable conscious effort/veto, sometimes only indirectly, by doing something else.[7]

Insofar as the reactive attitudes in their primitive first-nature forms can be modeled on perceptual modules, they differ in both their affective qualities and in their close connection to action. Other input systems, reflexes for example, instigate action tendencies as do moral modules, but they typically, consider the knee jerk, do so without any emotional involvement and are cognitively empty. Startles—for example, to a car backfiring—meanwhile are heavily affective, but not, at least initially, cognitive. The car backfiring or unexpected fireworks or gunshots cause a startle, and mental alarm bells go off. The startle or alarm has no content. But it instigates thinking about what that noise was, where it came from, whether danger lurks, and so on, which results eventually in a contentful thought: "That must have been fireworks." In the case of the child falling into the well the entire episode starts with a cognitive-intentional state: One sees that the child is falling into the well, and this contentful state produces the alarm and compassion. Mencius's view is not one where the sprouts are mere bodily happenings, they are intentional psychophysical states (M. Kim 2010).

Moral sprouts or modules, if there are any, are cognitive and affectively loaded. Indeed, a quick survey of every important list of basic moral attitudes or attitudes that are sometimes relevant to morality depict them as partly emotional. For example, the seven Ekman faces, happy, sad, scared, surprised, angry, disgusted, and contemptuous, are reactive, expressive, and communicative. I see a snake and I am scared. You see the fear on my face and infer that there is something scary at the location where my gaze is fixed. I glare hostilely at you as you approach my food, and you understand that you ought to back off. Likewise, explicitly moral attitudes such as compassion involve cognitive appraisal, the thought that this is a child falling into a well. But once this is grasped, or better, as this is grasped, the emotional reaction is automatic. Even King Herod, who set out to kill Jesus by killing all first-born Jewish children, can't immediately override his impulse to save the child falling into the well. The feeling of distress and the impulse to save the child will happen, and that much is pretty much what is meant by talk of "cognitive impenetrability" in cognitive science. Of course, Kind Herod can, as he did, think it is a good idea, all things considered, to proceed with his policy of genocidal infanticide. But doing so, especially if the killing is up close and personal, will involve overriding or circumventing powerful impulses not to do so.

If we look at Figures 4.1 and 4.2 proposed by "five modules," we can see that each module has these three properties that Strawson's reactive attitudes have:

1. It is automatic, fast acting, and easily activated.
2. It involves affect (feeling), cognition, and conation, that is, an action tendency.
3. It has features of cognitive impenetrability despite itself being cognitive, for example, the cognitive-affect-conation triplet is hard to turn off or keep from being activated; the action can be stopped but only with conscious effort/veto, or sometimes only indirectly, by doing something else.

In addition, each module of "five modules" has these two features that Strawson's reactive attitudes don't necessarily have:

4. There exists a well-defined class of stimuli that trigger it.
5. There is evidence that the foundation (or reactive attitude as linked to what it is a reaction to) is universal, that there is an evolutionary

rationale for its existence, typically in ancestral species and near
relations on the evolutionary tree; and that some form of it (a
sprout, a seedling) shows up in the very young, or as part of normal
psychobiological maturation.

This last is the demand for an evolutionary explanation, an explanation for
why the original equipment is as it is given a background commitment to
Darwin's theory of evolution. Why? Because Darwin's theory of evolution by
natural selection is extraordinarily well confirmed.[8]

It is worth noting that according to Figure 4.1 of "five modules," each foundation has associated with it certain specific emotions or sociomoral attitudes,
which constitute in some measure the beginnings of the associated virtues.
These are compassion and love for care; anger, gratitude, and guilt for justice; loyalty, belonging, betrayal, and cowardice for in-group affiliations and
associations; obedience, respect, and deference for authority; and contempt,
indignation, and disgust for purity and sanctity.

One important difference between "five modules" and Strawson's reactive
attitude inventory is that Strawson doesn't link or tie down his reactive attitudes to distinctive domains of life nor does he say anywhere that a well-
defined class of stimuli triggers each attitude. The weal and woe of oneself and
others activates the reactive attitudes, but what constitutes the weal and woe
is abstract, requires interpretation, and is not tied down to specific concrete
triggers. Many different states-of-affairs associated with things not going so
well for me and/or my loved ones can cause sadness. It seems plausible that
the emotion of sadness might have had a similar dynamic structure when the
ice melted at the end of the Pleistocene. In which case, we might sensibly say
that the sadness sprout or module is universal, fast acting, has an evolutionary
rationale in terms of motivating me to step up my game, watch for chances to
improve my situation, and so forth, but would not say that it is triggered by a
well-defined set of stimuli. I think the same sort of point can be made about
the causes of feelings of gratitude, forgiveness, and friendliness. If this is true,
then it follows that some basic emotions are not very modular because a well-
defined class of stimuli does not trigger them, at least not until a form of life
sets those parameters by modeling reactions of anger and gratitude starting
with the newborn.

A related issue is that in "five modules"—but perhaps not in real life—
different emotions are linked quite specifically to distinct domains of life.
Anger is associated primarily with affronts to justice; rage with disloyalty; fear
with abuse of power in hierarchies. The specific reactive attitudes are depicted
as doing their work primarily inside a module as it were, not across the modules. But this does not seem to be how the reactive attitudes actually work.
Even in something like the original evolutionary situation, anger would seem a
natural response to violations of any protomoral norm violations. That is, I see

that you do not reliably save children falling into wells, I experience anger; you try to take my food or my bride, I experience anger; you are cowardly when the group needs you to show courage, I experience anger; you never defer to others, I experience anger; you use my sleeping spot in the cave as a toilet, I experience anger. On the other side, shame and guilt would seem to be both common and appropriate reactions to one's own moral violations across all five domains (Gibbard 1989; Williams 1991).

Another question is this: How is it possible that emotions can be extended to new triggers inside a module or, what is different, across modules to states of affairs normally governed, according to moral foundations theory, by processors that specialize in different "characteristic emotions" (see Figure 4.1)? Extensions inside each module are not hard to explain. Fear for alpha males back in the day (hierarchy module 3) is now fear of you because you have power to fire me and take away my livelihood, even though you could not win a fight in the old-fashioned way and are not alpha at all outside the office. This extension of fear from bullies back-in-the-day to bullies in present-day capitalistic economies is easy to explain so long as there are simple psychological laws of association that track resemblance, contiguity, and cause and effect, or the organism learns via Pavlovian classical conditioning, or Skinnerian operant conditioning, or most likely both. A key question about the underlying architecture is whether such learning or conditioning regimens are conceived as placed redundantly inside each module (assuming there are modules), or whether these laws are placed in the mind just once and permeate across the modules. In both cases, there would be a ready explanation for extensions of the modules, but the second architecture has an easier time explaining associations across modules (I think you are compassionate but repulsive), while at the same time it would provide reason to think the modules are not as autonomous as is sometimes suggested. There is horizontal interpenetration across the modules from the start. Neurobiology teaches that synapses do not respect silo structures perfectly.

Darwin and Moral Sprouts

Was Darwin himself a sprout theorist, or a moral modularist? Maybe. Here is what he says in the *Descent of Man* ([1871] 2004) in his most explicit gloss on human moral sense:

> In order that primeval men, or the ape-like progenitors of man, should become social ... they must have acquired the same instinctive feelings.... They would have felt uneasy when separated from their comrades, for whom they would have felt some degree of love, they would have warned each other of danger, and have given mutual aid in attack

or defence. All this implies some degree of sympathy, fidelity, and courage.... To the instinct of sympathy ... it is primarily due that we habitu-
ally bestow both praises and blame on others, whilst we love the former
and dread the latter when applied to ourselves; and this instinct no doubt
was originally acquired, like all the other social instincts, through natural selection.... With increased experience and reason, man perceives
the more remote consequences of his actions, and the self-regarding virtues, such as temperance, chastity, &c., which during earlier times are ...
utterly disregarded come to be highly esteemed or even held sacred....
Ultimately our moral sense or conscience becomes a highly complex
sentiment—originating in the social instincts, largely guided by the approbation of our fellow-men, ruled by reason, self-interest, and in later
times by deep religious feelings, and confirmed by instruction and habit.
(498–500)

The fact that Darwin uses the word "instinct" is promising for reading him
as a modularist. But the fact that he doesn't specify the class of triggers for
the instincts very precisely speaks against reading him as the kind of modularist who tries to meet the strong conditions on modularity as specified in
Figure 4.2 above, where the triggers are supposed to be well defined (4) and
there is a clear evolutionary rationale for its initial form and structure (5).
Then again, one might claim that Darwin does speak precisely enough about
the triggers. They involve separation, danger, and need for mutual aid. But
the fact that he adds that with "increased experience and reason, man perceives the more remote consequences of his actions" indicates that the "highly
complex sentiment" that emerges in actual worlds is not only complex, as he
says, but also a heavily cognitively and historically conditioned competence.
All of which suggests that even if Darwin might be attracted to a modular substrate view, he would resist a modules "all-the-way-up" view, because he sees
an important role for reason, heart/mind, history, conscience, Mencian *zhi*,
and Aristotelian *phronesis*, and also because he himself foresaw the distinction
between a trait that is an adaptation in the fitness-enhancing sense(s) and one
that is adaptive, functional, conducive to happiness, flourishing, and, what is
different still, good or right; or in a thicker idiom still, what is compassionate,
just, fair, loving, faithful, patient, kind, and generous.

One unfortunate consequence of speaking in terms of the ballistic reactions
of the reptilian brain or the powerful intuitions of System 1 is that it makes
it seem as if all control and modification of initial settings must come from
the discipline and punish regimens of a relatively weak System 2. But Daniel
Kahneman, the main defender of the dual process model, insists that it is an
explanatory model, and the two systems are not psychobiologically distinct
and thus neither one is really real. This means, among other things, that we
can think of the initial settings of what is modeled as System 1 as, in reality,

variable, fluid, and messy, as a system that can adjust and learn on its own (Railton 2014). Fruit flies and sea slugs can learn from experience, so there is no reason to think that whatever it is that System 1 names can learn, adjust its initial settings, and sophisticate itself. This would mean that in the human case, as seems to be the case with nonhuman animals without large dorsolateral prefrontal cortices, such as dogs, "the more complex sentiment" of which Darwin speaks can be understood as emerging in social commerce at either the System 1 level itself, so long as it can learn, or at the locations where System 1 and System 2 interact and blend due to social experience.

Variation

I have been speaking as if there is such a thing as original human nature, something like our species nature. I think the idea makes some sense. But there is this caveat: Ever since Darwin, we are encouraged, indeed required, to conceive of variation across populations. Some traits, height, for example, distribute themselves normally in a bell-shaped curve. If we separate the male and female populations, we get two distinct but overlapping height curves. One possibility is that different humans have different settings of the original modules, high original tunings for some modules, low tunings for others. Perhaps like height, facial hair, and upper-body strength the tunings are linked to biological sex. Variation in the initial settings might be widespread and important. Some people like novelty more than others, some are shyer, some more impulsive, and so on.

Also, there are almost certainly likely to be gender differences in the initial settings due to selection pressures that might have made for consequential differences in the male and female bodies. Tania Singer et al. (2006) claim that women experience empathy as measured by brain images for both generous sharers and ungenerous sharers in economic games if they are in pain, while men experience it for the generous sharers but not for ungenerous ones even if both are in pain. Assuming this is true, no one knows if this is a consequence of biological sex or socialized gender.

Any theory that thinks that there is a baseline or platform for morality in some kind of shared human first nature needs eventually to face up to this problem of variation. We should assume such variation for both "four sprouts" and "five modules," for example, in how precisely attuned the sprout or module is to what is supposed to activate it, and whether and how intensely it responds when activated. Some people, like some canines, are excessively deferential from the get-go. Newborns who sustain an elevated heart rate in response to novel stimulation are likely to be judged shy by themselves and others later on. There is variation in temperament, novelty seeking, just as there is in eye color, hair color, height, and so on.

Moral Specialization?

Once we understand how much variation there is, we can consider collectively how to deal with it. We ought not underestimate variation in the sprouts or modules in our natures, if there are any, but we also don't want to make too much of differences in the initial settings if these settings are also very plastic. This has happened. Many actual moralities have built themselves around the idea that different individuals are naturally suited to display or develop a virtue specialty but not all the virtues. Neo-Confucian philosophers thought that most animals were like this, uni-virtuousos.

> The benevolence of tigers and wolves, the dutifulness of bees and ants, the ritual propriety of badgers and otters, the wisdom of seasonal insects, and the trustworthiness of ospreys and hawks: since each of these only attains one [virtue] one cannot say that other creatures possess a complete endowment of benevolence, dutifulness, ritual propriety, and wisdom. . . . since other creatures never attain the excellence of the five types of virtuous conduct and their minds are not capable of intelligent reflection, it is simply groundless to say they fully possess benevolence, dutifulness, ritual propriety, and wisdom; this is just contrary to basic reason. (Ivanhoe 2015)

The idea that animals are exemplars of single virtues also occurs in some of Aesop's *Fables*, Buddhist *Jakata* stories, and the Hindu *Panchatantra*, as well as in the *Wizard of Oz*. Turtles are slow and steady, rabbits are fast but easily distracted, dogs are loyal, and lions are courageous. One sees a related idea in some role moralities, where skills and virtues are assigned narrowly—there are womanly virtues, heroic virtues, and the virtues of particular classes and castes. Each individual might be assigned a particular moral specialization, a virtue or a small cluster of virtues, based on sex, gender, race, profession. Alternatively, the moral community might be on the lookout for the normally limited virtuous potential of each individual and develop it along with the individual's station and duties or it might tell a noble self-fulfilling lie as to what those natural abilities are in order to gain the same results. The idea is that there is no expectation that all individuals develop all the virtues, whatever these are deemed to be. A world with divided moral labor works, if it does, in roughly the same way a world with an economic division of labor does.

Deep Structure

According to "five modules," from a dedicated system of five shared sets of intuitions, various cultures develop moralities that extend, shape, and moderate the modules, in order to create a system of appropriate, socially certified dispositions of perception, feeling, thought, and behavior. The shaping of first nature yields second nature, the set of human individuals with moral character, with systems of values, who know and abide certain norms, who possess a repertoire of virtues, and who often, at least in modern times, have a certain moral ideology. They are Catholic, Buddhist, Hindu, Confucian, Daoist, communist, consequentialist, Kantian, Jewish, Muslim, atheist, secular humanist, and so on.

Moral foundations theory sometimes depicts these different moralities as "incommensurable" (Haidt and Joseph 2004, 56). If by "incommensurable" they mean incomparable, this seems unlikely if there is a universal basis of all moralities in the common sprouts or modules.

According to moral foundations theory, the modules, like classical Chinese sprouts, underwrite virtues, but they are not themselves virtues. They are "an essential tool in the construction of a virtue" (Haidt and Joseph, 2004, 63). We can think of the modules as potential virtues or protovirtues or as housing potentials for the virtues. One interesting question is whether the modules also provide the seeds or sprouts on which vice grows or can grow. And the answer is "yes." In fact, moral foundations theory is explicit about this basis for vice with respect to the modules. So, for example, the loyalty/in-group module is the basis both for the virtue of attentiveness to the needs of loved ones and for various familiar kinds of nepotism and chauvinism. MacIntyre's "Is Patriotism a Virtue?" (1984b) is a lovely exploration of just how difficult finding the balance or mean here is. We want people to care specially about their community or society in part because this is the best practical way to produce the greatest good for everyone. But we don't want such care and concern to become chauvinistic, blinkered, and so on. The same goes for the other foundations; in each and every case there are ways that one can under- or overdevelop the initial sprout, or activate the module deficiently or excessively. Care or compassion may seem like the exception, in the sense that there can never be too much of it. But for Aristotle it was clear that the "care" or compassion foundation can be developed excessively (Nathaniel West's novella *Miss Lonely Hearts* provides a picture of such a case). And I think that this is a not uncommon view among many citizens of liberal democratic states, who think that justice does the heavy lifting.

One could of course be skeptical that there is any real moral force to designations of "virtue" and "vice." All naturalistic accounts of morality can be taken (although it is not necessary) to show that such designations as "virtue" and "vice" are to be read as honorifics (or pejoratives) pinned on different ways of extending or growing or cultivating the modules. Different societies favor different extensions of the modules. A minor or subordinate speaking up can be a virtue or a vice depending not only on context but also on culture. Compassion can be pegged as weakness or sentimentality, as courage can be viewed as foolhardiness, and a strict sense of justice as stiffness. Some think that there is no deep answer to the question of which way of doing things, of designating virtue and vice, is the right way.

The question remains whether developing all five foundations to some small or large degree is typical or necessary for an adequate morality. If "five modules" is true, then the surface structural differences among moralities, about which a significant amount of moral disagreement turns, are different extensions, expressions, modifications, and tunings-up or tunings-down of the same underlying deep structure. Furthermore, the evidence suggests that either some cultures or subcultures build morality mostly on a subset of these five foundations, or that if and insofar as all five intuitive modules are appealed to in all societies, they are hooked up with different domains of activation beyond the domains they are innately set to respond to, and/or they are tuned up-down (higher or lower) to different activating conditions.

This perhaps is enough about the ways that "four sprouts" and "five modules" conceive the foundation of morality. It is time to speak about whether these models are good models of first nature, about their relative and absolute strengths and weaknesses. Remember, we are on a mission to develop a more adequate philosophy of psychology that is helpful to the project of morality.

5

Beyond Moral Modularity

Sprouts and Modules

There are several issues that can now be addressed, two immediately: First, are the five modules more or less the same as the four sprouts, in terms of what they are set to do and why they are set to do that, in terms of what their function is or what their functions are? Second, are the five modules of moral foundations theory Mencian, in the sense that it is desirable normatively, to grow all of them, to develop all of them to the same extent, as it is, for example, to grow and develop all four limbs?

To answer these questions it will be helpful to line up Mencius's sprouts alongside moral foundations theory's modules (see Figure 5.1). Assuming that moral modules—sprouts in Mencius—pick out a small set of universal phenotypic traits that are adaptations[historical] and that serve in their extended forms as a basis for morality, one might expect the sprouts and the modules to map cleanly onto each other. The reason is that smart, observant people can see adaptations without knowing anything about the Darwinian theory that explains what an adaptation is, how one works, and so on. But the lists differ and not just because Mencius has only four sprouts, not five modules as moral foundations theory does. Mencius does not have a sprout for justice/fairness. This, of course, doesn't mean that Mencius doesn't recognize some such moral competence or universal feature of moral life. It is certainly not there on the surface.

Also, the assumption that Mencius is looking for universal traits that are adaptations in the biological sense is probably wrong and not only because it is anachronistic. He seems to be looking for universal traits or capacities that are productive of what contributes to flourishing, or what is good or right. He is not looking for the beginning or sprouts of vice. That is something his successor Xunzi (314–217 BCE) is better at. Even so, one might think that a sprout for "justice as fairness" should be highlighted since it plays such an important role in fitness, on the one side, and flourishing, goodness, and rightness, on the other. But it is not marked off and treated much or very directly in classical

FIGURE 5.1 Mencian Sprouts Compared to Modern Modules

REN	BENEVOLENCE	CARE/HARM
LI	PROPRIETY/DEFERENCE	AUTHORITY/RESPECT & IN-GROUP/LOYALTY
YI	RIGHTEOUSNESS	PURITY/SANCTITY & IN-GROUP/LOYALTY
ZHI	WISDOM	?
?		FAIRNESS/RECIPROCITY/JUSTICE

Chinese philosophy.[1] If there is in human nature a justice/fairness sprout that pertains at least to me wanting my fair share, as there is among capuchins or canines (Brosnan and de Waal, 2003), but it shows up neither as a sprout nor a virtue, we are owed an explanation as to why it wasn't seen in the fourth century BCE by Mencius.

One idea is that it is not missing and that we can find the sprout "justice as fairness" in Mencian righteousness (*yi*). If so, then *yi*, now understood to include justice as fairness, would be certified as an important virtue, but it would be understood as having different roots in Mencian moral psychology than it has in moral foundations theory. The reason is that in Mencius the virtue of *yi* is rooted in the sprout of purity/shame, a sprout that for moral foundations theory is a whole different deal. It supports not judgments of fairness but judgments about whether marrying first cousins or being an atheist makes one dirty or yucky.

Bryan Van Norden writes this of Mencius's moral psychology:

> Righteousness (yi) is the integrity of a person who disdains to demean herself by doing what is base or shameful, even if doing so would reap benefits. So, for example, a righteous person would not accept a gift given with contempt (6A10), beg in order to obtain luxuries (4B33), or cheat at a game (3B1). As with benevolence, the capacity for righteousness is innate, but its growth is first stimulated in the family, where respect for the opinions of one's elders is internalized as the ethical sense of shame. (2008, xxxii)

It is worth noticing that the examples Mencius gives in these passages of the structure of *yi* are not easily read as expressions or outgrowths of a beginning with modular structure as, for example, *ren* can be understood as the cultivated outgrowth of basic compassion (2A6). A toddler will eat a cookie even if it is given in great annoyance or exasperation, a well-formed adult will not. Somewhere along the way from being an infant to being an adult we acquire complex norms governing righteousness, *yi*. Similarly, there may be no innate disposition to express deference or propriety by, say, averting one's eyes over bowing over kneeling over handshaking. The specifics of rites must be learned, which is why they often stymie outsiders who are trying hard to pick up local customs of proper, decorous, courteous behavior.

Furthermore, although "four sprouts" has a hierarchy module in "deference," the sprout for propriety, which maps nicely onto the authority/respect/hierarchy module of moral foundations theory, there is no sprout in Mencius that maps onto the in-group/out-group module of moral foundations theory. Then, again, one could make a plausible, but not decisive, case that the Chinese tradition makes much ado about filial piety (*xiao*), which is a paradigm case of an in-group virtue—that starts with one's parents and older siblings and which then generalizes to other elders inside one's culture.[2] This, if true, might lay the basis for an argument to the effect that the in-group/out-group module is a subspecies of authority/respect/hierarchy, or vice versa.

One might worry that we are down to only one bona fide sprout in Mencius, only one module-like beginning, the sprout of compassion (2A6) that does the mother lode of work in specifying by its first nature its own second nature form. This is a good, sensible worry to have. The rest of the moral equipment that is said to consist of sprouts or to be sprout-like start to look like very general, complex abilities and orientations, beginnings, perhaps, but beginnings that radically underspecify their own final form. That, their final form, is now being largely left up to the particularities of distinctive moral communities.

Practical Wisdom

When the four sprouts and the five modules are lined up, Mencian wisdom, *zhi*, stands out as a clear loner. The reason is informative, speaks in favor of one feature of Mencius's moral psychology over "five modules," and reveals a weakness in any modules-all-the-way-up view. Mencian wisdom, *zhi*, appears to be a meta-skill, largely cognitive, akin to Aristotelian *phronesis*, practical wisdom, which involves the abilities to read complex situations, other people's character, to skillfully coordinate means and ends, to apply a doctrine of the mean between excess and defect, and that is familiar from both classical Greek and classical Chinese philosophy (Van Norden 2007, 123). Wisdom, *zhi*, as a mature virtue, competence, or set of competences, is not fast acting, nor is it automatic, and it is not seen in newborns (M. Kim 2010). A morally skilled individual might, like a practiced athlete, respond in skillful interpersonal ways, but there is nothing automatic about their response. The five modules of moral foundations theory "produce flashes of approbation and disapprobation," but mature moral judgments produce something more complex, very different from a flash (Appiah 2008, 128). The morally mature person will assess things as they are and respond appropriately. Whatever moral clarity they experience comes perhaps with a deep intuitive sense of rightness or fittingness, but almost never with a flash of approbation or disapprobation.

One can see the extraordinary usefulness of *zhi*. A standard difficulty for virtue theories is to break ties. What should I do when I am called on to be compassionate and just at the same time or when my powerful desire to ostracize the slimy scumbag (purity) conflicts with my impulse to be compassionate? Which is trump? It is not clear how modules solve such problems among themselves except by sheer strength. Imagine the order of trump just went from left to right according to the order in which the sprouts or modules are introduced by the respective theories, "four sprouts" or "five modules," which we might, for the sake of argument, say reflects the temporal order according to which they evolved. So, all else being equal, the output of the older trumps in case of ties, or whichever module reaches the highest intensity on a 1–10 scale trumps. In Figure 5.2 in-group/loyalty is activated the most, and thus its response rules the roost.

The modules might reveal their outputs in consciousness or outside it. If their deliverances are conscious there are still many possibilities. An individual might feel the force of both her disgust for the way a certain person dresses and a dollop of sympathy for her being so uncouth but reveal only the first reaction in behavior. Or she might show her disgust in a patronizing way, the outcome of the two modular reactions, disgust and sympathy interpenetrating at the level of behavior.

A practical general reasoning ability (*zhi*) could help if it operated with a rationally worked-out, as opposed to evolutionarily worked-out, trump rule to the effect that if/when there is conflict between, say, the purity and compassion

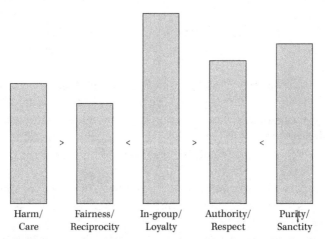

FIGURE 5.2 In an all modular (modules all-the-way-up) system, trump relations among the modules could be determined by intensity of activation or by the evolutionary order of emergence, so that in a competition, the most strongly activated or the oldest module activated wins.

modules, the latter (or former) is trump. Such a practical reasoning ability might sometimes look away from the modules altogether to some higher standard, to God's law, the Golden Rule, the categorical imperative, the principle of utility, or the wisdom of the ages.

Indeed, a close reading of Mencius indicates that he endorses such trump rules. For Mencius, benevolence (*ren*) and righteousness (*yi*) are the two most important virtues, more important than propriety (*li*) (Van Norden 2007, 273).[3] How does Mencius gain this ranking hierarchy? The best answer is that it is seen or discovered by wisdom (*zhi*), where wisdom is conceived not only as a virtue of persons but as a social virtue, and does not, at least in its mature form, have any modular features. It is not simply that *ren* and *yi* trump *li* because that is the way the system is built or designed—so that you will be caused by the force of the strongest module to save your drowning sister-in-law even though this requires improper touching (4A17), or to tell grandpa that you intend to marry whom you choose despite the fact that he is not one of us. Rather it is that you can do these things because they are reasonable, rational, the right thing to do under the circumstances. In these cases, benevolence (*ren*) and right (*yi*) provide stronger reasons than decorousness or propriety (*li*).

There is a reply to my objection (due to P. J. Ivanhoe) that Mencian *zhi* is akin to reason, which is not modular. The issue of modularity is in the first instance about the sprouts, not about their mature form. And, according to Mencius, *zhi* is the mature form of an ability that begins in an innate tendency to respond with approval or disapproval to simple cases of good or bad character and good or bad action. I like people who give me cookies, not those who hoard them. Very young children and perhaps other animals respond in these kinds of ways: approving—Yes! Yes! Smile, or disapproving No! No! Scowl. It is this sprout that yields *zhi* in its mature form, where *zhi* has become a flexible and far-ranging ability that allows sophisticated evaluation and judgment of character and types of action. But still, on this analysis, *zhi* begins as a module or as a cluster of minimodules. So the modular basis of virtue is still a contender.

This objection is helpful and it would protect the most general version of the moral modularity thesis, which says that some set of modules forms the basis of all moralities. But it undermines the modules all-the-way-up view, since it pictures the sprout that yields *zhi* not simply as expanding in content and scope during development, but also as yielding a higher order capacity that is no longer remotely modular in form. One advantage of accepting the picture that conceives mature *zhi* as emerging from the sprout of approval and disapproval is that it explains why Chinese *zhi* is not understood as dispassionate. *Zhi* is passionate reason.

In any case, whether wisdom (*zhi*) is conceived as an independent System 2 meta-skill or a hypertrophy of a System 1 sprout or some sort of System 1 and System 2 hybrid, and if in addition benevolence (*ren*) and righteousness (*yi*) trump propriety (*li*) in importance, then the analogy in "four sprouts" with growing and coordinating all four limbs starts to break down, unless, that is, some limbs are to be stronger (or longer) than others and one limb (wisdom, *zhi*) is less like a limb than like the mind. Wisdom (*zhi*) is more like the motor cortex or even DLPFC (dorsolateral prefrontal cortex) or System 2, which controls the limbs (via motor areas), than like one of the limbs (now three), or like the charioteer's relation to his chariot and his two steeds in Plato's famous analogy, or like the horseback rider in a favored Korean neo-Confucian analogy, or to the elephant rider in an analogy deployed by advocates of "five modules" (Haidt 2012).

If one attraction of "four sprouts" from a contemporary modularist perspective is that it seems to maintain a smooth relation between "is" and "ought," between description and normativity, then in fact, upon reflection, it doesn't do this. What we ought to do, how we ought to weight the outputs of the modules, is not determined by the modules themselves. The modules, if there are any, are shaped, grown, moderated, suppressed, and integrated by and in a preexisting but ever-changing cultural ecology. The ecology is the normative force field in which we grow and develop, and it is authorized, regulated, and maintained outside the head, in the common, but possibly fractious, social ecology.

If another attraction of "four sprouts" is that it anticipates the modern modularity view, then in fact it doesn't quite do that either. There is not a match between the list of philosophy's first great moral modularist and its twenty-first-century mate—between "four sprouts" and "five modules." In the end, Mencius is not a "modules-all-the-way-up" theorist, because he sees that a general purpose meta-skill, namely, wisdom, *zhi*, emerges (either from a sprout or independently or through some sort of hybrid process) and exerts cognitive control over first-order dispositions whatever the number and nature of these might be. This is an important insight about the need for and role of non-modular elements for successfully negotiating the sociomoral domain in most actual worlds.

The upshot is that "four sprouts" does not succeed, upon close scrutiny, in describing moral competence as fully modular, nor does a credible moral analogue of the four limb analogy emerge. Becoming virtuous is not just like growing one's arms and legs. And this is a good feature of Mencius's model: placing *zhi*, or something like *zhi* (*phronesis*), in the driver's seat, describes a capacity that we seem sometimes to actually deploy in real moral life. How *zhi* works is to be explained partly in terms of psychology and partly in terms of the social ecology.

Putting aside the special problem due to the nonmodular, non-limb-like aspects of Mencian wisdom (*zhi*), one way of explaining the lack of fit between the two lists, or possibly of explaining it away, especially given how perfectly the Mencian sprouts (imagining them again as perfectly sprout-like) yield exactly the four Confucian cardinal virtues, is this way: Mencius was noticing the sprouts that his culture valued, idealized, and amplified, but not all the sprouts available for valuing or amplification. In this case, Mencius makes no contribution to normative ethics generally—if there be such a thing—but only to ancient Chinese cultural anthropology or ancient Chinese moral psychology. The same could then be said of Aristotle. What Aristotle depicts as first nature is not all there is in human nature deep-down-inside-beneath-the-clothes-of-culture that can be cultivated, but mainly the equipment that is most relevant to cultivating excellent Greek men, just, courageous, witty, friendly, wise, philanthropic men. This suggests the possibility that if there are seeds or sprouts or beginnings or modules in human nature and they are comparable to limbs, then they are comparable to the limbs of a creature that either has many limbs only some of which are chosen to do work, or alternatively that has no determinate number of limbs, but some range that constitutes normalcy. Imagine that an octopus, now a "ploctypus," can have anywhere from four to twelve limbs depending on the local ecology.[4] The right number is determined relationally in terms of what number of limbs is best suited to the environment or what number the environment happens to serendipitously select. The idea is that first nature may be extremely plastic itself, at its own level, so that there might not—assuming there are modules—be any specific number of them until they are put into a complex set of environments (embryonic, geographic, sociomoral, economic, etc.). Another possibility is that what modules we think there are and assign to first nature may be interest-relative pragmatic constructs rather than objectively real special purpose sprouts, modules, anatomically or functionally canalized dispositions.[5]

The basic idea here is from Waddington (see Figure 2.1). Whatever human first nature consists in at the point of conception, it exists in an environment, first fetal, then parental and sociocultural, and there are causal influences in every direction. Two eyes, a nose, two arms, and two legs are robust phenotypic traits. They are produced across most every fetal environment. Speaking a language is also robust, although which language one speaks is determined by local rules. Most environments present a landscape with channels that draw first nature to be formed in certain ways. Not all possibilities are equally probable. However, over world historical time most human landscapes have been transformed both in terms of their natural features and in terms of what sociomoral channels we are directed toward and that mold us. If when the ice melted at the end of the Pleistocene we were uncouth, sexist cavemen, we are now, at least superficially, more couth and less sexist. The social environment channels us that way. A similar set of problems arises when considering moral foundations theory's modules as both descriptive and normative, as containing information about both what the innate moral dispositions are and what the extended competence is supposed to be. Recent work indicates that the political morality of American Liberals rests primarily on considerations of harm and fairness (modules 1 and 2), whereas the morality of American Conservatives rests on considerations corresponding to all five modules (Haidt and Graham 2007; Haidt 2012). Cultures or, as in these cases, subcultures inside a culture, nation-state, or small community, "can specialize in a subset of human moral potential" (Haidt 2001, 827). According to "five modules," divergent conceptions of the appropriate boundary conditions (domains) of the modules, or divergent relative priority among the modules, or over- or underdevelopment of the modules would each deliver us divergent moralities, which are nonetheless built from the same suite of modules. So what is the right way to grow and/ or tune the modules, assuming again, for the sake of argument, there are any? If the answer is not in the modules where—if anywhere—is it?

Taming First Nature

Suppose (implausibly) that the original scope of compassion is attuned only to children of one's own kind falling into wells, but can be extended to unrelated kids, old folks, and so on. This will require extension of scope. Likewise, suppose what is not implausible, that disgust is originally attuned to rancid food or excrement, but can be extended to strangers, communists, and homosexuals. Some think that there are no deep moral "reasons" to favor a society that does not extend the scope and content of a sprout in one way rather than another. There just are the different ways different groups extend the foundations, and then the various contingencies that bring about interest group "nudges" to adjust, extend, moderate, and modify the scope and content over which the modules range. I think there is a normative principle that one can use to evaluate extensions.

> *The Anti-Extension Principle*: Allow a module, if there are any, some permission to range over the contents it was originally designed to range over and to have the scope it was designed to have by Mother Nature. But resist further extensions, unless there are good sociomoral reasons for them. When there are extensions in place that have occurred under the radar, or that are unreflectively delivered on the wings of some tradition, feel free to examine their genealogies looking for dubious moral sources. Finally, require when it seems necessary, for example, when there are challenges, that the extensions be justified or rejustified morally, that reasons that pertain to what produces well-being, or what is good, or what is right be publicly produced and certified or recertified.

The "some permission" clause is intended to give a module a prima facie pass to do what it is supposed to do on grounds that it was presumably an adaptation when it evolved. But this permission is revocable for a variety of reasons. The trait may no longer be an adaptation, or exercising it might enhance fitness but not be morally good. In the latter case, we might understand the tendency and then need to work hard to mitigate or overcome it. Bloom (2013b) and Greene (2013) emphasize how easy it is to arouse xenophobic, ethnocentric, and racist feelings in babies. This is because first nature is designed to be small-group focused, possibly tribal. But the dispositions can be mitigated by wise care and instruction. And they should be.

Suppose the disgust reaction is set by Mother Nature to be triggered by more than dangerous fluids and waste, but also by incest within the nuclear family (Strominger, 2014). Allow disgust to range over rancid food, sour milk, human and animal waste, incest, and such easy extensions as masturbating on food that you then serve to guests. But don't raise the kids to think homosexuality is disgusting. The rationale is that there is a prima facie reason to think that evolved modules were, at least, once adaptations, plus we know that germs are bad for you, and that some fluids and substances carry germs more easily than others.[6] In extending its scope or content to cover new situations, require that good reasons, reasons of the right kind, be offered.

Disgust for homosexuals will not pass such a test, nor will disgust for communists or strangers, which, however, is compatible with wanting reassurances that the communists and strangers do not have bad intentions. In the other direction, if an ancient setting on a module starts to be questioned because it is no longer an adaptation in current environments or because it is still fitness-enhancing but is in tension with other ends—flourishing, goodness, rightness—then consider suppressing it or sublimating it. Some think that for evolutionary reasons men have tendencies to want to outcompete other men in reproduction, and also to be relieved of child-rearing duties. If true, this would be an example of an adaptation (it enhances fitness) that ought to be suppressed or sublimated for reasons of flourishing, goodness, and rightness. If, as part of this same adaptationist cluster, young men in particular are prone to violence and this tendency once served to keep peace, but no longer does so in the modern world, we ought to work to minimize or remove catalysts to violence such as economic inequality, lack of educational opportunity, and easy availability of guns. Basic common sense.

Unlike Mencius's sprout view, moral foundations theory might be judged to assume too readily (it is part of the scientific zeitgeist) an adaptationist prejudice. The initial settings of the modules are presumed to have been "selected for" because they enhanced fitness (Sober 1984; Brandon 1990). That is, they were selected for because of ties they had to the fitness of ancestral species and early hominids. *Homo sapiens* in its modern form emerged 250,000 years ago. But only in the last 12,000 years, since the domestication of animals and invention of agriculture, did people start to live in groups bigger than 150, to develop markets between tribes and capitalistic exchanges that bring unrelated people into regular relations with each other. The sprouts or modules that do the work of morality for us were selected for their contribution to fitness in environments entirely unlike modern ones. Furthermore, as I've been insisting, even if we assume that fitness is necessary for flourishing, goodness, and rightness (in the weak sense that you need to exist, to survive, in order to enact or realize these things), it is not sufficient. Fitness reasons have to do with maximizing genetic profit—with getting more copies of my genes or the genes of my people into the future gene pool than those of others. Flourishing reasons have to do broadly with the quality of lives, not their length or biological fecundity, with such things as decency, education, literacy, happiness, and social support. Goodness and rightness reasons are considerations about what advances the flourishing of all, the virtues, and the recognition of equal worth, rights, and dignity.

Consider again, the disgust module. Disgust is designed to be triggered by such things as excrement, rancid food, disease, and incest. As an adaptation, disgust has little to do initially with morality, or with interpersonal commerce beyond disgust for incest. The fact that we can and do easily extend it to people who sometimes carry bad odors, germs, and so forth, or to people with unseemly sexual preferences may not itself be a biological adaptation, but simply an easy extension of one. The same goes for extending warm fuzzy Mencian 2A6 feelings to cartoon figures with large heads and big eyes, or to pandas and puppies. The compassion system can easily do that, but it does not contribute to either fitness or, possibly, to morality, assuming we are already respectful of the life of all sentient beings.

One reply here for the proponent of "five modules" is to claim that the relevant basic reactive attitude for the purity/sanctity foundation is contempt not disgust. This move has potential, since the Ekman contempt face is very close to the disgust face involving only a slight difference in one corner of the mouth, but unlike disgust, contempt is a response to people who are morally slimy. As for extending compassion and any other initial setting beyond its initial fitness-enhancing scope, it makes sense to require different kinds of reasons, reasons that pertain to other goods than fitness. For example, the fact that it is easy to extend compassion to pandas and puppies because they have the look of a human baby is a cause of extending compassion, not a reason for extending compassion. A reason would be that they are sentient beings, feel pain, have social lives, and as such, have interests that deserve protection and promotion.

Evolutionary biologists and psychologists distinguish among adaptations that were selected for and various kinds of exaptations, spandrels, and free riders. A heart that pumps and oxygenates the body is an adaptation. The sound it makes while pumping is a free rider; it comes automatically with a muscle that expands and contracts in a cavity to send blood throughout the body. Using the heart rate in medical diagnostics is adaptive in the sense that it is good for us, but not an adaptation in the sense that there are genes for it, that it is hereditable, and so forth. We discovered that listening to heart rate tells us something about heart health. But Mother Nature did not make heart sounds so that we could do that. Likewise, even if Mother Nature set us for adaptive reasons to form strong bonds with in-group members and even if that trait can easily be extended to distrust, even to despise, out-group members, does not mean that it was selected to do that. Nor, more importantly, does it mean that it is smart or good to do that.

One response is to say that I am too hopeful that disgust, as well as in-group chauvinism, can be contained, possibly that many familiar forms of it can be eliminated. The disgust module is like a tropism, reflex, or instinct. If activated there will be a ballistic straight shot that produces disgust. But this is not so. When social psychologists study the response, they see that its contours are highly responsive to socioeconomic status, education, and zip code (Haidt et al. 1993).

Interpenetration and Hybridity

I've been arguing that if there are modules in human nature they are subject to hybridity and interpenetration, as well as to all sorts of relations to nonmodular features of the heart-mind, for example, to thinking and imagination, as well as to the wider sociocultural ecology. Kwame Anthony Appiah asks us to consider how little we experience our own moral responses as running up and down silos of the sorts depicted in Figures 3.1 and 3.2 of "five sprouts." Appiah writes:

> Now, you will already have started to wonder how modular these hypothetical modules really are. If you cheat me—or treat me without dignity—am I not harmed? In Shakespeare's *Richard II*, Thomas Mowbray says, "Mine honour is my life; both grow in one / Take honour from me, and my life is done." We have already remarked on the fact that people of low caste are regularly represented as being impure or polluted (a condition that blends considerations of hierarchy with their outgroup status). Is ingroup solidarity free of a sense of reciprocity? What about the resurgence of interest in "stigmatic" punishments among legal scholars: when we punish someone in this way (for example, by requiring the drunk driver to advertise his status on his bumper), is stigma best understood on the pollution model ("cooties") or on the hierarchy model (dishonor; the "white feather") or on the outgroup model (as with "shunning")? Is gratitude—if it is to be more than a felt obligation to discharge a debt—reducible to reciprocity or does it not borrow from elevation, buoyed by the sense that we have been helped by an act of supererogatory kindness? Is the awe that we experience when contemplating the venerated moral saint entirely different from the awe commoners once experienced in the presence of royalty? . . .

Our interrogation could continue indefinitely. So we should be clear that these conjectured modules interact in countless ways, and we shouldn't pretend that they "cut nature at the joints"; tomorrow, someone might come up with a different and more persuasive taxonomy. The best case to be made for such modules is just this: when we try to reduce one of these categories to another (or another set of these categories), there always seems to be some residue left. And the same holds on the level of moral theory: parsimonious theories that aim to reduce everything to a reckoning of harm and fairness, say, just don't account for the full range of our moral intuitions, including reflection-resistant ones. (2008, 145–47)[7]

Appiah raises four concerns about moral modularity. First, the phenomenology of moral experience involves massive interpenetration and admixture of moral qualities, not single-minded ballistic responses of allegedly canalized response systems. Second, the system triggered by fitness-enhancing or fitness-detracting situations from the original evolutionary situation, cannot know what its responses are supposed to be in new worlds that are nothing like that world. Third, we call now on that old fitness-advancing equipment, whatever it consists in, to concern itself with new ends, goodness, rightness, and flourishing. Affronts to one's honor and dignity, for example, only arise inside a system of social practices that are entirely modern and which only recently created those very concepts. Fourth, the principles that govern the division into five distinct modules are not entirely precise.

When a novice or mature individual experiences a strong protomoral or quasi-moral reaction to a stimulus or situation, how does the system activate? How does the system know which module is violated when something bad happens? One answer is that the modules know a priori, in advance of experience, presumably thanks to the way they, the modules themselves, have been built by the regimen of natural selection (here intended to include both functional historical adaptations as well as quirky nonadaptive constraints, exaptations, and so on). Another possibility is that the modules are not very fixed, but are designed to absorb what the culture teaches about norms, values, wise choices, and apt feelings. This information is not in the head, but in the cultural surround. It is a sociohistorical product and comes in a different, more flexible form than what is packaged in genetic and neural structure and computed by fixed psychobiological structures. This would explain more easily perhaps than modular structure, how and why massive interpenetration across silos is possible.

Consider the family. The family is a universally important sphere of human life, a domain of enormous practical and moral significance, and it is recognized as such across traditions. The family is a laboratory in which every social situation type occurs. There are dramas that pertain to care, compassion, love, loyalty, us-them, and so on; similarly for spheres such as friendship, romantic relations, work, and religion. "Five modules" can handle family relations, but the way it does so looks a bit ham-fisted and ecologically invalid. Some situations that occur in the family activate the care/compassion module, others the justice module, others the in-group/out-group module, others the hierarchy/respect module. The alternative is to say that family life activates complex dispositional tendencies that from the start interpenetrate to a greater degree than any industrial-strength modularity view can permit.

Delusions of Rational Justification and Control

I have explained an advantage that Mencius's "four sprouts" view has over contemporary "five modules." It explicitly acknowledges the existence of some nonmodular cognitive competence as part of the ordinary architecture of the moral mind. *Zhi,* for the curious, is similar to what Aristotle calls *phronesis,* although perhaps it has more oomph since Chinese philosophy does not separate reason and emotion the way most Western traditions do. It is not entirely clear that "five sprouts" is committed to the thesis that the moral architecture is modules all-the-way-up, but if it is, this is a weakness. But it is best not to read "four sprouts" as advancing such a strong thesis. There is too much in Mencius that emphasizes self- and social-cultivation to think that his sprouts do all the work.

Jonathan Haidt (2001, 2012) commonly expresses skepticism about reason's role, especially its power over the outputs of the modules, sometimes claiming that it is a "rationalist's delusion" that reason plays much of a role in guiding morality and resolving moral issues. One widely accepted reading of his "The Emotional Dog and Its Rational Tail" (2001), is that rational moral discourse is epiphenomenal post facto rationalization. Smart college students can provide all sorts of reasons why they will not PUSH in FOOTBRIDGE, but the evidence is that they are just feebly trying to explain a System 1 gut reaction that they themselves don't understand, that dumbfounds them. So they say a lot of stuff, make a lot of verbal noise, go scholastic and casuistic to account for lower brain parts that just say NO!

In his recent work (2012), Haidt argues that there are two roles that reason plays, where reason isn't naming anything highfalutin, just thinking, deliberating, trying to figure out what is for the best, deciding what to do, and doing it.

1. A strategic or instrumental role in rationalizing and framing actions, norms, or policies in order to win friends and influence people. Haidt calls the view about the role and power of reason "Glauconian"; but he should call it "Thrasymachean" since Glaucon, Plato's brother, describes the view in the *Republic* without endorsing it, whereas

Thrasymachus, himself a sophist, endorses it. This represents the social role of reason.

2. An animal trainer-like role, that involves tricking and treating an unruly animal into compliance. Reason sometimes plays a role akin to that of the elephant driver who guides, cajoles, and encourages an unwieldy elephant, that represents the rest of you, to do what you, the driver, want it to do. This represents the individual role of reason.

The picture that Haidt rejects is that reason plays the role of truth-seeking or conjuring up or offering good justifying, public reasons for action. He denies in addition that moral self-control, self-cultivation, and sociomoral policy are exercised typically on the basis of such reasons. Sometimes he seems skeptical that thinking can in principle play such justifying and controlling roles. The elephant is not obedient because he gets the driver's reasons but because he succumbs to the driver's power, treats, and training. This may be true about the elephant, but it is beside the point. The driver has his reasons, which he can justify (he gets paid if the elephant rides the passengers successfully) and he demands that the elephant respond to them. It is no different than when I decide to go to the movies and go.[8] I have my reasons and my body cooperates.

Haidt calls the view he opposes "the rationalist's delusion." He writes: "worship of reason is ... one of the most long-lived delusions in Western history. ... The rationalist delusion ... is not just a claim about human nature. It's also a claim that the rational caste (philosophers and scientists) should have more power, and it usually comes with utopian programs for raising more rational children" (2012, 88).

Here we have two hyperbolic claims at once: that we overrate the role of reason, the delusion part, and that the rational caste uses the delusion to gain control over the hearts and minds of the youth. As I said earlier, we must separate the components of Haidt's own program from what moral foundations theory as a communal research program says, implies, entails, or requires. My recommendation is to read "five modules" as a theory about some of the sources or roots or sprouts of morality, but not as a theory about the whole of moral psychology. What proponents of moral foundations theory have proposed so far is that there is a modular system in first nature, and that it can explain a fair amount about the structure of moralities across the earth. The beginnings are cultivated in the multifarious ways that yield all the moralities that exist. But moral foundations theorists have not dedicated themselves to studying the role or the efficacy of reason in the allegedly delusional sense or the roles of culture and history in shaping the moral mind. Haidt's famous "Emotional Dog" paper (2001) is a one-off that does show that there are some cases in which reasoning looks to be mere rationalization, and even worse like post facto confabulation, about why we judge a tricky moral dilemma as we do. But we know and knew in advance that some people, especially verbally adept college students who are invited to say more than they can know, sometimes do that.

If Haidt and his fellow moral foundations theorists think that this shows that the modules do most or all of the work in determining the fine-grained texture of individual moral personality, feeling, and behavior in real life, they would need evidence that they simply do not have. Meanwhile, thousands of years of philosophy across traditions, thousands of years of testimony of individuals who do not do what is wrong even though they are powerfully tempted, as well as nascent but compelling work in cognitive neuroscience that tests the alleged delusion of rational justification and control, yields a different picture (Greene, 2013). Reason, usually in tandem with imagination, can and does sometimes play the role that philosophers say it does. This clears space for saying it would be better still if it played more of a role in both justification and control, and not just for some imaginary power-hungry rational caste, but for everyone.

Individual Reason and Social Reason

There is another point that needs emphasis: There are two senses of reason that overlap and interpenetrate. One sense is psychological; the other sense is social-historical. The first refers to certain inner resources of individuals. The second refers to communal resources, considerations, and practices that individuals depend on to structure and order their lives. Once a polity decides that there should be public education and welfare for the poor, that there are reasons to mitigate fate's arbitrary rule, it sets up mechanisms and bureaucracies to provide education and other public goods without depending on each individual's reason and will to do what the polity has determined is rational, makes sense, is wise and good. The resources are in social relations, in the culture, in public institutions.

It is a weakness of moral foundations theory or at least of Haidt's version of it that it underestimates both kinds of reason. Denying reason's role in justification and control dramatically overreaches as a descriptive psychological claim relative to the evidence. It is a claim for which moral foundations theory has no interesting evidence, nor that its proponents have even tried to test in any large-scale or systematic way. Those who have studied this matter in a systematic and large-scale way claim that there are two systems, System 1 and System 2, the so-called dual process model, and that they interact in complex ways. The view in its modern form is said to originate with William James ([1890] 1950), and is all the rage in contemporary cognitive science (Kahneman 2011). But even Kahneman insists in his book on the two systems that they are merely useful fictions. They provide a model for analysis. They do not exist separately. They are not real (77).

Thus, it is an empty, unwarranted, possibly dangerous rhetorical conceit, to claim that we shouldn't try to use reason in the way philosophers recommend, because we can't. The dialectical situation is such that the burden of proof for advocates of the view that reason's fans are deluded is on them to show that reasons don't play a justificatory or controlling role, and that they can't.[9]

Multiple Teleologies

There is one advantage that "five modules" has over "four sprouts," namely, it makes better sense of the multiple options for building second nature out of the original sprouts in virtue of being less confident that they wear their end (*telos*) or function (*ergon*) or aim on the label that comes with the sprouts they are. Moral foundations theory also acknowledges, perhaps more clearly than the Mencian view, the tendencies they have to support vice, as well as virtue.

This latter point is important and needs emphasizing. The sprouts that serve morality are set in Mencius, or perhaps it is better to say, are understood by Mencius, when cultivated properly, to produce exactly the virtues that the Confucian form of life aims at. This is the *ergon*, the proper function, and the *telos*, the goal, of the Mencian sprouts. In good environments the sprouts realize their destiny and constitute the virtues of a *junzi*, a *Ru* gentleperson. This seems, with several thousand years of experience of moral diversity and the ever-present abundance of ill-formed, even bad people, under our belts, too good to be true.[10]

"Five modules" is a better model for seeing that and how the sprouts of morality, whether conceived along Mencian lines or in contemporary terms, radically underdetermine mature moral psychology. "Five modules" is intended to model what we know to be actual and not merely possible: that people, subcultures and cultures, differ in terms of how much any module is developed, what it is extended to cover, how much it is favored or disfavored, and so on. Furthermore, the modules contain within themselves the potential to be exploited excessively or deficiently; each module has vices, as well as virtues, associated with it.

Seeds and Weeds

Many traditions and many views, including ones that never explicitly entertain modular architectures, acknowledge the existence of what Buddhists call the poisons in human nature. Alongside whatever prosocial, altruistic, good tendencies in human nature are antisocial, egotistic, bad tendencies. In Buddhism, the three poisons are (1) ungrounded fantasies, illusions, and delusions that I will get what I wish for and that I deserve it (*moha*); (2) avaricious, greedy, rapacious, thirsty desires for all sorts of stuff I think I really need (*lobha*); and (3) hatred, anger, and resentment (*dosa*) when I do not get what I want, when others stand in my way. Like Mencius's four good sprouts, these sprouts come with our natures, as a sort of Buddhist original sin (Flanagan 2011; Ivanhoe 2015a). There are not only good seeds in our nature, but bad seeds as well, kudzu, which, if given the chance, will grow unconstrained and suck the life out of the good sprouts.

Call any view that is like this a "seeds and weeds" view. How do we distinguish between the good seeds and sprouts and the bad ones, the weeds? Weeds, after all, are just plants that for multifarious reasons we don't like or want in the garden. Are the bad ones always bad? Confucius distinguishes "petty impatience" from principled anger, and in the *Analects*, he sometimes loses his temper with his students for good reason and with good effect. Some Buddhists think that violence can be warranted as part of a quiver filled with "skillful means."

The point is that when we do a clear-eyed, normatively neutral inventory of human first nature, we will see not only Mencian sprouts with a noble teleology but also various tendencies, especially emotional ones, that are equally natural but normatively more suspect or worrisome. This complicates the work of the moral psychologist in providing a complete inventory of first nature. It also complicates the work of the moral community and the moral self-cultivator to grow what is good and weed or suppress what is not good, as well as to explain why and how some gifts of Mother Nature, which may well have become fixed because they were fitness-enhancing adaptations, are not conducive to flourishing or goodness, not conducive at all or not conducive in certain forms. On every place on earth, and at every time, there have been debates and disagreements about what Allan Gibbard (1992) calls "wise choices and apt feelings," about the norms governing behavior, what to choose and do, how to be, and about the norms governing emotional feelings, emotional expression, and the regulation of the economy of human desire and action. It is not only between moral communities that there are disagreements about apt feelings, but often, at least in modern times, inside them. I say you are rude. You say you are honest and direct. I say you are immodest. You say you appreciate beauty, and that you are simply not uptight or a prude.

Thanks to work at the intersection of ethics and the human sciences, there has been progress in developing more psychologically and anthropologically robust and realistic moral psychological models. We should, in fact, call some of the models on offer "bio-psycho-social" models. We have a more robust and adequate philosophical anthropology than we did when Elizabeth Anscombe expressed her lament over a half century ago that ethics suffers from the lack of an adequate philosophy of psychology. This more adequate philosophical psychology and anthropology provides abundant evidence that the possibility space for human psychology and development is vast and much of it, most of it, perhaps, is still untapped. We are not moral tabulae rasae. Our species nature and common problems across space and time constrain what is good, right, and what conduces to flourishing, without determining what is good, right, and what conduces to flourishing. And excellent work on human first nature from across the disciplines is filling out the picture of both the good sprouts and the bad sprouts, the angels and devils in our natures, as well as the sometimes surprising zones of fragility and strength. In some cases, as in the case of revisiting great thinkers like Confucius and Mencius, Plato and Aristotle, the Stoics and Epicureans, it is a matter of revisiting and reminding ourselves of what is already known, embedded, and worked-out in our own and other traditions.

On the consensus view, we all to some degree contain the seeds to display the virtues of a saint or the vices of a devil. There are seeds, say, for generosity, love, justice, courage, honesty, and respect on the one side, and seeds for miserliness, meanness, thievery, sloth, dishonesty, gluttony, and contempt, on the other. The seeds that are fed are the ones that grow into mature plants, the virtues or vices that will make up the distinctive ecology that is each one of us, which makes up our character.

Moral Science and Normative Ethics

"Five modules" claims that there are (at least) five dispositional foundations in human nature. The modules underwrite cognitive-affective-conative reactions that coevolved with certain specific kinds of states-of-affairs. The right kinds of states-of-affairs activate the dispositions in normal environments and produce "intuitions," as well as impulses to act.[11] The initial dispositions are then grown, moderated, modified, channeled, and harmonized in distinctive ways across—and even within—social environments. The original dispositions plus their extended phenotypes form a fair amount, possibly all, of what are recognized across cultures as morality. These dispositional foundations, or better the disposition/environment activating condition pairs, are first nature.

Second nature is what you get when you take all the individual and small-group variation in the initial settings of the dispositional foundations, and mix them with the multifarious vagaries of fetal development, local natural and social ecologies, family, economics, religion, politics, history and culture, plus all manner of unforeseen disruptions, famines, tsunamis, wars, and unexpected good discoveries, electricity and iPhones.

There are many questions that remain, some are about the way first nature yields, if it does, to second nature. Other questions are more normative, about which way or ways given the constraints and directionality of first nature, and all the ecological contingency and variability we ought to seek to develop, build, or otherwise direct, including self-direct, first nature to become a certain variety of second nature. Is second nature only the emergent product of the modules? Is it only a matter of the initial modular settings percolating up through the soil of some antecedent natural and social environment? Or are there other sources of morality than just the modules and the local soil? Might there not be some nonmodular general purpose abilities that also come with human minds and that affect second nature "from above," reason, or what they are now calling "System 2" in cognitive science, for example?

A key normative question is: How do we tell when the outcome, or better, some set of outcomes of the initial settings of the modules, assuming there are any, mixed with all that contingency produces what we want and are correct in wanting? How do we tell whether some configuration or some set of configurations, but presumably not all configurations of second nature, are good, worthy, what we ought to want? How do we tell when a genealogy of morals has not just produced a morality—that is guaranteed—but a good one, a morality that is ethical, an ethical morality, a truly good way of living, of being human?

Merit and Promise of Sprout and Module Views

So what in summary is my view of sprout or modular theories? There are some strengths and some weaknesses. On the positive side, there is some merit in establishing an analytic vocabulary for the basic psychological disposition-situation pairs that are activated across worlds in very similar ways, and which are then cultivated, enhanced, modified, and weeded, in somewhat different, often surprising ways across moralities.

Regarding Mencian modularity: If there are sprouts in our natures, they are definitely not all good. I am agnostic about whether the Buddhist poisons or Christian original sin, or something like Xunzi's view that human desire is undisciplined or Hobbes's view that we are natural-born egoists gets the poisons right or describes the relevant tendency or tendencies better. There may be distinctive kinds of poisons—distinctive settings for food lust and sex lust—that disrupt social relations or it may just be the general tendency to selfishness that does so. But there are some such tendencies.

Regarding interpenetration, autonomy, and completeness, here is a generous scorecard: If there are modules, and if they really are like taste buds, a favored analogy among moral foundation theorists, then there is interpenetration already at the level of perception. A taste, even for a baby, is a unified experience: the taste of mother's milk, even absent the vocabulary for tastes, is sweet, salty, and umami. Because drinking mother's milk involves tactility as well as taste, it, the liquid, has an experienced texture, the texture of milk. Even in a newborn, the experience of the flavor and the taste is what-it-is, molar, holistic, unified, with a certain phenomenological structure or texture, which is detectable, somewhat experientially decomposable, but blended. The experience is the joint production of a modular taste-bud system, a (possibly) modular tactile-kinesthetic system that unifies and "binds" the output of the modules. Moral experience seems like this. As experience, it is like this. Modular outputs, if there are any, interpenetrate and yield their autonomy and isolation in experience from the get-go.

There are two more important points that bear repetition and emphasis: First, if there are moral modules, then in addition to the features of interpenetration just mentioned, they are not remotely fixed or set at birth. Even if taste buds compute sweet and salty, and the eyes compute color and light, newborns do not decode the social world in terms of justice, compassion, liberty, and the like. Second, whereas the output of modular sensory processors may be mandatory and cognitively impenetrable—the cilantro tastes soapy and I cannot think or will away the soapy taste—moral perception is penetrable by thinking. I might experience you powerfully and viscerally as someone who is alpha status-wise to my omega, but I may nonetheless decide that you are not worthy of my deference and stand up to you. This much militates against any extreme fixed modules all-the-way-up view.

The Role of Thinking and Imagination

The strongest reason to oppose a view that insists that the system is modules all-the-way-up is because we consistently reveal, across many domains of life, that we are rational social beings, a special kind of animal who has long ago embraced new kinds of reasons beyond reasons of fitness—reasons of flourishing, reasons of goodness, and reasons of rightness. No one who has reflected for a second about their own experience, let alone familiarized themselves with the wisdom of thinkers like Plato and Aristotle, Confucius, Mencius, and Xunzi was in need of twentieth- or twenty-first-century cognitive science discovering that we have in us these two capacities, System 1, fast, intuitive, and powerful, and System 2, slow, deliberate, and often hard to get into the driver's seat, where the latter houses *zhi, phronesis*, or reason.

A modules all-the-way-up view lacks resources to explain the possibility of what we know is actual, namely, that we do sometimes show strength of will and reason our way to justify and enact moral or political policies that go against System 1, our quick, intuitive gut reaction system (Bloom 2013a, 2013b; Greene 2013). Classical philosophers like Plato and Aristotle and Confucius and Mencius were right to emphasize the actual and normative roles of reason, *phronesis*, or *zhi*. Of course, one might hear smart-aleck cognitive neuroscientists say that speaking of reason is a philosopher's antiquarian affectation, and commits what Antonio Damasio (1994) calls "Descartes' error," advocating the "abyssal separation" of mind and body. The straightforward response is that speaking of reason doesn't imply, entail, or in any other way align oneself with a dualism of mind and body. It is simply a useful way of marking off in common parlance a capacity or set of capacities that we humans have. Classical Chinese philosophy especially cannot be a target for the "abyssal separation" charge since reason, *zhi*, is emotional, originating in a system that feels powerfully about what it approves and disapproves of, what it likes and dislikes. *Xin*, heart-mind, is or houses a passionate reason.[12]

We are creatures who live in spaces of reasons, as well as spaces of causes. Ethicists, as well as scientists, are in the business of giving justifying reasons for their views all the time. For the ethicist: Why is it good to be honest? Why ought I care about the well-being of others? For the scientist: How does this evidence support this hypothesis? Why should I trust this statistical measure rather than that one? Why care about understanding nature? We are not asking the ethicist or the scientist to tell us merely what causes the relevant belief or explains the overall commitment, but to explain what makes it sensible to hold the belief or to have the commitment.

So, I read the evidence for sprout or modular views of morality as mixed. What seems fairly clear is that there are in first nature a variety of dispositions that are implicated in what we call morality. How exactly to describe and individuate these dispositions is tricky. One way is to attempt to isolate modules, which are individuated/defined/characterized in terms of a well-defined, concrete, and limited set of prototypical triggers (seeing a child falling into the well) of basic affect-cognition-conation triplets (alarm, compassion, and impulse to save) at the lowest level or at the lowest morally relevant level. This is what moral foundations theory does, and perhaps what Mencius does as well. What I mean by the lowest morally relevant level is the level at which some tendency worth cultivating—where cultivation is initially ambiguous among grow, moderate, modify—is judged to occur in something like a moral or protomoral guise, for example, disgust at incest, which is moralized, but not disgust at sour milk, which is not moralized.

These points explain why and how moral foundations theory makes room for moral diversity. The initial fitness-enhancing settings of the sprouts, modules, or foundations radically underdetermine the shape, extent, strength, and scope that the realized, full-grown forms of them can and do take across human ecologies.

Whereas moral foundations theory is congenial to relativist and pluralist genealogies and perhaps also to normative relativism and pluralism, to the view that it is fine, acceptable, possibly good that different moral communities grow the sprouts/modules in their own ways, Mencian modularity expresses a kind of confidence that there is one way to grow the sprouts properly. That is, whereas moral foundations theory says that there are different ways to tune the modules, and that there may be no good reasons to prefer one way of tuning them over another, and thus no reasons for preferring one way of achieving second human nature over another, Mencius is plausibly read as thinking that the sprouts have a natural teleology, a proper function, which is to yield Confucian *junzi*.

Alternative Models

One result of this inquiry is to open up the possibility of other ways to model moral development than mainly in terms of sprouts or modules that consist of powers inside persons. Two additional models are visible now. The "domains of life" model and the "basic equipment" model. A "domains of life" approach involves thinking of the development of first nature into second nature as involving bringing a distinctive cultural form of life to a set of domains that are universally moralized or moralized "around here" by us. The focus is on domains in the world, birth, sexual coming of age, death or certain kinds of economic, political, religious institutions that will inevitably demand attention rather than on equipment inside persons.[13] A "basic equipment" model starts with the observation that it is persons-in-community (ies) who are transformed in a variety of holistic and interpenetrative ways as they develop into skilled, smart, gifted, and decent folks, and the equipment that yields such souls is whatever it is—modules, blank spaces, exotic thinking abilities—that the communities that aim to develop whole human beings work with.

One sees the "domains of life" approach across philosophical traditions, as well as in sociology and anthropology (Winch 1958; Nussbaum 1988; Fiske 1991, 1992, 2004; Shweder and LeVine 1984; Shweder 1991; Shweder et al. 1997). Pretty much every moral philosopher recognizes family and citizenship as zones of morality; and also that such events as birth, sexual coming of age, reproduction, and rituals for burying and remembering the dead are marked as significant and embedded in webs of sociomoral normativity. If one starts with domains of life, then one will focus on how to develop the beliefs, norms, and dispositions that will yield the virtues, apt feeling, wise choices, and correct behavior for each domain. There will be dispositions, such as respectful attention, for example, that will be required of each domain and thus across domains, and some that will be domain specific—joy at birth, grief at death, and so on.

Alan Page Fiske's (1992) influential theory of the four elementary forms of sociality can be read as being in the "domains of life" family of theories even though he describes the four forms as "psychological." How so? Across the earth people are born into preexisting cultural forms and normative ecologies that have in place certain norms of who is boss in what situations (hierarchy), when parties are equal and can demand equal treatment (equality matching and communal sharing), and what things cost in terms of money and effort (market pricing). The preexisting normative ecology presents new persons with its solutions to dealing with the main domains of life—family relations, marriage, civic life, and getting and spending.

A "basic equipment" model says that what you start with is whatever—the kitchen sink, as it were—there is in first nature, and that whatever you end up with in second nature is the emergent product of whatever all the dispositional resources of first nature can yield when mixed with the forces of the environment, history, and culture. What is the basic equipment? It consists of all the blank space for social learning, as well as all the fixed and canalized dispositions plus the more fluid, inchoate ones (that enable selfishness and/or fellow-feeling, for example), plus some number of reactive attitudes that one sees in the taxonomies of classical Chinese, Stoic, modern Korean neo-Confucian, and Buddhist philosophies, as well as Darwin's and Ekman's basic emotions, and Strawson's reactive attitudes. The basic equipment strategy makes things more unwieldy than either a modular approach or a domains approach, but it will claim for itself greater psychosocial and ecological validity. We, the socializers of the youth, the keepers and purveyors of communal moral standards, really do in self-cultivation, in the moral education of the young, and in setting and modeling the norms of our shared form(s) of life, deal with creatures who just are, at the bottommost level, critters with an enormous number of massively interactive dispositions and equipment. Sure, the equipment is canalized in certain respects: A child falling into a well will give a ballistic output: "Alarm → Save that child!" But the greater part of moral life is such that, even at the start, thoughts, feelings, and action tendencies interpenetrate. Even Mencius observed "four sprouts, one mind."

Of course, one could, without inconsistency, recommend the merits of each model and of operating with all three models for now, going forward, seeing which one, or which hybrid view is most explanatory and predictive. I hereby do so.

Natural Teleology

Finally, none of these three models—"five modules," "domains of life," or "basic equipment"—tells us, by simply specifying the equipment and the typical problem space, what most philosophers want to know about. What is the best way for second nature to be? What is the right way for human moral personality or character to be developed to create excellent human beings? Each model will yield a causal explanation—or more likely, a causal-explanation sketch—of how second nature develops from whatever first nature there is. But if it is any good, it will do this equally well for King Herod, Hitler, Stalin, and Pol Pot and for Mary, mother of Jesus, St. Teresa of Avila, Gandhi, and Nelson Mandela.

One thing seems clear: there is no longer any warrant in the first part of the twenty-first century (if there ever was) to believe that simply bringing people into the world and providing basic sustenance yields morally good people. Furthermore, even in decent physical and sociomoral ecologies, first nature radically underdetermines second nature, by which I simply mean that there are—or in cases where the life form is extinct, were—communities of good Stoics, Epicureans, Christians, Muslims, Jews, Confucians, Hindus, Jains, Buddhists, pantheists, pagans, secular liberal humanists, communists, atheists, and so on. And if you doubt this because, for example, you disapprove as a Jain of Abrahamic folk eating animal flesh, make them vegetarians. Or if as an egalitarian you disapprove of these historical examples because they are or were sexist, patriarchal, or warmongering, make them not so. Or if you think that communists always trample individual rights, imagine them as not like this, think of them as having learned from past mistakes and now as master moral educators, not as repressors or oppressors. I claim that even if you imagine each person or life form as improved along the dimensions you think it needs improvement on, it can remain distinctive as the moral form of life it is. For example, the ideal Buddhists, as you imagine them, will still rate the virtue of compassion higher than liberal secular humanists do; and the Buddhists and Confucians, on one side, and the Christians on the other, will have different ways of answering the question "Why be moral?," while agreeing across a wide class of cases about what it takes to be a good person.

That said, this radical underdetermination of second nature by first nature is not, according to the views I have been examining, complete underdetermination. First, we are not moral tabulae rasae, not blank slates. Humans have some sort of first nature, not crayfish first nature or rhesus macaque first nature or dolphin first nature. First nature has some structure; it is not featureless. The traits we model as species traits are subject to normal variation. Second, the epigenetic landscape is a landscape with certain channels set in part by ever-changing environmental features, by demography, natural supply and demand, scarcity and abundance, and, in part, by previous normative solutions to problems of social, moral, and economic life. Third, there are reasons that can be offered for why some ways of developing youngsters into certain kinds of people are good. Some reasons are impersonal—everyone needs to learn to share, to be honest. Some reasons are ecologically specific. There are geographical catchalls that reliably yield differences in the psychological economies of virtue and vice. Confucianism is terrific on respect for elders, on gratitude for the wisdom of the ages, but less strong on freethinking. Buddhism excels on compassion, but is weaker on inculcating and theorizing justice. American liberalism is strong on individual liberty but, possibly because of this, less good on mitigating the role of economic bad luck. We see these strengths and weakness most clearly and constructively when we also see the contrastive spaces, the zones of alternative possibilities as lived by other people from other traditions.

Sometimes the situation is the moral analogue of the QWERTY keyboard. This was a great design when there were mechanical keys that could lock. QWERTY separates letters by frequency in English and reduces the likelihood of lockdowns. QWERTY is not optimal for speed on electronic keyboards. Apparently KALQ is better for phones and tablets and DVORAK is better for typewriters. But QWERTY is so entrenched in both technology and in muscle memory that no one knows a way to move away from it to what is better, at least not quickly. Morality is like this. It often requires generational change. We see a better way to be. But we don't see a quick, low-cost way to get there.

One way to see the cup as half full rather than half empty is to focus less on the parts of life where people differ and disagree and more on the parts that contain the vast agreements about what virtue and vice are, how good people feel, think, and act, and so on. Natural teleology is not a live view if it is taken to mean that first nature "knows" where it should head, and that, in addition, all it needs to achieve its telos is free and open space. Not so. We are gregarious mammals, and persons develop only in communal spaces with dynamic life forms already in place. The development of first nature takes place inside a sociomoral community that carries a history, often a specific tradition, increasingly in some places, multiple interacting traditions, as well as all the multifarious contingencies that the natural and social environments offer up. If we know which direction to take first nature it is largely because of discoveries, both mistakes and successes, over world historical time, which pertain to making ourselves better, more focused, more aim-filled than we naturally are. In this sense, natural teleologies are all there are, but there is a large range of decent, possibly good outcomes, not just one (Wong 2006b), and it is good that there is moral diversity, a marketplace of actual and possible ideas and practices from which to learn what the options are (Ivanhoe 2009). Just as there are good and bad ways to grow plants and crops, including some that just don't work at all, there are some sensible standards for developing excellences in our charges. These ways are not simply available to intuition or known by gut reactions. They require rational attention to the lessons of culture and history. And most importantly, they require the wisdom and the permission to engage imaginatively with alternative ways of doing things, sometimes with alternative ways of being.

6

Destructive Emotions

Opening Cans of Worms

A debate about natural teleology, about whether first human nature contains inside its packaging a code or recipe or set of instructions about how it is supposed to develop ideally, arose in the Korean neo-Confucian tradition in the sixteenth century, and is known as the "Four-Seven debate." It arose separately in Buddhist discussions of wholesome and unwholesome, or as they are sometimes known, afflictive and nonafflictive mental states between the fourth century BCE and the first and second centuries CE. These discussions are highly relevant to the contemporary discussion of first and second nature, whether the original equipment is good, bad, or neutral, whether it is best conceived as sprout-like or not, and if it is, how many sprouts there are, and finally to debates about how to develop whatever sprouts there are, to make for good persons in good communities.

The Four-Seven Debate

First, the four-seven debate: The question of whether or not human nature consists of a heterogeneous set of tendencies or dispositions, some of which are good, some not, some that compete with the good ones, that can strangle them, and if not, how bad people are possible, has been an important topic among Korean neo-Confucians starting in the sixteenth century during the long-lived Choson 朝鮮 dynasty (1392–1910), especially in discussions between Yi Hwang 李滉 (Toegye 退溪) (1501–1570) and Gi Dae-seung 奇大升 (Kobong 高峰) (1527–1572) over the relation between the four sprouts and the seven emotions. Confucianism was the official philosophy of the Choson dynasty, and thus South Korea is to this day the most Confucian country on earth.

In a nutshell, the debate revolves around the connection between Mencius's claim that first nature consists of the four noble sprouts and the inventory of seven basic emotions provided in another authoritative classical text, *The Book of Rites*. The four sprouts are:

- Compassion
- Shame/disgust
- Deference
- Approval/disapproval

The seven emotions are:

- Happiness
- Anger
- Grief
- Fear
- Joy
- Liking/disliking
- Desire

The rub is that the four sprouts seem to be fairly uncontroversially good, and worth developing, whereas the seven emotions that also come with the first nature equipment are a mixed bag normatively. Even if the four sprouts aim to be excellences, the seven emotions are undisciplined and can go every which way. How do we discipline the emotions, possibly eliminate their most destructive forms, and where do the norms for doing so come from? Obviously, they do not come from ways of the emotions themselves.

It is inevitable that this conflict between authoritative sources would get noticed and be considered important, because by this time in Korea and in other parts of East Asia orthodox Confucianism had met with Buddhism. Indeed, the esoteric version of the four-seven debate arises naturally when Mencius's four sprouts doctrine is mixed with influences from Huayan Buddhism.[1] Huayan Buddhism claims, on the one hand, that all persons have within them a perfect Buddha nature (Dao mind) that can be reclaimed, realized, and "recovered" (Ivanhoe 2015a), but also that we contain at some level in first nature the familiar poisons of false belief, avarice, and anger. The first, perfect nature, comes with or as some sort of heavenly gift, *li*; the poisons come with our psychophysical nature, our *qi*. The seven emotions discussed in *The Book of Rites*, even if not obviously poisonous, are not obviously good sprouts either. They come with *qi*.

Pure Li and Impure Qi

The incident that touched off the debate was the presentation of the Diagram of Heavenly Fate drawn by Chong Chiun 鄭之雲 (1509–1561) in 1554 in which he said that "the Four Beginnings are initiated by Principle, and the Seven

Feelings are initiated by Material Force." A fellow philosopher Yi Hwang 李滉 (Toegye 退溪) (1501–1570) worried that this separated the two things "too deeply" (Xe Dejin 1987, 350). The debate is further developed in correspondence between Seong Hon 成渾 (Ugye 牛溪) (1535–1598) and Yi I 李珥 (Yulgok 栗谷) (1536–1584). The two-on-two teams then consisted of Toegye and Ugye, on one side, and Kobong and Yulgok, on the other.

The four-seven debate turned largely on the metaphysical relation between *li* and *qi*. In contemporary Anglophone philosophy no one accepts the classical *li-qi* metaphysics, which makes sense of what is to us an esoteric debate. Many of us take Darwin's theory to be well established, and thus think first that we are 100 percent *qi*, and second, that even if Huxley's "red tooth and claw" picture of our nature is not entirely true, it is not entirely false either. First nature contains dispositions to crush rivals, as well as to save children falling into wells.

The question is, even if we set aside *li-qi* metaphysics, can we make sense of the debate and learn from it? I say yes. Indeed, there are two ways to frame the four-seven debate that resonate with debates familiar to us. First, everywhere around you there is *qi*. Physical stuff is everywhere. But *qi* is not a disorderly, chaotic mess. *Qi* has systematic properties. Acorns grow into oaks, caterpillars become cocoons then butterflies, and some people become *junzi*, saints, and sages. There is the periodic table of elements, the inverse square law of universal gravitation, $E = mc^2$, and there are the laws of planetary motion. These are expressions of the patterning principle, *li*, which expresses pure principle, law, norms, and natural teleology. The question arises: How do *li* and *qi* relate, how is it possible for pure, immaterial principle, *li*, to affect, interact with, or form what is impure, and material, *qi*? One idea is that there are different ways of speaking about one unified nature, the world. *Li* is not an extra thing beyond nature in addition to *qi*. Speaking of *li* is just a way of thinking and speaking about the order that *qi* abides. There is not the world and then the laws of psychology or botany or physics. There is the one world, a world of *qi*, inside which the norms or laws (*li*) operate. How the world got that way, how order, *li*, came to be is an entirely different question. Another road, the one that most Korean philosophers went down (by way of philosophers like Zhu Xi and the Cheng brothers) was to think that the laws or norms were in fact somehow above, outside of, transcendent to the world of *qi*. So there is *qi* and there is a world of *li*, pure patterning principle, trying to reveal itself through *qi*. Compare: The Abrahamic God decides outside of time to make a world in which the laws of physics, biology, and psychology eventually apply. Before God creates *qi*, the laws and norms, *li*, are pure ideas. After creation, there are still two worlds—one, *li*, is immaterial, the other, *qi*, is material. *Li* is transcendent, not imminent. On the second view, there are interaction questions: How does a nonmaterial force express itself in a material force, how does it cause anything to happen in the material world? And, most importantly for the present debate, is *li* all good and is *qi* an obstacle, a source of normative disharmony? At the limit, is *qi* bad? Or does *li* need *qi* to perfect itself?

A different way to understand the *li-qi* debate, and the one I develop here, is one about the causal and constitutive relationship between two moral psychologies, two inventories of first human nature. Do the Mencian sprouts contain tendencies that support vice as well as virtue? Or is it the reverse, where the seven emotions are actually the roots, or subroots, of the four sprouts, which as described by Mencius display only their four normatively promising forms? Or are the four sprouts and the seven emotions to be added together to form eleven dispositions that make up first nature and are the materials that sociomoral development works with? Or are the four sprouts and the seven emotions orthogonal, the way the Mencian sprouts and the five senses or the digestive organs are orthogonal to each other, designed for different kinds of work than sociomoral commerce and excellence?

Here are several models that depict some of the possibility space. I doubt that any of the participants in the traditional Korean four-seven debate held any of them exactly, but one sees something like each view expressed at times. They are not in all cases mutually incompatible. *Growth* comes in two flavors. *Outgrowth* and *Ingrowth*:

1. *Outgrowth* says that there are in first nature only four seeds or sprouts. The seven emotions name various possible expressions of the sprouts, at least some of which are suboptimal or malfunctions, for example, divergences from the mean -- the trait, disposition, or action that is between excess and defect. Imagine a plant like basil that from one kind of seed grows a stem, leaves, and which also has a tendency—if leaves are not clipped and harvested—to develop a top growth that is what we call "going to seed." Each of these three states or conditions are outgrowths of one type of seed. But only one outgrowth, the edible leaves, is the good one. According to *Outgrowth*, a person who is respectful of an evil leader—Stalin, Hitler, Pol Pot—or who feels shame for being physically handicapped or female or gay has had her good sprouts of deference or shame grow unnaturally (because her *qi* or that of her socializers is turbid and led to mistakes in self-cultivation or socialization).[2]

2. *Ingrowth* says that the seven produce the four in ideal environments. In not so favorable environments, the seven don't realize this best form. It would take work, but one might try to make an argument that the emotions of liking, desire, and grief yield the good reaction of compassion in 2A6, and that it is this particular hybrid that deserves cultivation into *ren*. How might this work? Any normal person likes children, desires their well-being, and would experience fear/grief at thinking great harm was to befall a child. When

such positive mergers or hybrids of the seven emotions, or some subset of the seven emotions, occur, we, the moral community, encourage it. What about vice? Same story. Suppose a child refuses to share her toys with her sibling. This results, let's suppose, from liking, desire, and fear. This merged sprout (now conceived as a hybrid ingrowth and thus not as atomic), we discourage. So, according to *Ingrowth*, the four sprouts are the young morally approved seedlings that grow from various hybrid possibilities of the seven lower-level seeds in human nature.[3]

3. *Addition*. There are between seven and eleven sprouts in human nature comprising either the seven emotions alone (assuming as on *Outgrowth* that these can produce by growth in favorable soil, like the basil, the four sprout-related excellences) or the seven emotions plus Mencius's four sprouts. The four sprouts are names for the realizations of this expanded list of sprouts that are excellent. If addition were true, and there were taken to be eleven beginnings, then we might be led to see things as Buddhists do, and judge some of these as bad seeds or weeds that need to be removed, or as likely, that we simply see the construction of the four or five cardinal virtues (and whatever number of subsidiary ones there are) from the seven to eleven (or whatever the right number is) as requiring enormously careful tending—some weeding, some careful horticultural disciplining, and some experiments with hybrids in order to produce persons who are good, societies that are harmonious, beautiful, and so on.

4. *Subtraction*. One starts with the taxonomy of $4 + 7 = 11$ and examines it for any redundancies, for members that are the same or overlap. Redundancies are then eliminated or subtracted to get the final list, which could be anywhere from four to eleven. Possible candidates for redundancies might be the Mencian sprout for propriety with such things as emotions of appropriate grief, for example, grief at the loss of a loved one, or for appropriate happiness for excellences in oneself and others. In cases where matches are secured or reductions occur, the redundancy is eliminated, and the final list of basic dispositions in first nature consists in what is leftover. Good and bad outcomes of the remaining beginnings are explained in all the various ways mentioned above.

On both *Addition* and *Subtraction* some of the beginnings, seeds, or sprouts on the final list might need to be weeded out and treated as poisons, or alternatively kept under careful shaping regimens as in a Japanese topiary (*bonsai*). According to *Addition* and *Subtraction*, cases of respecting evil leaders, and shame over things that do not warrant it, could be explained by the development of an imperfect basic disposition (probably with sources in *qi*) such as fear of powerful leaders, liking charismatic bad people, or anger at oneself for possessing characteristics that a power or numerical majority disapproves of. Both *Addition* and *Subtraction* are committed to allowing the entire range of human emotion-laden dispositions as revealed empirically, whatever these turn out to be, to constitute first nature and to be grist for the mill of moral development. So, although anger is not on Mencius's list of four sprouts, it might with the right evidence be promoted to the status of a basic sprout. Then we would have to decide whether it has normatively acceptable forms, and, if so, what these look like. The same would go for grief, desire, and so on. The role of the moral community is to modify, moderate, grow, and channel first nature to express the best side of this nature—whether it be expressed in terms of four, seven, or eleven competences or virtues—that is built on the basic equipment whatever it is.

All these possibilities leave open the question of why certain forms of development of somewhere between four, seven, and eleven basic dispositions are considered good and some not so good. *Li-qi* metaphysics provides an answer: The dispositions aligned with *li*, principle or heaven or spirit, are good, the ones aligned with materiality (*qi*) are suspect.

No matter how the four-seven debate is resolved as a debate about the ingredients of moral psychology, the question will arise: How do we judge what is the right form, the best form for human nature to take? If we have access to *li*, how does that work and how is such insight made public, shared so that we agree about norms and values, about what is good, bad, worthy, unworthy, and excellent? How does a mostly imperfect *qi* critter like me overcome my tendencies to disrupt the world with my untamed emotions? The question is perennial. A contemporary form is this: Nature gifts us with traits that were perhaps once adaptations, but that are no longer adaptations, or that even if they still are biological adaptations in the sense that they enhance fitness, are not conducive to happiness, flourishing, and goodness. How do we see through and beyond fitness norms to ones that advance flourishing? How do we convince animals like ourselves with powerful interests in fitness to see beyond it and work to enact, abide, and maintain forms of life that are compassionate, loving, and just?

Buddhist Moral Psychology

Classical Buddhism is another gold mine for sensitive thinking about human nature and the human good. Buddhism is a treasure trove for excellent phenomenology, refined analytic taxonomies of mental states, and at the same time, is normatively opinionated about which states of the heart-mind are destructive, unwholesome, and afflictive. Buddhists hold a "seeds and weeds" view of human nature,[4] and identify the source of most, some say all, human suffering in poisons in our nature.[5]

Orthodox Buddhists usually cite the three general poisons already mentioned of false view (money will make me happy), avarice (I need that BMW), and anger (you cut me off, prick!). But Buddhists are also known for lengthy lists and nuanced analytic inventories in which the initial three poisons ramify into—as Buddhists like to say—84,000 kinds of destructive emotions.

The three poisons consisting of the tendency to false views, thirst and acquisitiveness, anger and resentment, are thought to give rise to "the Six Main Mental Afflictions," which then give rise to the "Twenty Derivative Mental Afflictions." Do not worry about what might seem like repetitions, the key is just to see what an inventory of first nature will look like once gifted, observant taxonomists are let loose. First, there are the six afflictions:

- Attachment or craving
- Anger (including hostility and hatred)
- Pridefulness
- Ignorance and delusion
- Afflictive doubt and afflictive views

And then the twenty derivative afflictions that the six can spawn:

- Five types of anger: wrath, resentment, spite, envy/jealousy, and cruelty
- Five types of attachment: avarice, inflated self-esteem, excitation, concealment of one's own vices, and dullness
- Four kinds of ignorance: blind faith, spiritual sloth, forgetfulness, and lack of introspective attentiveness
- Six types of ignorance produced by ignorance plus attachment: pretension, deception, shamelessness, inconsideration of others, unconscientiousness, and distraction

These elaborate analyses reveal how the poisons ramify, how they mutate into, and how they germinate and generate new poisonous offspring, which create ever new obstacles to flourishing and, what may be different, goodness.

Normally, Buddhist taxonomists go on to distinguish states of the heart-mind that are wholesome and unwholesome, afflictive and nonafflictive, in terms of four features: the attitudes themselves, their contents, their fit with the world, and whether they produce or alleviate suffering and misery. Sometimes it is the attitude itself that is suspect regardless of its intentional content. Many Buddhists think that anger, at least of the resentful sort, is always unwholesome, poisoning the heart of the one who harbors it, as well as the relationship between the subject and object of the resentment. The wholesomeness or unwholesomeness of other mental states depends largely on the attitude, its content, its fit, and whether it produces or diminishes suffering. Happiness that my friend has entered the bodhisattva path is wholesome. Happiness that I can afford a Rolex watch and will now buy one is not wholesome.[6]

Emotion researchers ask questions about which emotions are basic and which ones are culturally constructed, and thus best conceived as hybrids or composites. The brilliant taxonomies of the ancient Buddhist psychologists raise exactly such questions. Even cursory examination of the ramified list will make one think about the degree to which some of the emotions on these various lists come with equipment, which ones require social development and learning to be possible, and which ones also require a particular kind of culture to arise.

Basic Emotions and Reactive Attitudes

It will complicate, in a helpful way, our discussion of the shape and structure of human first nature, and its possible second nature forms, to reintroduce some ideas from Paul Ekman's inventory of basic emotions and P. F. Strawson's inventory of the reactive attitudes.

Ekman was a student of Margaret Mead's, and initially was set the task, under her tutelage, of putting to eternal rest Charles Darwin's proposal in *The Expression of Emotions in Man and Animals* (1872) that there are universal emotional expressions that have been naturally selected for because of their contributions to fitness, possibly in ancestral species. Instead, Ekman confirmed Darwin's hypothesis, disappointing Mead, who had placed bets on expressive relativism, the idea that all facial expressions are constructed locally and vary in the way linguistic expression does (at least at the surface).[7] These are the seven emotional expressions that at present are thought to pass muster of universality[8]:

- Anger
- Sadness
- Happiness
- Surprise
- Fear
- Disgust
- Contempt

Independently of Ekman, indeed a decade or so before Ekman's research, P. F. Strawson proposed this list of reactive attitudes, which he also suggests come with the equipment in the way induction does:

- Indignation
- Resentment
- Gratitude
- Approbation
- Guilt

- Shame
- Hurt Feelings
- Feelings of Affection and Love
- Forgiveness

The first point is that it is entirely possible that Ekman and Strawson are both right about the basic equipment since their lists are not inconsistent. Ekman was looking for basic emotions expressed facially, and Strawson was looking for basic or commonplace, possibly universal dispositions to react with feeling, judgment, and action toward the weal and woe of others, and at our own or others' failures and successes at meeting the multifarious expectations of sociomoral life.

Each Ekman emotion and each Strawson reactive attitude involves or is an intentional mental state. They are about something in the mind of the experiencer. I am scared of the snake. I am angry that you took the last cookie. I am ashamed that I lied. Disgust might be the exception, since, although every instance of disgust has a cause, for example, the sour milk, the disgust is not about the sour milk (the subsequent thought that it was the milk that caused me to feel that way is about the sour milk; but that is a different matter). This possible exception aside, I claim that insofar as traditions assess mental states and dispositions morally, as for example neo-Confucianism and Buddhism do, they always do so in terms of a quartet of relations that include (1) the mental attitude itself (anger, fear, contempt); (2) its content, what it is about (that you won the prize, that I will be fired, that you lied to me); (3) the fit of this attitude with its content to the way the world is; and (4) some set of normative standards, possibly culturally or tradition specific, about what behaviors that kind of mental state typically gives rise to, what effects it produces.[9] If this is right, then moral disagreements, at least ones about the proper configuration of a good heartmind, can be diagnosed by critically examining the locations in the quartet that are contested. We can use this diagnostic tool to explain why certain basic emotions as expressed by Ekman faces or on the neo-Confucian seven emotions list or the Buddhist afflictive and destructive emotions lists are not certified as normatively pure, while others, the Confucian virtues of *ren, yi, li,* and *zhi,* Buddhist virtues of compassion (*karuna*) and lovingkindness (*metta*), as well as certain forms of Strawson's reactive attitudes are certified as morally pure, or at least acceptable, on the path to a good life, as it were. A common, but not universal, feature of a good, worthy disposition, trait, or emotion - a virtue - is that it is other-regarding rather than merely self-regarding.

Self-Regard and Other-Regard

Korean neo-Confucians and all varieties of Buddhists are highly attuned to features of moral psychology at any of the four locations that display tendencies toward egoism. P. J. Ivanhoe notes the connection between Ekman emotions, which can be thought of first pass as mostly self-regarding—they almost all involve "me-noticing-something-that-pertains-to-my well-being-now," especially as it pertains to fitness, and the seven emotions that the Korean neo-Confucians worried about, which also seem self-regarding.

Ivanhoe writes:

> [T]he Four-Seven Debate remains relevant and highly pertinent to contemporary philosophy. . . . Among the first things to note in this regard is that the traditional Confucian list of emotions is quite close to what one highly influential contemporary psychologist, Paul Ekman, has argued is a list of six basic, universal emotions, all of which find standard expressions in different facial muscles. Ekman's list of emotions contains five out of the most traditional lists of Seven Emotions found in the Chinese tradition. (2015a; see Figure 6.1)

Ivanhoe then asks:

> Is there, as Toegye and Ugye insist, a systematic and significant difference between the Four Sprouts and Seven Emotions, granting that all of these are in fact emotions? One plausible way one might draw such a distinction is between other and self-regarding emotions or, in terms closer to those used by neo-Confucians, emotions that tend to separate the self, morally, from others and those that tend to connect the self with others. The emotions identified as the Four Sprouts, as well as their corresponding virtues, i.e. "benevolence" (K: in Ch: ren仁), "rightness" (K: ui Ch: yi 義), "ritual propriety" (K: ye Ch: li 禮), and "wisdom" (K: ji Ch: zhi 知), all involve emotional responses about how to treat or what we owe other people, creatures, or things. In contrast, the Seven Emotions of pleasure, anger, grief, fear (or joy), liking, disliking, and desiring are all concerned with the self and its needs, desires, and interests.

Ivanhoe's interpretive recommendation is extremely helpful for understanding the significance of the four-seven debate in terms that make sense for those of us who cannot quite feel the appeal of the neo-Confucian *li-qi* metaphysics. The debate can be understood in large measure, even for the neo-Confucians,

FIGURE 6.1 Ekman Basic Emotions and Classical Basic Emotions (Ivanhoe 2015)

Paul Ekman	happiness	anger	sadness	fear	(null)	disgust	(null)	surprise
Book of Rites	xi 喜 happiness	nu 怒 anger	ai 哀 grief	ju 懼 fear	a i愛 approval	wu惡 disapproval	yu欲 desire	(null)
"What Master Yan Loved to Learn"	xi 喜 happiness	nu 怒 anger	ai 哀 grief	le 樂 joy	a i愛 approval	wu惡 disapproval	yu欲 desire	(null)

as about self-regard versus other-regard. Mencius's four sprouts and the virtues associated with them pass normative inspection because they are other-regarding, whereas the seven emotions are self-regarding or have persistent self-regarding features.

What about Strawson's reactive attitudes? Strawson says that they can be self-regarding or other-regarding. Each reactive attitude, recall, has these three features:

1. It is automatic, fast acting, and easily activated.
2. It involves affect (feeling), judgment (thought), and conation, that is, an action tendency.
3. It has features of cognitive impenetrability despite itself being a cognitive state, that is, the affect, associated thought, and action tendency triplet are hard to turn off or keep from being activated; the action can be stopped but only with considerable conscious effort/veto, sometimes only indirectly, by doing something else.

These three features are not enough by themselves to mark off the moral reactive attitudes from many nonmoral reactive attitudes that also satisfy 1–3. Again Ekman emotions come to mind. Or consider the snake detection system in rhesus macaques. It satisfies the three conditions above. Snake-sensitive neurons respond more quickly to snakes than to the faces or hands of fellow rhesus monkeys (Van Le et al. 2013). The system involves an intentional state, the perception that there is a snake; it has oomph; it feels scary and it engenders action—"get out of here." It is not part of the criteria for satisfying 1–3 that the attitude has anything to do with morality. Of course, a snake detection system that alerts an individual rhesus macaque to the fact that it is in danger is also good for its compatriots if it is tied by evolutionary design to a communicative facial or vocal expression system.

That said, our natural reactions to snakes, sour milk, stomachaches, tickles, itches, and sharp pains are eventually implicated in sociomoral life. We teach all sorts of norms about how to march ahead morally even when huge distractions that ought not to distract us occur. The soldier who lets food poisoning affect his duty in battle is a coward; the person who sees the snake and runs before saving the child in the revised version of *Mencius* 2A6 is a fool, ill-formed, a monstrosity. The starving person who accepts food from the fat cat who spits on him has no sense of worth. It is hard to see what parts of human life are not implicated in moral life.

Superwide Reflective Equilibrium

Thanks to work at the intersection of ethics, comparative philosophy, and the human sciences, we have a more robust and adequate philosophical psychology and anthropology, one that includes abundant evidence that the possibility space for human psychology and development is vast and much still untapped. At the same time, we are neither moral tabulae rasae, not infinitely malleable. Our species nature and common problems across space and time constrain what is good and right. The beginnings that foster other-regard; Mencius's four sprouts; what the Buddhists call *bodhicitta*, the well of compassion and lovingkindness that competes with the three poisons that serve ego alone; and Strawson's other-regarding reactive attitudes are all consistently cultivated across the traditions we have examined. The seven neo-Confucian emotions, the three poisons, self-regarding reactive attitudes like resentment, and the basic fitness-enhancing emotions as revealed naturally in Ekman faces, all get a lot of sociomoral attention because they are self-regarding or can easily swing that way.

I think Elizabeth Anscombe would be pleased, or, if not that, at least a bit more optimistic than she was in 1958 about the prospects for profitable normative reflection with sensible partners in psychology and anthropology. But there are still reasons to worry about parochialism.

Most research on human psychology is based on North Atlantic samples, on college sophomores from Western Educated Industrialized Rich Democratic nations (Henrich, Heine, and Norenzayan 2010). The WEIRD populations are among the most unrepresentative in the history of humankind. This suggests extreme caution in extrapolations about first or second nature from findings based largely on one group of people who are living now and "around here." Such limited resources impoverish moral imagination. Add to this the fact that almost all academic philosophy in the North Atlantic and Oceana is self-consciously, often proudly, "Western," and there are the ingredients for a perfect storm that defeats moral imagination (Park 2013).

On the normative side of things, regarding questions of which, if any, of the universal or widespread dispositions in our natures ought to be cultivated, suppressed, modified, and how, as well as which novel dispositions or hybrids are possible, things are no less complicated for us now than they were for the ancients. For us, unlike for the ancients, it is easier to see the multiplicity of forms of life that are the array of second natures displayed across the earth, and it is harder to have confidence that our way(s) even in its idealized form(s) is the right way. Still some people and social groups muster such extreme confidence, which at least in certain forms is a problem with education, with failures to grow in our selves and our charges anthropological curiosity, skills of self-criticism, and optimism about our capacities to change for the better.

We can read Plato or Aristotle or Confucius, Mencius, or Xunzi as still live sources for us. Of course, it is also hard not to be struck with this observation: Each philosopher sees the ethical project as grappling with the transformation of first nature into a kind of second nature that despite some aspirations to universalism best suits a people at a time and in a place.[10] The conception of the good life is normally discussed in terms set by an antecedent tradition that has its own special problems, weight and force, and that provides identity to a people. Ethical inquiry, even at its best, is normally the project of finding an ecological equilibrium for a people, at a time—sometimes only for some people at that time. Calls for radical transformation are responsive to the ethical ecology in place. This may mean—it is not decisive—that one feature of a morality that is a conditional virtue for the morality itself, is coherence with its own best thinking and practices. This is the familiar idea of reflective equilibrium. Philosophers who defend wide reflective equilibrium normally take the set of norms, values, theory, and practice that need equilibration to come from a stable form of life, a stable tradition, from resources internal to a constitutional polity or nation-state. This is almost always a sensible practical tactic. But I am suggesting something different, which is in part motivated by the fact that the very idea or premise that there are such things as stable forms of life or singular traditions is itself in question, at least in the many places on earth where muticulturalisms reign.

Some see the situation as one of sociomoral Babel, as one of moral disarray, even chaos. I recommend that we view the situation in a cup-half-full way. The combined resources provided by travel, migration, international economic relations, large cosmopolitan cities, increased consciousness of variation in the nature and quality of the moral ecologies of different genders, races, and social classes, and by anthropology and comparative philosophy, reveal varieties of moral actuality often unseen, and varieties of moral possibility worth entertaining. Once we allow ourselves comparative resources, wide reflective equilibrium encourages attention and attunement to good ideas from both occluded places inside our traditions as well as in other traditions.

Morality is an accommodation to interpersonal life in social worlds that are not the same as the worlds in which the original equipment evolved. What to do? Use your head. Pay attention to what you, or we, or they sensibly aim to accomplish, be open to learning from others, and keep deadly conflict to a minimum. The basic equipment inside you is designed to make you fit and to react quickly and decisively to threats to yourself and those most near and dear. This gives you a headstart in being a prudent self-regarding organism, to being attuned to what is good for yourself and near kin. This might make you feel cocky, confident and assured that you see things correctly, and that you are as wise about other-regard as you are about self-regard. Doubt yourself. The sheer size of modern social groups along with global interaction makes entirely different demands on us than did the ecologies of the first 240,000 years of species life. We live in different worlds now than then. So keep your eye on whether your moral confidence really has warrant in this world, in the one you're actually living in, or even better in the world that moral imagination can conjure and see would be even better than the actual world, kinder, gentler, and more just.

This recommendation to use your head, your reason, your imagination, and your powers to change the structures of everyday life along the way is, of course, an old idea. But it reconnects the cognitive science of morality with normative ethics in a way that involves an understanding of what we have some power to do. Despite all the recent talk about ancient mental systems running the show, we have overwhelming evidence that we are highly malleable and that we possess capacities, both individual and social, for changing ourselves, sometimes for the better. The fact that there is the incredible variety of normative communities across the earth, sometimes even in our own neighborhood, is to be expected, and nothing that should trouble us. We can learn from difference rather than disdain it. The varieties of moral actuality are testimony to the fact that our natures are not fully specified by our biological natures. The existentialists had this right. We humans in virtue of being social, cultured, and very smart and because of the plasticity of human nature have numerous options for the kinds of persons we can be. It is an enormous responsibility to cocreate ourselves, to choose the better paths, and nothing less that the quality of one's being and the contribution one makes to the well-being of others depends on how well one succeeds in this daunting project.

Bibliographical Essay

3. Classical Chinese Sprouts

My own education in classical Chinese philosophy has been done mostly under the supervision of two sages, P. J. Ivanhoe and David Wong. In 2003 Wong and I taught an undergraduate comparative philosophy course together, which was my first systematic exposure to the tradition. I repaid David by teaching him a bit more than he knew at the time about Buddhism. Hagop Sarkissian, whom David and I shared as a graduate student, shared in the adventure. A little later, P. J. Ivanhoe, Ted Slingerland, and I started talking about classical Chinese views of human nature and the many resources they provide to analytic philosophy of mind and cognitive science. Classical Chinese philosophy is a useful source for thinking about problems of human nature and conduct because there is historically less theological overlay in Chinese discussions on these matters than there is in Western conversations on them after the advent of Christianity.

There are now excellent translations of the classical Chinese philosophers into English. I recommend P. J. Ivanhoe and Bryan W. Van Norden's *Readings in Classical Chinese Philosophy* (2nd ed., 2005); Ted Slingerland's translation of Confucius's *Analects: With Selections from Traditional Commentaries* (2003); Bryan W. Van Norden's translation of *Mengzi: With Selections from Traditional Commentaries* (2008); Eric Hutton's translation of *Xunzi: The Complete Text* (2014); and Brook Ziporyn's translation of *Zhuangzi: The Essential Writings with Selections from Traditional Commentaries* (2009).

The recent scholarly works that I have benefited most from in my readings of Mencius include P. J. Ivanhoe, *Confucian Moral Self-Cultivation* (2nd ed., 2000), *Ethics in the Confucian Tradition: The Thought of Mencius and Wang Yangming* (2nd ed., 2002), and *Confucian Reflections* (2013); Bryan W. Van Norden, *Virtue Ethics and Consequentialism in Chinese Philosophy* (2007); Kwong-loi Shun, *Mencius and Early Chinese Thought* (1997); David Wong, "Early Confucian Philosophy and the Development of Compassion" (2015);

May Sims, *Remastering Morals with Aristotle and Confucius* (2007); and Myeong-seok Kim, "What Cèyǐn zhī xīn (Compassion/Familial Affection) Really Is" (2010).

These two papers in moral psychology engage contemporary moral psychology and show how philosophically and psychologically sophisticated classical Confucianism is:

- Hagop Sarkissian, "The Problems and Promise of Situationism in Moral Philosophy" (2010)
- Ted Slingerland, "The Situationist Critique and Early Confucian Virtue Ethics" (2011)

4. Modern Moral Psychology

On "Five Sprouts": The best statements of moral foundations theory in the form I discuss it are in these three papers:

- Jonathan Haidt and Craig Joseph, "Intuitive Ethics: How Innately Prepared Intuitions Generate Culturally Variable Virtues" (2004)
- Jonathan Haidt and Craig Joseph, "The Moral Mind: How 5 Sets of Innate Intuitions Guide the Development of Many Culture-Specific Virtues, and Perhaps Even Modules" (2008)
- Jesse Graham, Jonathan Haidt, et al., "Moral Foundations Theory: The Pragmatic Validity of Moral Pluralism" (2013)

In *The Righteous Mind* (2012), Jonathan Haidt extends "five modules" to include a sixth module, liberty/oppression, which involves a quick reaction system to constraints on liberty, to bullies and oppressors. He then uses this six-module scheme to explain the differences between the political moralities of liberals, conservatives, and libertarians, and forcefully argues for his skepticism about reason.

Modular views and dual process models of mind tend to go together, but there is no necessity. Many people from time immemorial have noticed that humans are good at computing what is in one's immediate, short-term self-interest. Such a system can operate without modular silos as long as it is equipped with an effective "what is in my interest now" app. Daniel Kahneman's *Thinking, Fast and Slow* (2011) is a clear introduction to the dominant dual process model and the research behind it.

Peter Railton's "The Affective Dog and Its Rational Tale" (2014) is a deep, sensitive exploration of the place where moral philosophy and moral psychology meet that brings nuance to the dual process discussion. Railton gets that System 1 and System 2 are models that make a host of simplifying assumptions.

The actual functional architecture of what they model is complex and unwieldy. He explores the possibility that so long as both Systems 1 and 2 can learn, then the alleged properties of fixed triggers and their ballistic intuition-emotion-reaction profiles can be adjusted by sociomoral experience, including self-adjusted. One upshot is that moral intuitions and moral gut reactions are malleable.

These three important, pedagogically useful papers discuss the possible implications of dual process models for normative ethics:

- Jonathan Haidt, "The Emotional Dog and Its Rational Tail: A Social Intuitionist Approach to Moral Judgment" (2001)
- Joshua Greene, "From Neural 'Is' to Moral 'Ought': What Are the Moral Implications of Neuroscientific Moral Psychology?" (2003)
- Joshua Greene and Jonathan Haidt, "How (and Where) Does Moral Judgment Work?" (2002)

In *Moral Tribes: Emotion, Reason and the Gap Between Us and Them* (2013), Joshua Greene advocates the dual process picture, thinking that typically we see/respond to the sociomoral world in "point and click mode," but that we can also go into manual mode when we want to see things better. Greene also thinks there are some "modules," but he never commits fully to the modules of moral foundations theory. System 1 is evolutionarily old and thus tribal and chauvinistic, thus Greene recommends a System 2 morality that is consequentialist along the lines of Peter Singer's (2011) preference utilitarianism.

5. Beyond Moral Modularity

Kwame Anthony Appiah's *Experiments in Ethics* (2008) is an extremely smart, judicious, and beautifully written discussion of recent trends at the place where moral psychology and moral philosophy meet. Appiah is especially good on the situationist challenge and on moral modularity.

Two classics on the "domains of life" approach, which focuses less on dedicated systems inside the head and more on common ecological challenges of morality, are:

- Martha Nussbaum, "Non-Relative Virtues: An Aristotelian Approach" (1988)
- Alan Page Fiske, "Structures of Social Life: The Four Elementary Forms of Human Relations" (1991). Fiske describes his elementary domains as "psychological," but for reasons I explain in the text, I think they are better read as involving typical ecological challenges.

6. Destructive Emotions

Daniel Goleman, *Destructive Emotions: How Can We Overcome Them?; A Scientific Collaboration with the Dalai Lama* (2003), is a fine report on the discussions in Dharmasala, India, in 2000. I try to offer a useful analysis of the relationship among Buddhist moral philosophy and its epistemology and metaphysics in *The Bodhisattva's Brain: Buddhism Naturalized* (2011).

The best paper in English on the four-seven debate is P. J. Ivanhoe, "The Historical Significance and Contemporary Relevance of the Four-Seven Debate" (2015).

Two other debates inside Korean philosophy are the Horak debate, which pertains to the nature of animal minds, and the general debate between neo-Confucians and Buddhists about how best to live. Both debates are deeply philosophical. For the first, I recommend Richard Tail Kim, "Human Nature and Animal Nature: The Horak Debate and Its Philosophical Significance" (2015). For the second, I recommend A. Charles Muller's translation, *Korea's Great Buddhist-Confucian Debate: The Treatises of Chong Tojon (Sambong) and Hamho Tuktong (Kihwa)* (2015). In fourteenth-century Korea, Confucianism and Buddhism were both live options and commanded a certain amount of mutual respect. The "Great Debate" is a terrific resource for what remain even today some of the main stakes between the two philosophies: The Buddhists accuse the Confucians of drinking too much, being partial to their own family, and not being attuned to the suffering of animals. The Confucians accuse the Buddhists of being nihilists, advocating odd ideas about rebirth, and introducing a foreign philosophy, and claim that Buddhist monks are parasites. It is a very modern discussion.

PART III

Collisions

7

When Values Collide
PIDGINS, CREOLES, AND SMASHDOWNS

Holism of Beliefs and Values

Virtues, values, norms have local coloration, texture, and shape. They are fitted normally inside equilibriums of other good qualities and things. It is rare for a virtue in one culture to be considered a vice in another, for something of high value in one moral ecology to have zero or negative value in another ecology. But it happens. Tibetan Buddhist and Stoic views on righteous anger and warranted indignation appear to deny what is affirmed by a fairly common, possibly standard North American view. We think anger and indignation are sometimes morally required; Buddhists and Stoics say anger and indignation are always immoral.

It is much more common for there to be agreement about abstract virtues and values, about compassion, justice, and honesty and the like, but for there to be disagreement about particular practices. Most Americans believe in monogamous marriage. My students think that polyandry, one wife–many husbands, as practiced among some South Indians and some Himalayan peoples is "gross" and that polygyny as practiced in Saudi Arabia is sexist. But note that there is agreement among these three cultural groups that marriage ought to exist and be regulated. There are peoples who don't think that.

Every culture believes in respectful treatment of family members. Ancient Hindu practices like *sati*, where a wife self-immolates on her husband's funeral pyre, or the old Japanese practice of *Ubasute-yama* 姥捨山 (literally "Grandma Forsaking Mountain") in which, according to lore, the eldest son would take the beloved seventy-year-old grandmother to the mountaintop, where she would sit in full lotus to die of exposure, are judged as weird, alien, and awful. It is an open question whether they are judged as awful because they are inherently disrespectful or because they are practically unnecessary, or because they embed vice, sexism, and coercion.

When one group of people says V is good and another group of people says V is not good but bad, it is worth wondering how there could be such fundamental disagreement, such an inversion or transvaluation, which group has made a mistake, and what the mistake consists in. Or, if there is no mistake, it is worth wondering how something like the form of life taken as a whole creates the conditions under which an inversion is only apparent, not real, or alternatively, how the overall ecology of some form of life creates the conditions under which the disagreement or inversion makes sense. Many who display the proper liberal mix of shock and bewilderment over *Ubasute-yama* or *sati*, will acknowledge that in times of scarce resources such rituals might have made a certain amount of sense and might have even embedded and enacted certain forms of spousal and parental respect.

In epistemology, holism is the view that individual beliefs have their place in a system or a web. In the web, some beliefs are more central and structurally important than others, and many beliefs are interdefined and dependent for their meaning and status on the meaning and status of other beliefs. For example, the beliefs that everything is itself, A is A; that a proposition cannot be both true and false; and that there is an external world, which contains physical objects, are more central to the web, its stability and integrity, than the belief that an hour of daily strenuous exercise is good for you, which is more peripheral. You could give up the belief about the strenuous daily exercise without it rocking your world.

Second, beliefs do not do their work one by one, but mean, refer, and are true or false in relation to each other. Sense, meaning, reference, and truth depend on location and fit in a web. Newspapers and weather channels provide the exact time of sunrises and sunsets, but sunrises and sunsets only occur strictly speaking in a geocentric universe, not in a heliocentric one, the actual one we live in. But we get what is meant by speaking about sunrises and sunsets, and it is true that on July 4, 2020, the sun will rise at 5:30 a.m. and set at 8:30 p.m. in New York City, even though there are no such things as sunrises and sunsets, or, as we might say more gently, given that there are such things given a certain common-sense, but strictly speaking, incorrect, frame of reference. Sunrises and sunsets happen inside a certain common-sense way of worldmaking, but they never ever really happen in the actual world, the one we live in.[1] What really happens is that the earth moves in and out of positions where the sun can be seen or not. Earth moves, sun stays still. When you move beyond our solar system, then that's not true because our solar system orbits the center of the Milky Way galaxy, which itself is always on the move. What can be said, what is true about most everything depends, as we say, on one's frame of reference. One might legitimately conclude that even the concept of 'the earth' was different, possibly inconsistent, between the geocentric and heliocentric theories. According to the first theory, earth is stationary. According to the second, it moves at high speed in two orbits, around its axis daily and around the sun annually. Situations like this lead philosophers of science to worry about the difficulties of communicating easily, even at all, across or between grand theories. Conceptions that differ greatly in core assumptions are said to be incommensurable, where this word points to deep differences in core beliefs, difficulties in translation and mutual comprehension.

At the center of our web of belief is the invisible truth, worn like eyeglasses, that there are physical objects, substances. There are things and these things have properties or qualities. The world is chock-full of four-dimensional hunks of matter. At the center of the Buddhist web of belief, the Buddhist way of worldmaking, there are only processes and events. There are no substances. So who is right? Which are there really? One way out of requiring one side to be right, and the other to be massively wrong or what could be worse, just conceding complete incomprehensibility, is to say that internal to both ways of worldmaking are resources to eliminate the ontological divide. Buddhists make a distinction between conventional and ultimate perspectives, and from the conventional perspective there are things, tables, chairs, people, planets, and galaxies. From the ultimate perspective these "things" are just slow-moving events that lack stability and thing-hood. And Western philosophy is chock-full of reminders that talk of substances is instrumentally useful but can overreach when it reifies particles or objects or minds or God. In *Science and the Modern World* (1928), A. N. Whitehead worried about "the fallacy of misplaced concreteness," the tendency to reify slow-moving processes, as if they were substantial, permanent things. Perhaps, in ecumenical frames of mind, the Buddhist metaphysician and the Western scientific realist can agree that some events or processes have enough stability to be treated as things or substances while recognizing that all such things are perishable. Glass some think is best conceived as a slow-moving liquid, and even diamonds, which people say are forever, are not forever.

Ethical holism is similar to epistemic holism. Some ethical beliefs are more central and categorical than others for a people—killing for fun is wrong versus marrying without parental approval is wrong. Also, some, possibly many moral beliefs make sense only against a background of other beliefs and commitments, possibly only inside a form of life. In the North Atlantic many people nowadays think male circumcision is unnecessary, possibly barbaric. Among the Maasai of Kenya and Tanzania, male circumcision in a cohort plays a role related to group formation rather than to hygiene, and thus its function, meaning, position, and importance in the normative web is entirely different than in northern Europe or America. Circumcision isn't the same thing in Kansas and Kenya, Texas and Tanzania.

There is not holism of beliefs on one side, and value holism on the other side or in a separate space.[2] There is holism of beliefs, values, practices, norms, and virtues. The commandment "Thou shall not kill innocents" is widely shared across cultures. But obeying it depends on complex, ever-changing beliefs about who is and who is not innocent, for example, criminals, enemies, sociopaths, psychopaths, nation-state actors who have perverse values by our lights or who want our resources. Judgments of moral responsibility including differences between cultures depend on beliefs about where control over actions and outcomes is located, for example, in the individual or in unseen spirits or in the culture or in the cosmos or in admixtures. Americans were puzzled when a ferry sank in South Korea in 2014 drowning over two hundred school children and, when in addition to charging the crew with negligence, the entire nation expressed shame and collective responsibility, the vice principal of their school hung himself, and the prime minister resigned. In America, we don't think that a country has the kind of control necessary to be held responsible or sensibly feel responsible for a ferry sinking (Sommers 2012).

There are many other cases where thinking holistically, in terms of the wider ecology, would bring deeper understanding of what a practice is, especially before a practice is given a thumbs-up or thumbs-down, sensible or stupid, oppressive or not, final judgment by people who do not like being inside its regime. The role and meaning of arranged marriages and the burka in Islamic societies are good examples. Lila Abu-Lughod (2013) writes, "In kin-based social orders, marriages are far too important to be left to individuals." And Abu-Lughod, as well as Unni Wikan (1982) and Martha Nussbaum (2012) have done important work revealing the role and meaning of the burka, and in Wikan's case of various kinds of hijabs, its many styles, and the way it is thought to enhance individual style, features, and reveal rather than conceal beauty. What the burka is, says, and does depends on its function inside the societies where it plays that role, those roles, whatever they are. And more often than not, outsiders who are simultaneously appalled, intrigued, and aroused by the burka haven't a clue as to what those roles are.

A Taxonomy: Pidgins, Creoles, and Smashdowns

Cultures, cultural groups, and individuals collide and interpenetrate in many ways with many results. There is an analogy between linguistic collision and moral collision. A *pidgin* is a simplified version of a language that results when two groups who speak different tongues need to communicate for some mutual end, for example, trade. A *creole* is a full-fledged language that emerges from mixing two or more languages or from a pidgin that is enhanced and passed on over generations. A *smashdown* is when a dominant language is imposed and local language is extinguished.[3]

Holism and Disagreement: A Smashdown

In *Radical Hope: Ethics in the Face of Cultural Devastation* (2008), Jonathan Lear writes about the end of the Crow Indian way of life in America in the late nineteenth and early twentieth century and provides one kind of example that might be a case of incommensurable values or, what is different, fundamental disagreement. The Crow were nomadic hunters in what are now Montana, Wyoming, and North Dakota. War to protect hunting lands for beaver and buffalo from Blackfeet and Cheyenne, but especially the Sioux, were major features of Crow life. Among Crow, "scoring coups" was a virtue of men, es- pecially young men. Coups came in many forms. One kind involved striking an enemy in battle with a weapon; another involved capturing the horses of an enemy and planting a coup stick at the site. Planting the coup stick at the place where Sioux horses were taken, said to the Sioux enemy: "You are on Crow land. Here I stand. I will fight to the death." The number and magnitude of coups were represented in feathers in headdresses and elaborate face painting on the warrior and his bride.

During westward expansion, the white man prohibited the practice of stealing horses and they made the Crow know that there would be hell to pay for stealing horses. But to the Crow, there had never been any horse stealing. What there was, was scoring coups and that involved capturing and moving Sioux horses and parading the bounty to signal pride and express an insult. The horses themselves had low value to the Crow because they had plenty of horses. By bringing the weight of the law down on the behavior required to score coups, namely, moving horses from Sioux lands to Crow lands, the white man eliminated scoring coups. Scoring coups was a virtue that gave meaning and significance to the Crow. The behavior happened to be the same as the behavior of, say, white men, who steal horses. But the action performed by the white horse thief and the Crow scoring coups are entirely different even though both involve moving horses from someone else's campsite to one's own. Sacred ceremonies, festivals, and dances for both the Crow and the Sioux cel- ebrated winning battles, scoring coups, and capturing various kinds of bounty. But these things did not involve stealing. Stealing was wrong, capturing enemy bounty was not.

It is puzzling, hard to know how exactly to describe this situation. What action is performed when the Crow "capture" Sioux horses and plant the coup stick? They say it is scoring coups. The white man says it is stealing horses. The behavior can be described or seen on videotape, for example, for what it is, but it is not clear that there is a neutral description of the events involving Sioux horses being "captured" by Crow. It is thievery to the white men and scoring coups to the Crow, possibly to the Sioux as well.

In her powerful ethnographic fiction work *Waterlily* (1988), Ella Cara Deloria, herself a Sioux, specifically Dakota, more specifically Teton, writes about the substantial parts of Sioux-Crow warfare that were devoted to "adventure and glory." *Waterlily* is the story of Sioux life from the perspective of a female from girlhood to adulthood. It contains, in chapter 11, a breathtaking description of the sun dance ceremony, a several-day frenzy of dance, petitioning, placating, cutting, and self-mortification. Deloria describes it as "a great corporate petition" for well-being, which is performed in full acknowledgment of the fragility of life and the necessity of good fortune, being graced by Mother Earth, and the spirit world. The sun dance ceremony was "unspeakably holy," "the holiest moment in the life of the people."

In Deloria's nonfiction work *Speaking of Indians*, she writes that "the two systems in question [white man and Indian culture] are irreconcilable." Why? "One says in effect: 'Get, get, get now' ... The other said: 'Give, give, give to others'" ([1944] 1998, 120). The slaughter at Wounded Knee in 1890 marked the official end of this irreconcilability. "Get, get, get now" pretty much dissolved "Give, give, give to others," as the form of life it was. Deloria writes:

> War dances lost their "kick" after intertribal warfare was forbidden. "Civilized men did not kill each other." Ceremonies, too, were difficult to manage now, because of the cramped life forced on the people. Without any war deeds to extol, there was no longer any point to war dances. ... When the sun dance, their greatest corporate ceremony, was stopped by the authorities because of the self-torture essential to it, the people gave it up. It would be pointless without sacrifice. (88)

When Sun Dances and Scoring Coups Lose Their Meanings

Power explains how the description of Crow practices as "horse thievery" defeated the Crow's way of describing what they were doing as "scoring coups." But that outcome, the smashdown, is compatible with both descriptions, both valuations, being true—scoring coups is not horse thievery and it is a necessary condition for a good Crow life, and scoring coups is horse thievery—before power decided on "the right interpretation," namely, that scoring coups just is stealing horses.

Miranda Fricker (2007) distinguishes two kinds of epistemic injustice that are relevant here. Testimonial injustice is when prejudice causes one to give another's testimony less credibility than it deserves. Hermeneutical injustice occurs when the larger community, a power or numerical majority, refuses to allow the experiences of a person or community to be described fairly. Fricker gives the example of a woman who suffered from a colleague who jiggled his crotch, brushed against her breasts, and tried to kiss her on the elevator, who became depressed because of it, but who couldn't get others to understand that she suffers from "sexual harassment." At the time, neither that idea nor that particular set of descriptions or interpretations had yet been invented or permitted. Hermeneutic injustice in the Crow case is where the white man got to describe the practice of "scoring coups" his way, not because it necessarily made more sense, but because he had the power. The analogy is to the crotch-jiggler, elevator-kisser who describes himself as just flirting. Colonialism is almost always guilty of hermeneutical injustice, missionary practices may or may not be, tourism is usually not, and postcolonialist anthropology tries never to commit hermeneutical injustice.

Was what the white man judged a vice, horse thievery, a virtue for the Crow, scoring coups? Is this just a contest for the power to interpret the situation, as between the harasser and the flirter? Is this a case of fundamental disagreement where one community values V, and another group values *not* V? That is probably not the best way to describe the situation. Why? Because for the Crow "capturing" Sioux horses was not theft. The Crow believed that stealing is wrong. In principle, all sides might have charitably understood scoring coups as a kind of courage or bravery or a way of displaying courage or bravery, as well as a practical solution to the problem of dividing hunting lands among seminomadic groups. This is surely the way the Crow conceived it. On this interpretation, it would be best to say that both cultures share virtues and values at a deep level, courage and bravery, and caring for the sustenance of one's people. They simply count very different behaviors as instances of the virtue and values at the surface level.

This result has its advantages. But one downside is that it permits by parity, dual descriptions of what the white man did to the Crows. It was stealing Crow lands from the Crow perspective, and it was conquering the frontier, achieving his manifest destiny from the white man's perspective. All of which might make one think that all this "taking" under whatever description it occurs and whatever side does it, is itself not for the best.[4]

Aliens and Incommensurabilities

What should we think, say, and do if and when radically different values, inversions, revaluations, and transvaluations occur, especially when they confront each other and, at a minimum, a modus vivendi is required, as was the case among the Crow, Blackfeet, Cheyenne, Sioux, and white man? Incomprehensibility comes in many forms. Sometimes persons or two peoples do not even get what another is doing. This was the case between the Crow and the white man. Other times there is puzzlement over why you value what you do, or as you do. The Achuar of Ecuador find architectural magazines showing New York City real estate extremely interesting, but they find it weird that anyone would want a bathroom in their home. In my youth in the suburbs of New York City, the clash between communist values, unfree, atheist, but equal, and democratic-capitalistic ones, free, Godly, but unequal, was the talk of the town. These two ways of worldmaking could not coexist in the same world, nor could they be blended to produce some sweet synthesis. So we were going to have to obliterate each other.

Clashes like this can be global, between peoples, or they can occur in an individual life. In *Either/Or* Kierkegaard described the life of the hedonist, Don Juan, and the ethical person, whose virtue is marriage, as incompatible. In *Fear and Trembling* he offers vivid exploration of a third way of living and being that is incompatible with both the hedonistic and ethical life, namely, the religious life. It is impossible to be a Lothario, a married person, and a Catholic priest. They are mutually incompatible inside one life. Similarly, if I want to maximize pleasure, I will not also be able to maximize knowledge, unless I am the extremely unusual type who finds learning Sanskrit grammar a thrill.

The Crow–White Man case has this kind of structure between two forms of life. Scoring coups contributes to the meaning and significance of Crow lives. Peace on the range is of value to the white man, and the way Crows score coups causes a bloody ruckus. The two forms of life cannot be fitted together, cannot coexist in the same place. One way of doing things has to go.

Another sense of incommensurability, not fitting, also suits the case. Imagine that we have videotapes of what the Crow call "scoring coups," and what we—looking at exactly the same behavior—call "horse thievery." Suppose we decide to have a mixed jury of peers, six Crow and six white men, figure out how to correctly describe what is seen, what is truly going on. There will be a conceptual stalemate. Each group knows how to evaluate the videotapes from their own perspective, "scoring coups" and "horse thievery," but not from any neutral perspective that could help decide which way is the right way. They could agree that "horses are moved by those guys (pointing)," but not on what action those bodily movements are or produce. That determination depends on concepts and permissions given by the overall web of normativity each lives inside.

One kind of mismatch, mutual incomprehensibility, or incommensurability occurs when two worldviews are so different that there is no non-question-begging way to precisely measure or evaluate the two descriptions, "scoring coups" versus "horse thievery" on some common way of speaking or common scale of value.

Consider these questions: Which is better blue or four? Apples or square roots? The questions make no sense because there is no common unit against which to measure, rank, or otherwise evaluate colors, fruits, and numbers. Elizabeth Povinelli (2001) calls cases like these "radical alterity."

The hedonist-scholar case is an either/or case, where the ends of maximal pleasure-seeking and maximal knowledge-seeking can't be satisfied inside a single life. The Crow–White Man case is one where the life-form that requires "scoring coups" and the one that requires no horse stealing cannot coexist, not because scoring coups is horse thievery, but because it requires behavior that is materially equivalent to horse thievery. In the North Atlantic, married friends often greet other married friends with hugs or kisses on the cheek. This is not sinful, certainly not adultery. In other cultures, it is sinful, adultery.

Sometimes, but not always, radical alterity can be understood in terms of there being no non-question-begging method to describe, measure, evaluate, or rank the things, phenomena, or thingamajigs in question. For any things that have length, there are rulers and such; for any things with a temperature, there are thermometers. Such things are commensurable lengthwise and temperature-wise. If everything were a physical object then everything would have a temperature and they would be commensurable in that respect. But since numbers are not made up of molecules, they have no temperature and they are incommensurable with physical objects temperature-wise.[5]

Some say that all value can be measured by monetary worth, and thus that the value of everything can be ordered that way, by how much money the things are worth. Others disagree and say that some things, for example, the value of friendship, the lives of sentient beings, and conscious experiences, cannot be measured in terms of monetary value. Clearly, one could decide to do this and stipulate that there is some dollar value to a human life, to each kind of experience, and so on. But it is not clear how stipulating that there is a dollar value for something that others say is priceless resolves the disagreement in the moral sense, as opposed to settles it for practical purposes, for the actuaries and lawyers. It is not clear how to settle in a neutral manner the debate between those who say that some goods, lives, rights, truth, beauty, goodness, have no monetary value and those who say they do, that everything must have monetary value, in a way that does not beg the key question. It is at precisely such locations, at the center of the web of belief, that different forms of life stipulate their axiomatic beliefs, and then stand by them.

If there are values that can be measured by a common unit and others that cannot, these latter values are incommensurable, orthogonal to each other at least with respect to that measure. When incommensurability is conceived this way, individuals can face incommensurable value conflicts, as can cultures or cultural groups. Bernard Williams's (1981) quasi-fictional case of Paul Gauguin involves a choice between his marriage and his artistic project. If Gauguin conceived his marriage as a moral obligation endorsed by a sacred ceremonial vow and his desire to paint in Tahiti as a personal project of monumental existential significance, deemed them incompatible, and furthermore, saw no neutral measure or trump rule that did justice to the situation, then his choice was between subjectively incommensurable goods. Gauguin made the choice, so incommensurability does not rule out choice. Likewise, in the Crow–White Man case, a decision was also made. Whereas we could think that Gauguin made the best choice for himself, all things considered, despite the incommensurability, the Crow did not participate in the decision. The decision was made for them.

The values of "scoring coups" for the Crow and "manifest destiny" for the white man played similar sacred or central roles in their moral systems. But there was no common measure of value—or at least none was seen—that would do the situation justice from both perspectives. One interpretation had to go.

This case may be a particularly deep kind of incommensurability. Suppose all parties, the Crow and the white man in the present case, agreed that moral value should be measured by an instrument sensitive to the contribution a practice makes to the meaning of a people's life, to how much the practice matters and especially to sacred value. Now the Crow say that scoring coups contributes greatly to their quality of life, is essential to it, sacred and good. The white man says that "stealing horses" contributes a lot to the Crow's quality of life, is essential to them, sacred, and bad. But to use a measure—importance, mattering, sacredness, and the like—to evaluate a practice or two practices, we have to agree on the description of the practice(s) being measured by that standard. But we don't. The Crows call the action to be measured "scoring coups," but it's stealing horses to the white man.

It is easy to understand what goes on in situations where power determines interpretation and imposes normative order. It is more puzzling how inside an individual life or inside the lives of a people or cultural group, ordering and choices between incompatible or incommensurable good are made. Even if life, love, and friendship are not worth a dollar amount, and even though all the tea in China is worth a dollar amount, I might still say that life, love, and friendship are worth much more than all the tea in China. I might say this on grounds that some priceless things are worth more than many priced things, possibly, each priceless thing is worth more than all the priced things taken together.[6] I seem then to have compared and ranked values that have no common measure. Life is more important than money. Good health for sentient beings is more important than the total number of grains of sand on the earth's beaches. We say such things, make such comparisons, but it is not entirely clear what we are doing and what the warrant is.

Comparability involves the question of whether A is better that B according to some feature or other, some ordering or other. Is Van Gogh's *The Starry Night* more beautiful than Bach's Cantata BWV 51? This is an odd question, odder even than asking us to compare apples and oranges, which at least are both fruit. But it is not as odd as asking us to compare apples and square roots. Which is better: Tolstoy's *War and Peace* or T. S. Eliot's *The Waste Land*? Same situation. We don't know how to measure novels against poems in a way that doesn't favor from the start one genre over the other. Which is better, Tolstoy's *War and Peace* or Jane Austen's *Pride and Prejudice*? This makes more sense because we are inside a genre. Still, one response, not at all strange, is that both are great novels, but that they are incommensurable because there is no non-question-begging way to measure the quality of Russian novels and great British novels, or at least these two great novels. This could, of course, be interpreted to mean that they really are commensurable, measurable by a single scale, "the great novel scale," but seem tied or too close to call in my mind, for me to make that determination. Either way they are comparable if you specify some narrow properties to do the comparison. If you want to learn about the mores of British landed gentry, Austen is better. If the Napoleonic era appeals, if you are interested in the lives of Russian aristocracy during the French invasion of Russia in 1812, find philosophical excursions interesting, and have lots of time, read Tolstoy.

What about the comparison of Van Gogh's *The Starry Night* to Rembrandt's 1629 *Self-Portrait*? We might think that here, too, there is no common measure of beauty according to which we can rank these paintings, in which case we judge them to be incommensurable (or, what is different, that they are commensurable, but when I try to apply some supreme platonic standard of beauty, it seems to me a draw). Still, we might agree that these paintings can be compared across a host of dimensions, for example, in terms of which painting has more yellow in it, which would look better in the study, which is worth more money, which is better as a portrait (Note: We could do the same in the Van Gogh–Bach case and say that the Bach cantata has more sound in it than the Van Gogh; but it is weird to order qualities according to a standard according to which one item lacks what is being measured altogether and on purpose). It would be like saying my iPhone is warmer than the $\sqrt{17}$.

Jean Paul Sartre's famous example of the young man who must choose between joining De Gaulle and the French Resistance in London or staying with his needy mother in France is often said to be an example of radical choice. And it is, if we believe that both goods matter a great deal to the young man, are incompatible, and that neither one ranks higher or trumps the other according to a common measure that he knows or avows. The Gauguin case, another case of intrapersonal incommensurability, also involves radical choice. It may just be that radical choice is choice when there is incommensurability in the sense that there is no single standard or measure to determine the value of the incompatible options relative to each other, but where one end or goal presents itself to the chooser as the right one, the best one.

Still, the situation is puzzling. If there is no way to determine relative value, how are we to understand Sartre's young man's choice or Gauguin's choice when they make it? A choice just is a determination. How did they make it? How are we to understand choice when there is incommensurability? What does it even mean to say that one end or goal between incompatible or incommensurable ones presents itself as the right one, the best one? There seem to be several possibilities: the strongest impulse won, a coin was flipped, or the two incompatible ends were compared and the one judged to have higher value was chosen. The first two methods will work to produce decisions even when there is incommensurability and incompatibility. But they do not seem rational. The third way keeps the decider in the decision but the mechanisms at work are on the mysterious side. What do the young man or Gauguin see or understand about value that helps them choose? Without answering that question, and leaving it to the psychologists, it is possible on the first and last scenarios (strongest desire wins or most choiceworthy option, all things considered, wins) that despite the incommensurability, the choices were not even close calls. Suppose Gauguin did the comparison and judged correctly that pursuing his artistic project in Tahiti mattered to him much more that his marriage, then the artistic project won the comparison of goods, according to the scale that measures "mattering most to oneself," and it won hands down. He performed the intrapersonal comparison of two incommensurable goods and the result was clear, a no-brainer, as we say.[7] The idea that Gauguin made the right choice for himself is compatible with thinking that he made the wrong choice, that he was selfish, morally negligent, and so on.

Similarly, one might think that the value of the Crow scoring coups by way of capturing Sioux horses and the value of the white man conquering the Crow by decimating horse and buffalo populations and taking their lands involve incommensurable values, but not totally incomparable ones. Remember two items are comparable if there is some value or some dimension, some values or some dimensions according to which they can be compared. The Crow and the Sioux were in Wyoming, Montana, and North Dakota long before the white man, so their claims to the land have greater weight or higher priority than the white man's according to the value of who was there first. This way of ordering the land claim would presumably have some weight in the white man's way of thinking since it is very Lockean: One has rights to land and its bounty if one got there early on and has mixed one's labor with that land to produce that bounty. But comparability is not a panacea. The white man might claim that since he brought the horses to the Americas in the first place, he has greater say than the Indians in whether and how they are moved. And the white man can agree that the Lockean proviso means that there are "some" Indian land rights, but that these are outweighed by bringing the Crow, and the other indigenous peoples, Christian values and the like.

Verstehen

One reason to engage the project of comparative philosophy is to explore the space of moral possibility, to respectfully understand what people are doing inside other forms of life, and consider whether and how ways they think and do their lives might be good for us. Holism means that to get what others are doing will require getting a sense of the whole, their form of life, something more than just a particular practice. Thinking about whether a practice could be for us, requires thinking about how the "really good idea" might be imported given that it will have to be fitted into our form of life. Sometimes we can adopt good ideas without changing our form of life in a wholesale way. Suppose one thinks that it would be good if young Americans were more like Confucians in respecting the elders, trusting that the elders have wisdom about living that they, the youth, lack. One can't just import this idea without also adjusting views about what kind of knowledge matters for a good human life, possibly changing educational practices so that in fact each generation of elders actually deserves such respect, and so on. But with those kinds of adjustments, one might add the good Confucian ideas to our ways of worldmaking and without ourselves becoming Confucian.

One might be skeptical of the very idea of understanding or really getting another culture or form of life, especially once we have absorbed our own way of seeing and being, once our form of life is in our blood and bones, once our way of seeing and being is our life world. There are reasons for humility, but the obstacles are not insurmountable. There is a host of inscrutabilities and various kinds of ontological relativity.[8] The skeptic can always point to such zones. But the facts are that everyone has learned their form of life, so it is learnable, at least by the youth before their minds are fixed. Furthermore, there are few examples in the history of science or anthropology where serious patient inquirers, especially when they give the other room to speak, cannot make sense of what seem at first alien ways of thinking and speaking. Consider the example of the geocentric and heliocentric theories discussed at the beginning of the chapter. This is a standard example offered in epistemology and the philosophy of science for incommensurability. Suppose it is. That has caused no trouble, exactly zero, for philosophers who have worked to reveal how the concepts of 'earth,' 'sun,' 'sunrise,' and 'sunset' are used across the two theories. It has also caused no trouble for the epistemologists who offer reasons for why one way of worldmaking is superior to the other. The heliocentric theory better fits the facts. Now this last feature, "better fitting the facts," may not be a tool that the ethicist can use in comparing theories, at least not in the way science uses it. But the point for now is that, hard as it might be, there are no obstacles for getting what others are doing and why they are doing it. The word 'justice' is not the same concept when liberals use it and when libertarians use it. But we know how to understand each other, what the other is saying, what they assume, even if we think they are wrong, confused, missing something.

Getting each other is not sufficient to produce agreement about the best conception. There are what Alasdair MacIntyre ([1981] 1984a, 1988) calls "interminable disagreements" between, for example, liberals and libertarians over whether the demands for justice are demands for fairness or demands for freedom. The fact that Confucians and Dinka and Shia and Achuar have somewhat different conceptions of justice than either the American liberal or the American libertarian ones, just adds complexity to the situation.[9]

The first lesson is that there are often complicated questions for the comparative philosopher about commensurability and comparability and thus we need to beware of overconfidence at the level of description of a morality, including our own. Ethical beliefs, norms, values, virtues, and vices are eco-logical items. Holism reigns. Understanding differences and the location and source of disagreement is not something that can be had at a low-level physi-cal description of events. On a thin description, Crow moved Sioux horses. But this is neutral between whether scoring coups or horse thievery occurred. Such cases bring us into situations where concerns about radical alterity and incommensurability are legitimate.[10]

Fundamental Disagreements and Inversions

Inversions and fundamental disagreements depict a different, not unrelated, set of distinctions. Inversions and fundamental disagreements have this sort of surface structure. I say V is a virtue or a good value or norm, you say V is a vice or a bad value or norm.

Fundamental disagreements might be ordinary, mundane, and common, such as the debate between people who believe that active physician-assisted euthanasia for consenting terminally ill adults is moral versus those who believe that active physician-assisted euthanasia for consenting terminally ill adults is murder and thus immoral, a great evil. In 2014 in Doha, Qatar, I listened to Muslims discuss fundamental disagreements inside Islam about third-party sperm and ova donations. Some say such practices are categorically wrong, a violation of God's will, lineage norms, and absolute responsibility for one's offspring. Others think that such donations are morally acceptable if they are not anonymous and involve gifting of sperm and ova inside families. Such fun-damental disagreements occur often enough within a generally shared form of life.[11] There are some fundamental disagreements that have their source in deep differences at the center of different webs of belief and value. Buddhist metaphysics of No-Self, the belief that the self is an illusion, expresses a funda-mental disagreement with views that put the belief in the self, and the self's fate and its good at their core. This is itself a fundamental disagreement, and it is connected to, possibly it lends inductive support and thereby sustains, certain fundamental disagreements of the V and not-V sort further from the center of the web, for example, that anger is bad. Q: How could that be so? A: Because anger is based on fear of one's self losing something. But there is no self, so there is no one, no substantial essence that is your self to lose or gain anything.

An inversion is a fundamental disagreement that has a certain genealogy; specifically, an inversion is a case where there is a fundamental disagreement, V and not V or not V and V, where the change occurred over time and inside a tradition.

Gay marriage may be a good example of a fundamental disagreement that is also something of an inversion. In Europe and North America, there has been a rapid shift in the early twenty-first century from a majority view that gay marriage makes no sense or, what is different, is wrong, to the majority view that gay marriage makes sense and is fine, even good. The change of view is not yet universal, but it is moving in that direction. Furthermore, it looks as if this happened inside the cultural traditions that changed, that flipped their views. There were not pressures from Asia or Africa to change our views and attitudes. What happened? The change was multifaceted, part conceptual, the concept of marriage isn't so fixed as to exclude the gay marriage possibility; another attitudinal, gay and lesbian sex and love matter; another ethical and legal, regarding the values of freedom and autonomy; another psychobiological, there is natural variation in sexual preferences, and so forth. Thinking of the change this way raises the possibility that what looks to be a fundamental disagreement and change to the contrary over time—V to not V—is actually not quite that. Why? Because the change at the level of moral belief was created and enabled by all sorts of small, unnoticed adjustments elsewhere in the system that changed.

Compare: Suppose you changed your belief from eggs are good for you to eggs are bad for you back to eggs are good for you. This actually has happened in my lifetime. Each time the change of belief was less about eggs as ordinarily conceived, at least as eggs were conceived at the time of each belief change, than about hidden, heretofore unknown properties of eggs, about cholesterol, kinds of cholesterol, and the relation between kinds of cholesterol and heart disease (good and bad cholesterol). It is hard to know exactly how to describe the situation. One could say that the concept of an egg, what an egg is, stayed the same, but that we changed our beliefs about the properties of eggs. Or we might say that the concept of an egg changed given that the concept itself involved certain ideas about the goodness or badness of eggs. Given the varieties of holism, this kind of uncertainty about what changed, how, and why, might be the normal situation.[12]

Are there any examples of genuine global inversions in the West? Candidates include the inversion from prizing sexual liberty to prizing chastity; from treasuring pride, one's personal magnificence and feeling contempt for the small and the weak to honoring humility, pity, and sincerity; from valuing faith and obedience to authority to admiring skepticism, self-discovery, and personal autonomy.

Nietzsche's Shadow

The concepts of "inversion," "transvaluation," and "revaluation" have their home in Nietzsche, in texts such as *The Antichrist, The Genealogy of Morals*, and *The Will to Power*.[13] Take "inversion" to refer to cases like this: Classical Greek and Roman society prized sexual pleasure and sexual virtuosity.

Christianity inverts this and prizes chastity instead. It is an interesting question whether this inversion is true or real, whether it involves an actual denial that sexual pleasure is a good, in which case we have a true flip-flop, a genuine contradiction, or whether the situation is more one of a demotion—chastity is at least as good as sexual virtuosity, maybe better—plus a restriction to the effect that sexual pleasure is good, but only inside a marriage. "Transvaluation" and "revaluation" involve disclosure as well as reassessment. Chastity in addition to being an "inversion" of classical hedonistic morality is revealed—this is Nietzsche—to have its source in hatred for life, for the flesh (the disclosure). If you think this ill-advised or sick (the reassessment), then there is reason to rethink how you judge the virtue of chastity and the values and norms associated with sexual restraint and modesty. A different example that reveals how similar surface structure of values might not be grounded in similar deep structure is this: Christian charity and Buddhist compassion look similar on the surface. But genealogy reveals them to be entirely different at a deep, psychic level. Buddhist compassion is motivated by the perfectly sensible wish not to suffer and is thus based on a sincere, genuine desire to alleviate suffering for oneself and others who suffer. Christian love (again this is Nietzsche) is motivated by hatred for life, the flesh, joy, and fun (these are all "sinful"), involves deep hatred for the winners of the world, who the weak, filled with envy and resentment say will burn in hell for all eternity, as well as self-mortifying delusions of a disembodied afterlife.

Nietzsche was a genius, but his genealogies, disclosures, and revaluations are contentious, polemical, frequently uncharitable and mean-spirited. But it is a deep point that both the nature and value of, say, asceticism may upon disclosure be seen as an entirely different constellation of virtues or values, entirely different ways of being for the Buddhist, the Christian, and the philosopher or the strong poet despite looking very much the same in all three cases. Furthermore, because the histories, motives, and aims of asceticism differ across these communities they may deserve different valuations. Think of it this way: real property is subject to reassessment and revaluation. Many houses in a city may look the same, have the same square footage, have been constructed at the same time, and so on, but their value will vary over time based on certain intrinsic properties, such as the age and condition of the infrastructure, electrical, heating, and cooling systems, the foundations, as well as certain relational properties such as the neighborhood, the schools, safety, the overall housing market, and so on. Christian pity and Buddhist compassion might look very similar, but they are constructed from different materials, embedded in a different metaphysic, and they sit in relation to other virtues, values, norms, and aims that are not the same.

One might be skeptical that any of the cases mentioned so far are true global inversions or transvaluations on grounds that the former virtues and positive values, turning one's cheek, chastity, pity, and love, are not nowadays considered vices or disvalues, which one might expect in a true inversion. There is perhaps some controversy about the proper forms of these values, and the associated virtues, but not as I see it a true contradiction, V and not V.

Righteous Anger?

In the case of righteous anger, the dominant view is that it is justified, probably a virtue if certain conditions are satisfied, certainly not a vice. The American Psychological Association says this: "Anger is a completely normal, usually healthy, human emotion." "Healthy" is the kind of normative judgment psychologists are entitled to give. If the American Psychological Association had a joint taskforce on anger with the American Philosophical Association, then they could issue a joint communiqué saying, "Anger is normally healthy and normally morally acceptable." Allan Gibbard defends the view that anger is one of two key, indeed essential moral emotions. "Morality concerns moral sentiments: the sentiments of guilt and resentment and their variants" (1992, 6). Actually, it is even stronger than that since the sentiment of anger is the master key to the zone of morality. According to Gibbard, guilt is anger turned inward. "Moral convictions . . . consist in norms for anger and for the first-person counterpart of anger, guilt" (126). We identify a morality in other cultures in terms of what aspects of life the aliens think it makes sense to be angry or guilty about (128).

There is a nonparochial reading of this hermeneutic strategy. Even if an alien culture does not in fact advocate regimenting morality by way of anger and guilt, we identify their morality by seeing what their norms are in the spaces where we would think it would make sense (for us) to feel anger and guilt. The aliens, however, need not feel those emotions.

One common strain of thinking says that experiencing righteous anger and giving voice to it is a way of standing up for what is valuable and good, a way of respecting oneself and even a way of respecting the righteousness and autonomy of the one at whom one's anger is directed. Perhaps we should treat the racist, or sexist, or rapist, or murderer, or thief nonviolently, rather than violently. But he deserves our righteous indignation and we would be pusillanimous, sycophants, pathetic cowards, were we to hide, stuff, or sublimate these sensible, noble feelings. So it is said.

Stoics and Buddhists say this is all wrong. V and not V. We have a fundamental disagreement between, shall we say, us and two thems.[14] Righteous anger is good; righteous anger is bad. Is this a core disagreement with sources at the structural centers of the forms of life in dispute, in which case we might have incommensurability? Or is it a fundamental disagreement further out, somewhere between the center and the periphery? Or is it some of each? Even if we decide that it is a fundamental disagreement with sources at the center of the webs, and thus involves incommensurability or radical alterity, we cannot automatically conclude that the two forms of life are incomparable or that particular judgments about righteous anger are incomparable. The Stoic and the Buddhist might agree with the North American that righteous anger can get things to happen fast, so righteous anger and its absence can be compared against a "get things done fast" or "quick fix" measure. But the Stoic and the Buddhist can claim that this measure is not a good measure, all things considered, and presupposes precisely the sort of impatience, sense of urgency, and egoism that the claim that righteous anger is bad is designed to question and undermine.

Furthermore, the Stoic and Buddhist views can be seen as either a fundamental disagreement or an inversion with the accepted view where we live, depending on how we fix the lineages, the time frame, the geography, and so on. Neither the Buddhist nor the Stoic views that righteous anger is a vice inverted Christian views about righteousness since they came before Christianity, or better, in the Stoic case, just as Christianity was emerging. But the Buddhist view can be understood sensibly as a reaction to the constant strife of ancient Indian life that divided families as depicted in the *Mahabharata* and the *Bhagavad Gita* that sits inside it. Thus, it could be viewed as an inversion inside certain South Asian lineages. And the Stoic view is a response to strains of thought widely available across the Greco-Roman world, in Homer, classical tragedy, and Aristotle. Some of these sources celebrate jealous rage, prideful wrath, petty revenge, and overwrought retaliation. Others, specifically Plato and Aristotle, favor more astute rational control of anger. But never its elimination. The virtuous person gets angry when what is good or right is threatened.

What should we think and do when there is fundamental disagreement of this sort where I say V is good, a positive value, a justified norm, a virtue, and you say V is bad, a negative value, a bad habit or trait, a vice? Should we think that one way of valuing must be right, the other wrong? Or should we think to each his own and different strokes for different folks? The answers depend in part on whether the confrontation is notional, in history books, anthropology books, table top, in *National Geographic* magazine, or whether the confrontation of different values is real and occurs right here in River City, among neighbors, coinhabitants of a place, a village, a metropolis, or a nation-state. The debate about righteous anger and justified indignation occurs somewhere between the *National Geographic* on the coffee table, and the spaces of vivid public discourse in North America. But it would be good for us if it moved in that direction. I say this because, even on the containment view, the dominant Aristotelian view, there seems to be something wrong. Large numbers of people are ever at the ready to be annoyed, angry, resentful, and bitter. Road rage is discussed as if it is normal, natural. Politicians in America express and thereby model perpetual sanctimonious disdain. Television shows with high ratings and blogs steam disdain and contempt, and the targets of this disdain are often misrepresented, characterized, not interpreted with any charity or loving attention. In certain quarters there is recognition that being prone to anger is bad for an individual's serenity and cardiovascular heath and such regimens as yoga and mindfulness-based stress reduction are sought out to soothe the soul, and of course there are various lamentations about the level of disdain, contempt, and anger in public discourse. But no one wants to take the lead and suggest that there are reasons to stop giving permission for all or almost all of this.

Varieties of Anger, Precursors, Fuel, and Effects

Anger is the topic of the next two chapters. To prepare the way, I offer a brief philosophical psychology of anger, a taxonomy of the terrain, a template for speaking of anger. A full analysis of the structure, contours, and function of anger in different ecologies, would require more fine-grained analysis, which I do not pretend to provide.

- *Anger* or *angry feelings* refers to the phenomenal state(s) that is/ are experienced as anger, the phenomenal state(s) that feels/is angry. It includes whatever psychophysical states the angry person experiences, reddening, heat, and the impulse to strike out.
- *Angry behavior* is any behavior in the world that results from anger, for example, strong words, criticism, gossip, shaming, striking. Angry behavior is normally linked to feeling angry, but not always, as when a parent or teacher feigns anger to get the kids to behave.
- *Anger norms*: permissions or recommendations about appropriate anger, both phenomenal, how angry one is allowed or supposed to feel in different circumstances, and behavioral ones, what it is legitimate to do given those feelings.
- *Anger scripts*: socioculturally and normatively specific scripts for anger and angry behavior. In "Three Stooges" comedies, the brothers Moe, Larry, and Curly displayed this syndrome: harm → anger → I hit you on the head with a frying pan.
- *Justified anger* is anger that is at least permitted by anger norms; normally the justification involves there being considerations that warrant or speak in favor of anger.
- *Righteous anger* is anger, the phenomenal state and the psychophysical accompaniments, which is warranted or considered warranted by high values, especially justice violations.
- *Righteous indignation* is sometimes used as a synonym for righteous anger. But here I intend it to refer not to what is a variety of phenomenal anger in the usual sense(s), but rather to the judgment

that there has been disrespectful or insulting treatment of someone, others or me. The judgment, as I conceive it, involves feeling, the feeling that disrespect, insult, or injustice has occurred. It comes with a certain impatience that a wrong be righted. But it is not angry.

- *Punishment, violence, war.* These are all practices that may or may not be motivated by anger, as are rudeness, sarcasm, snark, irony, and passive aggressiveness.
- *Annoyance, frustration, resentment, disdain, and contempt.* These are all attitudes that seem to be, are likely to be, in the anger family. They have negative valence, are heated, directed at an insult, obstacle, or impending threat, and typically come with a desire to harm the source, to kick the flat tire, tell you that you are racist slime. Depending on one's purposes, one might say these are varieties of anger or that they are precursors or fuel for full-on anger, possibly fuel for the kind or kinds of anger, for example, out-of-control rage, which we ought not want to experience or enact.

The taxonomy enables us to see and reflect on some worrisome features of the economy of anger inside cultures and traditions, as well as several possible ways and locations that we might at a minimum better contain or tame it. First, anger norms and anger scripts are often transparently asymmetrical. The powerful are permitted to experience anger and to behave angrily toward those who are weaker, master to slave, men to women, bosses to workers. The powerless are not given similar permission. Second, justified anger can be governed by high standards of justification or low ones. Where I live, they are low, very low. If you annoy me in the slightest, I can be pissed. If you cut me off, I can give you the finger, although prudence (you might be dangerous) might lead me to restraint. If you don't hire me or give me a raise, you are a "fuck-head."

"Justified anger" is the kind of anger and angry behavior we find common or normal, the kinds we have normalized, the space of venting we expect and permit. Sometimes, perhaps often, we say to others, or ourselves, "You ought not to be so angry," which expresses norms of aptness or proportionality. Other times we say, "You ought not to be angry at all, period," which expresses an objective standard, one that appeals to more than your subjective feelings and perceptions.

There are three features of the taxonomy to which I call special attention. First, there is the possibility of prising apart behaviors or practices that involve injury, punishment, and even war from feelings of anger or the angry behaviors that typically accompany it in our psychology. Anger may usually involve the disposition to strike out, to do harm to the source. But the connection is not necessary, not inevitable. There are abundant historical and contemporary examples of decisions to punish individuals or attack and conquer nation-states that involve no anger at all, where cold calculations of public safety, or the desire for your resources motivate us to lock you up, take your gold, or your oil fields. Foucault famously explores cases where punishment is motivated not by anger, but by boredom and sadism. This disconnect, which perhaps is not usual, opens the possibility that one might think anger is rarely, even never, justified, but not be particularly loving or compassionate nor be a pacifist. One might, like the Stoics, and to a certain extent even the Buddhists we'll meet in the next chapter, think that anger is always unjustified, unwholesome, bad, vicious, but think that punishment and war are sometimes justified. On the other side, one could be a nation-state pacifist, a vegan for moral reasons, and be against every form of retributive punishment, or punishment, period, but think anger—both the emotion and certain expressions—is natural and must be given its space to roam in everyday life. Perhaps that is the position of the American Psychological Association when they speak of anger being "usually healthy," which by the way, is compatible with it not being good, all things considered.

Second, these points relate to the distinction between righteous anger and righteous indignation. Righteous anger is wrathful. One is furious, outraged. The righteous part involves high normative standards. Unlike ordinary anger, which is governed by pathetically low standards of justification, righteous anger is at least supposed to be governed by high standards. Grave injustice, racism, sexism, trampling on my sacred values, all warrant righteous anger.

"Righteous indignation" of the sort that is not equivalent to, just another name for, righteous anger is a state where one judges that grave insult or injury has taken place or is likely and speaks out against it, engages in civil disobedience, possibly civil war or war between nations to right the wrong.[15] Some doubt that pure righteous indignation is possible, which it would be if it did not involve any affect at all. The question is whether there can be judgment that such-and-such state of affairs is grievously wrong, the wrong ought to be righted, and a powerful emotional disposition to want to participate in righting the wrong without being angry. I think it is possible.[16] One might object: Even if one starts with the calm judgment that, for example, Jim Crow laws are racist and thus warrant mass civil disobedience, one will not be able to keep the lid on one's emotions and one will get fired up as soon as the demonstrations begin.[17] But here one conflates being angry for a righteous reason and getting angry when one starts to do something to right the wrong. I am not entirely sure about the prospects of pure righteous indignation. But it would be a mistake to think that because it is rare, possibly never sighted around here, it is a weird psychic twist or some kind of impossibility. We have not explored that space recently.

Third, it can help open ourselves to possibilities of being different, better than we now are, if we recognize that our ways of doing anger and being angry, our anger norms and anger scripts make themselves seem normal, natural, the way anger is, the way things are with anger, when in fact they are not normal. They are the way WEIRD people do anger.

Even if at the end of the day, anger is inevitable, different peoples have it and do it differently. In *Unnatural Emotions* (1988), Catherine Lutz discusses *song*, "justified anger," among the Ifaluk of the South Pacific. For the Ifaluk, unlike for us, anger is never justified or righteous, never *song*, if it is the result of a mere personal injury. There is normative permission to feel it and act on it only when there is a social norm violation that can be recognized by everyone not just by the wounded party. More importantly, the expression of *song* in the face-to-face moral ecology of the Ifaluk is an invitation to make peace, to repair and renew communal commitment to these shared norms. Whereas American anger follows a script in which the object of anger is threatened with injury, exclusion, and harm, the Ifaluk are socialized to meet the object of *song* with *fago*, a complex emotion of love-compassion-vulnerability, and to indicate to him that his norm violation is seen, spoken of, and gossiped about, but that he is welcomed back to the moral order without fanfare and without much in the way of what we would call angry behavior, insults, or aggressive displays. Whereas our anger script involves hurt, injury, sometimes humiliation, Ifaluk *song* involves fear of ostracism (*metagu*). The point is not that the norms of justified anger are entirely different across life-forms, between, for example, native New Yorkers and the Ifaluk. Whether and how anger norms differ is a delicate empirical question. The point is that there are differences in the way anger seems or feels, the actions it gives rise to, the feelings it arouses in targets, and the way it is resolved or dissipates, and these differences depend on differences in the overall moral ecology.

Equilibrium, Harmony, and Decency

Holism has important implications for both ethics and the project of comparative philosophy. It is fair to say that most moral systems that live long enough to be noticed achieve some kind of functionality or equilibrium. If a moral system is stable in the sense that it contributes to the maintenance of social order, peace, and harmony, it is functioning well in one sense. It is contributing to the maintenance of social order, peace, and harmony, and that is one common reason people cite for why a moral code is needed, and why they judge their moral code as a good one. The trouble is that ethically bad practices can serve peace and order, even harmony, if there are also well-honed beliefs in place about the station and duties of particular groups. Plato recommended a collective hallucination, the "noble lie," that some people are made of gold, others silver, and others brass to help people accept, understand, and perform in a way that produced the ideal harmonious state. And morally dubious systems can do that. Many societies have accepted slavery and worked well enough for a long time with that institution in place. Many societies function well with asymmetric norms: the master is behaving according to the right norms and script if he speaks harshly to the slave and gives him his comeuppance, while the slave, also in normative conformity, bows his head, averts his eyes, and accepts his insulting treatment. The system is in equilibrium, functioning smoothly, but is ethically awful. How do we see this?

There are several possibilities. Sometimes we don't see it at all, nor do we reason toward a better practical or moral equilibrium. It just happens, under the radar, due to the multiple ways complex systems change, develop, accrete, and degenerate. Blue fabric bleeds into white fabric and the whole cloth becomes lighter blue. The climate changes, people stop growing cotton, slaves are less valuable, the institution changes. The Portuguese, unlike the British, explicitly approved of sex with slaves. As a result, skin color is a less good marker of ethnic origin in Brazil than in America, and this makes ongoing racism based on skin color a bit harder to sustain in Brazil than in America. There is natural wear and tear in most complex systems, and ebbs and flows, in which some subsystems strengthen and others weaken. Like graying hair, it happens gradually over time. One day when looking at photographs from ten years ago, one sees that there has been a big change, constituted by little changes, none of which were seen or noticed, as they happened day-by-day.

Sometimes, however, there are tensions, possibly contradictions that exist or develop inside a tradition, internal to it, and they are noticed, spoken of, and debated. Ideals of compassion and common humanity were always in tension with the institution of slavery in America, even if they were tinkered with in self-serving ways, suppressed and ignored during the slave age, and even if those who pointed this out were largely silenced or ignored. Often, again America in the eighteenth and nineteenth centuries is a good example, there are pressures produced by nearby or interacting moral systems to reflect on the quality of aspects of the way one lives and values. A nearby system can have an influence by being seen, visible, noticed, and judged to provide an alternative, a novel possibility—a small adjustment or a radical makeover—to some norms, values, or practices. An interacting system is one where the alternative is not simply seen from afar, but is having a say, a public influence because of immigration, trade, the way neighborhoods are bumping up against each other, and so on.

In sum, there are two points: First, there are two senses in which a moral system might be said to be functional, one practical, and the other moral. A system is practically functional or in equilibrium if it produces stability for the society in question. It is morally functional or in ethical equilibrium if it is defensible from a moral point of view. The second point is that there are normally two perspectives from which to judge moral quality, internal and external. When a challenge is raised to a moral tradition or an aspect of a tradition, there is almost always a defensive reaction, akin to an immune system response to a germ. People inside a tradition are normally pretty good at saying why and how their values make sense, how they work and make sense both practically and morally. The slave owners speak of a flourishing economy and of compassionate paternalism, explaining how the slaves are better off, and the slaves, perhaps as a result of immobilizing fear or a group hallucination or the effects of the Stockholm syndrome, or all of these, nod compliantly.

Pressures from the outside do not create direct challenges to a moral order—in part because modern people often abide different-strokes-for-different-folks attitudes—so much as they provide opportunities for reflection and imagination by those inside a moral order. At these points, issues of commensurability and incommensurability, radical alterity, comparability and incomparability, and superficial and deep contestation, all come to the fore. In the next two chapters, I examine a fundamental disagreement between two ways of worldmaking on the single question of the value of anger. WEIRD psychologists say that anger is "normally healthy," and WEIRD philosophers say it is morally justified. Stoics and Buddhists say it is unhealthy both to the person who experiences the anger and to her relations, and that it is wrong because it aims to injure, and no virtue does that. There is a fundamental disagreement. To understand its contours we will need to enter deeply into the forms of life inside which the different normative views arise and make sense.

8

Moral Geographies of Anger

Parable 1: Himalayan Foothills

In March 2000, I visited Dharamsala, India, for four days of meetings with the 14th Dalai Lama, Tenzin Gyatso, some of his fellow Buddhists, and a group of Western scientists, mostly psychologists and neuroscientists, to discuss the topic of "Destructive Emotions and How to Overcome Them." Daniel Goleman's (2003) book on these meetings with that title is a good report. There was much to learn at these discussions in the Dalai Lama's residence and many surprises. Here is one unforgettable one.

It became clear after a day or so of talks that Tibetan Buddhists believe that anger, resentment, and their suite are categorically bad, always unwarranted, wrong, "unwholesome," as they are inclined to say. That was surprising by itself. We have many norms for appropriate anger, such as "Don't get too angry" or "so angry" as we sometimes say. And wrath is a deadly sin. But we do not think that one, indeed, no one, should never get angry, that anger is always wrong. For us, the right kind of anger reveals that you see and care about something of value. Everyday, not-so-warranted anger shows that one is normal. Minimally, we expect and tolerate a certain amount of it.

But then there was this kicker, even more mind-boggling. These Buddhists also believed that anger could be eliminated in mortals, that there are practices that actually work so that it is possible to not experience anger, practices that can extirpate anger, cleanse the soul of tendencies to anger. I got that there are practices and rules of decorum—"counting to 10," sublimation, or "stuffing it"—norms of apt anger that keep us from expressing anger and that work to contain it, but not experiencing anger at all seemed unnatural, weird, not human. Again, self-work to keep from getting pissy over small frustrations makes good sense and is possible. But except for a rare saintly bird of maximally even temperament, not experiencing anger at the cosmos or the gods for the slings and arrows of outrageous fortune, and especially at evil people for their awfulness seems close to a psychological impossibility. Then there is the fact that most people I know were raised to think it OK, permissible, possibly sometimes required, to feel and express outrage. Righteous anger is something we ought sometimes to experience and express, something that certain people or states of affairs deserve.

So I found myself posing this thought experiment to the Dalai Lama. Imagine that one were to find oneself in a public space—a park, a movie theater—where one realizes that one is seated next to Hitler—or Stalin or Pol Pot or Mao—early in the execution of the genocides they actually perpetrated. We, my people, think it would be appropriate first to feel moral anger, possibly outrage at Hitler et al., and second, that it would be OK, possibly required, to kill them supposing one had the means. What about you Tibetan Buddhists?

The Dalai Lama turned to consult the high lamas who were normally seated behind him, like a lion's pride. After a few minutes of whispered conversation in Tibetan with his team, the Dalai Lama turned back to our group and explained that one should kill Hitler (actually with some ceremonial fanfare, in the way, to mix cultural practices, a samurai warrior might). It is stopping a bad, a very bad, karmic causal chain. So "Yes, kill him." "But don't be angry."

What could this mean? How did it make sense to think of one human being killing another, being motivated to kill another human being, without feeling, without activating the suite of reactive attitudes such as anger, resentment, blame?

Stoics, excellent warriors, thought something similar, that when effective action is required against an enemy including his elimination, emotions like fear and anger get in the way, immobilize, under- or overreach, and undermine skillfully achieving one's aims. In *De Ira*, and in a direct challenge to Aristotle, Seneca writes, "It is easier to banish dangerous emotions than to rule them" (7). The mature person is disciplined and thoughtful, whereas the angry person is undisciplined and sloppy; "anger is excited by empty matters hovering on the outskirts of the case."[1]

Seneca like other Stoics thought that we confuse the occasional necessity of severe punishment and war with the necessity of anger. Aristotle, he says, claims that anger is useful for the soldier, although not for the general. But good soldiers, good Stoic warriors are never angry; otherwise they make a mess of what sometimes sadly needs to be done. Seneca's recommendation for anger: "Extirpate root and branch . . . what can moderation have to do with an evil habit?" (42).

Parable 2: Johannesburg

I have visited South Africa twice, first in 2007 and then in 2009 as the country prepared to host the World Cup in soccer. Apartheid has been on my mind since I was twelve and my friend Johnny Estenfeld and I would plot after school how we would end it. Both times I visited, but especially the first time, I found myself feeling awe that Nelson Mandela and his comrades had found it in themselves not to kill all the white folk. Even fifteen years after the end of apartheid it was hard for me not to feel vicarious outrage against the white population who still largely controlled the wealth and lived in fancy houses in gated communities in the major cities of Durban, Johannesburg, Pretoria, and Capetown. It amazed me that apartheid ended, that it could have ended, without an even worse bloodbath than had already occurred, and that South Africa found its way to enter an era of "truth and reconciliation."[2] There was visible damage to hearts and minds of white, black, and colored people, and to the economy, but somehow Mandela, inspired by Mahatma Gandhi, who himself was inspired by Jainism, let go of some of the anger, resentment, and fury that I, again vicariously, thought was normal and appropriate, even required for justice's sake. The best explanation is that I was not raised to see how ending a practice like apartheid was psychologically, morally, or practically possible without a bloodbath. I didn't see that this was a variety of moral possibility. Or better, I saw that a world in which people settle peacefully disputes like this one where grievous moral harm is at stake is a good and worthy one, an attractive moral option, better than the world of righteous angry bloodstained warriors. But I was not attuned to its actual possibility for human beings. I was raised in a world where every tale of the victories of the forces of good over the forces of evil involved righteous fury, death, and destruction. Even biblical angels are fierce souls. Satan, recall, was once an angel in heaven. And he did not leave peacefully.

Possible Moral Worlds

The first story raises the possibility of a world in which anger is eliminated and the thought that this would be a better world, even if that world still contains injuries, insults, and injustice. The second speaks of a world that is actual in certain places and where righteous anger is allowed but overcome, resolved, or set aside in nonangry ways, through communal rituals of forgiveness and reconciliation. Now, with both stories in mind, I proceed to the heart of the matter: Are there credible cross-cultural sources that could help people like me see, and understand better than I did, than I now do, the possible ways anger and its relations can be configured in human moral psychology, the various ways anger can be shaped, molded, and expressed, and the worth of adjusting, modifying, possibly eliminating certain, even all forms of anger?

Most philosophers as well as most ordinary people in the West are Aristotelians about anger. We think that anger can be a virtue if it is moderate and contained. Anger, like every other virtue, admits of a mean between defect and excess, and its virtuous forms are all kept at the mean or in its vicinity.

Whether moderation is required of the feeling of anger, its expression, or both is a matter of some dispute. Some think that it is perfectly OK for you to be pissed that the barista is slow making your triple macchiato with virgin spring coconut shavings, but that you should stuff it, not express it. Others think that you have lots of self-work to do on what you are disposed to feel, possibly on what you think it is normal, OK to feel, possibly on your assessment of how hard it is to make that drink. Containment can mean the same as moderation or it can refer to the requirement that one ought to control and encapsulate behavior no matter what one feels (frustrated, pissy, angry); or relatedly that one ought not to allow emotions, especially negative ones like anger, to penetrate one's heart, mind, or behavior beyond what they are aimed at, the novice barista. Otherwise, you might get mad at me for the barista problem—project, displace, and so on. Then I get pissy. Next, the kids are a mess; all of Williamsburg feels the pain, and eventually it is the end of the world, as we know it.

For ease, I'll refer to views like ours as containment views. Anger is or can be a virtue if it is moderate, at the mean as determined by proper assessment of the situation, and so long as it does not spill over into places in one's heart, mind, and behavior where it does not belong. Anger is a virtue when moderate and contained, otherwise it is a vice.

Anger's Nature and Texture

There are complex taxonomic questions about anger and its relations that I do not try to answer, or claim to know the answers to, although I sketched some distinctions among its varieties in the previous chapter. Here again for ease of reference is an abridged version of that taxonomy.

- *Anger* or *angry feelings* refers to the phenomenal state(s) that is/ are experienced as anger, the phenomenal state(s) that feels/is angry. It includes whatever psychophysical states the angry person experiences, reddening, heat, and the impulse to strike out.
- *Angry behavior* is any behavior in the world that results from anger, for example, strong words, criticism, gossip, shaming, striking.
- *Anger norms*: permissions or recommendations about appropriate anger, both phenomenal, how angry one is allowed or supposed to feel in different circumstances, and behavioral ones, what it is legitimate to do given those feelings.
- *Anger scripts*: socioculturally and normatively specific scripts for anger and angry behavior.
- *Justified anger* is anger that is at least permitted by anger norms, normally the justification involves there being considerations that warrant or speak in favor of anger.

- *Righteous anger* is anger, the phenomenal state and the psychophysical accompaniments, which is warranted or considered warranted by high values, especially justice violations.
- *Righteous indignation* is sometimes used as a synonym for righteous anger. But here I intend it to refer not to what is a variety of phenomenal anger in the usual sense(s), but rather to the judgment that there has been disrespectful or insulting treatment of someone, others or me. The judgment, as I conceive it, involves feeling, the feeling that disrespect, insult, or injustice has occurred. It comes with a certain impatience that a wrong be righted. But it is not angry.
- *Punishment, violence, war.* These are all practices that may or may not be motivated by anger, as are rudeness, sarcasm, snark, irony, and passive aggressiveness.
- *Annoyance, frustration, resentment, disdain, and contempt.* These are all attitudes that seem to be, are likely to be, in the anger family. They have negative valence, are heated, directed at an insult, obstacle, or impending threat, and typically come with a desire to harm the source, to kick the flat tire, tell you that you are racist slime.

In linguistics there are superordinate terms, like 'vehicle,' that subsume lower-level terms, like 'car,' 'truck,' 'train,' 'plane,' 'bike,' and so on. My Volkswagen Jetta and my Trek bike are vehicles, and they are tokens respectively of the types automobile and bicycle. Is 'anger' a superordinate term covering all the varieties above, so that wanting to extirpate anger would be the sociomoral equivalent to issuing an edict against all vehicles? Maybe.

Rage and fury seem, the way I use words, to be kinds of anger. That's OK, because rage and fury are definitely on the extirpators' minds. What about resentment, indignation, contempt? I am not sure that these are best classified as kinds of anger, although speaking for myself, they seem to share some central phenomenal properties with anger. The same holds for being frustrated, annoyed, and pissy. They have an angry-ish feel to them. But I am not sure if they are types of anger or simply close relations. If they are just close relations, then arguments against anger might leave them untouched if the arguments are that all and only the kinds of anger should be eliminated. What about revenge? It seems mostly behavioral to me, and I can imagine saying that someone got revenge without implying anything about angry feelings. The Mafia, according to a common trope, is good at getting revenge in accordance with a "don't get mad, get even" business model. The same is true for retaliation and violence. Suppose 'anger' is a superordinate term like 'vehicle,' where most members of the family truly fall under it as varieties, one might mark some types or varieties as good, some as bad. Imagine that some municipality issues an edict that says that one ought not to take vehicles to work that have a carbon footprint above some measure *m*, which we'll suppose rules out driving a car or flying to work, but not taking the bus, train, or bike. Likewise, one could cull anger into its permissible and impermissible kinds. This is what the Aristotelian does; permissible anger is at the mean, and it is also what the adjectives 'righteous' or 'justified' modify among people who speak a certain way. I assume nothing very precise about how to classify the members of the anger-family. But I do assume that the foes of anger intend that ordinary anger, righteous anger, righteous indignation, resentment, and contempt, as well as lots of everyday feelings of frustration, annoyance, impatience, and pissiness, ought to go, or at least that they ought to go in the varieties that involve anger. This way I can finesse the taxonomic question while making the arguments for extirpating anger maximally strong, interesting, and radical.[3]

Now I examine two views, a Buddhist view, then a Stoic view, which express a fundamental disagreement with the containment view. Anger is vicious, period, full stop. Siddhartha Gautama, the historical Buddha, and Seneca explore the farthest edges of human possibility space, the space where there is no anger, or something in that vicinity.

The Bodhisattva's Way of Life

The bodhisattva is a Buddhist saint. In Mahayana, we are naturally drawn to be a bodhisattva, at least once we are presented with the ideal. We are drawn to the ideal of being a morally much better version of ourselves in the same way that we are drawn to the idea of more perfect weather on any day that we see or are reminded that the weather is less than perfect, very stormy, much too hot, humid, cold, or just a bit too stormy, too hot, humid, or cold.

Buddhist psychology posits three poisons in human nature, which create dis-ease, the socio-moral equivalent of uncomfortable and unpredictable weather within and between beings:

1. Greed, thirst, avarice (*lobha; raga*) for all the things I want (which is a lot);
2. Anger and resentment (*dosa; dvesa*) when I don't get what I want;
3. Illusion (*moha*) believing such things as that I deserve to get what I want, and that other beings or the impersonal universe warrant my anger when they don't deliver.

The core illusion that runs through and sustains the poisons, a kind of Buddhist original sin, is that I am EGO, *ĀTMAN*, that what I get, gain, acquire, or own accretes to the SELF, solidifies its strength, its resilience, and its permanence, all of which further secures my impression that I am the center of the universe. This illusion needs to be crushed. It is a metaphysical mistake. I am not a permanent, cosmically important thing. I am, at most, a psychophysically continuous thing or process. I am impermanent, not a SELF in the puffed up sense of *ĀTMAN*. I am *ANĀTMAN*, not *ĀTMAN*. I am less *I* than a procession of *i*'s, more e. e. cummings and bell hooks than a big name in the big lights on Broadway.

Everything will go better including my prospects for living a good life, as an impermanent being, if I cease grasping stuff for myself and seek to alleviate suffering whenever and wherever it exists, including of course in me, such as *i* am.

Once the possibility of being out from under the grip of the ego illusion is seen and experienced as worthy, one finds oneself wanting to develop the altruistic potential in oneself.[4] The awakening of this intention is *bodhicitta*. Once awake and aware that *bodhicitta* expresses a worthy, indeed an excellent intention, one is ready to enter the bodhisattva path and to take vows to work to alleviate the suffering of all sentient beings whenever and wherever it exists, which is always and everywhere.[5]

If one believes in rebirth, one vows to return to this world for as long as it takes to alleviate the suffering of all the sentient beings.

> For as long as space endures
> And for as long as living beings remain,
> Until then may I too abide
> To dispel the misery in the world. (Śāntideva, 10.55)

If and when that aim is achieved, the highest good, the liberation of all sentient beings, has been achieved. And then, "mission accomplished," all enlightened souls can rest, be dissolved, absorbed back into the bosom of the universe, freed finally of the last attachment, and the only sensible and worthy one for mortals, the one that aims to liberate all sentient beings from suffering. Universal salvation. Nirvana.[6]

Two things are worth noting. Salvation in Buddhism is not an individualistic project. The aim is the salvation of all sentient beings, not just me.[7] Second, and possibly because of the first, the Buddhist time horizon is very long. I once asked a wise lama how long enlightenment would take for a normal guy like me. He asked that I imagine a mountain range 84,000 times the size of the Himalayas and imagine that each day corresponds to a life of normal length. Each day I touch the nearest point on the range with a soft piece of cloth. I will need as many lives as it would take for those touches to make the entire range erode. A long time. Not infinite perhaps, but long.[8]

It is in the context of the bodhisattva ideal that the reasons for the categorical rejection of anger are voiced most clearly.[9] Śāntideva's eighth-century masterpiece, *The Bodhisattva's Way of Life* (*Bodhicharyāvatāra*) is a classic work that explains why anger is the very worst of all the unhealthy states of mind and why one "should totally eradicate" even the smallest discontent or frustration lest it seed full on anger and hatred. These beginnings are fuel for uncontrollable and destructive anger, "which has no other function than that of causing harm" (6.8).[10]

The Bodhisattva's Way of Life is at once a beautiful poem, a liturgy, and a self-cultivation manual that begins with the invocation of *bodhicitta*, the aspiration to see things rightly, and to work on one's self, one's ego—to deflate it—so that one can benefit all beings.

The path from wanting to benefit all beings to doing so requires confession, some sort of self-reckoning, purgation, and resolve to follow a better path. I dedicate myself to follow the example of those who have conquered vice (2.8) and "I leave behind previous wrongdoing completely; never again shall I do another wrong" (2.9).

Once *bodhicitta* is awakened or reawakened, and I have confessed and renounced my past misdeeds, I am purified enough to take the bodhisattva's vows:

> I am medicine for the sick. May I be
> both the doctor and the nurse,
> until the sickness does not recur. (3.7)

> May I be an inexhaustible treasure for
> impoverished beings.
> May I wait upon them with various forms of offering. (3.9)

Eventually, by trying to embody the vows, I come to see that[11]

> All those who suffer in the world do so because
> of their desire for their own happiness.
> All those happy in the world are so
> because of their desire for the happiness of others. (8.129)

But before I can really understand this, that egoism has never made anyone happy, especially the egoist, whereas altruism makes many happy including the altruist, I must learn to eliminate anger and this requires a multifaceted toolkit of mindfulness skills, meditation techniques, verbal reminders, and recitation exercises, as well as learning some Buddhist metaphysics.

Rx: Antidotes to Anger

The sixth chapter of *The Bodhisattva's Way of Life* is entirely devoted to anger and its antidotes, the three pills, or the triple concoction, that are incompatible with it, that deactivate it: compassion, lovingkindness, and patience.[12] First, we are told that anger is worse than all other vices. It alone can "undermine thousands of eons worth of merit" (6.1).

In his teaching on Śāntideva called *Healing Anger* (1999), the 14th Dalai Lama explains the reasoning this way. Greed, hubris, lust, jealousy, closed-mindedness, and many other states of mind are both personally afflictive and destructive of relations. But, bad as these other vices are, they are compatible with experiencing and sustaining the project of *bodhicitta*, the overall commitment to seek enlightenment in order to benefit all beings. Greed is wrong, but it does local damage, not global damage as anger does. Greed might require that I aim to get some of what you have, need, or are owed—more than my fair share, as we say—while possibly also, at the same time, being an overall (or otherwise) nice enough guy. I pay you a living wage, care that your family is OK, give you a fruit and rum cake basket at Christmas, and so on. Lust, in a common fantasy version, involves my having at you, possessing you for as long as it takes, while you are also quite pleased about the whole thing, even as we both violate obligations to others, norms we avow, reason, and decorum. But anger is a wholesale obstacle to *bodhicitta*; it performatively undermines it by aiming to wound, possibly destroy the other. The idea behind the remedy, the powerful mixture of compassion, lovingkindness, and forbearance is that it is some kind of psychic impossibility to be in a state of compassion, lovingkindness, and forbearance and to be consumed by anger or hatred at the same time.[13]

Bodhicitta is the unqualified desire that you do not suffer, that you flourish, whereas anger wishes you harm, pain, possibly that you be crushed like a bug, painfully, with no mercy. In every instant that there is anger, patience, compassion, and lovingkindness are dissolved, and in the person who is always angry, the one Seneca describes as "irascible," and whom we nowadays call "an angry asshole," these positive states of mind are pretty much always missing, simply characterologically unsustainable. Such a person is hateful. There is no room in their being for other virtues.

An Attitude of Gratitude: Adopt as Needed

In addition to compassion, lovingkindness, and patience, Śāntideva also recommends gratitude as an antidote for anger, as well as for all variety of subtle ego-centered inconveniences, frustrations, and resentments that seed or fuel it. When there is even the arising of anger, think of all one is grateful for, and it will extinguish the anger by taking all its fuel away. Śāntideva meets head-on an obvious objection to his recommendation. Imagine someone who says that he is grateful for many things, his parents, education, friends, a roof over his head, and so on, but claims complete justification for despising his irascible neighbor who is always starting disputes. Suppose the individual is right: the neighbor is incorrigibly mean and angry. Śāntideva writes:

> Those who wish to cause me suffering
> Are like Buddhas bestowing waves of blessings
> As they open the door for my not going to an unfortunate realm,
> Why should I be angry with them? (6.101)[14]

The question is rhetorical, of course. The individual who has awakened *bodhicitta*, taken the bodhisattva's vows, and learned some Buddhist metaphysics gets that he ought to meet his enemy with compassion. The irascible neighbor is broken, damaged. Perhaps the law needs to be involved to restrain him. Perhaps the mental health authorities need to look in on him, even institutionalize him. Deal with these practical problems wisely. As for the angry person, love him, and help him heal.

Metaphysical Reasons to Eliminate Anger

There are several reasons to want to eliminate anger. The destruction of eons of good karma is one reason. The natural attraction of the bodhisattva ideal is another reason to abhor anger and to want to be rid of it. Buddhist metaphysics, seeing things as they really are, gives additional and decisive reasons to want to eliminate anger.[15] Special importance is given to understanding the metaphysical thesis of "dependent arising" or "dependent origination," and it helps explain why the Dalai Lama said what he said to me about Hitler. Śāntideva writes:

> Whatever transgressions and evil deeds of various kinds there are, all arise through the power of conditioning factors, while there is nothing that arises independently. (6.25)

> Hence everything is governed by other factors which in turn are governed by others. And in this way nothing governs itself. Having understood this, I should not become angry with phenomena that are like apparitions. (6.31)

> Therefore, even if one sees a friend or an enemy behaving badly, one can reflect that there are specific conditioning factors that determine this, and thereby remain happy. (6.33)

Buddhist metaphysics runs this way: (1) Everything is impermanent. What there is and all there is, is a great cosmic unfolding. (2) You are among the things that unfold, appear, and that are impermanent (No-Self). (3) The existence of everything, each action, thing, event, or process in the unfolding depends on prior conditions. Dependent origination is the thesis that each thing, each event in the flux, emerges out of a field of relations. Nothing occurs ex nihilo, on its own, with causal powers that are self-generated ("nothing governs itself"). (4) Nothing that acts, occurs, or happens has an intrinsic, nonrelational essence (*sunyata*, emptiness).

Some of this will remind the Western philosopher of familiar discussions and debates about the one and the many, being and becoming, change and stability, the self, personal identity, and free will and determinism.[16] For present purposes, the focus is on how the distinctively Buddhist way of seeing things affects the Buddhist view on anger. Remember, the Dalai Lama said that I could, indeed, I should kill Hitler, but I shouldn't be angry with him. The reasons perhaps are now obvious. Hitler and his ilk are bad nodes in the unfolding of chains of dependent originations. They should be stopped, otherwise I am, by inadvertence, allowing a horrible karmic chain to unfold. But Hitler is not a bad person in a familiar sense of bad person, where a person is a self-initiating agent, a *causa sui*, a demigod who is a prime mover himself unmoved. No one is one of those.

> If disregarding the principal cause, such as a stick or other weapon, I become angry with the person who impels it, he too is impelled by hatred.
> It is better that I hate that hatred. (6.41)[17]

Two Challenges

Śāntideva anticipates two testy challenges to the elimination of anger. Surely, sacrilege and harming my loved ones are intolerable, deserving of righteous anger, fury, and the harshest retaliation. In March 2001 the Taliban destroyed two monumental standing Buddhist statues in Bamiyan, Afghanistan declaring them idols. What to do? How to respond? As far as the destruction of the altars at which I pray, the sites I hold sacred, Śāntideva writes:

> And my hatred towards those who damage sacred images and stupas or who abuse the true teaching is not appropriate since the Buddhas and Bodhisattvas are not distressed. (6.64)

Buddhas and bodhisattvas are enlightened, they are not attached to ephemeral things, themselves, their desires, even their temples. Tibetan Buddhists model and enact the right attitude when teams of gifted monks build elaborate and colorful sand mandalas over the course of a week, and then let the wind take it away, disperse it, eliminate it.

In the case of harm to my loved ones, I need to remind myself again of dependent origination. He writes:

> When people harm one's teachers, relatives and others dear to us, one should, as above, regard it as arising on the basis of conditioning factors and refrain from anger towards them. (6.65)[18]

These two responses invite the question of what is possible for unenlightened souls. Minimally, we should try to be this way.

Rebirth Is the Rub

No doubt readers who are not Buddhists will have many questions and objections to the idea that we should work to eliminate anger. Some obvious ones will turn on objections to aspects of Buddhist metaphysics:

- The idea that anger destroys "eons of merit" presupposes rebirth and laws of karma. I don't believe that there are impersonal karmic laws and that there is any sense in which *I* or even *i* go on across lifetimes, let alone eons.[19]
- The doctrines of No-Self and Emptiness lead Buddhists to allow too much time, eons, for goodness and justice to be served. The quality of my life, for me, depends on all the rewards and payback coming in this life, between my birth and my death.
- Anger is an adaptation. It contributes to fitness.
- It is psychologically impossible to eliminate anger.
- Righteous anger is warranted. When anger is justified it reveals the angry person to be a sensitive detector of cruelty, injustice, and what matters.
- Righteous anger is necessary. It gets things done. It gets the attention of bad guys and oppressors; puts fear in their hearts, possibly it leads them to act well.

I'll deal with some of these objections in the next chapter. Here I mark one natural and very general concern that the reader may have. Buddhist arguments for the elimination of anger involve several distinctively Buddhist metaphysical beliefs: Impermanence, No-Self, Emptiness, Karma, Rebirth, and Nirvana. These concepts are not ours, so these arguments against anger won't work for us.

Here is the sketch of a reply: The doctrines of Impermanence, No-Self, and Emptiness are not metaphysically all that strange. Many classical and contemporary naturalistic philosophers defend views such as Impermanence, No-Self, and Emptiness (Flanagan 2011). That leaves Karma, Rebirth, and Nirvana. The scientific naturalist will say that belief in rebirth, the quality of which is orchestrated by impersonal karmic laws, is unacceptable. Scientific reasons militate equally, one might say, against belief in any kind of postmortem survival, Abrahamic heavenly afterlives, or Buddhist rebirths. At this point, one could go either of two ways. One might say that the Buddhist arguments for eliminating anger do not depend on its theory of salvation or, not inconsistently, that the theory of salvation is poetic or metaphorical and need not be interpreted literally. I leave this work of figuring out the exact logical relations inside the Buddhist way of worldmaking as they pertain to anger to others.[20]

But if my suspicions are right that there are good Buddhist reasons for extirpating anger associated with the underlying psychology and the metaphysics, and if, furthermore, the remaining metaphysics, that is, the metaphysics minus rebirth based on a system of karmic accountability, is plausible, then there are neutral or non-Buddhist reasons to extirpate anger. And such reasons could be reasons for us, too.

Seneca "On Anger"

Before saying more for or against the Buddhist arguments for extirpating anger, I examine a different argument for the same conclusion that anger is always bad, categorically unwholesome, worth eliminating from the earth. Then in the next chapter, we can take stock of the best replies from the Aristotelian containment side to the Buddhist and the Stoic.

"On Anger" (*De Ira*) is a sort of dialogue between Seneca, the Roman Stoic philosopher, minister to Nero, and his brother Novatus, who is not actually present but whose view on anger is presented with utmost care and sensitivity. Novatus plays the role of the Aristotelian who is morally serious and wishes to learn how to moderate anger, to learn "how anger can be soothed." Seneca thinks that "soothing," or "moderating" anger is a lost cause. "It is easier to banish dangerous emotions than to rule them." The literary pose of two brothers who disagree, signals that this is a loving disagreement about a sensitive topic, a difficult matter.

Seneca begins his teaching by offering a physiognomy of anger: Anger is "above all other [passions] hideous and wild . . . greedy for revenge . . . awkward at perceiving what is true and just." Then he draws this comparison: "They who anger possess are not sane, look at their appearance." There are "distinct symptoms that mark madmen . . . the signs of angry men too, are the same." Again, "look at their appearance." Susan Brison, a philosopher who survived rape and attempted murder writes, "I have seen the face of a killer set on exterminating a fellow human being. It is not a face I want to see when I look in the mirror."[21]

Seneca agrees with his Aristotelian opponent that what motivates anger is suffering; injury; insult; threat of injury to oneself, loved ones, members of one's polis; suspicions or worries about injury; and envy that you have more than I do.[22] The aim of anger is transparent. Anger is the "desire to repay suffering." There are episodes of anger and there are angry people, the latter Seneca calls "irascible." The episodically angry person and the constitutionally angry person are compared to the person who drinks too much once in awhile, and the alcoholic who is always drinking or disposed to drink. Anger comes in varieties, and the Greeks are better than the Romans at naming them.[23] There are episodes and persons that we describe as "bitter, harsh, peevish, frantic, clamorous, surly, [and] fierce." "Sulkiness," Seneca says, is "a refined form of irascibility."[24] Irascibility, we are told, is "angry with the truth itself." The thought is that anger almost always overreaches and overreacts; it is incontinent. Suppose you are preoccupied with a matter of concern (to you) and are short with me. I think, possibly I say, that you are an inconsiderate prick. But you are not that. I don't really even think that. You were short with me; that's all. But as soon as anger gets its grip, I can't see things—you, our relationship—as they are. I overreact, and things are spinning out of control, especially if you react angrily to my unjust behavior.

"Aristotle stands forth in defense of anger and forbids it to be uprooted, saying it is a spur to virtue." Seneca denies this. Anger is a response to injury that aims to cause pain, and causing pain is vicious.

One part of Seneca's reply is that anger is almost always messy, undisciplined, and sloppy. It retaliates against aspects of persons and situations that have nothing to do with the injury or insult. The angry person brings innocent bystanders into his hissy fit. The angry person is furious about a specific injury and tells you that you are worthless scum.

The second part of Seneca's argument that anger is worthless is that it is practically useless. "See the foundations of the most celebrated cities hardly now discerned; they were ruined by anger." This point is related to the first about anger almost overreaching. You hurt me with a lie. Immediately, everything about you is hateful. Nothing you say can be trusted. Nothing about me, what I did, how I treat you, is visible, in play. There are not—contrary to the way things really are—two sides of the street. There is only (from my perspective) your side; and you better clean it up. Two nations disagree about their mutual history, about certain fundamental political and religious values, and then suddenly the other nation personifies all that is false, ugly, and bad. The other is an "evil empire." Seneca says, "Irascibility . . . is angry with the truth itself." Anger cannot hear or see what is there. Or, as likely, it sees more and worse than is there.

The third strand in Seneca's argument is to cast doubt on the idea that anger serves as any kind of "spur to virtue," as Aristotle says. Seneca writes, "Virtue, argues our adversary, ought to be angry with what is base, just as she approves of what is honorable." His reply: "To rejoice and be glad is the proper and natural function of virtue . . . [it is] beneath her dignity to be angry." The standard for Seneca is never what is given in undisciplined first nature, if anything is, but what is in the blood and bones of the person who is practiced in virtue. What is natural is what is natural for the morally developed person, akin to what is natural, what comes naturally, in other domains that require expertise, for the accomplished dancer, the virtuoso musician, the expert decathlete. Only the bad person gains pleasure from the feeling of anger and from revenge and retaliation. To repeat: "To rejoice and be glad is the proper and natural function of virtue . . . [it is] beneath her dignity to be angry." Seneca's recommendation: "Extirpate root and branch . . . what can moderation have to do with an evil habit?" (42).

But, But, But . . .

There are several obvious objections, many of which come to the tip of the tongue of readers. In my experience, what is coming to the front of your mind and the tip of your tongue "But, but, but . . ." presupposes or assumes a form of life that rationalizes anger rather than producing evidence for that form of life. We Aristotelians will say things that are truisms inside our way of seeing and making the world. Seneca responds at length to two common objections, the first of which involves arguing on something like neutral ground, that is, on grounds that do not presuppose the truth of either the containment view or the extirpation view: (1) Anger is automatic; (2) Anger is sometimes necessary, often useful.

Anger Is Automatic

Suppose one argued that we ought not to allow the pupils of our eyes to contract to light. This would be crazy, idle, since pupils (actually it is the irises) contract and expand reflexively to light and darkness. In dual process language, pupil contractions are impenetrable, self-contained, System 1 responses. But Seneca insists that anger is not System 1 behavior. He writes: "The question before us is whether anger arises from deliberate choice or from impulse." His answer is that it "cannot be a mere impulse which is excited without our consent." Mere impulses include pupil contractions as well as "shivering when cold water is poured over us, or shrinking when we are touched in certain places." But anger is not like that. "Our [Stoic] opinion [is that] to conceive of a wrong having been done, to long to avenge it, and to join the two propositions . . . cannot be a mere impulse which is excited without our consent."

Seneca thinks that the language of deliberate choice and the stark divide between impulse and deliberate choice is overdrawn. An anachronistic but charitable reading is to understand Seneca's claim as that anger always involves System 2.[25] It involves cognition, what philosophers call "intentionality," thinking about and assessment of states of affairs. If a person hits me on purpose, it is an injury, and I get angry. If a person has a seizure and hits me in exactly the same way, it is an accident and I don't get angry. I am startled in both cases. The startle perhaps is a "mere impulse." But the quick assessment of what happened, they hit me versus they had a seizure, and my reaction to this assessment is cognitive, intentional. But it happened so fast, one might say, it cannot be cognitive. The right response is that of course it can be cognitive. Expert cognitive systems operate swiftly and largely unconsciously. The expert chess player looks and sees immediately that his queen is vulnerable. The modern pinball wizard sees instantaneously what the pixels in a video game mean and reacts accordingly.[26]

Another piece of evidence that anger is not a mere impulse comes from reflecting on the fact that "anger can be put in flight by wise maxims." What Seneca has in mind can be put in terms of mindfulness practices. Suppose one meditates every day on the fact that from the point of view of eternity, nothing much is worth getting fussed up about. Both Epicureans and Stoics recommended the study of physics and astronomy precisely for gaining such perspective, sub specie aeternitatis. Or suppose one practices the mantra "excellent people never get angry," or that "one ought to be indifferent to indifferent things," or that one is in AA and constantly says the Serenity Prayer to evaporate, release, or control resentment ("the number one offender" to inner peace). The claim is that such practices can put anger "in flight." There is overwhelming evidence that this is so. People who practice mindfulness-based stress reduction and other forms of cognitive behavioral therapy cannot control pupil contractions, but they can control blood pressure, anxiety, and tendencies to get frustrated and angry over small, indifferent matters. And people do learn to count to ten before getting angry, or to dissipate anger as it arises. Reflexes and pure impulses are cognitively impenetrable, but anger can be penetrated, sometimes directly by minilectures to oneself, other times by indirect means, by taking a deep breath.

This much is not enough to respond fully to the automaticity objection since everything said so far is compatible with anger arising and gripping one's inner self, and only its expression being blocked. Perhaps the world we are imagining is one in which anger is not extirpated, but simply stopped in its tracks, held inside, repressed or suppressed, or maybe, if one is lucky and wise, sublimated or made to evaporate quickly by consciously taking something like the recommended Buddhist concoction of compassion, lovingkindness, patience, and gratitude.

Seneca acknowledges that the remedies for anger are twofold. One set prevents us from doing harm when we are angry, the other set prevents anger from arising, digging its tendrils in, and causing an inner psychic mess even if not a worldly one. Seneca is clear that extirpation is only possible in a world in which, among other things, children are raised to judge anger always and everywhere to be wrong. He did not live in such a world nor do we, surrounded as he was, and as we are, by the heirs and heiresses of the containment view, the view that there are norms of apt anger, that anger is OK, good, even necessary, especially when it is justified or righteous. Containment says that anger is to be "soothed" and moderated. If anger is defective, one is a wimp, a pushover. If it is excessive, one is irascible, an angry asshole, out of control.

The first set of remedies, which are in fact compatible with containment, include controlling wine consumption (it heats the heart), memorizing some maxims, and being less prideful and self-centered. The strong pill that would extirpate, rather than contain, soothe, and moderate anger is, like the Buddhists' medicine, really a concoction. It consists first in listening to the reasons offered by Seneca for why we ought to want a world without anger. Anger seeks to harm and injure. Only vices do that. Second, we examine the claim that anger is a "mere impulse," or a reflex, and we see that this is not obviously so. Children are not born angry. Adult anger is cognitively penetrable. "Anger management" involves leveraging ("use all that angry energy to clean the house"), distraction ("make a gratitude list"), and penetration and quelling techniques ("acknowledge the anger; now let it go"). Finally, there are saints and sages, all manner of indigenous peoples, Hindus, Buddhists, Jains, Sufis, and Christians, who claim to have extirpated anger, completely washed the disposition to be angry from their souls. Admittedly, the extirpators are rare, and most reports are self-reports.[27] Furthermore, they have never existed in such numbers that we can speak with confidence of communities of people who do not get angry.[28] But then again, in the West, we have not been encouraged to extirpate anger. The Stoics have lost that argument several times, first to Aristotelians, and then to all three Abrahamic traditions, which combine containment with powerful convictions about the legitimacy of righteous anger, God's righteous anger, and the anger of those who are on God's side.

The world in which anger is extirpated is not a nearby possible one. It is, at best, a notional possibility for those of us who are already formed inside worlds that give anger wide range. Bernard Williams (1985) marks a difference between real and notional possibilities. It is a real possibility for an indigenous unassimilated !Kung hunter-gatherer of the Kalahari to get a scholarship to MIT or CalTech. It could happen in the real world (although there are very few unassimilated !Kung). It is a notional possibility for a literate and numerate MIT or CalTech student to become an unassimilated !Kung. They could feign it, dress the part, live in a small group, try to learn the clicking language, but they could not undo her literacy and numeracy, and whatever effects these have had on their psyche.

Seneca believed that a world without anger is a genuine variety of moral possibility for *Homo sapiens*, even if it was not a real sociological possibility in his or nearby worlds.[29] We are asked to imagine a world in which people still say perhaps of terrible actions and events "That is outrageous" or "That is infuriating," but where they are speaking of their passionate judgment, what I call "righteous indignation," not expressing their personal feeling. Sometimes when macaque monkeys are forced to move because of mining or deforestation, the youngsters learn new survival techniques—how to eat oysters on the half shell. The elders can't learn this, but the youngsters share the bounty. The next generation all learn how to crack open oysters as a birthright. One thought is that the elders raised inside a moderation or containment ethic cannot learn how (or why) to live in the world without anger (it would be at best a notional option for them), but that unjaded youth raised by Stoics and Buddhists could.[30] Maybe.

Stoic Psychology

Behind and beneath the Stoic claims that anger is not automatic and that it is possible to extirpate anger is a psychology that is empirically plausible by modern standards. According to the Stoics, there are four basic states of mind or emotions. One sees these states of mind in children.

> DELIGHT: Judgment that what is here now is good ("I like it").
> DISTRESS: Judgment that what is here now is bad ("I don't like it").
> LONGING: Judgment that a future event/state of affairs is good ("I want it").
> FEAR: Judgment that a future event/state of affairs is bad ("I don't want it").

A semester in Psychology 101 might lead one to say that we now know ("know," deep throat) that first nature has much more specific structure than that. For example, we know that there are seven basic emotions—fear, anger, happiness, sadness, surprise, disgust, and contempt, or we know that there are five or six innate moral foundations—compassion, justice, in-group/out-group, hierarchy, and disgust.

Do we actually know that? It is not obvious. Do babies experience anger and contempt? I have never seen any reputable psychologist claim that they do. Do babies experience any of the well-known determinate emotions that adults do? Do babies make any, some, or all of the Ekman faces? Or, more likely, do they only make precursors to some of them, for example, faces and body language that express distress and delight, which is what the Stoic psychologist expects? What about the alleged moral foundations or modules? There is good work showing some fellow-feeling in infants, but it would be odd to think of distress over the crying of other newborns in the hospital nursery as compassion, as opposed to something like a seed that can be cultivated to yield compassion. Do babies show a sense of justice as fairness, the way even juvenile capuchins do? Do feces and urine disgust newborns? Not so much.[31]

The point is that a psychology that posits four emotions—delight, distress, longing, and fear—that differ along only two dimensions, positive or negative attraction, wanting or not-wanting, and time frame, now or later (or three, if one adds positive or negative valence), is not implausible especially when set against views of first nature that posit emotions that are highly canalized, modular, and differentiated from the get-go. Distress that mother's milk is not flowing as quickly as I want to consume it (but not under that description) is the same as, or a first cousin of, frustration, and it along with first nature fear that mother's milk will not come when I want it (again not remotely under that description), are the psychic roots of what perhaps eventually becomes anger. But there is no anger until there is a judgment that I have been injured joined to thoughts of its source, possibly joined to thoughts of "passing pain," of retaliation and revenge. Anger, like the other reactive attitudes, requires cognition. Or better, anger just is a heavily cognitive emotion. Or, if it makes a difference, it is a heavily emotional way of thinking. It requires understanding what is happening as an insult or injury rather than an accident, and it requires identification of the source. Finally, it requires two kinds of normative permission from one's community, one to allow its phenomenological potential to be experienced subjectively, possibly to glory or wallow in it, to revisit it as in resentment, and second, a separate kind of permission to express it or act on it.[32]

Anger Is Sometimes Necessary, Often Useful

Anger gets results. This is the second objection. Seneca offers the evidence of constant war, the destruction of city upon city to rubble as evidence that anger doesn't work. On Seneca's own terms, this evidence of civilizational warfare, conquest, and colonization could be as easily, perhaps more easily, attributed to greed than to anger. And in any case, the very idea of the Stoic warrior is premised on the idea that war can be justified. But the good soldier, be he general or infantrymen, is not angry. He does not rape and pillage. Those are signs of angry soldiers.

It is essential to Seneca's argument that we can distinguish anger as an emotional state from the angry behavior it often or typically gives rise to in our lives. Anger is always wrong, but correction and punishment are sometimes justified, including correction and punishment where we feign an angry face. The key is not to be or feel angry.

> We may sometimes affect to be angry when we wish to rouse up the dull minds of those we address, just as we rouse up horses who are slow at starting with goads and firebrands . . . we must sometimes apply fear [of retaliation] to persons upon whom reason makes no impression.

This line of argument, which requires drawing careful analytic and psychological distinctions between, anger, angry expression, punishment, retaliation, and revenge starts in the very first book of *De Ira*, when the two brothers, Seneca and Novatus, ask themselves what if our father was murdered, our mother raped? The answer is immediately given. "He [the good man] will not be angry, but will avenge them, or protect them." There is an obligation here that must be met (Kant was steeped in Stoicism). Sons, daughters, citizens have duties, and sometimes these will require retaliation, revenge, and payback.[33] But one should not be angry. Anger is a despicable emotion. In *The Princess Bride* (1987) there is the famous scene, when the lovable character played by Mandy Patinkin announces: "Hello. My name is Inigo Montoya. You killed my father. Prepare to die." The sword fight ensues. The murderer begs for mercy. None is given. Justice is served. And now, having gotten even, Inigo can get out of the "revenge business." Or, perhaps, if one thinks revenge entails past anger, even if not presently held anger, think of him getting out of the avenging business.[34]

In daily life, correction is often needed. The aim of correction is to improve and heal, whereas anger aims to wound, and to make its object skittish and fearful. We start with "gentle words" and only move to more severe words to advise and guide more difficult souls. Occasionally, for certain incorrigible souls who commit terrible crimes, capital punishment might be necessary, but not, as Seneca says, "because the [good person] takes pleasure in any man's being punished, for the wise man is far from such inhuman ferocity, but that they [the extreme punishments] may be a warning to all men."

Seneca can be read in a highly individualistic and rationalistic way: If you are convinced that anger doesn't work, is never admired by the virtuous, and also that it is not a mindless, uncontrollable impulse, then extirpate it by way of your reason. In this beautiful passage, he praises reason's patience and concern with the truth:

> Reason gives each side time to plead; moreover, she herself demands adjournment, that she may have sufficient scope for the discovery of truth; whereas anger is in a hurry; anger wishes its decision to be thought just; reason looks no further than the matter at hand; anger is excited by empty matters hovering on the outskirts of the case.

Seneca almost certainly overrates individual reason. Martha Nussbaum, in her study of Hellenistic philosophy, *The Therapy of Desire* (1994), emphasizes an aspect of Stoic psychology that, I am pretty certain, is empirically implausible. This is reason's sensitivity to the force of valid and sound deductive argument, to arguments which, if the premises are true, the conclusion must be true, must be believed. Seneca doesn't try, as far as I can tell, to give deductively valid arguments that anger is bad, a vice. Anger's viciousness is not a theorem of his philosophy as offered in *De Ira*. But it is credible, and various considerations are offered to think that it is so.[35]

A Friendly Amendment

A charitable way to extend and update Seneca's program for extirpation, given that we are not as optimistic about the power of pure reason, and better understand than he did that major adjustments in moral psychology are required would be to read him as calling for both individual work and social and political action. Pay attention to the awfulness of anger, to its heavily cognitive features. Stop giving each other permission to be angry.[36] Teach the youth that anger is vicious and give them ways to sublimate precursors to anger or mental states that fuel it.[37] Also work on nearby states of mind, frustration, irritability, and the like, as well as on external states of affairs that fuel anger. Reduce social and economic inequality so that occasions for envy are diminished. On the metaphysics side, acknowledge the ubiquitous hand of fate and luck, and use this acknowledgment as a spiritual tool to deflate the beliefs that seed pride, beliefs that I am self-made and deserve more than others because of circumstances of my birth, my education, and my work ethic. Eliminate vicious practices like racism and sexism, so that historical reasons for righteous anger dissipate. Deflate the ego by trying to see one's petty desires from the perspective of the cosmos.

If this multipronged set of personal, social, cultural, and political beliefs, values, practices, and norms is given time to root, it might eventually penetrate the normative structures of everyday life, become taken for granted and possibly self-sustaining. Obviously, one cannot just change the belief that anger is sometimes morally permissible, even at times a virtue, to the belief that anger is a vice, without making adjustments in other places in our moral system, most likely in beliefs about free will, responsibility, and the legitimacy of punishment, as well as to the norms of expectable behavior when conflict arises.

Community Immunity

A legitimate worry involves scaling up. It is possible to imagine a few people, saints, sages, and bodhisattvas, who cultivate nonanger, and are able to sustain the state. But it is hard to imagine that nonangry practices for resolving disputes, disagreements, hurt feelings, and so on, could root in environments in which they are not expected or common, and especially in environments in which angry feelings and displays are approved, the norm. True. Consider this analogy. Treating a disease like measles requires almost universal vaccination, which produces herd or community immunity. If 90 percent get vaccinated, the whole system can go into disequilibrium if one person gets the measles. First, the 10 percent who didn't get vaccinated are all susceptible, and measles is extremely contagious. Second, 10 percent of those vaccinated will not have developed the immunity, which is not a problem if they are not exposed, but is a problem if there is even one contagious person. Thus, one case can blossom into an epidemic with 20 percent of the population coming down with measles, even if most everyone is vaccinated. Likewise, a twenty-person bus queue will become a chaotic pushing match if only a couple of people break queuing rules. Eighteen people waiting for the bus are full normative conformers, but they cannot hold the line together when a couple of people start playing by different rules. This insight about scaling up and the importance of shared schemes of valuing was not lost on the Hellenistic philosophers. The Epicureans and the Cynics sought to create communities of like-minded people, fellow Epicureans or fellow Cynics, acknowledging the fact that the desired equilibrium of values, norms, and practices will be most, possibly only, sustainable in such moral ecologies. The Stoics, interestingly, were cosmopolitans, possibly overconfident that their wise counsel on anger and disruptive emotions generally, could win the day and withstand pushback from Aristotelians who favored moderation but not elimination.

Because the Stoic disagreement over a fundamental value occurs inside our tradition(s), it might be easier for us to accept Seneca's arguments for extirpation than the Buddhists' arguments, if we were inclined to accept any such argument. It involves more familiar ways of thinking and speaking in the surround. There are none of the alien concepts of *anātman*, karma, and nirvana.

What would our world be like if we taught the youth that anger is vicious? How far could we get if we tried to explore the possibility space that Seneca and Buddhists say is in fact open to us, but unexplored?

I now examine some main objections that advocates of the moderation and containment view give to exploring this possibility space. We WEIRD folk, we Western Educated Industrialized Rich Democratic folk, are anger aficionados, easily annoyed, resentful, and pissed off. We are proud, morally puffed up about our righteous angers and indignations, even as we are edgy, suspicious, worried about the resentments of the nonrich and oppressed among us, of those people who also in virtue of being raised as children of Aristotle and Abraham get anger and know how to do it.[38] The objections to extirpation I now consider are ones that one is as likely to hear across the North Atlantic and its Oceanic outposts.

9

WEIRD Anger

Western Educated Industrialized Rich Democratic Anger

In the previous chapter, I discussed a canonical text in Mahayana Buddhism, Śāntideva's *The Bodhisattva's Way of Life*, and a key text from Seneca the Stoic, "On Anger," that both offer arguments from distinct traditions for the extirpation of anger. Both texts offer a psychology of anger, its varieties and close family relations, frustration, resentment, indignation, and so on; a phenomenology of the varieties of anger, how they seem, what they have in common; and a theory of anger's normal causes and normal effects. Then there is the normative claim that anger, at least in some of its most familiar forms, ought to be eliminated, and then finally, another psychological claim: It is possible to eliminate anger. We are, as I put it perhaps too crudely, to imagine a world in which people still speak of moral outrages, still denounce degradation and disrespect, and cruelty, still defend themselves against attack, possibly even engage in bloody revolt or war; but they do these things without anger in their hearts.[1] Such people get that anger is vicious, harms the person who feels it, its target, and innocent bystanders, and they have developed and absorbed practices that have modified their moral psychology. The world, if not at peace, is at least a better place.

In my experience, friends as well as philosophers and psychologists line up at this point with objections both to the empirical claim that anger can be eliminated and to the normative claim that it should be eliminated. One objection is that Śāntideva and Seneca were then and there, and we are here and now. We live in radically different worlds, inside different forms of life, with several thousand years' worth of additional experience under our belts, and we need the tools that suit our world, and anger is one of those tools. Another objection is that what Śāntideva and Seneca offer are theories, possibly purely utopian ones, and there is no space in those theories for the histories of particular peoples who suffer degradation and oppression, nor for the idiosyncrasies and particularities of the real lives of ordinary people interacting in multifarious complex, demanding, and unpredictable ways. Then there is the objection that saying that something is outrageous without feeling the rage requires displacement or detachment, which we know from depth psychology, is unnatural, twisted, and bad for mental health. Finally, both Śāntideva and Seneca won various lotteries of life and it is easy for the winners of the world to lecture others about virtue and staying calm. They are still doing it.

There is much to these sorts of responses. Nonetheless, I'll try to give a fair hearing to some of the main objections and defend the Buddhists and Stoics, as best I can. I grew up inside the form of life that knows most of these objections inside out. But I have come to think that they are surprisingly hard to state without assuming what it is that we should be trying to show. Anger does suit us, especially righteous anger. It fits well into our form of life and supports and is supported by other features of the whole.[2] My overall opinion about the method of much moral philosophy is that it is often and mostly a clean-up operation for ways of thinking and being that we already assume and prefer. By and large, it speaks with a voice of universality and embodies and enacts with a certain bravado, even hubris, the confirmation bias, "the my-side bias," seeing evidence in favor of the view we or people like us already hold, and discounting evidence against it. Sometimes this is what we are asking for, making sense of our practices in terms of their own logic and our form of life. But the method of seeking what is known in the business as reflective equilibrium is not the best for exploring new possibility spaces, unless it is what I call super-wide reflective equilibrium, which, especially in times of trouble, looks to the best thinking and best practices in other traditions.

A common enough view on the moral psychology of anger is one like Allan Gibbard's (1992), where we recognize moral violations by whether it would make sense to be angry about an action.[3] Defenses of anger in my experience are typically reminders or appeals to the work that anger does inside our form of life, reminders that eliminating anger will be costly, requiring adjustments in how we think about and do things other than anger, for example, how we do affection, love, and loyalty, and mark injustice and oppression, and especially about how we think of the self, agency, action, responsibility, credit, and blame. This is not surprising given the holistic features of ways of worldmaking.

Four Arguments Against Eliminating Anger and My Scorecard

There are four main arguments against eliminating anger. "Impossible," "Attachment," "Injustice," and "Catharsis."

"Impossible" claims that anger is original and natural, an adaptation, and that extirpating it is not really possible. It is a philosopher's fantasy. The next three arguments are normative. Even if anger could be eliminated, it would be bad to eliminate it.

"Attachment" claims that living a good human life requires deep attachments to certain people and to worthy projects. Dispositions to be angry, as well as fearful and sad, automatically go with such attachments. If we think that great goods, possibly essential conditions of human flourishing, come from worthy attachments, friendship, love, loyalty, passions for art, music, or philosophy, then we believe in making ourselves vulnerable to certain kinds of injury. Anger is one appropriate, morally acceptable, response to harms or injury to ourselves, to persons we love, and to projects we are committed to.

"Injustice" focuses specifically on the importance, the normative significance of righteous anger and indignation. Righteous anger and indignation signal that matters of great moral significance are at stake; that we are witnesses to harms or clear and present danger of intolerable harms that must be marked, acknowledged, and overcome; and that anger is the proper vehicle, the best vehicle, possibly that it is necessary, to mark, acknowledge, and overcome injustice. Some think that anger is required even to detect certain kinds of harms as the kinds of harms or evils that they are.

"Catharsis" is an extension of the last argument, but involves an additional claim about the laws of psychology. Whereas "Injustice" is an argument about the moral necessity of anger primarily to detect and respond to problems of injustice that groups or collectives face, "Catharsis" focuses on the necessity of anger in the service of individual healing. The argument is that some injuries are so grievous that the individual who suffers them, will, as a matter of the laws of psychology, need to experience, express, and resolve their anger in order to heal.

My final scorecard is this: "Impossible," the psychological claim that anger is original and natural, possibly universal, and a psychobiological adaptation is worrisome for the Buddhist and the Stoic, but is typically overstated by anger's fans. The "Attachment" and "Injustice" and "Catharsis" objections do not establish necessary connections, that is, they do not show that making oneself vulnerable by seeking deep attachment to other persons or projects requires anger or a disposition to anger, nor that resistance to injustice or healing from violence or injustice, require anger.

Furthermore, "Attachment," "Injustice," and "Catharsis" are hard to state and defend without begging the question. That is, these objections work in part by appealing to taken-for-granted assumptions inside WEIRD forms of life, which antecedently rationalize anger in pretty much the ways the objections assume. If we question, as Buddhists and Stoics do, those assumptions, some about human flourishing, some about the hydraulics of mind, some metaphysical, about time, the self, free will, some soteriological or eschatological, about my fate, my salvation, the afterlife (or not), others about the order and trumping relations among the virtues, it is less obvious that the objections go through.

For the remainder of this chapter, I discuss the Impossibility Objection, the objection that anger is part of the original and natural equipment and thus that it cannot be eliminated. Then, in the next chapter, I take up the "Attachment," "Injustice," and "Catharsis" objections.

Nature's Ways: The "Original and Natural" Reactive Attitudes

It is a commonplace in the philosophy and psychology of the North Atlantic to speak as Peter F. Strawson (1962) does when he writes that certain basic emotions, what he calls the reactive attitudes, come with the equipment. The reactive attitudes include anger, resentment, indignation, contempt, hurt feelings, gratitude, shame, guilt, love (both *eros* and *philia*), pride, gratitude, and forgiveness. There are five claims: (1) The reactive attitudes are part of the normal and original conative repertoire of members of the species *Homo sapiens*; (2) the reactive attitudes express normal human reactions to acts, traits, or dispositions, or to whole persons; (3) the normal expression of the reactive attitudes involves interpersonal relations where benevolence or malevolence is displayed or, at least, where they are at stake; (4) the reactive attitudes are both other-regarding and self-regarding; (5) the reactive attitudes are attitudes through which we express our common humanity, recognizing others as persons, and according them the positive and negative reactions that come from seeing and treating them as persons.[4]

Strawson says that the reactive attitudes are "original and natural" in the way inductive reasoning is, something we could not ever give up. They are psychobiological givens, universals that appear in some form in the psychological economy of every human individual, probably for excellent evolutionary reasons (Brown 1991). The idea that anger and the other reactive attitudes are original and natural in the way induction is, is a key premise in the argument that the extirpation of anger is impossible.

We need to ask: What kind of psychobiological givens are the reactive attitudes, exactly? In what way are they "original and natural"? All babies cry from discomfort. Let's say that crying from discomfort is a psychobiological given because newborns do it, and because we see exactly why they do it, why it is an adaptation; it calls the attention of caretakers to important needs. If the reactive attitudes are psychobiological givens, it is not because they are just like a newborn's experiencing cold or chafing or pain, or like crying because of such discomforts. Newborns do not experience or display anger (the "terrible twos" come later), resentment or pride, guilt, gratitude, and forgiveness. But eventually, perhaps, a normal human will experience these attitudes or be disposed to them, if they develop in the normal way.

A better example of the kinds of psychological givens that the reactive attitudes are than the infant's crying from discomfort might be sexual coming of age. Puberty will come in the teens. It is developmentally programmed, and barring extreme internal or external disruptions, secondary sex characteristics will develop, and an individual will become sexually mature and feel sexy. That said, coming of age sexually—going from the broad sensuality of the infant to the genital sexuality of the adolescent—is a very long distance from determining such things as gender, sexual preference, degree of genital focus, and the amount of sexual activity or sexual expression (Mead 1935; Fausto-Sterling 1992).

A theory that says that reactive attitudes are psychobiological givens owes a theory of emergence. Puberty we understand. The story is given mostly by developmental epigenetics, although various aspects concern nutrition and such. Even if some basic features of the reactive attitudes are also explained by the theory of evolution and developmental epigenetics, cultural psychology and sociology play a large role in their content, what it makes sense to be angered by (scared of, disgusted by, loving toward), their forms, and the rules for expression. The reactive attitudes, like the Ekman faces to which they may or may not be related (I am agnostic), have a significant amount of socially variable structure and content, as well as local display rules.[5] There is excellent reason to think that even the phenomenological texture, how emotions feel, varies. When the Ifaluk are angry they lose their appetite (Lutz 1988). When Tahitians lose a loved one they say they are sick; they have no word for sad (Levy 1973). The German word for disgust, *Ekel*, refers to feelings associated with recoiling, as from a snake rather than from excrement or vomit or rancid food (Wierzbicka 2014).

William James ([1890] 1950, 485) writes of the multiplicity of possible emotions and the complex interplay between the discernment of emotions and the language of emotions:

> If one should seek to name each particular one [of the emotions] of which the human heart is the seat, it is plain that the limit to their number would lie in the introspective vocabulary of the seeker, each race of men having found names for some shade of feeling which other races have left undiscriminated. If we should seek to break the emotions, thus enumerated, into groups, according to their affinities, it is again plain that all sorts of groupings would be possible ... and that all groupings would be equally true and real.

In her novel, *The Map of Love* (1999), the Egyptian novelist Ahdat Souief gives beautiful testimony to James's point about the subtle phenomenological texture of the emotions inside different cultures:

> "Hubb" is love, "ishq" is love that entwines two people together, "shaghaf" is love that nests in the chambers of the heart, "hayam," is love that wanders the earth, "teeh" is love in which you lose yourself, "walah" is love

that carries sorrow within it, "sababah" is love that exudes from your pores, "hawa" is love that shares its name with "air" and with "falling," "gharm" is love that is willing to pay the price. (386–87)

Ratcheting Attitudes: Oysters-on-the-Halfshell and Affronts to Dignity

Once a practice, including an emotion or affective syndrome, is culturally entrenched, it can seem necessary (Tomasello 1999, 2014; Boyd and Richerson 1985, 2005; Richerson and Boyd 2005). Michael Tomasello calls the process of cumulative cultural evolution the "ratchet effect." Ratcheting occurs when "modifications of a cultural practice stayed in the population rather faithfully until some individual invented some new and improved technique, which was then taught and conformed to until some newer innovation ratcheted things up again" (2014, 83). The "ratchet effect" models selection for cultural practices. A ratchet turns in one direction only, and over time moves whatever it is ratcheting—a screw, a bolt, or a fishing net—very far from its starting point. In the case of cultural learning, ratcheting can result in the development and normalization of beliefs, habits, traits, and practices that are a long distance from the beliefs, habits, traits, and practices of the original humans. Actually this is so, even if the practice is not a "new and improved technique"—the practice might only serve the interests of some powerful elite. But if the elite has the power to enforce the beliefs, habits, and practices, they will spread, accumulate, and normalize.

In Myanmar and Thailand, rhesus macaques that have been forced to move from their native habitats in jungles to the seashore, face problems getting the foodstuffs that constitute their normal diets. But being smart, opportunistic, and playful, juveniles almost always accidently learn to open oysters and clamshells. Once they realize that these are a nutritious and delicious bounty, they perfect opening such shells, usually with tools. The elders want to participate in the banquet and encourage the youth to keep bringing them oysters and clams on the half shell. But the adults can't seem to acquire the skill themselves. Within a generation, as the elders die off, every single seaside macaque is an accomplished clam and oyster shucker. It seems as if this skill is a birthright. And it is, but not because it is original and natural in the biological sense. Oyster and clam shucking is a birthright as a result of ratcheting inside a culture.

Ratcheting helps explain why some ways of doing and being that have attained the status of being normal and widespread, the way we do things around here, might seem original, natural, and necessary, without in fact being so. Sometimes what is true of local psychology, "must-dos" around here, "for us," can yield overconfidence that everyone does it "our way," that all peoples settled on the same solution to some common ecological problem, for example, regulating sex, or even that they saw that common ecological problems as we do. Anger at affronts to my dignity is probably like this. The very idea that there could be such things as affronts to a person's dignity requires an unusual, nonmandatory way of thinking about persons.

In *The Anatomy of Melancholy*, Robert Burton (1632) wrote of a familiar script, what might seem to be a law of the psychology of jealousy: "those who are jealous [because of sexual infidelity] proceed from suspicion to hatred; from hatred to frenzied; from frenzied to injuries, murder, and despair." The trouble is that this familiar script isn't a universal law. There are many cultures that do not enact this jealousy pattern, the Toda of South India, certain Artic peoples, and certain Himalayan people either do not define infidelity as we do, do not get jealous about it in the ways we do, or do not go the "frenzied" route when they do get jealous (Hatfield, Rapson, and Martel 2007).

Is Anger Like Induction? Not Something We Could Give Up

Anger and the other reactive attitudes are, Strawson says, like induction in two respects: they come with the equipment, or better, emerge naturally, and they are not features of our natures for which we can demand justification, as we can for most other social practices. "Justify the right to free, unfettered speech!" is a sensible demand. "Justify your nose!" "Justify the color of your eyes!" or "Justify puberty!" makes no sense. Asking for a justification of the reactive attitudes is like asking for a justification of induction.

Strawson writes, "Compare the question of the justification of induction. The human commitment to inductive belief-formation is original, natural, and non-rational (not irrational), in no way something we choose or could give up." The idea is that what goes for induction also goes for the reactive attitudes—they are "original, natural, non-rational (not irrational) ... [and not something we ever] could give up" (1962).

Imagine that the original people, when the ice melted at the end of the Pleistocene, reasoned about hunting and gathering by applying the straight rule of induction, which says: If I/we perceive that A's are/lead to/co-occur with B's to m/n%, then I/we infer that unseen A's are/lead to/co-occur with B's to m/n%. Walking south brought us to the water yesterday, we infer that it will do so tomorrow. Newborns are straight rule inductivists. Classical and operant conditioning depend on making associations between stimuli, responses, and reinforcers. Mommy nurses me; mommy is the best, most important, most desirable person on earth.

Induction has another feature worth noticing. It self-improves or, better, it delivers feedback that would lead a straight rule inductive system to adjust and improve the application of the straight rule, for example, by yielding new rules, subsidiary rules or metarules, that relate to sample size and representativeness. Applying the straight rule will lead to noticing that when my sample is too small or unrepresentative—suppose I predict the general election results from a sample of my colleagues who also work in the coal mines—there is a pattern. Predictions based on these samples have the characteristic of often being wrong. Induction itself discovers that small and unrepresentative samples yield poor inductions. Applying the straight rule to itself will lead eventually to principles of inductive logic, statistics, and probability theory, if anything will. Strawson writes, "Yet rational criticism and reflection can refine standards and their application, supply 'rules for judging of cause and effect.'" The idea is that we have made induction more sophisticated over world historical time as evidenced by the development of the canons of inductive logic, and probability theory. If we operated only with the original and natural version of the straight rule we would commit fallacies of unrepresentative and small samples all the time. But we are taught, thanks to the straight rule's own discovery of these fallacies, to beware of them.

The straight rule was selected for, and by deploying it in its natural and original form, possibly over many centuries, we came to see or discover ways in which the application of the rule needed to be constrained. There is no interesting sense in which the canons of inductive logic, statistics, and probability governing sample size and representativeness were selected for. But if you aim to accrue firmly grounded knowledge, to do science, or to make accurate predictions in elections, you better apply the relevant canons. In this nonbiological sense, the canons are adaptive, as are the abilities to read and write. Applying the norms of good reasoning yields firmer and more accurate knowledge, and literacy makes for richer and more pleasant lives than do the alternatives. But neither excellence as a sophisticated reasoner nor literacy is interestingly fitness enhancing. Indeed, the best predictor in the modern world for low birthrate is the average level of education attained, the two having an inverse relation. The main point is that a trait, such as being a whiz at applying the sophisticated canons of inductive reasoning—think of the master election prognosticator—or being an avid reader or writer, can be rightly understood as being adaptive in the sense that possessing the relevant trait or ability contributes to knowledge, flourishing, happiness, and the like, without its being adaptive in the sense that it was selected for because it contributed to inclusive genetic fitness.

There is a similarity and a dissimilarity of induction with anger and the other reactive attitudes. The similarity is that the initial settings of the reactive attitudes are somewhat plastic and adjustable over world historical time as is the straight rule of induction. We are angry, grateful, and forgiving not only about different things, but in different ways than the original people were. The dissimilarity is that whereas there are inductive pressures internal to induction to improve inductive practices, there are no similar pressures internal to the reactive attitudes to improve themselves. What there is are pressures inside various sociomoral ecologies to form and regulate the reactive attitudes in ways that make sense internal to those various forms of life. This might mean that functional equilibrium—peace, order, and harmony—is aimed at. But whether any particular orderly, functional, well-lubricated social system is morally good, in moral equilibrium, is an entirely different question.

Somehow or other the reactive attitudes emerge according to some sort of reliable developmental program, and then distinct social regimens bring them under normative discipline. We learn to tweak our attitudes and bring their undisciplined expressions under a sociomoral regimen that is understood and expected by our compatriots. For example, we learn to deflate, moderate, adjust, or expand our anger as is considered appropriate, to expand our affection beyond our immediate family (or not), to contain our lust, not to get too puffed up, and so on. Inside a particular moral ecology, normative rules are often assigned along with other normative assignments that pertain to one's stations and duties as determined by sex, gender, education, race, ethnicity, immigration status, job description, and zip code. So the standards of a white man getting angry and puffed up (these go together) and a woman or a member of an underclass getting angry and puffed up are different in America.

There seems to be this further asymmetry between thinking inductively and experiencing and expressing anger and the other reactive attitudes: No one thinks it is advisable, even if it were possible—which it is not—to stop thinking inductively. But some Tibetan Buddhists and Stoics think it possible and advisable to overcome, even eliminate, what is, or might be, 'original and natural,' in the case of certain reactive attitudes, possibly four that Strawson mentions, anger, resentment, indignation, and contempt.

Ought and Can

"Impossible" says that anger cannot be extirpated because anger is evolutionarily entrenched in human psychobiology. One ought not to demand that people do what they cannot do, or to be as they cannot be. Is this the death knell for Śāntideva's and Seneca's recommendations that we ought to extirpate anger? No. Ratcheting is one reason to give us pause in concluding that anger, or at least our familiar ways of being angry are original and natural. Plasticity is another reason.

Consider being a carnivore. Humans are not born wanting red meat, but in normal environments where meat is available as a source of protein the desire for meat will develop. Human teeth, the digestive system, and taste preferences are all channeled in this direction. But many modern humans think there are reasons not to eat animals. There are challenges, but not many for the well-off, to getting proper nutrition by being vegetarian or vegan, and many people choose successfully to go against human nature in this way. Many vegetarians report not only not wanting meat, but also eventually finding it disgusting.

Vegetarianism is a good example of a case where there is a plausible causal story for why humans normally like meat, which explains why the desire for meat is an original and natural one. But for which there is also a story about the discovery of reasons not to honor this natural desire. And, finally, for which there is a story about how many people have deployed these reasons, individually or at the level of a whole culture, to override the original and natural desire.

Evolutionary biologists and philosophers of biology standardly make a distinction between the question of whether or not a trait is an adaptation in the strict sense, this being largely a matter of history, in particular a question of whether the trait was fitness enhancing when it evolved, and the different question of whether it is adaptive in current environments, where the relevant sense of adaptive is tied to current fitness-enhancing features (Godfrey-Smith 1994). Then there is the entirely different matter of whether any trait, a natural psychobiological one or a socially constructed one, conduces to well-being, flourishing, happiness, and the excellence of a community.

Even if we take it for granted that anger and the other reactive attitudes, or some subset of them, can be plausibly defended as adaptations according to the criterion that weights most heavily the causal contribution of a trait to fitness in the original evolutionary situation in which the trait evolved and proliferated, it does not follow that the trait is now adaptive, where the meaning of adaptive is tied to being fitness producing or enhancing now. Finally, it does it not follow in any of these cases that the trait is morally good, or, what is different, that it cannot be overcome.

Cultural Coloration

I have insisted on something P. F. Strawson himself concedes, namely, that the reactive attitudes are subject to forces of cultural learning. Some of the reactive emotions, indeed the very names he uses for all the reactive attitudes, reveal a certain amount of local color, a color one might expect from a famous Oxford philosopher, a great admirer of Kant, and a knight of the British Empire. To speak a language of indignation, approbation, disapprobation, resentment, and gratitude is to speak in a different and less widely understood idiom than to speak of anger, fear, sadness, happiness, surprise, disgust, and contempt.

It is worth emphasizing that the normative notions of a person, and in particular of a good person or good persons, are different from, possibly orthogonal to, the normative notion of a maximally fit individual. At eulogies when we remember a person for having been good, we almost never focus on their reproductive fitness, and this despite the fact that we might well talk about their deep and abiding love for their children, if, that is, they happen to have had any.

John Locke, famously, distinguished between being a human being, a member of the species *Homo sapiens*, and being a person, the kind of agent whom we hold accountable and responsible. Picking out an individual as a man, as a conspecific, is pretty much a straightforward empirical matter, and the term 'human being' is straightforwardly descriptive. But the concept of a person is more than a biological concept. And it matters.

Strawson says that anger and its suite are attitudes toward persons. We might accept this, but doubt that the original and natural versions of these attitudes evolved to deal with personal relations. Why? Because there is reason to believe that the reactive attitudes evolved in nonhuman primates long before we existed. But if anger and the other reactive attitudes evolved as most think they did, they were designed to do work in small communities with compatriot apes, eventually fellow *Homo sapiens*, and only very recently to regulate relations among persons. The idea that humans are persons in any of the normative senses one sees across moral traditions—as agents with certain intrinsic rights—is a modern invention, a good invention perhaps, but an invention nonetheless.

Indeed, some of the reactive emotions on Strawson's list clearly require development, discovery, and canonization over some segment of world historical time. Feelings of pride, dignity, and respect fit this bill. They require development of a certain conception of a person, of norms governing behavior—dos and don'ts, oughts—institutions governing moral praise and blame, and methods for punishment of those who stray too far from the right path.

It is an interesting question whether we should think of the moral conceptions that are developed, and the more complex attitudes that figure in living according to a specific moral conception, as involving modifications of the original equipment or the creation of wholly new equipment. Consider Catherine Lutz's (1988) work among the Ifaluk of the Caroline Islands in the South Pacific. Lutz argues plausibly that the Ifaluk have moral emotions different from standard American ones. In one case, the case of the reactive attitude of *song*, which Lutz translates as justifiable moral anger, the Ifaluk experience and express *song* differently and in response to somewhat different situations than we do. The Ifaluk expect and display greater gentleness than your average American and live according to less individualistic norms than we do. So what a native New Yorker would hardly consider rudeness would be judged as a violation of norms of expected gentleness, which would lead to *song* and that might include as part of its display a refusal to eat. An angry American might inadvertently forget to eat or not feel like eating if she is morally outraged, but it is not an expected component of the expressive display of American moral anger. Despite being tuned differently than American moral anger, Ifaluk moral anger is familiar; it belongs to the same family as our anger. That said,

Ifaluk anger is rarely expressed as viciousness, nor does it seem to seek to pass on pain.

Another case Lutz discusses is an emotion called *fago*. The Ifaluk use the word *fago* to express love, compassion, and sadness. One might think there are actually three words for three emotions here and that the Ifaluk disambiguate the homonyms by context, so that *fago* uttered in a romantic situation means love, at a funeral it is an expression of personal sadness, or if uttered to the grieving spouse, it is best understood as a display of compassion. Lutz argues that there is actually only one complex emotion here, one that combines feelings of love-sadness-compassion all at once. The short explanation for why the Ifaluk link these three emotions, or better, so as not to beg questions about genealogy, experience them in a unified way, has to do with certain historical facts about the fragility of their lives due to widely remembered bouts with deadly diseases, typhoons, earthquakes, and tsunamis. When an Ifaluk looks his beloved in her eyes and declares his love for her, he simultaneously experiences feelings associated with prior losses of his own or of his beloved (or ones held in recent communal memory); he recognizes that eventually he will, in all likelihood, be lost to her or her to him, or even if they do not lose each other, their children might die young, and so on. It is hard to know whether we are dealing with new culturally created moral emotions here, or with a somewhat unusual configuration of already familiar ones.

Perhaps, there are clear cases where unusual ecological landscapes and cultural ingenuity have created stable affective states that are utterly new on the face of the earth in the way unusual landscapes have clearly created new social practices with powerful affective dimensions. Recall the picture of a Waddington ecological landscape, reproduced in this chapter (see Figure 9.1). Imagine such a landscape with only one very deep central valley, and that it depicts something like the state of Europe prior to 1517, where the valley draws people into the Roman Catholic form of life. Then imagine that there is a geological seizure, a *caesura* in the landscape, represented by the eruptions of reformers like Luther and Calvin and Zwingli, which we can suppose occurred because of tensions and contradictions internal to Catholic practices, some seen and some unseen, below the surface. Now, suddenly, the landscape consists of new valleys, which, depending on where those valleys are—Northern Germany and Switzerland versus Italy and France—draw people into the catch basins of new religious forms of life. Each form of life, each way of being, can then ratchet itself up and out in ways and directions that develop and strengthen it as the form of life it is. Once a form of life becomes a way of being, a culture, it is like a huge ship that can be turned but only very gradually, not on a dime. Deep-seated sociomoral and religious practices clearly have this much plasticity. They can and do change, but normally only very slowly. Our question is whether and to what extent emotional states and practices such as anger have the same kind of plasticity.

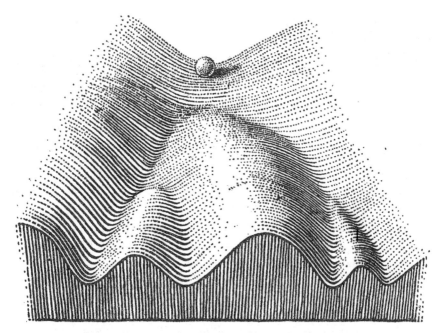

FIGURE 9.1 Waddington Landscape.

Modifying and Moderating Anger

In thinking about whether anger or any other reactive attitude can, and what is different, ought to be extirpated, these four questions are relevant.

1. Did the reactive attitudes arise as adaptations?
2. If so, are they still adaptive?
3. How modifiable are these attitudes?
4. If they are modifiable, are there any reasons to work to modify, moderate, or otherwise adjust how, when, and under what circumstances we experience or express the reactive attitudes?

The answer to the first question is a qualified yes. Many of the reactive attitudes, although not all of them, on Strawson's list are variations on, or reasonable facsimiles of, what many evolutionary biologists, primatologists, and psychologists say are robust, possibly universal emotions, which can be viewed as original and natural. They, or more likely something like them, will emerge in most ecologies. Certain emotional dispositions in their original inchoate (newborns), semichoate (children), and choate forms (socialized adolescents and adults) are likely to emerge in most, possibly all, epigenetic and social-ecological landscapes. Furthermore, the reactive attitudes in whatever original form they have, and with whatever developmental trajectories they have and plasticity they possess, arose as adaptations. In saying that the reactive emotions are original and natural and adaptations to boot is not to say that they evolved in *Homo sapiens*. Remember, it is possible, even likely, that the reactive emotions, pretty much in the form we are naturally disposed to display them, were delivered by gene sequences that belonged to and evolved in ancestral species, in earlier groups of hominids, or, even more likely, in some non-hominid ancestor.[6] It is likely that the kinds of reactive attitudes we judge to be normal and natural, in terms of how they feel, what triggers the attitude, and what action it motivates, are very different from the original and natural ones.

Even if the reactive attitudes come with the equipment, there are many unanswered questions. How strong or weak are the original settings in terms of intensity? What about individual variation in initial settings? What about variations dependent on sex, gender, and age? How similar or different are the shapes of contemporary ecological landscapes from each other and from the original one or ones?[7] We will want to know what sorts of situations standardly elicit the reactive attitudes. Saying that they are elicited by benevolence and malevolence says little until we know what sorts of things were perceived originally as benevolent or malevolent, and which ones are now. We can make some plausible, educated guesses here. But much information is missing, especially once culture is introduced, because we know different cultures and cultural groups conceive of benevolence and malevolence differently. A warm, friendly, and welcomed smile in America can be a lewd and lascivious violation in Mecca.

Despite lacking this information, we might still be inclined to say that in current environments, especially with certain technologies at our disposal, we need to be wary of some of the original and natural reactive attitudes. Expressions of anger in an environment filled with guns have, all else being equal, more dangerous and more deadly potential than in a world in which the standard expressions can only go as far as fists, sticks, and stones. Many people worried, and worried rightly, that being poised, even willing, to fight a nuclear war that might have resulted in species extinction was caused in part by the facelessness of the enemy. Remember, we are attuned to feel emotions of anger, as well as compassion to faces, but not to large chunks of, even inhabited, land on maps. On the other side, mass communication, it is often said, gives face to suffering. We see starving children halfway across the globe and are, at least sometimes, moved to help. Having said this much leads in the direction of a mixed verdict about whether in the world, as we know it, the reactive attitudes are well-suited for doing the jobs for which they were designed, most likely food, mate, and child protection.

What we do know is how to answer (3) and (4). Regarding (3), the reactive attitudes are modifiable, plastic to some degree. The evidence for this claim abounds. Contemporary moral educational practices aim at and sometimes succeed in moderating what are judged to be excessively angry displays, and benevolent dispositions can be developed and enhanced, although it is a variable matter how hard we try to do so. Different cultures, different moral communities work in different ways to increase or decrease anger, resentment, guilt, and so on. Getting a haircut the day after one's father dies is not something an orthodox Hindu ought to do; it comes close to sacrilege and will result in strong sanctions (Shweder 1991). For us, getting a haircut is a perfectly reasonable thing to do in preparation for any funeral. The fact remains that in both cultures there are ways of behaving at the time of the death of a close relative that will elicit disapproval, possibly angry disapproval.

The reason (4) gets a positive answer as well, namely, that we should work to modify, moderate, or otherwise adjust the original reactive attitudes, has to do with the fact that there came a time in every place on earth when a conception of a person and a conception of a morally good life was discovered, developed, and articulated. Every conception I am familiar with—whether the wisdom is that contained in the Torah, in the Old and New Testaments, in Confucius's *Analects*, in the Puranas and the Bhagavad Gita, in the Qur'an, in the Pali canon or other Buddhist texts, or in secular or sacred moral theory of the sort we get from Aristotle, Augustine, Aquinas, Mill, and Kant in the West—puts forward all sorts of wisdom and advice about how we ought to structure our affective-cognitive-conative economies, how best to live a good life, what virtues are the best expressions of our common humanity, and which feelings and vices we need to be most watchful of and ready to fight off. Each of the traditions I have mentioned, despite sometimes displaying parochial, xenophobic, sexist, and racist attitudes, identifies problems with living our lives according to our biological first natures, and provides considerable wisdom, each in their own way, for being better than we are naturally prone to be, even wisdom that might help us to be good, really good.

There is a tendency to think that what is original and natural is fixed. Some work in evolutionary psychology looks resolutely at our seamy side, highlighting certain unsavory tendencies we may in fact have in virtue of being animals, and makes it seem that because these traits are part of our nature—for example, male promiscuity, possibly male tendencies to violence—they will be very hard, if not impossible, to take control of, to modify, suppress, or redirect. But again, the evidence abounds that we are plastic, and that both culture and we as individuals can work with our natural equipment, as our norms require. Almost nothing in human nature is fixed until epigenetics, development, and a distinctive human ecology have at us and we at them. The skeptic might respond to this paean for plasticity and modifiability, by reminding us that there are limits. A good gardener can create a completely unexpected topiary. The gardener and her desire to be playful, to do novel things, combined with all variety of aesthetic judgments create an unusual epigenetic landscape and she creates trees in the shapes of animals. She makes trees shaped like bears and foxes, but she cannot make the trees into bears and foxes. So it is with anger and the other reactive attitudes. Anger can be shaped in surprising ways in unusual ecologies, but it cannot be extirpated in any ecology. Or so the skeptic says.

A Tale of Two Strawsons

P. F. Strawson can be read as a skeptic who thinks that anger and the other reactive attitudes cannot be extirpated, but only moderated, contained, and properly targeted. Galen Strawson, however, explores the extirpation possibility. One angle comes from the patriarch's own pen. P. F. Strawson points out that we sometimes take the "objective attitude" and subjectively disengage. The piano is out of key. I am angry at the piano, but I realize it is foolish to be angry at the piano even if it makes sense to be angry at the piano tuner. Likewise, I disengage or try to disengage when a toddler or mentally ill person commits a wrong. I seem to disengage or try to disengage for a reason, specifically, pianos are not persons at all, and toddlers and mentally ill persons are not full-on persons, not competent persons in the sense that is required to assign blame and responsibility. A person who regularly gets angry at physical objects needs help. A kindergarten teacher or a psychiatrist who gets mad at the students or the patients needs a new job. Psychologists teach that humans are so attuned to look for agency (possibly in order to regulate other agents), that we see intentional agency even where it doesn't exist (Bloom 2004; Gopnik 2009).

Person, when used in the normative sense, as a moral or legal term, can be understood in two ways, one theoretically innocent and close to common sense, the other conceptually sophisticated. The commonsense view is that a person is a creature that displays competence in absorbing and acting according to the normative order, and who is held accountable by us (and normally also by themself) because they display this competence. The strong view is that a person is a creature who displays such competence because he possesses free will. P. F. Strawson is best read as suggesting that the weak view is all that matters, and that the discussion of the metaphysics of free will is beside the point. But Galen Strawson thinks that the strong view of free will, where a person is a prime mover of their own will, motives, and actions, a *causa sui*, an agent who rises above both causal necessity and physical randomness and makes rational choices, is the view we in fact assume.[8]

One way of understanding the difference of opinion is this way. Both Strawson-the-Elder and Strawson-the-Younger agree that the reactive attitudes come first, as ancient equipment, before any view about free will is sensed, thought, articulated, or theorized.[9] But Galen Strawson emphasizes in a way P. F. Strawson does not the way that a strong view of free will has come to play a powerful role inside our form of life in justifying the deployment of the reactive attitudes and in building them out, ratcheting them up, in certain ways. This allows Strawson-the-Younger to think about modifiability of the attitudes in novel ways. At a minimum, there is the possibility that we could work to get rid of cultural encrustations that seem to justify the reactive attitudes, but don't really justify them (Remember: nothing justifies them in their 'original and natural' form; they are "arational"), and see what remains at the core, in these emotions in their chimp form. At that point, we can look again, to see what further practical work can be done to adjust, modify, rechannel, possibly even to eliminate, the attitudes in something(s) like their original form(s).

In a volume celebrating the fiftieth anniversary of his father's essay "Freedom and Resentment," Galen Strawson writes:

> I'm still inclined to disagree with "Freedom and Resentment" on certain points, in spite of the value of the whole. So (for example) I still think that working to give up the ordinary strong belief in free will, in such a way as to resile from the natural human commitment to the personal reactive attitudes, is a possible and genuine project, even if it can be undertaken only indirectly; and I still think that such an attempt can be justified—or even forced on someone—by something like a desire to believe the truth. So I disagree with [P. F.] Strawson when he says that if we could choose between retaining and abandoning the reactive attitudes, "we could choose rationally only in the light of the gains and losses to human life," and that "the truth of falsity of a general thesis of determinism could not bear on the rationality of this choice." (2014, 5–6)

Strawson-the-Younger agrees with Strawson-the-Elder that the reactive attitudes may come with the equipment and that their causal history may explain why we have them in something like their chimp form, namely, they contributed to reproductive success, and so on. But humans live in the space of reasons as well as the space of causes. Even if the reactive attitudes evolved in ancestral creatures for no reasons that those creatures thought of or had, but only due to the blind force of the regimen of inclusive genetic fitness, we have evolved to the point that we can and do ask for reasons to justify any and all adjustable practices. We ask for practical reasons: Do they work? And for moral reasons: Are they good? Furthermore, we can use such reasons, considerations for or against the wisdom of any practice or set of practices, to work to adjust the epigenetic landscape by attending to malleable features on both the person side of the ledger, and in the ecology inside which persons exist and that we can affect.

Specifically, Galen Strawson thinks that inside our form of life the strong view of free will plays a role, an ill-advised one, in the wide swath we give to certain reactive attitudes. First, agreeing with P. F. Strawson, he writes, "The grounds of the mechanisms—the feeling-mechanisms—of conscience and responsibility are ancient. They predate the Diachronic [narrative, historical] sense of self, both phylogenetically and ontogenetically, and they are in that straightforward sense independent of it and can operate without it." But then he adds this point of disagreement: "It seems plain that such reactive attitudes are unwarranted, inappropriate, out of place, fundamentally mistaken, if people do not really have 'strong' free will . . . it seems plain that the reactive attitudes depend logically on the belief in strong free will for their full appropriateness. There is, however, an extremely powerful argument . . . that shows that strong free will of this sort is incoherent, logically impossible (G. Strawson 2008, 218–19).[10]

He then asks, "Does this mean that we should give up the reactive attitudes? The question does not really arise for us, as [P. F.] Strawson points out, for it raises the question whether we can give them up, and the answer to that question is, for all practical purposes, No" (G. Strawson 2008, 218–19).

But Strawson-the-Younger seems ambivalent about this point concerning modifiability or unmodifiability. First, he consistently expresses the view that we can take some of the wind out of the sails of the culturally extended forms of some of the reactive attitudes by doing therapy on the beliefs that extend, support, and encrust them, specifically, the belief in free will. If we can extirpate the theoretical belief that humans have strong free will, we can retain blaming and shaming perhaps, but not the whole edifice of retributive punishment, stories about eternal reward and damnation, oppressive guilt, and so on. What is left after this work is done remains to be seen. Second, Galen Strawson is sympathetic to practices of modification that are unfamiliar in the West, but come highly recommended by other peoples. He writes:

> The suggestion that one's commitment to belief in freedom and the reactive attitudes may be of such a kind that its abandonment is practically speaking impossible has not so far been challenged, but it has been suggested that one might be able to engineer (or might simply undergo) partial but not total erosions of this commitment; and that it is perhaps not equally unrenounceable in all areas. . . . Consider certain Buddhist philosophers who argue, on a variety of metaphysical grounds, that our natural notion of the persisting individual self is a delusion. Having reached this conclusion, they set themselves a task: that of overcoming the delusion. . . . Delusions delude, after all; and the ordinary, strong sense of self (and of self-determination) is a particularly powerful delusion. They therefore recommend the adoption of a certain practice—that of meditation—the eventual effect of which, they claim, is to cause the delusion to dislimn. . . . A decision to adopt the 'objective' attitude to oneself and others cannot be implemented overnight, given the nature and strength of the framework and our commitment to it, but there is no such difficulty with a decision to initiate some practice which may more gradually undermine or alter the supposedly inflexible constraints

of the framework. And if we admit the possibility of partial alterations in attitudes or habits of thought to which we are . . . deeply committed, then this points to the possibility of a progressive abandonment of these attitudes or habits of thought which, gradually achieved, amounts to a total abandonment relative to the original position. It is not implausible to suppose that Buddhist monks and other mystics have succeeded in altering quite profoundly their experience of themselves (and others) as acting, thinking, and feeling beings. Nor—finally—is it implausible to say that they have in so doing achieved what is in certain respects a more correct view of the world, precisely to the extent that they have ceased to regard themselves and others as truly self-determining sources of actions, and have thereby come to adopt the objective attitude. (G. Strawson [1986] 2010, 101–2)

This seems like a large opening for the Stoic or Buddhist or any opponent of WEIRD anger. It may be that inside our way of being-in-the-world, our commonsense framework, that we see no way to get rid of our anger norms and practices overnight by "intellectual fiat." But perhaps there are practices that could engineer the result if there were good reasons to do so.

Roman aqueducts, suspension bridges, and airplanes all defy the laws of gravity, but we engineered them.[11] *Payback*, a book on the evolutionary psychology of "pain-passing" is filled with strategies for mitigating anger in conformity with what its authors Barash and Lipton call an eleventh commandment: "When evaluating alternative actions, I will ask myself whether each is likely to increase or decrease the total amount of pain in the world, and I will always choose the latter" (2011, 199). They think that anger will almost always lose its rationale if measured against such a norm.

Major modification of the reactive attitude of anger is possible. Even if anger has contours that are 'original and natural,' I doubt that we know what they are. So work at modification, even major overhauls, of anger is not destined for failure. There are, as in ordinary engineering, many angles of approach, self-adjustments, Weltanschauung adjustments, as well as social, economic, and political adjustments (I leave aside genetic and neural tampering), or all of these at once or over time.

Perhaps this much will give pause to the critics who say that the reactive attitudes are not modifiable or not, at least at the limit, entirely eliminable. Maybe, maybe not. The fact that so far the Stoics and Buddhists are not among the winners of the world proves nothing, exactly nothing. In 1902 every aeronautical engineer knew that a winged plane could be lifted and glide some distance in the air, but most were skeptical that physical laws would allow an engine to power a plane over any distance. The inverse square law, the law of universal gravitation would defeat that project. And so perhaps it is, or might be, with what we think are the psychophysical laws that govern anger and the other reactive attitudes. Suppose, therefore, that anger can be radically modified, possibly extirpated in some of its forms, there remains the normative argument that some say anger, some forms of anger at any rate, are good, morally good. I turn to this line of defense of WEIRD anger.

10

For Love's and Justice's Sake

THE ATTACHMENT, INJUSTICE, AND
CATHARSIS DEFENSES

Extirpation Is Possible

We have considered the argument that extirpating anger is impossible. It is not as strong as it seems. Even if anger is original and natural in some forms, those forms are inchoate until a moral ecology speaks, forms, and authorizes them. Ifaluk *song* is a gentle healing anger that does not aim to pass-pain. And Stoic and Buddhist communities authorize punishment, even execution and war when absolutely necessary, but never with anger's feel, never with anger's sadistic tone, its desire to pass-pain.

We can now turn to the three other objections to extirpating anger, which are each entirely normative, and claim for anger a role in sustaining and repairing the most important relations we humans can have, relations of love and relations of justice, and a role in healing from hurt, from the ill will of bad people and evil treatment. The arguments are "Attachment," "Injustice," and "Catharsis."

Anger and Attachment

The Attachment Objection, "Attachment," for short, says this: Every contender for a good human life, every way of being that provides minimal conditions for flourishing, goodness, decency, rightness, and so on, recognizes some goods of attachment. Attachments are produced and sustained by passions, and they engender passion. If one loves one's partner, children, village, hobbies, or career, then one will be disposed to anger if they are threatened, injured, killed, or taken away. Attachment and passions such as anger, fear, and sadness, are psychologically intertwined in such a way that extirpating passions would require eliminating worthy attachments, the ones that make life worth living, and thus is a bad idea. Eliminating attachments might reduce the possibility of some vulnerabilities, but not old age, pain, death, and at the much too steep cost of making life not worth living, not a meaningful human life.

Every culture has views about the things that matter and the things that don't, the things that are good and the things that are bad. And every conception of the good life recognizes that love and friendship are good, and hatred and enmity are bad. Well, almost every conception. Despite claiming that no one would choose to live without friends, Aristotle discusses views about the good life that seem to involve making oneself invulnerable to the sorrow, grief, and anger associated with losing what one loves by loving nothing and no one. One can see a similar strain in some forms of Theravadan Buddhism where the *arhat* goes to the mountaintop without anything or anyone other than himself, which "self" he then tries to detach from, meditate away, reaching a state in which he experiences "emptiness." Neither option is open to the Stoic, who is a communal creature, a political animal, nor is it open to the modern Buddhist, who is socially engaged and avows the bodhisattva ideal.

Varieties of Detachment

David Wong (2006a) discusses the connection between attachment and vulnerability, and some strategies that philosophers have recommended for balancing the two. Wong provides a useful set of distinctions:

1. Extirpation of the emotions
2. Detachment with encapsulation
3. Detachment with resilience

The first strategy, extirpation of the emotions, is to minimize one's vulnerability to losses of meaningful projects or loved ones by choosing not to become attached to projects or persons in the first place. But this is a nonstarter for most of us because it would undermine the quest for value and meaning, and make for a life not worth living.

"Detachment with encapsulation" involves "calibrat[ing] the strength, depth and dissemination of [an individual's] attachments according to the fragility and transience of the objects involved. It is not wise to attach deeply to a mayfly . . . the main constraint on attachment is that it not be maximally strong, deep, and disseminated (that it not have maximal ramifications throughout all spheres of one's life)" (2006a, 211).

Wong thinks that a Stoic will endorse the encapsulation strategy (2). The Utku Eskimos are a living example of people who have norms to keep them from loving their children "too much" on grounds that it can lead to pain for the person who loves (Briggs 1970, 70–71). A certain type of cost-benefit reasoner might serve best to picture the encapsulation tactic, where one engages, but only to the point where one is not too vulnerable. So the cost-benefit reasoner consciously calculates and calibrates such things as her degree of commitment to a relationship based on rational expectations. Perhaps she marries knowing that there is a 30 percent chance of divorce, 60 percent chance her partner dies first, and so forth, and that she then reminds herself of the updated relevant statistics once a week. This might (I guess) work to keep loss of a loved one from producing immobilizing sorrow or anger, but it has the downside of requiring less than full absorption in the relationship, which will reduce the yield of the relationship on the meaning-of-life side of the ledger. And, of course, if one party, the Stoic or the cost-benefit calculator, in an otherwise good marriage, is not fully engaged, but her partner is, this, on its own, might ruin the marriage.

If detachment makes sense, then Wong advocates (3) "detachment with resilience," which allows one's love for one's partner, children, and parents, even one's artistic or philosophical projects, to be maximal in degree, to interpenetrate everything one is and does, but in such a way that one is capable of responding to a loss without reverting to "bestial" or infantile and incapacitating states.

Wong offers this famous passage in the *Zhuangzi*, where Zhuangzi's wife has died and his friend Huizi visits to pay his respects as an example of detachment with resilience:

> When Huizi went to mourn her, he found Zhuangzi squatting with his legs splayed, drumming on a tub, and singing. Huizi said, "You lived with her, brought up children, and grew old. Not to cry at her death is indeed enough already. But you even drum on a tub and sing. Isn't this going too far?!" Zhuangzi said, "It's not so. When she first died, how could I not grieve like everyone else? But I looked into her beginnings, and originally she had no life. Not only no life, but no body. Not only no body, but no *qi*氣 ("energy-stuff"). Amidst the mysterious chaos, something changed and she had *qi*. The *qi* changed and she had a body. Her body changed and she had life. Now there's been another change and she's died. These changes are to each other as the procession of the four seasons, spring and autumn, winter and summer. She was going to sleep quietly in a giant bedroom, while I in turn was wailing and weeping—I took this to show I was incompetent with respect to fate. So I stopped. (*Zhuangzi* 18.15–19)

The amazing story of the passing of Zhuangzi's wife and Zhuangzi's reaction reveals the metaphysical perspective that enables a Daoist sage to go on after such grievous loss. Of course, Zhuangzi grieved "when she first died." His reaction was normal. He never extirpated sorrow. But his sorrow, a certain kind of Daoist sorrow, dissipated more quickly than it does for the average person.

Why did his sorrow dissipate more quickly than the sorrow of a normal Chinese person, a Confucian or a Mohist? How was it able to dissipate more quickly than normal Chinese sorrow? The answer given is that Zhuangzi rehearsed constantly over the course of his life the wisdom of Daoist metaphysics that nature has its ways of proceeding that is at once beautiful, sad, tender—ashes to ashes, dust to dust; stardust to life and back again—and not under human control. The metaphysical perspective is one of awe, appreciation, and acceptance, and it is strongly reminiscent of the Buddhist's insistence on recognizing the impermanence of everything, as well as Stoic training that encourages one to see one's affairs from the perspective of the universe sub specie aeternitatis. Zhuangzi's love, we are allowed to suppose, was maximal. His resilience accrues from having absorbed a certain picture of things taken as a whole—"from becoming competent with respect to fate"—not from consciously containing his love for his wife.

I will not fuss about the merits of the two kinds of detachment that Wong associates with Stoicism (encapsulation) and Daoism (resilience) respectively, except to say that 3. "Detachment with resilience" sounds much better than 2. "Detachment with encapsulation," for reasons Wong gives. Instead, I want to make a remark about 1. Extirpation of the emotions, and suggest a fourth possibility:

4.   Extirpation of some emotions/reactive attitudes
     and detachment with resilience

Remember Wong makes quick work of 1. Extirpation of the emotions, because according to "Attachment," there is a necessary connection between the attachments that make life worth living and passion and emotional vulnerability. But this much is not enough to establish which emotions are in play or necessary, nor does it establish that all the reactive attitudes are necessary.

Attachment is closest to love, and most familiar as a morally worthy passion in that form, in a form that wishes the very best for the beloved. So let's allow that loving attachment is a passion that is required for a meaningful life. This much rules out extirpating every emotion, passion, or reactive attitude since love, itself a reactive attitude, is necessary. Next, suppose that we add gratitude, forgiveness, and sadness as reasonable reactive attitudes required in the course of normal attached, loving human relations. Must we also add anger and its mates to the list? I don't think so.[1]

It seems perfectly possible for a modern Śāntideva or Seneca to single out anger as singularly destructive and worth eliminating. The modern Stoic or Buddhist will say that the passions needed to sustain worthy attachments ought to be formed and encouraged only in their noninfantile forms, only if they involve seeing things (such as agency and what really matters) truthfully, and also, practically, in ways that permit a certain amount of both encapsulation (the teacher who does not bring their own fraught relations with their teenage children to the classroom) and resilience. On what basis might we justify the demarcation of the passions and reactive attitudes worth maintaining and those, perhaps anger alone, which are to be extirpated, eliminated?

One answer is this: Sorrow, when it is good, flows from loss of something of value, something that matters. It is a response that comes from loving attachment. It is sorrow that something beautiful, good, and worthy is lost, gone. Sorrow, gratitude, and forgiveness acknowledge what is good, beautiful, and worthy. But anger is a response that marks injury and seeks to do harm. It is vengeful and spiteful. It does not seek to heal like forgiveness and sorrow. Nor does it encourage and compliment goodness as gratitude does. It is ugly and harmful, and in the business of passing pain.

In addition, there is no necessity in viewing persons according to a metaphysics that assigns them self-originating intentions to be cruel, and to do harm or evil, which might, if true, warrant anger, as opposed to a Stoic or Buddhist metaphysics that emphasizes a person's embeddedness in the causal history of the universe, and their relative lack of entirely self-originating good or bad character, intentions, or will. We are not mini prime movers, ourselves unmoved.

So the "Attachment" objection to extirpating all passions is met in this way: First, it is true that attachments to people and projects are what make life worth living across most, but not all, forms of life. Second, such worthy attachments are motivated, enabled, and sustained by passions. Third, these attachments make us vulnerable to experiencing various emotions, anger if you betray me or if you harm someone or something I love, envy if you have what I want, sorrow if my beloved dies, and so on. Fourth, this makes sense of practices designed to build encapsulation or resilience—these include metaphysical lessons of the sort Daoists, Stoics, and Buddhists recommend, various containment strategies and moderation rules of thumb, as well as self-help techniques from wise gurus and all manner of spiritual snake oil salesmen. Fifth, although a good life conceived in terms of worthy attachments requires passions and emotions, it does not necessarily require every passion or reactive attitude. Anger—disgust is my other main candidate for a suspect passion—might, all things considered, be worthy of extirpating as far as is possible.

Humanizing Rage?

In *The Therapy of Desire* (1994), Martha Nussbaum tells a story she heard secondhand about Elie Wiesel.

> Wiesel was a child in one of the Nazi death camps. On the day the Allied forces arrived, the first member of the liberating army he saw was a very large black officer. Walking into the camp and seeing what there was to

be seen, this man began to curse, shouting at the top of his voice. As Wiesel watched, he went on shouting and cursing for a very long time. And the child Wiesel thought, watching him, now humanity has come back. Now, with that anger, humanity has come back. (1994, 403)

Nussbaum follows the Stoic as far as agreeing that brutality and delight in vengeance are vicious and dehumanizing, but she sees "the central problem" with Seneca's view that it disallows virtuous anger, anger that is humane. She writes, "*not* to get angry when horrible things take place seems itself to be a diminution of one's humanity" (403). "Wiesel's soldier was no Stoic. But it was just on account of the extremity of his justified rage that the child Wiesel saw him as a messenger of humanity. . . . Can the Stoic have humanity while losing rage?" (403). The question is rhetorical. Nussbaum thinks that the answer "no" will be obvious to anyone who hears or reads the story. She might be right about how her audience will receive the question. But it might be so, because first, the story explicitly endorses that interpretation and second, because we Aristotelians, we containment theorists, are inclined to think that rage is sometimes required. This is the "Injustice" objection.

The Dalai Lama uses a similar strategy to object to a certain reading of Śāntideva. He writes that the Tibetan word *zhe sdang* can be translated as anger or hatred in English. He then says, "I feel that it should be translated as 'hatred' because 'anger,' as it is understood in English can be positive in very special circumstances. These occur when anger is motivated by compassion or when it acts as an impetus or a catalyst for a positive action. In such rare circumstances anger can be positive whereas hatred can never be positive" (1999, 7).

The title of the Dalai Lama's teachings on Śāntideva is *Healing Anger*, and it turns out to be something of a double entendre. First, there are practices to heal, repair, and restore the harms that most anger does, that anger often or usually does to both the individual who suffers it, and to those who are its intentional or inadvertent targets. But second, some kinds of anger, specifically outrage over injustice to others, can lead to healing (vii). Now Śāntideva does not, as far as I can tell from the translations available, make the second point. He seems to have thought that all anger is bad. Thus, if the issue is what Śāntideva meant or intended, then the fact that we, in the West, think that there is such a thing as "positive anger" is irrelevant, even though it is true that we in the West do think that anger motivated by compassion or anger that aims for social change, and also as I will discuss shortly, cathartic anger, are morally acceptable, even good, possibly required.[2] One thought is that the Dalai Lama is reinterpreting Śāntideva from the perspective of modern Tantric practices, which involve all sorts of esoteric rechannelings and sublimations of anger in rituals that involve wrathful gods. Chinese Ch'an and Japanese Zen also offer ritualized or metabolized anger practices, but without the divine props of Tibetan Buddhists.[3]

Another thought is that the Dalai Lama thinks that Śāntideva has an inadequate understanding of the nature of justice, which is, as a matter of fact, comparatively undertheorized in Buddhism, or that we now, with experience of more history—with the treatment of Tibetan Buddhist and Ulghar Muslims in China, the civil rights movement in America, the anti-Apartheid movement in South Africa, and so on—under our belts, see the practical necessity of expressing outrage, which may or may not (but usually does) come with feeling outraged. Or perhaps the Dalai Lama is just resolving this particular moral collision with Western values by conceding the WEIRD view. Still, it is not clear that the concession is consistent with Śāntideva, nor is it clear that positive anger is required even in cases where it works or seems to work to get justice accomplished.[4]

Consider the "outraged liberator" in Nussbaum's telling of Wiesel's story. It is a good story, and one can see how in the eyes of a little boy, scared and despondent in a death camp that reeked of cruelty and hopelessness, that the officer's vivid indignation restored a sense of humanity, a glimmer of hope for decency. One might also, or because of this, judge it to be a case of positive anger.

But imagine that instead of rage, the officer who was the first member of the liberating party to arrive at the concentration camp, had wept rivers of tears at what he saw. Suppose that instead of fury at the evidence of depraved racist inhumanity, he experienced compassion and solidarity and profound tearful sadness. One could easily imagine that this might have both diminished the young Wiesel's sense of hopelessness, allowing him to think that perhaps "humanity had come back," as well as served as a catharsis for the officer and his fellow soldiers. Imagine the soldiers shedding tears together; it is much easier to imagine than to imagine them all shouting and cursing. Could a contagion of tears rather than a contagion of rage be healing, could it restore hope in humanity? The answer seems clearly yes. And this means that anger is not necessary in the story, and thus that the answer to Nussbaum's rhetorical question, "Can the Stoic have humanity while losing rage?" is maybe. Why not?[5]

One objection to this reply is that it allows the Stoic something she is not supposed to have, namely, strong feelings, rage in Nussbaum's version of the Elie Wiesel story, deep sorrow in my version. Two replies: First, I am not very interested in what makes one a card-carrying Stoic. I used Seneca's treatise, "On Anger," to remind us that some have thought and provided strong arguments inside our tradition that anger is bad and that it can be eliminated. Even if a standard Stoic view (I am agnostic) is that all passions are bad and should be extirpated, sorrow as well as rage, then I am not a Stoic, which is fine, since I wasn't trying to be one. I am trying to reveal and explore the moral possibility space. Second, even if one is very fussy about doctrinal correctness, there are modern Stoics who interpret the doctrine, then and now, as allowing the full complement of constructive, wholesome passions.

Lawrence C. Becker, speaking as a modern Stoic, argues that no Stoic defended passionlessness, as we understand it, a purely rational, unfelt sort of agency, *apatheia*. *Apatheia* was prized not as general indifference, but as indifference to indifferent things (a shared conviction among Stoics, Epicureans, and Cynics). Stoic *apatheia* is equanimity, not indifference. According to Becker, Stoics, twentieth- and twenty-first-century ones, seek to flourish, to achieve *eudaimonia*, which requires and produces good feeling, *eupatheia*. Becker writes:

> Historically, most of our efforts to talk about our views on the passions have been directed to dealing with its dangers rather than its safe luxuries. But nothing in our fundamental doctrines (as opposed to therapies and moral-training manuals drawn up for the benefits of those at risk) opposes passion as such. Infantile or bestial passion, yes, insofar as it lacks (or subordinates) propositional content. Immature, unintegrated, or incapacitating passion, yes, insofar as it is incompatible with the perfection of agency. (1998, 131)

Becker's view is that Seneca should only be read as asking that we extirpate infantile, unintegrated, or incapacitating anger. Whereas my response to Nussbaum's version of the Elie Wiesel story is to ask us to imagine the soldier as sorrowful rather than rageful, Becker says in response to the same story that "the soldier may well have been a perfectly good stoic. . . . Nothing in the event as described implies the least compromise with the stoic conception of virtue. No duty was breached. No one suffered or was incapacitated by the soldier's anger; on the contrary, a suffering child was comforted by it" (132).

This may be right, but I think the tearful, sorrowful response, rather than the rageful response, the kinder softer response, would be more likely than the latter to console small children, to restore a sense of hope and trust. Anger, we remember from Seneca, tends to overreach, it is designed to injure its object, but often hits more than its target, what is nearby and innocent. A child in a concentration camp might easily misunderstand the rage of the officer and experience further terror, rather than a feeling of calm, and a sense that moral order is being restored.

In *Stoic Warriors* (2005), Nancy Sherman objects to Seneca's view by arguing that, "while some forms of anger are little more than destructive; others are constructive and morally healthy responses to injustice and wrongdoing. In their absence, we cannot properly record wrongdoing or morally prepare ourselves for forms of repair and healing" (67–68).[6] Like Nussbaum, Sherman doesn't think that Seneca allows for the constructive forms of anger, although tellingly she thinks that even though Stoics also think that fear is always irrational, the sage will experience "a kind of caution or wariness (*eulabeia*)" but not "ordinary fear" (101–2). One wonders why the Stoic cannot say the same about anger, namely, that there are some states that are related to normal anger, but involve a refined, focused, firm, and serious sense that there is injustice to be stopped or overcome, and the stern posture that indicates that I aim to do so.[7] These relatives of anger are acceptable, but not pissy anger at not getting my way or rage that loses a sense of itself, not the infantile, unintegrated, or incapacitating varieties of anger. This is Becker's interpretation.

A more important point is that Sherman's claim is too strong when she writes that in the "absence [of some constructive forms of anger] we cannot properly record wrongdoing or morally prepare ourselves for forms of repair and healing." It is too strong for the same reason Nussbaum's way of understanding the necessity of anger in the Wiesel story is too strong. It is not necessary that anger do the work of perceiving the injustice or restoring humanity in the Wiesel case, nor does recording wrongdoing and getting on with repair and healing require anger.[8] Anger might normally play this role, or typically do so inside our form of life. But it is not necessary. This matters because if anger was necessary or needed to play a central role in repair and healing then many great leaders like Leymah Gbowee, Ellen Johnson Sirleaf, Tawakkol Karman, Nelson Mandela, and Desmond Tutu, who were involved in the restorative justice and the truth and reconciliation movements would be seriously confused, misguided.[9] These movements work, but they do not give anger any sort of pivotal or sustaining role.[10] It isn't as if the experience of anger is denied. It is acknowledged and let go, because having it, holding it, and harboring it, are seen as damaging to all parties. Truth must be told, sorrow and tragic loss expressed, shame and guilt experienced, cowardice and fear and anger all acknowledged, in the service of mutual comprehension, compassion for suffering on all sides, and the restoration of trust and hopefulness.[11]

So "Injustice," the argument that anger is necessary for certain purposes, for marking or signaling that certain evils are evil, for restoring humanity after a holocaust or genocide, or for reconciliation, healing, and repair after serious injury or injustice, is not valid. What is true is that we, inside our WEIRD form of life, use anger for such purposes. And thus saying that righteous anger, moral outrage serves such purposes for us is true. It is also beside the point insofar as we are interested in exploring the space of moral possibilities.

Catharsis

There is another argument that claims that anger is necessary in human life. "Catharsis" is familiar from depth psychology, especially from psychoanalysis. But it predates Freud by several thousand years, is visible in Greek tragedy, and the basic mechanisms were discussed by Aristotle in the *Poetics*. Whereas "Injustice" claims that anger is required when there is social injustice, "Catharsis" focuses on the necessity of anger for restoring individual psychic equilibrium or mental health. The basic idea is that some, perhaps only extreme, situations call for a powerful emotional response, for rage, fury, weeping, wailing, incapacitating sorrow, and incapacitating anger on the part of the individual who is harmed and seeks to heal. Healing can occur only if, in the present case, anger, or something near enough, is released, vented.

Aristotle asks a good question: Why would any rational person want to go see a tragedy? His answer: catharsis. You pay money to have a psychic purgation. Antigone, Oedipus, and Hecuba are lost, beyond redemption. They express the gamut of powerful rage and sorrow, but their weeping and wailing, their rage and fury, accomplishes nothing. Their expressions of incapacitating emotion bear witness to the unmitigated awfulness of their predicament, but they serve not one iota to improve that predicament in practical terms. They do not, they cannot, regain what is irretrievably lost.

But we, the members of the audience, get why the tragic hero needs to express these incapacitating emotions. And we are purged of pity and fear vicariously through that tragic hero. These are the two emotions involved in tragic catharsis. The characters in a tragedy invariably express fury and rage, but these angry emotions do not, according to Aristotle, figure in any significant way in the first personal psychological purification of the audience. For the characters in a tragedy, there is no salvation. They weep and wail and are enraged. Perhaps this releases some of what must be released or vented before, what is normally, their final tragic end. But for the audience members, it is the vicarious feelings of pity and fear that are salvific, not the audiences' own rage. The audience is not enraged. It is in a state of deep, compassionate identification.

How and why is that? The answer is that the audience is assumed to be compassionate enough that it feels for Antigone's plight, and smart enough that it identifies with her plight in a "there but for fortune" sort of way. We get how what is happening to Antigone could happen to us. She is trapped between love for her two deceased twin brothers who fought on separate sides in the civil war, her duty to bury them, and Creon's royal edict that traitorous soldiers, and thus her brother Polynices, cannot be buried. She is attached, she is vulnerable, and either great injustice, or just plain old inexplicable cosmic awfulness has come her way. *Huis clos*. We get it, we vicariously identify with it, and in this way, we vicariously experience Antigone's tragedy (and Creon's tragedy, Ismene's, her sister's, tragedy, and Haemon's, her fiancé's, tragedy, as well as her brothers' tragedy, which sets the plot). The heart-wrenching purgation of pity and fear is restorative. It releases anxieties we have about our own vulnerabilities.

One might wonder whether what is revealed in Greek tragedy is really universal, or whether instead it models, endorses, and works to produce a catharsis for people of a certain sociocultural historical kind. Several distinct questions arise: First, is it a psychic necessity, a universal law of psychology, that any character in Antigone's, or Oedipus's, or Hecuba's position—or name your favorite tragic hero—would suffer incapacitating emotion? That is, are tragic situations such that anyone in such a situation would lose it? Would Zhuangzi lose it? Buddha? Second, accepting that tragedy works by a catharsis of pity and fear, what does it teach about catharsis generally? Does it show anything about the cathartic necessity of anger when actual, not merely vicarious, mayhem occurs to an individual? We might wonder about actual tragic heroes in the canon, whether, if they had reasons, they could have responded to their awful predicament differently, for example, more stoically? And if they could have responded differently, we might wonder whether it would have been better if they had responded differently.

Although Seneca agreed with Aristotle about the cathartic potential of tragedy, he emphasized more than Aristotle the cognitive component of the catharsis, the idea that tragedy is "a visual and horrific revelation of the truth" that fate is what it is, and does what it does (Staley 2010, 113). Furthermore, Seneca the tragedian, favored modeling and mimicking the behavior of people like Antigone, Oedipus, and Hecuba, who have lost it, not because he wanted us to see this sort of incapacitated response as normal and expectable when one is on the wrong side of fate. For Seneca, giving a "naked" image of the angry soul—"Let us picture (*figuremus*) anger . . . like the hellish monsters (*monstra*) poets create" (*De Ira*)—serves to allow us to see how a person who is not a sage will handle tragedy.[12] For the Stoic, as for Aristotle, tragedy produces catharsis, a purgation of pity and fear, but it is also ideally supposed to convey this message: "Losing it" is not the correct or inevitable response to tragedy; no one, even in extremis, should want to lose it the way Antigone, or Oedipus, or Hecuba do. I quite like this line of argument, insinuating, as it does, a strong suspicion about universalist psychological claims, but I'll focus on a different line of argument.

The form of "Catharsis" that I am interested in exploring briefly is more modern and says something like this: When great personal harm or certain kinds of great personal harm come to a particular individual or to those one loves, it is necessary for that individual to express anger in order to heal. The simple form is that, in the relevant types of situations, anger is normal and expressing anger is required for healing—possibly sublimated anger can work, for example, works of art that release anger—but denial, repression, or suppression of anger is harmful. The idea can be put in the form of a schema:

The Catharsis Schema: In order to heal from certain kinds of injury to oneself or loved ones, for example, assault, rape, attempted murder, torture, murder of a loved one, and systematic oppression, it is necessary to express anger about the injury, at the perpetrator, or if the perpetrator is not available, at something that serves as a sensible replacement for the perpetrator (his people, the cosmos, a punching bag) and in such ways, for example, in martial arts, philosophical debate, or pumping iron, that anger or something close enough to anger is vented and released.

The need for individuals in certain worlds to release anger as anger, or in something near enough, may be true as a matter of our social psychology, but it is parochial to think that it is so in all actual and possible worlds. In fact, there is now consensus among therapists who treat anger that punching pillows and the like does not diminish feelings of anger, but actually encourages it and gives practice to striking out from anger. Saying this much does not mean it will be good for us to give up our views and practices to the effect that cathartic anger is sometimes healing. But it encourages recognition that the possibility space is not as closed off to other ways of being and doing anger as we might think, and thus if one saw reasons to change our practices we could.

Victims of rape are individuals with complex individual and social psychologies, but there are some commonalities in postrape experiences: shame, embarrassment, guilt, fear, and anger. How does a victim of rape heal, how does she feel safe again, and get over unwarranted feelings of shame and guilt? What does she do with her anger at the rapist for the horrible violation of her body and her autonomy? It is hard to imagine that Stoics or Buddhists who are raped do not feel anger or rage.

One set of therapeutic goals for the victim of rape involves seeing things truthfully, understanding, for example, that she is completely the victim, and did nothing wrong. There are sadly whole cultures that make this almost impossible because of implausible, but widely accepted metaphysical or moral beliefs, for example, that the victim of rape deserves it because of bad karma in previous lives; or that a girl who has sex before marriage by choice or rape shames the whole family and deserves to die. In America, shame accrues from more insidious fears and falsehoods—the victim looked sexy or slutty; she made a bad choice being out; she was looking for it, deserved it, enjoyed it, and so on.

The therapeutic work involved in seeing these falsehoods as falsehoods is epistemic. It involves getting oneself, and possibly others, to see things as they really are. Epistemic justice is enormously important for both individual healing and social progress. Seeing things truthfully is often difficult, both because old but misleading ways of seeing and describing things are entrenched, and because there are typically interested parties, perpetrators of injustice, collaborators in injustice, who work consciously or unconsciously at concealment (Fricker 2007). But this work, the truth-seeking part, does not involve catharsis as such, which consists primarily of expressing or venting emotion.

Another aspect of healing besides seeing things truthfully involves overcoming traumatic fear and feeling safe again in the world that has declared itself vicious, and this may involve primarily expressing and venting anger. In *Aftermath*, Susan Brison's (2002) powerful philosophical memoir of her life after an attempted murder and rape experience, appropriately subtitled *Violence and the Remaking of a Self*, she writes:

> Although I didn't blame myself for the attack, neither could I blame my
> attacker. Tom [her husband] wanted to kill him, but I like other rape

victims I know, found it almost impossible to get angry with my assailant. I think the terror I felt precluded the appropriate anger response. . . . The anger was still there, but it got directed towards safer targets: my family and closest friends. My anger spread, giving me painful shooting signs that I was coming back to life. (13–14)

Brison explains that some of the work she did to overcome fear, which enabled her to have an "appropriate anger response," involved taking self-defense classes and doing political work. It was in such activities that she started "to experience justified, healing rage."

> Learning to fight back is a crucial part of this process, not only because it enables us to experience justified, healing rage, but also . . . to learn to feel entitled to occupy space, to defend ourselves. The hardest thing for the women in my self-defense class to do was simply to yell "No!" Women have been taught not to fight back when being attacked, to rely instead on placating or pleading with one's assailant— strategies that researchers have found to be the least effective in resisting rape. (14)

We are not now imagining a case like Wiesel's where the individual—the young Wiesel we can suppose—is terrified, bewildered, demoralized, and depressed, and someone else (the officer) does something, specifically, expresses rage at the heavens, which is healing (according to Nussbaum's rendition). We are imagining a case where an individual needs to do certain things to herself and for herself, specifically, express rage, in order to heal, in order to get beyond fear and rage, beyond emotions that spill over destructively into everyday life, into her relations with baristas, auto mechanics, and loved ones where they don't belong, and are not warranted one iota. She needs to express "justified, healing rage" in order to overcome the incapacitating fear and obsessive, immobilizing anger that seep into zones of her life where they make no sense, and are not warranted. "Justified, healing anger" is cathartic precisely in the sense that it helps purge the victim's soul of fear, perhaps also, depending on the particularities of the individual, shame and guilt, and it purifies her heart-mind so that an insidious, permanent well of resentment, distrust, and anger cannot root and poison her and her relations. Justified healing rage is forward-looking; it is healing rage not punitive rage. Its aim is to heal the victim's soul and make the world, her world, and the world of other potential victims, safe again.

Normally, catharsis is recommended within the bounds of what is morally acceptable and what is psychologically wise. These can come apart in either direction. What works to restore my mental well-being, killing you for harming my children, may be bad. And a morally good response to a serious injury, praying for you, might not restore my psychic equilibrium. Abiding the bounds of morality involves such things as expressing anger in accordance with norms that govern what the perpetrator deserves. Inside our form of life this might be anger, fury, and prison.

For Śāntideva, the rapist or murderer is the proximate cause of a terrible occurrence, inside something larger, some set of states-of-affairs, some unfolding that might be more worrisome, not just a one-off. Minimally, the perpetrator of the evil deed is broken, deserving of compassion and loving-kindness, as well as perhaps jail or death. But one plausible thought is that even Buddhists get that rageful catharsis is sometimes required for healing and is thus acceptable. Rageful deities are, on most every plausible view, externalizations, sublimations of something necessary, the karmic impulse that evil not pay, that neither I nor anyone else be subject to inexplicable pain at the hands of other sentient beings, or even, truth be told, at the whimsical hand of the indifferent universe.

The sort of catharsis that makes psychological sense involves expressions of feelings that are healing and that won't backfire onto me, or that won't generalize or seep out where they are not deserved, make no sense, and which then might come back to harm me and my relations further.

"Catharsis" claims that individuals must, of psychological necessity, express anger at great personal injuries (including to people they love), otherwise there is psychic hell to pay. "Catharsis" is a standard view, part of WEIRD folk psychology. But there are challenges to it as a psychological necessity, and not just from aliens like Buddhists and Stoics, who ask that we change many of our metaphysical beliefs, our beliefs about virtue and vice, and so on, and then reconfigure our attitudes about the necessity and role of anger. There are now challenges inside our form of life, from individuals who claim that love and forgiveness can work where once we thought only anger worked.[13] These cultural practices of forgiveness, and truth and reconciliation, are too young for us to know whether they can effectively do the work that catharsis has traditionally done.

Finally, it is important to recognize that it is a feature of justified, healing rage that it aims eventually at being released from that very rage. Thus, in a local, but not a global sense, catharsis seeks to extirpate anger, as well as perhaps some other destructive emotions, depending on the person, the particulars of her case, and her society.

Hating Hatred

In the case of both anger at social injustice and anger at individuals who cause grave personal injury, which are often interconnected, the Buddhist and the Stoic provide a recommendation, which if not fully eliminativist, incorporates their credible metaphysical perspectives. Śāntideva writes:

> Whatever transgressions and evil deeds of various kinds there are, all arise through the power of conditioning factors, while there is nothing that arises independently. (6.25)

If disregarding the principal cause, such as a stick or other weapon, I become angry with the person who impels it, he too is impelled by hatred.

It is better that I hate that hatred. (6.41)

Seneca also emphasizes the dependent origination of persons. To be sure, individuals do things, but the shapes of their minds and hearts that cause them to do what they do, are themselves products of natural and social worlds that both precede them, and surround and envelop them. Opportunities to leverage human agency in better directions often exist mostly in the social and natural surround, and not in the psychology of already formed or malformed persons. It is at such points that metaphysics and something in the vicinity of natural human reactions or culturally entrenched attitudes and practices can come to conflict. The moral philosopher, but perhaps not the psychologist or sociologist, will express hope that the right metaphysical view of things, of causation, the self, responsibility, and their suite, can lead us to leverage human plasticity in the right, morally better direction.

It would be foolishly anachronistic to say that Śāntideva and Seneca were structuralists, that they insisted on the embeddedness of individuals in the cosmos, history, and culture long before great thinkers like Karl Marx, Charles Darwin, and Max Weber showed the power of that way of thinking in terms of economics, natural history, and the ideologies of modern nation-states. But I will say it. Both Śāntideva and Seneca recognize that persons become who and what they are in a great unfolding of dependent origination, and that the picture of persons as self-movers themselves unmoved is false and dangerous. The belief in that kind of agency adds fuel to whatever sparks of anger that first nature, or various kinds of cultured nature, produce in the face of injury. It would be good to extirpate that view of agency and see what effect it has on our anger practices. Perhaps it will lead to compassion for the perpetrators of unjust practices on some sort of "they know not what they do" principles. They, racists and sexists, might be heirs and heiresses to forms of life they did not choose. If we can't get them to see this, then there may be hell to pay. Revolution and such. But perhaps even that revolution, those revolutions, and whatever violence they require, can be done of necessity, from compassion, with the aims of justice and equality, and not from or because of anger. As for the rapist, perhaps we can work to think that he is like Hitler, a terribly malformed creature deserving of compassion, and, not incompatibly, severe punishment. The metaphysics of dependent origination and No-Self do have some visible veins inside our traditions among people who speak of structural obstacles to goodness, for example, poor education, poverty, racism, and sexism, and among people who do not think that a person or self is a permanent thing that gets to keep what it acquires. And there are several well-known strands of Christianity that, like Buddhism, rank love and compassion as the greatest virtues. So there is reason to hope.

Conclusion: Holism, Overconfidence, and Question-Begging

The work of the last two chapters has been devoted to responding to four for-midable arguments against those who recommend that we eliminate destructive states of mind, anger first and foremost. The first argument, "Impossible," says this cannot be done. The second argument, "Attachment," says that anger is an appropriate response to certain kinds of harm to important persons or projects. The third argument, "Injustice," says that even if extirpating anger were possible it would be a bad idea, since moral outrage is required to over-come grave injustice. The fourth argument, "Catharsis," says that anger is re-quired to heal from certain great injuries to self or loved ones.

My overall assessment is that there are no arguments in philosophical psy-chology or cognitive science that show that anger, in the ways we do it, is origi-nal and natural, or that it cannot be modified. Furthermore, there are credible metaphysical beliefs and social practices in Buddhism and Stoicism that un-dermine the standard reasons we offer to justify anger; possibly, at the limit, these traditions provide reasons we ought to accept for wanting to extirpate anger altogether. There are strands of the relevant beliefs and practices inside our traditions, as evidenced by the truth and reconciliation movements, as well as certain strands of thinking among social democrats and progressives who typically reject the metaphysics of self-made women and men, and the as-sociated standard stories of the merited distribution of wealth and well-being.

As for the extirpation of anger, it may be an ideal that can't in fact be reached by anyone, like the ideal of any human running under 8 seconds in the 100 meters, or like an ideal that doesn't scale up well, like a 25-second 100 meters standard for everyone, which is out of the reach of many young children and most old people. But extirpation is underexplored terrain for us, and very few WEIRD souls have gone on a committed anger elimination program for a very long time.

I live among WEIRD people, probably most readers do as well. Philosophically, on a good day, we are Aristotelians about anger. We aspire to moderate it. Psychobiologically speaking, we say that anger is natural, normal, expectable, and an adaptation to boot. For some, that is enough to conclude that anger in roughly the ways we have it and do it, is morally acceptable and here to stay. Others see that the fact, if it is one, that a trait is natural does not entail that it is good, or even adaptive nowadays, or that it is unmodifiable. And thus we WEIRD folk have regimens to contain and moderate anger and we sort it into justified and unjustified kinds. This much makes us philosophi-cal Aristotelians. Scratch a WEIRD person and he can tell you all sorts of rules for apt anger, especially in others.

Even if this, moderation, is the philosophical background, the penumbra, the ideal normative landscape, contemporary anger practices in America are not moderate. They are excessive, sloppy, and permissive. People are angry a lot, and most everyone thinks that their anger is warranted. I strongly believe that we are both much too angry for our own good and largely complacent and thoughtless about how we might be better and do better. It seems we almost never give thought about being less angry, although there is an extraordinary amount of commentary about how others, significant others, the boss, retailers, the government, the people living in the Middle East, could behave better so that they didn't make me so angry.

But there are sources that have explored very high standards for anger, of working to not let it happen or get a grip, even the possibility of eliminating it altogether. Both Śāntideva and Seneca acknowledge the extraordinary difficulty of ridding ourselves of anger, but they provide many good reasons to think that we ought to try to eliminate anger and also for thinking it is or, at least at the limit, might be possible for creatures like us, some possible future *Homo sapiens*, and possibly even without genetic tampering or neuroenhancements. One set of reasons that I have emphasized are philosophical reasons, reasons that have to do with seeing human nature, the human good, and our place in the greater scheme of things correctly, truthfully, and without delusion.

I do not have a firm position on the topic I have been exploring for three chapters. I am trying to explore varieties of moral possibility that we rarely entertain, but which might be genuine possibilities for us. One reason that I have trouble declaring for the Stoic or Buddhist or Aristotelian sides in the debate about anger has to do with standpoint epistemology. I have not personally suffered racism or sexism, nor has anyone tried to rape or murder me. I have not been called on to heal from those kinds of awful injuries. Some friends who have suffered those kinds of harms say anger is required, others not so much. Their voices are the ones to listen to most carefully in our world.

A second reason I am hesitant to declare that Śāntideva and Seneca are right that anger ought to be extirpated has to do with facts about holism. Śāntideva and Seneca both presuppose and defend a certain way of seeing, making, and being in the world, as do the responses to them. The most familiar arguments against the Stoic and the Buddhist offer reasons that presuppose our WEIRD form of life, rather than justify that form of life. We say that injustice requires anger. This is what we think and say. It is an everyday truism for us. It is not a neutral reason that can serve as evidence between us, on one side, and the Stoics and Buddhists, on the other. We say that time is of the essence and that moral outrage is required to right this wrong, this injustice, now, in my lifetime. The Buddhist says that this attitude displays an excessive attachment to me, this guy, seeing the outcome now, as soon as possible, certainly in this very life. Buddhist time is very long, possibly infinite. Buddhists are patient. And, in any case, the SELF that is in a rush to accomplish some end is no longer there as that self when the hoped-for outcome is achieved. Likewise, for the Stoic, whatever positive short-term consequences outrage brings about, it undermines virtue, poisons the future, and rushes to get things done fast here and now, when sub specie aeternitatis "here" and "now" have no special status.

The point is something like this: There are arguments that all sides can give about the psychological and sociological economy of anger that describe why it suits them, how it fits into, possibly how it coheres with each tradition, how it fits inside its way of worldmaking. A Catholic or Jew or Aristotelian or secular WEIRD person cannot just decide to become a Stoic or Buddhist about anger, as far as anger goes—eliminate it!—and leave the rest of one's form of life intact. There would have to be adjustments, possibly massive, in other locations in the form of life, in how one thinks about the nature of the self, about the good life, about salvation and afterlives, about other virtues and vices.

The "internalist predicament" (Flanagan 2007) is the common predicament of justifying a way of being by describing how that way of being suits those of us who live inside that form of life.[14] For the philosopher who seeks deep justification, the predicament is a source of concern, since it reveals that what is presented as justification or reasons in favor of doing such and such, are often just reminders that this is the way we do such and such, and that this is why it makes sense for us. It is confidence undermining to understand that when one offers reasons for the way one lives and values, one is mostly repeating that this is the way we do things around here.

On the other hand, saying aloud or repeating our reasons for how we do things as we do, for why we think as we do, can be viewed as a sort of Weltanschauung maintenance program, a way of checking for damage or leaks or loose threads. When we repeat our reasons, and experience them as still secure, possibly because they are good reasons for us, possibly because we are stubborn or dogmatic, it resecures and cements our form of life. My own view about anger is that we should not feel at all secure about our reasons for doing it the ways we do it, and thus that we ought to think seriously about the vision of a world without anger offered by Buddhist and Stoics, which, lest the reader get teary-eyed and start humming John Lennon's "Imagine," need not be a world in which injustice is tolerated nor a world at peace, a world without war. Then again, it might be.

III Collisions

Bibliographical Essay

7. When Values Collide: Pidgins, Creoles, and Smashdowns

In *After Virtue* ([1981] 1984a), Alasdair MacIntyre adopts the language of incommensurability from Thomas Kuhn's (1970) work in the philosophy of science and applies it to ethical disagreement. Some moral disagreement, such as that between liberals and libertarians over whether equality or liberty is the most prized good of a just society, is interminable precisely because they mean something fundamentally different by the concept of justice from the start. Liberals start with the view that justice means that bad luck should be mitigated and economic equality should be prized first and foremost. Libertarians think that justice means maximizing individual liberty. The situation is similar to that of Ptolemaic astronomers who think that 'earth' means the heavenly body that is at the center of the universe. For the Copernican, 'earth' does not mean that.

In *Whose Justice? Which Rationality?* (1988), MacIntyre argues that incommensurability does not entail incomparability. He uses another tool from philosophy of science, this time Imre Lakatos's (1978) idea of progressive and degenerative research programs. Lakatos, a student of Karl Popper's, thought that for two scientific theories, A and B, both of which solve a certain set of problems, but where only B solves a new problem, say the appearance of the Higgs boson, then B is to be preferred over A. MacIntyre offers the tantalizing suggestion that, even between two moral traditions that do not think or speak in mutually understandable ways, there might be grounds for choosing one over the other, beyond where one is antecedently situated, on the basis of which one solves some new set of pressing moral problems.

Five excellent works by philosophers on issues of incommensurability, comparability, translatability, and their connections to debates about relativism and pluralism are:

- David B. Wong, *Moral Relativity* (1984)
- David B. Wong, *Natural Moralities* (2006)

- Michele Moody-Adams, *Fieldwork in Familiar Places* (1997)
- Ruth Chang, ed., *Incommensurability, Incomparability, and Practical Reason* (1997), especially Chang's introduction
- Ruth Chang, *Making Comparisons Count* (2002)

The following books and articles all take up the collision between the original peoples of the Americas and European colonizers:

- Jonathan Lear, *Radical Hope: Ethics in the Face of Cultural Devastation* (2008)
- James Maffie, *Aztec Philosophy: Understanding a World in Motion* (2014)
- James Maffie, "In *Huehue Tiamitiztli* and *la Verdad*: Nahua and European Philosophies in Fray Bernardino de Sahagun's *Coolquios y doctrina Cristiana*" (2012)
- Miguel León Portilla, *The Broken Spears: The Aztec Account of the Conquest of Mexico* (1966)
- Nicole Hassoun and David B. Wong. "Sustaining Cultures in the Face of Globalization" (2013)

8. Moral Geographies of Anger

Śāntideva's *The Bodhisattva's Way of Life*, chapter 6, and Seneca's *On Anger* are deep, beautiful, philosophically and psychologically sophisticated works that open up the space of moral possibility by proposing the elimination of anger.

Daniel Goleman's *Destructive Emotions: How Can We Overcome Them?* (2003) is a good overview of some of the main differences between Buddhist and North Atlantic views about the moral psychology of anger and other destructive states of mind. There are many ways a state of the heart-mind might be destructive. It might not be fitness enhancing; it might have negative valence, feel unpleasant; it might have harm as its aim; it might make the subject who experiences it worse off even if this is not what it intends; and it might harm others. Buddhists think anger normally has all these features, although biological fitness is not usually on their radar as particularly important sub specie aeternitatis.

Pierre Hadot's *Philosophy as a Way of Life* (1995), Martha Nussbaum's *The Therapy of Desire* (1994), and Michel Foucault's *The Care of the Self* (*Histoire de la sexualité, III: Le souci de soi*) (1978), are important books that defend what, among us, may be a lost conception of philosophy as a way of life. Hadot writes of this view that, "Philosophy is the art of living that cures us of our illnesses by teaching us a radically new way of life." He adds,

> In all the Hellenistic schools, the way of life is given form either in the order of inner discourse and of spiritual activity: meditation, dialogue

with oneself, examination of conscience, exercises of imagination such as the view from above the cosmos or the earth, or in the order of action and daily behavior, like the mastery of self, indifference towards indifferent things, the fulfillment of the duties of social life in Stoicism, the discipline of desires in Epicureanism. (1995, 30–31)

The idea that philosophy is or can be a way of worldmaking and provide what Foucault calls *techniques de soi*, methods of self-care, or what Nussbaum describes as "the therapy of desire," is a major and lively theme in much of Asian philosophy. There is constant discussion of self-cultivation among Confucians and Buddhists. P. J. Ivanhoe's *Confucian Moral Self Cultivation* (2000) and his *Confucian Reflections: Ancient Wisdom for Modern Times* (2013) are crystal clear introductions to Confucian *techniques de soi*, with many helpful extensions of Confucian ideas on self-cultivation to Western precincts.

On the Buddhist side, the fourteenth Dalai Lama's teaching on Śāntideva, *Healing Anger* (1999), is both an *explication de texte*, and an introduction to several mainstream types of Tibetan Buddhist meditation. *Tonglen* involves trying to inhale, literally breath in, the pain, suffering, misery, anger, boredom of another, and then to breath it out, so that neither she who was experiencing pain nor you who took it from her suffers. *Metta* involves consciously entertaining loving, compassionate, hopeful wishes for oneself, and then for others, including one's enemies.

9. WEIRD Anger

WEIRD anger is the normative penumbra, part of the psychosocial background that sets the norms for what anger is, what is allowed sensibly to trigger anger in the North Atlantic, and what actions are judged to partly constitute it or to sensibly emerge from anger once triggered. The norms for permissible or acceptable WEIRD anger are very low. People are allowed to be pissed off about most anything—long lines, traffic jams, bad grades, doing chores—although there are norms about not always expressing these feelings. Even on the view that anger is permissible when there is a violation of some sort, the question ought to arise, but doesn't arise, whether and how a long line at the coffee shop is a violation of any sort. The norms for "morally justified" anger are higher, but not much higher than those for acceptable everyday anger. Politicians, blogs, and TV news reflect, model, and perpetuate a culture of resentment, indignation, disgust, and contempt that is not the one that most, even WEIRD, moral philosophers defend.

Philosophical norms for anger are offered by philosophers from North America and the North Atlantic who "know" the WEIRD surround, live inside it, in part reflect these norms, but usually encourage new and improved versions of them inside our way of worldmaking that is committed to giving anger room. No one lately has defended eliminating all or most kinds of anger.

P. F. Strawson's "Freedom and Resentment" (1962) is, of course, the most influential article on the topic of reactive attitudes, anger, resentment, and their suite. The importance of Strawson's paper to the debate about anger is that he sets the ground-level assumption: Anger is a natural attitude, "not something we could do without."

Jean Hampton provides a useful taxonomy of anger in her dialogue with Jeffrie Murphy in *Forgiveness and Mercy* (1988). Hampton distinguishes simple hatred from spite from malice from moral hatred. Moral hatred makes sense when it is motivated by powerful concerns about justice. This is the dominant view among philosophers who live in WEIRD precincts.

In his must-read *Wise Choices, Apt Feelings* (1992), Allan Gibbard not only considers that anger is often "apt," but in fact offers apt anger as a test for the adequacy of moral judgment. We recognize moral violations by whether it would make sense to be angry about the violation in question.

Other important books and articles that give some sort of pride of place role to anger, or members of the anger family—indignation, resentment, contempt, and so on—include R. Jay Wallace's *Responsibility and the Moral Sentiments* (1994), in which he defends indignation over resentment as a generally acceptable moral attitude. Indignation is a response to a violation of legitimate expectations. Resentment is commonly caused by the world not cooperating with my individual wants and desires. Stephen Darwall's *The Second-Person Standpoint* (2006) makes a similar point, arguing that resentment can be too personal and egoistical, whereas indignation speaks more impersonally, about failures to abide the legitimate standards of one's normative community. It may also be the case—it is according to the way I use words—that indignation but not resentment can occur without angry feelings.

Michelle Mason's "Contempt as a Moral Attitude" (2003) is the first and best essay I know of that defends contempt as morally permissible, possibly required. Kate Abramson's "A Sentimentalist's Defense of Contempt, Shame, and Disdain" (2010) is extremely helpful on resentment and contempt in sentimentalist moral theory. In *Hard Feelings: The Moral Psychology of Contempt* (2013), Macalester Bell argues that, whereas resentment and indignation compel a hostile reaction toward the violator, contempt causes withdrawal from the perpetrator. Contempt is a member of a suite of attitudes comprising moral anger, resentment, contempt, disgust, and blame as well as forgiveness and reconciliation. Bell defends contempt as a morally appropriate response to the vices of superiority, arrogance, conceit, and its mates, what she calls "superbia." Indeed, Bell thinks contempt is not just understandable and, what is different, permissible, but that we should cultivate the virtue of apt contempt to deploy when we meet up with those who suffer superbia.

The best book I know of on the moral psychology of anger is David P. Barash and Judith Eve Lipton's *Payback: Why We Retaliate, Redirect Aggression, and Take Revenge* (2011). The book is an authoritative primer on the evolution of anger, the pain that anger causes the subject of anger and its targets, how it often overshoots, and why it may no longer be adaptive. It is also a heartfelt exploration of some practices that might help us overcome the "pain passing."

10. For Love's and Justice's Sake: The Attachment, Injustice, and Catharsis Defenses

Three excellent works by philosophers who question the dominant philosophical views about anger are Lawrence C. Becker's *A New Stoicism* (1998); Margaret Urban Walker's *Moral Repair: Reconstructing Moral Relations After Wrongdoing* (2006); and Lisa Tessman's *Burdened Virtues: Virtue Ethics for Liberatory Struggles* (2005), especially chapter 5, "The Burden of Political Resistance

Larry Becker is himself a stoic. He is also a handicapped philosopher, who suffered serious ravages from polio as a child. His book is a modern manual for what it means to be a stoic now, a "new stoic." Becker's stoic is passionate, but he works hard to purge himself of destructive emotions like anger, by all sorts of self-work, including by his commitment to stoic philosophy as a way of life.

Margaret Urban Walker's *Moral Repair* is a deep exploration of the philosophy behind truth and reconciliation, restorative justice, and transitional justice. These movements encourage treating festering anger in ways that vary among venting, forgiving, forgetting, forgiving and forgetting, allowing time to diminish anger, and resolving to live in peace. In chapter 4, "Resentment and Assurance," Walker accommodates resentment, "a kind of anger," while recommending diminishing the role that it is standardly given by philosophers. She helpfully explores the idea that there are other emotions, sadness and grief, for example, as well as practices of expressing outrage, mistrust, and plans to obstruct your plans, or crush your policies like bugs, and so on, that can serve as rebukes, possibly without the anger part, and which might be preferable, all things considered, to angry rebukes.

In *Burdened Virtues* Lisa Tessman explores the horrible predicament of oppressed people, especially of women and African Americans, who are unduly burdened by feelings of tremendous anger because of their treatment, and for whom anger may also be the best vehicle to "communicate their refusal to accept subordination." Tessman offers a deep meditation on five different arguments in favor of "oppositional anger" among feminists, while also giving voice to the possibility of practices of solidarity, firm rebuke, articulate and insistent claims of rights, and respect, without anger, as we know it.

Amia Srinivasan's "In Defence of Anger" (2014) is a meditation on the role of anger in racial and gender politics and gives powerful voice to the view that arguments against anger are often part of the arsenal of oppressors.

Martha Nussbaum's "Transitional Anger" (2015) marks some change in her view from the one I discuss from *The Therapy of Desire* (1994). Nussbaum's John Locke Lectures, given at Oxford in 2015, have just appeared as *Anger and Forgiveness* (2016) as this book was in press, and express further developments of her view about anger. Nussbaum is now more Stoic than Aristotelian— something of a reversal for her. Also watch for Myisha Cherry and Owen Flanagan, eds., *Moral Psychology of Anger*, which promises to be a good collection of new essays.

PART IV

Anthropologies

11

Self-Variations

PHILOSOPHICAL ARCHAEOLOGIES

The "category of the person" is, Marcel Mauss ([1938] 1985) teaches, a "delicate" one. It pertains to delicate matters, to who and what I am, to my sense of subjectivity, individuality, and privacy, to my most important relations, identity, aspirations, good, and fate. And it is historically delicate. The ways that what Mauss calls "conscious personalities" seem, to the subjects of those very conscious personalities, vary. Homeric persons are dutiful beings with disciplined minds. The Daoist sage experiences himself or herself as like a butterfly "fluttering about joyfully just as a butterfly would" accommodating the wind; as a creature who "does not engage in projects, does not seek benefit, does not avoid harm, and does not pursue happiness, does not follow any specific course" (*Zhuangzi* 2.39–48). The selves of Russian peasants in Tolstoy's short stories are simple, unreflective, and devout. The selves of the pietistic Lutherans for whom Kant speaks are selves governed by severe consciences, stern superegos. The Buddhist adept experiences himself or herself as No-Self (*anātman*), overcoming entirely the experience of separateness from other persons, the experience of himself or herself as an ego that wants, desires, and thirsts for things for itself. Some contemporary people have inner lives that mimic the bright lights and never-ending energy of the cities in which they live, selves in which there is a "24/7" bright lights performance of my very self for me.

Charles Taylor (1989) claims that the selves of modern people of the North Atlantic are—or at least are encouraged to be—highly reflective, opinionated, and judgmental, especially about one's own moral self and that of others. We are "strong evaluators." There is some Kant in our souls, as well as a fair dose of the ever-opinionated Nietzsche. But there is no Daoist butterfly in us (that would mean being a "wanton"). We are much too reflective to be simple religious people of the sort Tolstoy writes about, and there is no real market for serious Buddhist un-selfing, although there is a large market for New Age "buddhisms" of the ego-centered personal hygiene sort.

So, conscious personalities, what kind of selves there are, as well as conceptions of what kinds of selves ideally we ought to be, are historically variable and culturally conditioned. Furthermore, goods such as self-esteem and self-respect, including whether they are goods, vary in form and content. Some say one ought to feel self-esteem and self-respect only for actual accomplishment, getting an 'A' on the exam, others for effort, for studying, others for simply being alive and in school. Some think that self-esteem, self-respect, pride, and so on, ought to come with individual accomplishment; others that they should come only from participation in some collective accomplishment, in what we did, not in what I did or even what I did to bring about our collective achievement.

The idea that there is self-variation in various cultured ecologies, and that some of these reveal deep differences, not just superficial behavioral differences, trends, or fashions, serve as interpretive guides in this chapter. Understanding the nature of a self, a person, or an individual, how selves fit into various communities, what their stations and duties are, and with whom and with what values a person identifies, is delivered on the wings of an antecedent tradition, by way of a cultural history, in the form of something like a folk philosophy or, in heterogeneous societies, by amalgams of folk philosophies, which penetrate the blood and bones of participants in the form of life. These folk philosophies might, indeed they often do, appear in spiffed up, esoteric form among elites, among shamans, priests, theologians, and philosophers, charged with preserving the tradition in its pure form.[1] In both their refined and esoteric forms and in their folk and mundane forms, these, what Charles Taylor calls "inescapable frameworks," are penumbral; they are taught to us early on, seep into our consciousnesses, and are then carried by us, worn like lenses, through which we see, but barely notice. They frame and shadow what is there, determining whether what is there, is seen in high light or low light, focally or not.[2]

The Philosophical Penumbra

To better understand the archaeological method and its rationale, consider this analogy with a method deployed profitably in comparative cognitive psychology. In *The Geography of Thought* (2004), Richard Nisbett writes about differences in the cognitive psychology of East Asians and North Americans on a host of reasoning tasks, involving such things as sensitivity to figure and ground in perception. North Americans are better than Chinese and Japanese at remembering the number of fish in an aquarium, but less good at describing the surround. Or to put it the other way (note how the description matters to which group looks deficient), Chinese and Japanese are good at remembering the flora and fauna in an aquarium, but not as good as North Americans at counting the fish. Nisbett thinks that part of the explanation for such differences has to do with the relations among "folk metaphysics, tacit epistemology, and cognitive processes" (36). Chinese and Japanese metaphysics, epistemology, and aesthetics give relational fields priority over individual objects, whereas North American folk philosophical norms reverse the priority. This engenders different norms of attention, different preferred strategies for comprehending the world, which results in the differences in the aquarium exercise.

I hypothesize that self-variation across traditions, cultures, and subcultures, might be explained in similar ways. And I provide the beginnings of an argument that the hypothesis is credible, possibly true. I use the Buddhist view of No-Self as an example of a way of conceiving of "The Philosopher's Self" that is unusual by WEIRD lights, which reveals itself in the way ordinary Buddhists speak about themselves and that connects inside the Buddhist form of life with morality. No-Selves are metaphysically selfless and, according to the tradition, ought to work to be maximally unselfish in thought and action.

If we seriously entertain the idea that there are "inescapable frameworks" that orient peoples to conceive of the self and to be a self, then a natural method for understanding and evaluating self-variation suggests itself. The method is philosophical archaeology or genealogy. Nietzsche and Foucault are famous practitioners. The archaeological method recommends that we follow the normative philosophical structures of life, and try to understand self-variation in terms of difference in metaphysics, epistemology, ethics, and aesthetics.[3] Self-variations are always illuminated, sometimes best understood, in terms of the philosophical surround, in terms of the philosophical penumbra of a tradition, or in terms of intersections and interactions of traditions in a dynamic ecology.[4] The method does not assume remotely that a way of worldmaking is sufficient to explain self-variation, only that it is a useful explanatory resource.

As for normative disagreement and critique: if and when there is disagreement between conceptions or traditions about how best to conceive a self, how to be a self, what the characters of excellent selves are, how selves ought ideally to be, we can seek to understand and perhaps resolve the disagreement by locating and examining the grounds for these differing judgments in the background philosophy, in the way of worldmaking that makes sense of and warrants them. Does that way of worldmaking, that metaphysics of self, conceive of the self, its good, and its fate in a way that makes sense? Is it better than the alternative, the other option or options?

This method of understanding and critique has several advantages. First, it locates sources of normative disagreement in the ecologies in which such disagreements typically root, surface, and grow. Second, it help us understand what in addition to behavior needs to change if we want to change ourselves, the kind of people we are. We may have to change significant aspects of our form of life. At the limit, we may have to change the entire form of life and consider becoming entirely different kinds of persons—although obviously not in our lifetimes and not for our particular selves and cohort.

Self-Variations: A Dozen Examples

Here are twelve specific examples of self-variations that philosophers, psychologists, and anthropologists claim exist:

1. *"The Philosopher's Self."* There is disagreement among professionals, philosophers, psychologists, neuroscientists, and theologians, as well as among ordinary people the world over, about what it is that is the subject of experience, what I am, where I am, how I came to be, what my fate is, and how I keep track of all I am, do, as well as all that happens to me. The candidate list is vast and ranges from ψυχή, *anima*, *nephesh* (נפש), *nafs* (نَفْس), and *ātman*, to the human organism, the brain, a part of the brain, to the idea that there is no "Mind's 'I.'" The "I" is a tempting illusion produced by, again take your pick, the stream of consciousness, memory, the speed at which the brain keeps track of and updates information about what this individual organism is doing, or, in certain postapocalyptic circles, each of us is a simulation in the Matrix run by the Artificial Intelligentsia.[5]

2. *Porous and Nonporous Selves.* Clifford Geertz, the anthropologist, writes that the standard Western conception of the person is "a bounded, unique, more or less integrated motivational and cognitive universe, a dynamic center of awareness, emotion, judgment, and action organized into a distinctive whole and set contrastively both against other such wholes and against a social and natural background" (1973, 57). Social and cultural psychologists (Shweder and Bourne 1982; Markus and Kitayama 1991), contrast Geertz's "independent" self with the "interdependent" self. This contrast is also described as one between "individualist" and "collectivist" or "idiocentric" and "allocentric" cultures, typically North Americans and northern Europeans, on one side, and East Asians, South Asians, Amerindians, and Africans, on the other side (Triandis et al. 1988).

3. *Self-Constitution.* North Americans experience their traits of character as in them, inside themselves, as traits they have. "Wherever I go, there I am." I am shy, adventurous, creative, or whatever exactly the Myers-Briggs personality inventory or the Minnesota Multi-Phasic Personality Inventory says I am. East Asians experience themselves, their traits of character, as less matters of individual character or personality, and as more dependent on particular situations and relationships, as coconstituted relationally (Markus and Kitayama 1991, 2010).

4. *Storied Selves.* Many psychologists and philosophers, Jerome Bruner (2002), Paul Ricoeur (1984), and Alasdair MacIntyre ([1981] 1984a), for example, say that selves are essentially narrative, that narrative is the essential genre for self-making, self-understanding, and self-representing. But Galen Strawson thinks that some selves might be constitutionally episodic, and that, in addition, the demand of narrativity is a regimen of responsibility and accountability imposed by certain kinds of cultures, not a discovery of the way the self is necessarily, or the way responsibility must be conceived. A narrative or diachronic self "naturally figures oneself, considered as a self, as something that was there in the (further) past and will be there in the (further) future. . . . If one is Episodic, by contrast . . . one does not figure oneself, considered as a self, as something that was there in the (further) past and will be there in the (further) future" (2004, 430). There is evidence in anthropology that there is variation in whether and how much selves are diachronic, narrative, and understand themselves to be embedded in either or both a personal and cultural history, or, on the other hand, synchronic, present focused, and more ahistorical (personally and culturally). The Achuar of the Ecuadorean Amazon (Descola 1996) and the Piraha of the Brazilian Amazon (Everett 2009) might fit the episodic bill.

5. *Virtuous Selves.* The quality of a person and their character, the goodness of a self, is normally, across the globe, thought to be a function of virtue. Even if there are universal virtues, they are ranked differently in different traditions. Compassion (*karuna*) is the highest virtue among Buddhists, whereas justice as fairness holds pride of place among North Americans. Confucians rank family loyalty and filial piety (*xiao*) higher than Americans do, and so on.[6] If a good self is a virtuous one by the lights of a moral conception or tradition, then different ecologies call on us to be different selves.[7]

6. *Ideal Emotional Selves.* Children's books in different cultures and subcultures, for example, among peoples of Japan, Hong Kong, Taiwan, on one side, and the United States and Canada, on the other side, and between traditions such as Christianity and Buddhism, model different faces and emotional states as ideal. American books model "happy-happy-joy-joy" faces and endorse states that are high-arousal positive (HAP) ones—"excited, enthusiastic, and elated"; Buddhist books model low-arousal positive (LAP) faces, a look of calm, and endorse internal serenity and equanimity (Tsai 2007; Tsai et al. 2007a; Tsai et al. 2007b; Tsai et al. 2007c).

7. *Authentic and Inauthentic Selves.* North Americans value a kind of self we call "authentic," where this involves being true to one's personal values, more highly than do East Asians, who think that a

good person often stands down from their personal self preferences when the collective or the tradition demands it. There are many ways to describe this difference, every one of which expresses a clear normative preference for one side or the other: willful versus self-effacing; authentic versus inauthentic; egotistical versus communal.

8. *Self-Reference.* When four- to six-year-old children in America and China are asked to report on daily events, the proportion of self-reference is three times greater among the Americans. American kids focus on what *I* did and what happened to *me*. Overall, American children report on fewer events, usually only the ones that mattered significantly to them personally, and not neutral or third-party actions, such as that the teacher put all the toys away. The American children also make twice as many references as the Chinese children to their own internal states (not just their own doings and deeds), to what *I wanted*, whether *my desires* were met or thwarted, what *my feelings* and *my emotions* were (Nisbett 2004, 87–88).[8]

9. *Self-Recognition.* North Americans prefer jobs in which personal initiative is encouraged and individual merit is rewarded and publicly acknowledged, Japanese and Singaporeans do not, and Europeans are intermediate (Hampden-Turner and Trompenaars 1993). North Americans believe that individuals can pull themselves up by their own bootstraps more than individuals in other cultures believe this, and are less likely to think that good or bad luck is a major factor in accomplishment, success, and desert (Clark 1997).[9]

10. *Self-Comprehension.* Indians, Chinese, and Koreans are less susceptible than Americans to the *fundamental attribution error*, which involves overrating the causal influence of stable character traits and underestimating situational or contextual factors. An American is more likely to infer from an individual act of kindness, for example, giving a dollar to a homeless person—that he himself is a generous person, or that whoever did it (a third party) is generous, whereas an Indian is more likely to appeal to particular features of the situation—for example, the behavior of the homeless person (he asked politely) or his appearance (he looked as if he needed it for food, not drugs or booze) (J. G. Miller 1984; Flanagan 1991; Markus and Kitayama 1991; Nisbett 2004).

11. *Self-Serving Bias.* North Americans are more prone than Amerindians, Mexicans, Fijians, Southern Italians, and East Asians to the *self-serving bias*, thinking one is better across various dimensions—looks, intelligence, and so on—than others. Garrison Keillor calls this the "Lake Wobegon Effect," where everyone is, by their own judgment, in the top 5 percent.[10]

12. *Positive Self-Illusions.* North Americans are more prone than people
    of other cultures to believe that they are in control of outcomes,
    controlling the sex of babies at insemination, winning lotteries, or
    that bad things, getting cancer, divorced, in car accidents, and so
    on, won't befall them, than is sensible, given that they are told the
    relevant base rates. Technically, positive illusions involve mistakes
    (they are "illusions"), but they are good mistakes (the "positive" part)
    since people who make them are happier than those who do not (S.
    E. Taylor 1989; S. E. Taylor and Brown 1994). In North American
    populations only moderately depressed people are realists and do not
    suffer positive illusions.

WEIRD Mistakes?

The twelve examples embed and express metaphysical, epistemic, moral, and
aesthetic considerations. The method of philosophical archaeology recommends attempting to understand these self-variations by digging deep into the
philosophical roots of the form of life—which is often an amalgam or fusion
of multiple threads—that embeds, possibly causes, engenders, strengthens, or
even is produced by the self-variation in question. I am especially interested
in the connection between, on the one hand, the self, including whether there
is such a thing, and conceptions of the self, its nature and its good, and, on the
other hand, selfishness.

The first three self-variations (1–3) pertain to the fundamental or universal
metaphysical and psychobiological architecture of the self, including whether
there is such a thing. The next four self-variations (4–7) involve normative
self-variation, variation that involves ideals and norms for good selves, for
selves that are morally excellent, well put together, orderly, harmonious, ful-
filled, happy, flourishing, complete, and successful in the eyes of society, God,
or the cosmos. The last five self-variations (8–12) are epistemic, they involve
differences in ways of knowing and speaking accurately about one's self and
other selves.[11]

How should we evaluate these twelve self-variations? Has some group made
a mistake? What kind of mistake? How consequential is the mistake? Are there
any connections among the mistakes?

A quick review of 1–12 might lead one to think that some differences depicted are, as it were, just differences, options in logical, metaphysical, and
normative possibility space, where there is no mistake, perhaps because there
are no facts, or they are not known, or they are unknowable, which could or
do determine the best view. For example, the nature of "the philosopher's self"
(1) might be considered essentially contested. The question I leave off the present list but discuss in other chapters, of whether humans are devils or angels or

admixtures, the question of first human nature, might be judged as nowadays getting worked out by human scientists, but still not established. Questions about the proper economy of emotions and virtues and the proper hierarchy of values—whether justice or compassion is the most important virtue (5), whether a serene life is better than an ecstatic one, or perhaps whether this depends on one's personality, one's values, one's stage of life (6), or whether authenticity involves standing by personal or communal values (7)—are ones that decent, thoughtful peoples answer differently, and sometimes for good reasons that pertain to contingent facts about particular cultural histories.

Several self-variations among 1–12 might be judged the results of conventions that work well enough inside cultures that designed them, and do not involve any obvious mistake. For example, every culture wants to maximize useful information in the minds of individuals, as well as in social communication, given local norms, beliefs about what matters, and so on. This naturally leads to different kinds of memory, and different methods of reporting what I did, what others did, who did well, who did badly, whether norms were abided or not, and by whom. It is not surprising therefore that differences emerge in the norms of self-reporting and narration (4). On this way of thinking, the self-variation that involves high first-person reference relative to all that really happened (8) or the focus on the causal significance of certain individual traits as opposed to all the causal forces involved in what I did or what happened (10), might be understood as people simply abiding the norms of what we, the audience, think you ought to pay attention to, perhaps because we think it is what you have the most control over, such things as what you did at school, not what the teacher did, or what inside you caused you to hit your classmate, and so on.

Another less liberal and less tolerant interpretation is that some of the dozen self-variations really do depict mistakes by most anyone's lights. And we know who has made them, namely, WEIRD folk more than non-WEIRD folk. For example, the fundamental attribution error (10) is the error of overrating the causal influence of character traits compared to admixtures of multiple traits and situations. The self-serving bias (11) is a bias. And the tendency to positive illusions (12) is a tendency to illusion. Furthermore, these few clear mistakes look suspiciously contagious, as if they ramify into other self-variations on the list or, possibly, that they are all produced by some common root cause that leads to some WEIRD tendencies. The errors in 10–12 look like reasonable suspects for bad tendencies that spill over into, cause, or contribute to several other self-variations on the list, for example, in cultural differences in self-ascriptions of stable inner traits (3), high rates of first-person pronoun usage (8), beliefs about the importance of personal versus communal desires and preferences (7), how much individual, agent-centered credit as opposed to communal credit ought to accrue for one's accomplishments (9), and beliefs about individual immunity to luck (11). These can all be viewed as instances of more general mistakes such as are depicted in 10–12, and subsumed under them, or as I have just said, they can all be thought to have a common source in some single deep place in folk philosophy.

Insofar as there are some clear mistakes about the self on the list of self-variations, they are made disproportionately by WEIRD people rather than by the groups they are compared with. This ought to get our attention since tendencies to error, false beliefs, and the like, are generally thought, across the globe, to be a bad thing.

In order to assess what is going on here, we need to dig into the folk philosophies that in part embed and account for these variations, and that will often be called on by those inside a tradition, to explain why they think, speak, act, and value as they do. First, we ask whether there is something about a form of life or way of worldmaking that can account for a kind of self-variation. Then, we examine the merits of that way of worldmaking relative to alternatives. We look to see whether the reasons in the philosophical surround that support a particular kind of self-variation are good reasons—reasons of the right kind. My aim is to offer a beginning, an example of how to have this sort of discussion. My guiding principle is that if there are not good reasons for being or conceiving of the self in a certain way, we ought to consider changing or adjusting both it and the philosophical surround that sustains it, especially if there are alternative views that are better.

I do not try to examine the sources of each of 1–12 in the philosophical surround. I focus on 1, "the philosopher's self," and 2, the idea that some selves are porous and some not. And I focus on one example, the Buddhist No-Self view, which provides a pretty vivid contrast case to a more familiar neoliberal, individualistic view of self that is more common in WEIRD precincts. It is fairly easy to see that and how these ten other self-variations relate to the first two. I encourage others to continue the archaeological investigation on 3–10.

Contested Philosopher's Selves

The first self-variation (1) pertains to variation, différence, in conceptions of the "Mind's 'I'," in views about the metaphysical essence of persons. It is difference in conceptions of the "Mind's 'I'" that vary presumably, not what the "Mind's 'I'" really is, since, one might expect, there is some fact of the matter—a metaphysical fact—some right answer to that question, even if we lack agreement on what it is. One might also think that this debate is completely esoteric, a matter to be duked out between philosophers, theologians, and scientists, and utterly inconsequential to ordinary people and their lives. But if one had this thought, one would be wrong. Views about the nature of the "Mind's 'I'" are immensely consequential in ordinary life, people fight and die over metaphysical and theological matters, and school curricula in places all over the earth are battlegrounds for views on whether humans are en-souled or only embodied, whether my essence is everlasting or finite.

Indeed, in the West, the classical philosophical problem of the self is deeply implicated in philosophical theology, with the question of how it is possible that this embodied human individual can survive death and live an everlasting life in heaven.[12] If the ground of identity is, as naturalists say, an individual's complex human body-in-the-world, then I am the same individual so long as I have the same body, and I die with it—my eternal rest is one of being altogether gone, done, over. At death, I evaporate. Or, perhaps more hopefully, I recycle—from stardust, back to stardust, still around but dispersed, part of the impersonal cosmos. If, on the other hand, the ground of identity is my soul, then "I" might survive the transition from being embodied to being disembodied. My eternal rest might be one where I survive as me, possibly for all eternity.

There is a tradition in Western philosophy that asks this question: What is THE SELF? The pretense of the question, its very form, and the use of the definite article, suggests, perhaps it even assumes, that there is a self, that the self is a definite thing, something substantial, and that selves have a nature independently of how those very selves think of themselves. THE SELF, in this sense, belongs on the ontological tables of elements with other fundamental features of reality, perhaps in a trinity with GOD and MATTER.[13]

In some places on earth, and over the course of human history, many of the assumptions and presumptions that lie behind our quest to understand the self are absent. Among peoples of South, Southeast, and East Asia, especially Buddhists, Daoists, and neo-Confucians, there is the belief that all things, including all selves, are dependent, relational, emergent, and ephemeral phenomena—"arisings" that last awhile. Buddhism can serve as a master example of a tradition that conceives of the self in an unusual way, as No-Self (anātman), and claims a straightforward connection between conceiving of the self as No-Self and being compassionate toward all sentient beings.[14] Buddhists say that there is no self (ātman) of the immutable, indestructible, timeless sort.[15] Instead, there is No-Self (anātman). No-Self is a metaphysical view that is part of the "inescapable framework," the penumbra for Buddhists.[16] The metaphysical view of No-Self permeates Buddhist folk philosophy. Ordinary people in Thailand and Tibet speak the language of No-Self, Impermanence, and Emptiness. My hypothesis is that No-Self helps explain why Buddhists prize compassion and lovingkindness as the most important virtues (5), why serenity and equanimity rather than happy-happy-joy-joy states are preferred (6), why they are less prone to constant self-reference (7, 8, 9), attribution of essential character traits (3, 10), and self-puffery (5, 6, 8, 9) than WEIRD souls. No-Self is the name for a complex way of being-in-the-world that in both its explicit philosophical form and in its implicit sociocultural form(s), in what we call a worldview, plays a significant—not the only—role in explaining differences such as 1–12.[17]

I do not mean to make the point that we, the children of Abraham, think of souls as eternal gems inside impermanent bodies, and that Buddhists do not, and leave it at that. "Different strokes for different folk." Many WEIRD folk are secular thinkers who do not believe in Abrahamic souls. It is, however, an interesting and important question whether secular WEIRD people are not still in the grip of a certain concept of the individual who makes his or her own fate, and who succeeds as a person by himself or herself, which is originally a child of that tradition, where God determines our eternal individual fate on Judgment Day.[18] The purpose of the example is to invite the reader to reflect on the Buddhist view of No-Self as a good example of a deep philosophical difference that helps us understand and explain such self-variations as might occur between the way Buddhists, on the one hand, and WEIRD people, on the other, do 1–12, and also at the same time to call on the reader to consider what, if anything—beyond unfamiliarity—is mistaken about the Buddhist metaphysics of No-Self. If it is a good view, and if it warrants moral selflessness, then we have perhaps some reason to rethink both our metaphysics and our morals.

The Buddhist Way of Worldmaking

Buddhism is a comprehensive form of life, a complex way of being that exemplifies the ancient idea of a philosophy as a way of life.[19] Seeing the way reality is and seeing the way I exist or subsist, or unfold in reality, helps ground and motivate a certain way of being-in-the-world that we, from a Western perspective, would say is virtuous, good, and moral.[20] Being fully awakened involves, entails, or motivates goodness, selflessness. How is it that reality is, and how do I exist or subsist in it? Here is the Buddhist answer:

i. Impermanence (*anicca*; Sanskrit: *anitya*): Everything is impermanent. Nothing lasts forever. Good things pass; bad things happen (*dukkha*).

ii. Dependent Origination and Dependent Being
   (*pratītyasamutpāda*): everything is interdependent; there is no such thing as independent being; everything is becoming, an unfolding in various relational fields (coming to be, ceasing to be, child of, great grandchild of, sister of, taller than, faster than, nearby, far away, long before, long after, etc.), including relations of causes and effects (made by, formed by, killed by, loved by).

iii. No-Self (*annata; anātman*): A person is one of the dependently originating things, one of the constituents of the ever-changing flux that is the world, the sum of everything that is changing.[21]

A person, like all other things that seem to exist as independent substances (think of diamonds that are said to last forever but came from coal and that last a long time, but not remotely forever), has only conventionally or pragmatically endowed stability. And thus personal identity, being the same person over time, is not an all-or-nothing matter; it is a matter of psychobiological continuity and connectedness. There is no permanent diamond in the rough that is me, that makes me exactly the same person over time. One consequence is that even if I have perfect self-knowledge of what I want now, or, what is different, what I need now, the self that gets it, whatever it is—will be different, and may not like, want, or need what it gets.

iv. Emptiness (śūnyatā): The word śūnyatā comes from the Sanskrit word that means "hollow" and can be understood this way: First, start with the doctrine of No-Self and think of it as a doctrine about horizontal-diachronic decomposition or reduction, perhaps "blending" is the best word. My boundaries, conceived as the being-in-time that I am, are not clear. My identity or personhood today is different from my identity yesterday and tomorrow. Conventionally, I am the same guy I was yesterday and will be tomorrow, but ultimately (really) I'm not. Likewise, conceived at this moment in time, synchronically, I am a composite being. I am made up of organic parts. My organs are composite as well. The cells that compose the organs are composite too, and so on, possibly ad infinitum, or even if not ad infinitum, at least until the whole seems to dissolve into radically unfamiliar "things," events, and processes—bosons, fermions, and quantum information—and to lose its substantiality.[22] When the deconstruction proceeds this way, there are no things as they seem, indeed there are no things at all.[23]

The upshot is this: Because of (i–iv), it is a mistake to think that at the ultimate level, as opposed to the conventional level, there are any independent, nonrelational entities that exist or subsist on their own, outside of relations with other "things," events, and processes. In our terms this would mean that neither science nor first philosophy discovers or uncovers essences.[24]

But, one might object: Surely the periodical table of elements reveals essences. Reply: In cosmology and astrophysics, no one thinks that most members of that esteemed periodic table, aside from helium, hydrogen, beryllium, and lithium existed as the Big Bang banged 14 billion years ago. So, most of the 118 "essences" or elements on the periodic table are simply sightings of certain stabilities that occur over certain large swaths of space-time, but that are not forever, not eternal. One would have to see whether and how far one could take this sort of reply—for example, to the laws of nature itself, to the four early or original elements, or whatever there was, at the time of the Big Bang. I am not opinionated about this matter. The Dalai Lama says that he believes in the Big Bang, if that is where the scientific consensus is. But he also says that the Big Bang 14 billion years ago could not be the origination of all that there is, and thus it is more likely that there was an infinite number of Big Bangs all the way back. In my experience, Buddhists are almost always unimpressed by first-mover arguments for the existence of God, seeing nothing unsatisfactory with the prospect of an infinite regress of universes, each of which is not created by any agent.

The Moral of Metaphysics or the Metaphysics of Morals?

Buddhism is intended first and foremost as a way of thinking and being that works to overcome anxiety, frustration, and suffering. A key part of the therapy is to understand the way things really are. How's that? They are impermanent. "Things" arise and pass in fields of relations that encompass all that is unfolding, the mother of all unfoldings, Unfolding Itself. The unfolding unfolds. What there is, and all there is, is unfolding. Therefore, it is a fiction to think that I am a stable thing, especially that I am or possess a special eternal aspect, an essence that the unfolding, the universe, reality preserves, or even more implausibly, cares especially, or at all, about preserving.

Deflating myself, my diachronic and even my synchronic swath—the latter is the work or Emptiness, *śūnyatā*—seeing that whether I am conceived horizontally or vertically I am not a substantial thing but, rather, relationally constituted, as are you, and as are all other things, and also that we all suffer the slings and arrows, as well as the pleasures and treasures, of the unfolding, might make me care less about my own satisfactions and sufferings and more about yours.

Many Buddhists say these recognitions "should" make me more compassionate. Some think that really grasping Impermanence, No-Self, and Emptiness WILL make me more compassionate. Maybe. One might wonder why seeing or understanding this much will or should warrant virtue and unselfishness rather than a resigned nihilism or a frantic hedonism.[25] Sure, one might say, I am an ephemeral creature, but while I persist or subsist, I am a zone of *conatus*, of wanting and desiring, so I am going for all the gusto I can get, maximal pleasure in this vicinity, the vicinity that seems full of me-ness.

There is a range of responses to this question internal to the Buddhisms. Here are two familiar types of response:

1. *Metaphysics Lite* takes as authoritative the historical Buddha's insistence that the dharma he teaches is moral and practical. It is a way to overcome suffering, period. In famous scriptures (Ñāṇamoli

and Bodhi 1995, 63, 72), Siddartha Gautama, the historical Buddha, is asked ten metaphysical questions—Why is there something rather than nothing? Where does space begin and time end? Is the cosmos eternal? Is there an afterlife?—and says that these questions are unanswerable, even as he accepts and channels certain common cultural beliefs about reincarnation, karma, and so on. Once one has attended to the marks of existence: the ubiquity of unsatisfactoriness (*dukkha*), that everything is impermanent (*anicca*), including the self (*ānatman*), that what is bad will pass, that what is good will pass, that craving and being overly attached to certain outcomes rarely brings satisfaction, and so on, one will be in the mood to want to be less egoistic and selfish, more compassionate and lovingkind, and less anxious and fussed up about things that don't really matter. *Metaphysics lite* offers primarily this lesson: Look around. There is suffering. Those who suffer least, those who are happiest, are those who are not caught up in their own egos, they are compassionate, lovingkind, and unselfish. Life, yours and ours, will go better if you are less selfish, at the limit, if you are morally selfless, as you already are metaphysically in a different sense of selfless.

2. *Metaphysics Heavy* emphasizes the importance of cognitively absorbing the four deep truths of Buddhist wisdom—Impermanence, Dependent Origination, No-Self, and the Emptiness of all things— possibly by way of arduous meditation practice, where one grasps these truths by insight or intuition, in some ineffable way, or by grasping the rational arguments for these truths, which one can then teach and transmit over time to novices. Grasping Buddhist metaphysics conceptually (in texts, debate, dharma teachings) and nonconceptually (as meditative insight) will seed (not entail) the insight that there is no deep difference between my good and yours, and motivate me to become compassionate, lovingkind, and selfless. The metaphysics of No-Self, Emptiness, and their suite, seed and motivate selflessness in the moral sense.[26]

Readers will be familiar with this spectrum that runs from metaphysically lite moral training to metaphysically heavy moral training in our own precincts. Secular humanists typically try to raise their children to be good without much in the way of theological or metaphysical teaching, whereas orthodox Jews, Christians, and Muslims embed the ethics in a theology, metaphysics, and theory of salvation.[27] I was raised in an Irish Catholic family. My beloved father's favorite childrearing technique was a stern "Straighten up and fly right." This might seem to demand a metaphysically lite reading, but in our family, among people like us, it embedded the theology and ethics of the *Baltimore catechism*, which was the "inescapable framework" for us, and so it was in fact metaphysically heavy. Hermeneutics is required to get beneath the surface of many ways of speaking and acting.

Oneness

We might say that the highest Buddhist virtues of compassion and lovingkindness for all sentient beings are motivated inside a philosophical background of oneness that at once justifies, reinforces, and engenders deeper commitment to that very perspective of oneness.[28] In fact, the entire philosophical penumbra, as well as normative habits of a Buddhist heart-mind, can be framed in terms of oneness, which can be glossed in several, not incompatible ways:

- *Cosmic oneness*: I am part of everything that unfolds. My arising depends on everything that has arisen before, and my being and my passing will affect the quality of what comes after, it will affect the goodness or badness of the world after I am gone.
- *Historical oneness*: The well-being of all sentient beings now depends on the actions of sentient beings that are long gone. The well-being of future beings depends on what we do now, how we live at this time in the unfolding of the cosmos.
- *Sentient being oneness*: All "I's," all "selves" are impermanent, but there is a common feature that makes all sentient beings one, a common creature: We are all the same in having experiences of pain, suffering, ill-being, and well-being.
- *Care oneness*: I (we all do) naturally care about the suffering of others. I have some natural motivation that others not suffer. This is called *bodhicitta*.

These four ways of describing oneness in Buddhism differ in the following ways. *Cosmic oneness* depicts the maximal metaphysical interconnectedness of everything that there is. *Historical oneness* speaks of my (and everyone's) causal dependency on everything, including all those sentient beings that have come before me, and that of future creatures on the beings and doings of those that exist now. I am one of the lucky ones who got to be (something rather than nothing), most didn't and won't, that is, there is an infinite number of possible beings that are never made actual. *Sentient being oneness* speaks of our common, unified predicament, that we are (all) creatures who are impermanent and suffer. *Care oneness* depicts a universal natural motivational concern for the well-being of others, not just one's self. *Care oneness* says nothing about our causal interdependencies. Instead, it speaks about a relation that is just as fundamental to who and what we are as any causal relation. We are the kinds of creatures who have care or concern that at least some others not suffer. We are caring beings. There is some fellow-feeling in our hearts and minds from the get-go. Caring is a fundamental human disposition that we experience as a source of pure goodness, and might, if certain other conditions are satisfied, have a powerful desire to tap into and develop (*bodhicitta*).

Objection and Replies to No-Self

But, one says, "It is very hard to understand this, to comprehend that I am No-Self (*annata*; Skt.: *anātman*) and that I am empty (*śūnyatā*)," to which the right answer is that, yes, it is, especially for those of us who have been raised to think of ourselves and our selves in entirely different ways.

It is also very hard to understand why comprehending these metaphysical facts gives me reason to want to be a maximally compassionate and lovingkind being. The reply to this second concern, worry, or objection is to acknowledge that the metaphysical facts do not, on their own, provide sufficient reason to be maximally compassionate and lovingkind. Further cognitive and affective work is required to motivate virtue. This is where meditation and mindfulness come in. "Systematic meditation on the four Holy Truths, as on the basic facts of life, is a central task of the Buddhist life" (Conze 1951, 43). The goal is to fully absorb the Buddhist habits of the heart that engender (the four kinds of) oneness—Cosmic, Causal, Sentient-being, and Care oneness. Only if these are absorbed, is egoism mitigated.

Still the objection resurfaces: Even if I see that everything is interconnected, that I am not unless everything else is, and that I am causally dependent on what and who came before me, as those who will come after me are dependent on the world I leave, the world I have every so slightly affected, it is possible that I do not "give a shit" about anyone else or anything, about any worldly state of affairs—the future environment, the justice of the political economy—that does not affect me "such-as-i-am-now." One can even cite facts to support this egoistic attitude. What is done is done, what came before is over, those who came before are dead; none of the past can be undone or affected by what I do now. Furthermore, even if I am No-Self in the sense that I do not remain exactly the same going forward, even if self-sameness is a matter of degree, my No-Self going forward—the going forward of this "owen-flanagan-thingamajig," unfolding, event or process—is much more psychologically continuous and connected to me, to my No-Self now, to the self-stage of this-guy-i-am, and to the unfoldings of my loved ones, however cosmically insignificant they also are, than it is connected to you or to some starving guy or gal in Botswana, future Americans, and so on.

At this point in the conversation, as the egoist makes his case, Buddhism calls upon us to notice, to tap into a relation that is perhaps just as important as any causal or constitutive relation, the care relation, which directs us to the deep sources of fellow-feeling inside us (*bodhicitta*), to a side of ourselves, which even if not expansively or universally loving, is at least not radically ego-istic. It is not as if seeing that I am metaphysically No-Self, or noticing that I care for the well-being of some others beyond the boundaries of my own skin are sufficient to make me expansively or universally loving or compassionate. There is no sufficient analytic, deductive, or motivational entailment. What there is, and all there is, is some kind of seeing and reflective endorsement of what makes sense and what seems good to develop in my nature. There is also the fact, whose importance cannot be overestimated, that there is normally cul-tural permission, often encouragement inside Buddhist forms of life, to cul-tivate oneself in one direction, the unselfish direction, rather than the selfish direction. Neoliberals perhaps are not orienting their children in the same way.

Is to Ought? Selflessness to Unselfishness?

The question arises: How do Buddhists get from "is" to "ought"? How ex-actly do truths such as Impermanence, Dependent Origination, No-Self, and Emptiness imply, entail, or engender unselfishness?[29] The answer just given is that these truths do not by themselves imply or entail a way of life. These philosophical facts, despite being metaphysical and thus deep, are still just facts, whereas compassion and lovingkindness are not facts—they are values, norms, conative states, almost certainly in their mature forms, virtues. But how can compassion and lovingkindness for all sentient beings be grounded or again, what is different, how can these great (*maha*) virtues actually gain motivational bearing? One answer for how the motivating or engendering re-lation works inside the version of Buddhism that includes karma and rebirth is prudence. One gains liberation, *moksha* or nirvana, only if one achieves en-lightenment, where enlightenment involves deep comprehension or absorp-tion of the truths of Impermanence, No-Self, and so on, and also if one lives as a maximally virtuous person, a sage, a saint, or a bodhisattva in the last in a series of many lives that yield Buddhahood, and then—and only then—re-lease, *moksha*, nirvana.

My view is that there is no direct logical or motivational implication from the metaphysics of No-Self to selfless morality. Something additional is re-quired: The relevant insights about the metaphysics of personhood need to be paired with some kind of a grasping of, or calling to, something more moti-vationally powerful than even a deep philosophical truth. Here is a possibil-ity: What one grasps or experiences in the work of meditation on the truths of Impermanence, Dependent Origination, No-Self, and Emptiness is a calling—something akin to an overpowering desire, which, thanks to the prior work of philosophical preparation in No-Self and its suite, as well as tapping into *bodhicitta*, one sees no reason to refuse.[30] Once one has understood that we are all interrelated, that my good is tied up with the good of all other creatures, my ego's guard is down, and it is down for principled reasons. I am called upon to attend to the suffering of all sentient beings and I find the call appealing, possibly compelling.[31]

Porous and Nonporous Persons

So far I have focused on the Buddhist No-Self as a contrastive case of "the philosopher's self," to the picture of the self endorsed in the Abrahamic religious traditions as well as in the secular philosophical traditions born and shaped in Abrahamic precincts. The contrast provides evidence that there are unexplored (by us) ways of conceiving "the philosopher's self" that are credible in their own right, and that connect in complex ways to varieties of moral possibility that are good. Buddhist metaphysics of No-Self emphasizes impermanence and interdependency. We live in precarious worlds (*dukkha*) and how each of us fares as an individual depends very little on what I do alone, and almost completely on what we do together.

I now turn to #2 on the list of self-variations because it contrasts selves precisely along this dimension, interdependent, porous selves versus independent, nonporous selves. I am interested in what the contrast comes to and whether and how it captures some important differences between Buddhist and WEIRD selves.

Selves allegedly distribute themselves across cultures in ways that are described as more or less communitarian or more or less individualistic (interdependent versus independent, collectivist versus individualistic, allocentric versus idiocentric, autonomous versus relational), North Americans and northern Europeans, on one side, and East Asians, South Asians, Amerindians, and Africans, on the other. The alleged differences are described in many, not incompatible ways. Here is a picture that claims to depict or model these differences. Call it the PICTURE (see Figure 11.1).

There are two ways that the relevant kinds of self-variation depicted in the PICTURE and that matter to ethics are typically described in the literature in cultural psychology and anthropology:

- Some peoples conceive their well-being more in terms of how some unit larger (more inclusive) than their self is faring, the family, the firm, their church, their community, their nation-state, all humans, and even all sentient beings. So I am well only if I am well and my family (firm, community etc.) is well. I might, perhaps, never feel, think, or say I am fine if those I love are not well or, what is more, if the unit I love is not well, for example, not functioning harmoniously. One might naturally say that people who evaluate their well-being in terms of the quantity or quality of well-being beyond themselves

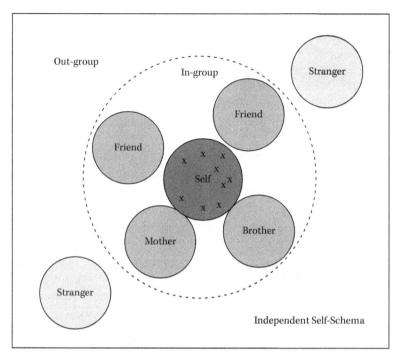

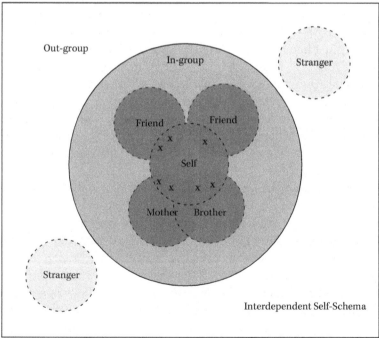

FIGURE 11.1 Independent and Interdependent Self-Schema. Adapted from Markus and Kitayama (1991) and Heine (2008).

are less selfish, more caring, and so on than those who evaluate well-being more narrowly.[32]

- Some peoples conceive their nature as *constituted* more by how others with whom one is in relation (certain others, many others) are, how they are faring, what they are doing, whether their projects are worthy, and whether they are succeeding or failing at their projects. One way of seeing oneself as actually constituted by (made up by) wide relations and a larger unit than myself comes from conceiving of oneself in terms of the totality of roles one occupies or enacts. Daughter of, mother of, sister of, girls' soccer coach, teacher of, and so on. The contrastive case is one where a person conceives herself less in terms of social roles and communal relations and more in terms of certain self-possessed features, her intelligence, her wit, her work ethic, her dedication to the girls' soccer team or to her students. The lives so conceived might look similar from the outside, but are experienced very differently by the participants. We might naturally speak of persons who are constituted more by relations and roles as possessed of fused identities (Wong 2006a).

Like the differences in views about the "The Philosopher's Self," differences along the dimensions of porous and nonporous persons ramify. First of all, if it is true that persons can differ along the porous-nonporous dimensions the way psychologists and anthropologists claim they do, then this reveals certain facts about first human nature, Namely, whatever human first nature is like, egoistic, altruistic, or mixed, it is plastic enough to allow a significant amount of shape-shifting. And this means that second selves can take on radically different forms in different traditions. Furthermore, 2 implicates 4, 5, 6, and 7, because if peoples differ along dimensions of porous-nonporous, independent-interdependent, individualist-collectivist, then they self-conceive and narrate in different ways (3, 4, 8, 9, 10, 11, 12), and abide different norms of human excellence (5, 6, 7).

The first important feature of the PICTURE is the way the boundaries, the borderlands, between the self, significant others, and out-groups are represented. Dotted lines indicate porous borders; firm lines indicate nonporous borders, fences that cannot be breeched. For porous persons, but not for nonporous persons, one sees by the overlap and open border design both well-being collectivism according to which I seem well to myself only if those I am in relation with are well, and wide, overlapping, constitution relations according to which I see myself as made up by certain essential relations to others not only by properties I possess as an individual. Interestingly, whereas independent selves have firm boundaries inside their group, they have more open borders than dependent selves have between the in-group and strangers and out-groups. Interdependent selves reverse the border design, open to in-group members, even coconstituted by them, but closed to out-group members.[33] Remember Clifford Geertz's claim that the standard Western conception of the person is "a bounded, unique, more or less integrated motivational and cognitive universe, a dynamic center of awareness, emotion, judgment, and action organized into a distinctive whole and set contrastively both against other such wholes and against a social and natural background" (1973). Balinese, Javanese, and Indonesian selves are not like this. How exactly they are, is complicated, but it runs along the lines of more interdependent, collectivist, and allocentric.

The second important feature of the PICTURE is the X's, which mark an amalgam of beliefs, desires, properties, and characteristics such as creativity, politeness, and courage. For ease, I call the amalgam depicted by the X's, "traits." Independent selves contain or own all their own traits. The X's are, or, what is different, are conceived to be, inside the firm borders. The X's of interdependent selves, of allocentric, porous persons are, or are conceived to subsist, at intersections where dyads, triads, and larger collectives of such persons come together.

The claim is that selves differ across two dimensions. The first dimension pertains to boundaries. Some selves have porous boundaries, some have firm(er) ones. The second dimension pertains to the location of mental states, dispositions, traits, and the like. Some selves have, or what is different, conceive themselves to have traits inside their selves, others conceive their traits as relational. What exactly are we to make of these two claims that pertain to the issues of the unit of concern, identification, and well-being, and the nature of constitution, respectively?

1. Some selves, North Americans (Amerindians excepted),[34] have firm borders, but other selves—East Asians, South Asians, and Southeast Asians—have porous borders. Concern, identification, and assessments of well-being are differentially narrow, internal to the boundaries of the psychobiological individual, or wide, encompassing the well-being of certain others.

2. Selves differ in the location (conceived location or actual location) of their traits. X's for WEIRD people are in them; X's for East Asians, South Asians, and Southeast Asians are between them. If traits constitute persons, then some kinds of people are constituted more individualistically, others more relationally.[35]

Self-Boundaries

One objection to a literal interpretation of the PICTURE is based on evolution and claims that in a basic metaphysical sense, a basic psychobiological sense, all selves in all social ecologies experience themselves, at least at some level, as individuals with firm, nonporous boundaries around themselves. Mother Nature designed them this way. The claim that all selves are subjects of experience and naturally understand themselves this way—for example, as having their own pains, seeing the world from one's own perspective—is compatible with porous boundaries when it comes to caring about the well-being of others, which Mother Nature also designed us to do (to a point). It is also compatible with extending the unit with which one identifies, and cares about well beyond one's narrow self. Indeed, the Abrahamic traditions teach that salvation is an individual matter, but that one gains it only by expansive love. So the objection to a literal interpretation of the porous image of persons says that there is a sense in which all of us might be interbeings, with many of our traits being best understood relationally, and our selves understood truly as communally constituted, without it also being true that our boundaries are literally porous and that all our psychological traits subsist in a space of interbeing that is in no one in particular.

William James provides a helpful template for thinking about these matters. First, he claims that there is "the fundamental fact" that "the only states of consciousness that we naturally deal with are found in personal consciousnesses, minds, selves, concrete particular I's and you's." James writes:

> Whatever I may be thinking of, I am always at the same time more or less aware of *myself*, of my *personal existence*. At the same time it is *I* who am aware; so that the total self of me, being as it were duplex, partly known and partly knower, partly object, and partly subject, must have two aspects discriminated in it, of which for shortness we may call one the *Me* and the other the *I*. ([1892] 1961, 176)

The idea is that the minimal organismic sense of myself as a subject of experience, as this *I*, is a gift of evolution and a biological adaptation to boot. When we speak or walk, we experience ourselves speaking and walking. When our stomach hurts or our knees ache, we experience that it is our stomach and our knees that are the source of our pain or discomfort, not someone else's stomach or knees. Bladders and bowels speak directly to their owners. No one ever thinks, "Lo, an orgasm just occurred, I wonder whose it was?" or "There is a headache or a need to pee in this café, I wonder whose it is?"

Still the basic facts about psychobiology of the *I* speak only about where and to whom experiences happen. They say little about what I ought to do, or what is different, what I ought to care about, and nothing much about the normative structure of life. Nor do they speak about the possibilities of moderating, modifying, and restraining the tendencies of the *I* to grow expansive and fat. These issues pertain to what *I* as a subject of experience identify with, what I care about and judge is important, matters, and so on.

Here, the distinction between *I* and *me* proves useful. James distinguished three me's. "The material me," "The social me," and "The spiritual me." If I conceive of my family as "flesh of my flesh, blood of my blood," then my family is part of my material self. Of course, one might conceive of a child as one's own flesh and blood in some ways that are literally true, and also in ways that are a kind of metaphorical extension and normative endorsement of a variety of self-identification that is more optional, where, for example, we truly share fate.[36] If parents, offspring, friends, loved ones, and business relations are not, in most contexts, conceived as literally parts of me, then they are not components of my material self. But they are still components of my social self, possibly several social selves, since I care about them more or less, self-evaluate in terms of the quality of these relations, fill roles that entail duties to them, and am evaluated by others in terms of culturally variable norms that govern such relations. I am a good father or not, a dedicated teacher or not, and so on. Finally, my deepest values, commitments, and attachments make up my spiritual self. If my commitments to my family, my country, my vocation, my moral code, and my religion are "deepest," then my material, social, and spiritual me intersect and overlap. James says "*In its widest possible sense, however, a man's Me is the sum total of all he CAN call his,* not only his body and his psychic powers, but his clothes and his house, his wife and children, his ancestors and friends, his reputation and works, his lands and horses, and yacht and bank-account."

Here, James is not intending to speak about what makes for personal identity in the thin sense, which might simply be having this particular genotype or nervous system. He is speaking about what makes for a self in the thick senses that encompass what an individual identifies with and cares about, what personality traits, beliefs, desires, projects, plans, roles, and relations that make an individual the person he or she is.

The constituents of the self almost always include the body, but "The material me," CAN encompass a person's belongings. There are people whose identity does in fact include their "yacht and bank-account." Recall the PICTURE above, where the independent selves have firm boundaries around their selves but porous ones between themselves and out-groups, whereas the interdependent selves have porous boundaries with respect to those near and dear, but firm ones between in-group selves and out-groups. If that PICTURE is right, then independent selves never literally experience or self-conceive in ways such that their children or parents or their yacht or bank account are part of themselves. Because interdependent selves have porous boundaries, they might literally experience other family members as part of themselves and these others might, beyond how they are conceived, actually be part of themselves. One idea is that these claims about what the material self CAN encompass should be read as claims about valuing and identification, not as claims about the basic metaphysical structure of the self, which I am pretty happy thinking is the basic psychobiological self, the subject of experience and their autobiographical memory, which one might insist is only held first-personally, as autobiographical memory, by its individual subject. The self, that self at least, is bounded, not porous, whereas what the self identifies with, cares about, can be expansive. A firmly bounded self can come to identify with his bank account or with all of humanity. Most everyone identifies with people, projects, and purposes beyond his or her self, and there are, no doubt, cases of parents and children, excellent friends, and long married couples, whose identities are fused. But this doesn't mean that we should conceive of their selves as literally fused, as not independent or not bounded in the minimal metaphysical or psychobiological sense. We might say that these are selves whose identities are fused, but whose psychobiological selves are not fused. It is an interesting fact, worth noting, that while independent selves are pictured as having firm, nonporous boundaries, they are also often pictured in the popular imaginary as avaricious, consumptive, and insatiable, as fattening themselves up by taking in what does not deserve to be inside the self. In theory and in actuality, selfishness occurs among independent and dependent selves. I won't argue for it here, but this entails that the metaphysical structure of the self and what grounds it might matter less to whether a person is good, lives well, has self-esteem and deserves self-respect than his or her identity, identifications, what he or she cares about, and what grounds these things.

Plasticity and Self-Shaping

It might be true that selves are normally metaphysically or psychobiologically bounded in the minimal sense such that each of us is a subject of experience, an *I*, and that this is so for good evolutionary reasons, while it is also true, say for Buddhist No-Self reasons, that we ought not to make anything or very much of this; or even that we ought to do work—cognitive, affective, meditative—to see things the right way, to see the self as blended, coconstituted, fate as shared and reality as ONE. And then, once we see things the right way, we should work to deflate EGO.

A certain kind of person impressed by research on the psychology and biology of morality might say that the metaphysics of morals cannot override the psychobiology of morality. Really? Consider this analogy. The earth feels stationary, but it isn't. The sun looks as if it rises and sets, but it doesn't. There is evidence that we are natural Aristotelians and Ptolemaics, not because we are innately opinionated about astronomical matters, but because it feels and looks as if the earth is stationary and the heavens move. But can we come to perceive the world as Copernicans and Galileans? Can we absorb the truths of astronomy so that we come to literally perceive the world as it is? Some wise philosophers—T. S. Kuhn (1957, 1970) and Paul M. Churchland (1979)—say yes. It takes some theory, some self-work, and some practice. But one can absorb a good, but counterintuitive theory, to the point that one can begin to see reality in its terms.

The idea in Buddhism is that seeing things as they really are (evolution doesn't deliver this any more than common sense does) might start to displace a certain surplus that involves an overflow from the experience of myself as a subject of experience, an *I*, to assigning autonomy, self-sustaining attributes, and importance to this fact. Ultimately, really, I am an impermanent, radically dependent being who suffers, an empty No-Self among other No-Selves that care about each other, and wish to end suffering whenever and wherever it is. So one idea is that some combination of metaphysical and moral therapy of desire and illusion might motivate taking the boundaries and fences down, identifying more with the well-being of all sentient beings, and being obsessed less with how I, conceived narrowly, fare. Try not to see the fences as there, even if they are, and even if it seems natural. The practice is the same in the case of the self, as it is in the case of seeing the external world, the world in which the earth seems to stand still, and the heavens seem to be in motion, the right way.[37] It requires cognitive-conative-affective therapy to align how one sees, experiences, and relates to one's self and the social and natural world with reflectively endorsed beliefs and desires.

X Marks What Spot?

I have said a fair amount about how to interpret the open versus closed fence design in the PICTURE, which contrasts porous and nonporous, individualist and collectivist selves. What about the X's in the original PICTURE? The X's, recall, are supposed to refer to the location of desires, beliefs, properties, and characteristics of persons. For ease, I'll call this bundle of heterogeneous items marked by X's "traits." The PICTURE could be read as intending that independent, nonporous selves, experience, or what is different, conceive (all, most, some) of their traits as inside them, whereas interdependent, porous selves experience or conceive certain traits as not in them, but as subsisting in between individuals, or, perhaps, what is different, subsisting relationally, only when they are enacted among individuals. Or the PICTURE could be interpreted as intending that some X's that are conceived as traits inside particular persons (by independent selves) are actually not inside those individuals. Such X's are better conceived as states of affairs or events that are nowhere in particular or that have a location that is best described as "in" the relationship, and in the relationship only when it is enacted. Imagine that two people treat each other courteously. Where is the courtesy? We might say that the virtue or character trait of courtesy is inside each individual, and that their relation, being together at this moment, activates it, and these facts collectively explain the courteous behavior. The courtesy is inside each person separately, and the interaction activates it. Or we might say that there is only one place that the courtesy is, in the interactive behavior of the two individuals as the courteous episode unfolds. As for what explains the courtesy, this involves socialization, internalization of norms, hermeneutics of interpreting body language and speech, and so on.

Here is what Markus and Kitayama say about interpreting the X's in their original paper on self-variation (1991):

> The X's are representations of the various aspects of the self or of others. In some cases, the larger circle and the smaller circle intersect, and there is an X in the intersection. This refers to a representation of the self-in-relation-to-others or to a particular social relation (e.g., "I am very polite in front of my professor"). An X within the self circle but outside the intersection represents an aspect of the self perceived to be relatively independent of specific others and, thus, invariant over time and context. These self-representations usually have as their referent some individual desire, preference, attribute, or ability (e.g., "I am creative"). For those with independent construals of the self, it is these inner attributes that are most significant in regulating behavior and that are assumed both by the actor and the observer alike, to be diagnostic of the actor. Such representations of the inner self are thus the most elaborated in memory and the most accessible when thinking of the self. (226–27)

Ramifying

The interpretation of the X's that occur in intersections of circles as depicting relational traits, and those that occur "within the self circle but outside the intersection represent[ing] an aspect of the self perceived to be relatively independent of specific others and, thus, invariant over time and context" ramifies. Independent selves conceive their traits as "invariant over time and context," but interdependent selves do not (3, 4, 5, 7, 8, 9, 10, 11). Independent selves are guided by personal preferences (3, 4, 5, 6, 7, 9), whereas interdependent selves are guided by shared, communal goals. Independent selves believe they are more autonomous, self-creating, and immune to luck than interdependent selves (9, 12). Some people (interdependent selves) consider other peoples' preferences and desires more that others (independent selves) when deciding what to do, even when deciding what they want to do together. Insofar as these differences are real, then, there is considerable self-variation across and between traditions, and much of it is of a morally consequential sort.

One might think, not implausibly, that many of these variations ultimately have little or nothing to do with the location of traits, but mostly to do with whether some kinds of people are more selfish or considerate than others.

Suppose two individuals each believe that one ought to be punctual and courteous, or that two individuals, a girl and her mother, are generous and shy. The pairs have the same beliefs and personality traits. They share beliefs and personality traits. But in saying this, we are not saying that the beliefs or the personality characteristics occur in some space of interbeing, betwixt and between the two selves. If courtesy is called for, then Jane is courteous. Such traits might be strong and reliable, like solubility of sugar in water, in which case we call them "standing dispositions." Still, these states, traits, and properties are at best multiply located, but not colocated. Consider hand-holding. If we are holding each other's hands we are each doing this, and we are both doing this, and we are both doing it with each other and it, the hand-holding, is in the exact same place for both of us (as well as from the point of view of the universe). But hand-holding is a physical state of affairs, which can be colocated. What about the desire to hold-hands? Or, the experience of hand-holding by both hand-holders? The first is a mental trait that explains what the couple is doing. The second refers to the shared feeling of intimacy that we hope accompanies or is caused by the hand-holding. Where is the desire to hold-hands? The answer is that there are two desires, one in me and one in you. We share the desire, but the desire is not colocated. What about the shared feeling of intimacy? It is shared. But there are two feelings not one in the single activity. It is similar with such things as sexual intimacy, playing tennis or soccer, and being a good citizen. In some cases, each party, occasionally everyone, is doing the same thing in the same place at the same time. There is dyadic or group coordination, and the well-being of each depends on what the others feel, think, and do. Sexual intimacy, the tennis game, the soccer match, and the election vote, are in no one in particular, but the experiences, thoughts, and feelings of these things are in particular individuals, in particular psychobiological selves that engage in the coordinated, valued activity. Each person has his or her own experiences. Many experiences are shared. But none are literally colocated. So, one interpretation of the X's is that the different locations—inside independent selves or in a space of interbeing for interdependent selves—are not really about location at all. The location is a proxy for differences in the content of traits and the connection of these traits to motivation. On this view, all the self-variation in 1–12 is consistent with the interpretation that independent selves and interdependent selves have beliefs, desires, and various kinds of dispositions that are located in the very selves that have those beliefs, desires, and dispositions, but that they have different contents in the two groups. Independent selves believe that personal goods matter more than social goods, whereas interdependent selves believe that communal goods matter more than personal goods. Independent selves tend to share the belief that I should do what I want or, what is different, what I think best, and interdependent selves share the belief that I should do what the collective thinks best. There is no colocation of beliefs in either group. There are group differences in how common the desire to fit in is, in whether people value the will of elders or social harmony or whether people are disposed to abide American versus Thai norms about courtesy. But in every case, the self-variations have nothing, exactly zero, to do with the location of the relevant dispositions in I's, or between I's, but rather with the content of these dispositions and how the traits and their contents figure in the hearts and minds of individuals in different communities. The claims about the location of the X's are best interpreted as a proxy for differences in self-variations that pertain to how much different kinds of selves care about the well-being of others (6–12). And this means that the evaluation of such differences as are marked by the X's must be referred to the tribunal of the normative sciences, to metaphysics and ethics.

An Inconclusive Conclusion

Human individuals are gregarious social animals, in and of the world. All persons, WEIRD people as well as South Asian, Southeast Asian, East Asian, Eurasian, the original peoples of Africa, the Americas, and Oceana, are psychobiological individuals. Individuals have their own experiences. This is compatible with individuals in different communities being differentially open to other people, to being attentive or inattentive to suffering whenever and wherever it exists, to taking the well-being of others as seriously as their own. Some reasons to do so, to be more open to each other, are offered by different background metaphysical, theological, and soteriological traditions. In this chapter I have used Buddhism as the primary illustrative example. I could have used other non-WEIRD views. Hinduism, Jainism, Daoism, Confucianism, neo-Confucianism, and indigenous Amerindian, African, and Oceanic traditions also offer metaphysics that emphasizes interdependency, shared fate, and various kinds of deep metaphysical oneness amidst conventional psychobiological individuality, and in this way encourage moral selflessness, or, more likely, less selfishness.[38] Such work is increasingly common in philosophy. My view is that such metaphysical differences make their way into the blood and bones of ordinary people and explain in part the dozen self-variations that are on my radar. It is an interesting question whether we, heirs of Aristotle's substance metaphysics, and of Abrahamic soteriologies that make salvation an utterly personal matter, could see our way to want to absorb and abide the credible lessons of views of metaphysical and psychobiological interdependency and oneness on offer in some other traditions and which might make us better, and better off, than we now are. It is something to think about.

12

The Content of Character

The Dream

On August 23 1963, Martin Luther King Jr. gave his "I Have a Dream" speech at the Lincoln Memorial in Washington, DC. This speech, perhaps the most famous ever given on American soil—its main competitors being Lincoln's Gettysburg address and his second inaugural address, both carved into the limestone in the alcove of that very monument—contains these words: "I have a dream that my four little children will one day live in a nation where they will not be judged by the color of their skin but by the content of their character."

In this concluding chapter, I offer some inconclusive thoughts, some conversation starters about how we might do this, how we might teach our children well, and by so doing create communities without hate and suspicion based on otherness, not on racial, ethnic, sexual, gender, and age differences, and not on religion or country of origin. I am interested in thinking about how we might help the next generation to be sensitively attuned to diversity as a positive resource for moral imagination, for exploring the varieties of moral possibility, for self-cultivation, and for social improvement. And, finally, I am interested in thinking about exposing the youth to a realistic, empirically well-informed picture of the crooked wood that is humanity, while at the same time exposing them to the idea that moral excellence is, based on the evidence, the most important aspiration they ought to have if they want to flourish.

We do not live in worlds like those we lived in for most of our species' history where normative conformity was guaranteed by small group size, the improbability of knowing about radically different others, and the impossibility of emigrating to entirely different worlds. Nowadays, all sorts of media expose us to the existence of different ways of worldmaking, and many of us interact with different kinds of people on a daily basis in schools, community colleges, and universities, in modern cities, and in commerce. How are we to think about the content of character in worlds where we cannot expect that we share entirely a vision of the good? What does the content of a person's character consist of, and what makes for good character? Or is this, as some say, none of my business, none of our business, once some minimum of not-being-awful is satisfied?

If I know that you are not racist or sexist, then you have a good character as far as that goes. But thinking well of a person normally involves much more than thinking that individual lacks certain common vices, or even less demandingly, does not enact these common vices, keeps those vices to themselves. You might not be racist or sexist, but you might still be a very bad person, a dishonest egomaniac, and an equal-opportunity trampler of other people's identities, hopes, and aspirations. Can a more positive conception of the content of character gain a foothold in liberal societies, in worlds in which the people who are to have those very characters have different worldviews, and who conceive of their selves in radically different ways? Can we expect more of each other than a modus vivendi, where we judge the quality of each other's character on the basis of whether we are both law abiding and, beyond that, whether we each give each other space to do our own thing?

What Is the Content of Character?

King's speech gives a partial answer to the question of what makes for good character. A good character requires minimally that the person is not racist. They do not let race, and we would nowadays add sex, gender, or sexual preference, make any difference in how they treat others. One reason is that these features of persons are, or so we now say, but did not always say, irrelevant to the content of one's character, to one's overall quality as a human being, and even more importantly inside a liberal polity, to each individual's possession of certain rights. But this is only a minimum, so we will want to think through the question of what the character of a person consists of and what makes for a good character.

One view of character is that it consists of whatever complement of virtues that a person has, and which they reliably reveal in their behavior. A view such as this is sometimes attributed to Aristotle in the West, and Mencius in the East. But this is not a view either held. Both thought that virtues were typical and necessary, but that practical intelligence or wisdom—*phronesis* in Aristotle, *zhi* in Mencius—was also essential. There are several reasons why they thought this, which I will not rehearse in detail, but two of which are worth emphasizing. Virtues come from socialization and habituation inside a culture that supports them. But it is hard to practice certain virtues, for example, the courage to stand up to oppressors and perpetrators of injustice if one lives in a time when conditions of social justice are relatively intact or, on the other side, when an oppressive regime will meet any hint of dissent as a flyswatter meets a fly. Second, some situations will involve conflicts between virtues, as when the demands of justice and mercy conflict. In such situations we need to think about how to respond, about what we ought to think, and feel, and do. Thinking about things, including what should be done in novel situations, and whether ordinary moral habits are doing what they are supposed to do, requires the use of moral imagination. Whenever we think about what we ought to do, what ought to happen, we are imagining possible moral worlds, we are thinking about how either we or the world, often both, might be different, how the content of our characters, that of our charges, or the structures of everyday life could be better and more supportive of the moral project.[1]

Most parents will say they hope that their children will become people of upstanding and reliable moral character, good people, with a substantial and resilient moral compass, a thick moral personality. What do we teach when we try to teach our children well, when we work to fill out their character, to give shape, content, and texture to their character? The answer is that we do a lot of different things. We inculcate an array of beliefs, norms, virtues, values, rules, principles, and views, and offer a philosophy as well as worthy ideals, historical or contemporary persons worthy of modeling and imitation. Here are examples of what each consists of:

- *Beliefs*: A good person tells the truth. Billy plays rough. Miranda is not trustworthy. That's against the law.
- *Norms*: Don't hit your sister. Tell the truth. Don't lose your temper.
- *Virtues*: Work at being kind (to your sister, your classmates, the dog).
- *Values*: It is good to be honest, fair, and kind.
- *Rules*: Use your indoor voice. Don't use foul language.
- *Principles*: Love thy neighbor. Maximize utility.
- *Philosophy*: Confucian, Unitarian, Pure Land Buddhist, Reform Jewish, Muslim, act or rule utilitarian, Kantian, secular humanist, libertarian.
- *Ideals and Exemplars*: Martin Luther King Jr., The Blessed Virgin Mary, Mother Teresa, Dorothy Day, Steve Jobs, Harry Potter, Jesus, the prophet Mohammed, Katniss Everdeen.

The kind of moral education for thick and excellent character I favor in the schools would involve teaching the beliefs that (1) One can learn from, and morally improve oneself, as well as help create morally better worlds in one's own vicinity by attending to how people unlike oneself conceive and do their moral life; (2) One can often do so without having to change entirely the kind of person or self one is, although one might have to change one's view about how important the aims of one's ego are; (3) One ought to understand the moral project to be sufficiently consequential to the meaning and overall significance of one's life, to well-being, that one ought to aspire to excellence, not just to what is sufficient, passable, or good enough.

In addition to encouraging these three true beliefs, moral education would expose young children to the diversity in their midst, or if there is no diversity in their midst, to stories, anthropologies, and philosophical tales that vividly reveal how people who are not like us do things. Often this will involve mostly understanding how others conceive the shape and texture of particular virtues we both admire, and how we differ in the relative priority we assign to shared values and virtues inside our somewhat different moral economies. In this way, we open schools to exploration of what most everyone will say is very important, perhaps most important—the quality of one's character. Such education would expose children to all the aspects of a morality just mentioned: beliefs, norms, virtue, values, alternative philosophies, debates about basic human nature and motives, as well as unfamiliar, but possibly attractive moral exemplars.

The guiding idea is simple: Some beliefs, practices, norms, and virtues of people who are not acculturated inside the dominant WEIRD forms of life have things to teach us, modes of moral possibility that we can learn from. But we can't benefit from what we don't know about. Here are a few plausible candidates:

- *Karuna* and *metta*, compassion and lovingkindness, as these are understood inside Buddhism;
- Indic practices (especially Jain versions) associated with *ahimsa*, nonviolence, as well as the rationales for *ahimsa* as they pertain to treatment of animals and conflict resolution between individuals and nation-states;
- Confucian views about why one should have gratitude and respect for the lineage to which one belongs, as well as respect for the wisdom of the elders;
- Stoic and Buddhist views about the destructive aspects of anger;
- African views about *ubuntu*, the idea that I am because we are, and the practices associated with this idea that a person is communally constituted by a lineage.

In these and every other case I can think of, there are children's stories that introduce these ideas as grist for reflection, imaginative play, and possibly for self-cultivation. Could this be dangerous? I doubt it. Would it mean that schools teach much more literature, history, geography, sociology, and anthropology, and also encourage ethical reflection based on such literature, history, sociology, and anthropology than they now do? Yes. But this is a good thing. Only eight states in America currently require civics education, and by the time students are in high school much of that is devoted to career and college counseling, nothing very normative. If anything, exposure to the varieties of moral possibility and reflection on moral development in schools has decreased in recent years. We live in times of enhanced testing regimes dominated by programs like "No Child Left Behind," where schools emphasize language arts and numeracy, and inside which teachers will say that what is not tested is not taught.

Spheres of Lives

I have not once tried to say what the moral domain is. Partly this is because I don't know, and partly because its boundaries are fluid. Sometimes there are contestations about whether a domain of life is inside the moral domain or not, and even if it is in the moral domain, whether it is personal moral matter or up for public scrutiny. Sex is sometimes said to be outside the realm of morality, or if inside it, a matter about which it is only the individual or individuals involved who have a say in how they live in that sphere of life.

What I did say is that most of the moral problems I face and that people I know face are not like trolley problems. They are not dilemmas and they are not emergencies. Most pertain to personal friendship, to civic friendship, to work for social justice, to being honest and reliable, to living up to one's own standards, and to creating conditions in which the youth develop into good persons, with the capacities and sensitivities that will serve them well in the moral project. The moral project takes place primarily in domains of life where there are no laws or written policies to structure action, but in which much of the work on goodness, decency, character, and meaning take place.[2]

One way to think about the moral domain in which the concept of character is most at home, is to define first the political level, which is also a zone or sphere of normativity, as the zone in which there is public legislation and typically formal written policy or, so as to capture the yet-to-be-enacted political agendas of ruling parties, the zone in which there are attempts to create legislation or clear public policy. The zone of ethics and morals, then, is the zone of normativity, where there is no public legislation or written policy.

The boundaries are not clear for two reasons. First, there are constant border disputes, for example, gay marriage, Planned Parenthood, immigration, and teaching ethics in schools. Second, the political framework creates by its political constitution and legislation the vastly influential set of structures that orient a people toward thinking and doing things in certain ways that may be both hidden (they are structuring causes) and extremely consequential for their moral form of life.[3] The political framework of a morality is one of the main ecological determinants of how the morality works, what it does, what it can do, and how it conceives the proper content of character in its vicinity. The contemporary American political sphere is set up to enable a capitalist economy, and it creates favorable conditions for a conception of the good life evaluated largely, but not exclusively, in terms of individual economic success.

One unfortunate feature of the political sphere in America is that it encourages a misleading impression of normative life overall through its noxious atmospherics. Politics models a picture of normative decision-making as fractious, shrill, and polarized, where every issue is decided by partisan demonizing of the opposition until the matter is resolved practically by the number of thumbs up or down on some matter of law or social policy. The focus in politics is on resolution and enactment. The ethical sphere operates with norms, but usually without laws. It also permits different individuals and small communities inside a nation of law to work for small incremental improvement in themselves and in their common life. No one needs to vote on those changes. They can be adopted and enacted by hearts open to being and doing better in their own time, and on their own time. A moral community, even more than a political community in which it inevitably subsists and is structured, can be highly attuned to learning from experience, and it can do so in subtle, nuanced, experimental, and piecemeal ways.

In America, we are encouraged to abide what John Rawls (1993) calls an "overlapping consensus," according to which people with different conceptions of the good life agree to a certain conception of political life, but possibly for different reasons. Secular people, Roman Catholics, and Buddhists can all agree with the language of inalienable human rights in the US Declaration of Independence, the US Constitution, and the UN Bill of Rights (1948), but for different reasons, which each can explain in their own terms.[4] In such cases, we get what Charles Taylor (1998) calls an "unforced consensus." The overlapping, unforced consensus, creates the context for, and thus is supposed to be compatible with, fairly wide space for personal and moral freedom. How each person or community of people within the polity choose(s) to be and to live is not legislated beyond whatever minimum is thought to be necessary for maintaining a common civic form. The common civic form is designed, if it is liberal, to keep necessary bureaucracies—for example, the transportation system, social security, banking regulations, and immigration—operating smoothly, so that all citizens can live well as they understand living well. Again, one might think that in a liberal community nothing can or should be said about the content of good character beyond that a good person is law-abiding.

One consequence in the American case of the liberal overlapping consensus, along with the separation of church and state, is a vacuum in public education for goodness, as well as what is stronger still, encouragement in the project of achieving moral excellence. One view is that the content of the character of the children is none of the state's business. And thus that public schools must maintain neutrality when it comes to morality. Outside of telling the kids that they cannot cheat on homework and exams, cannot use foul or abusive language, bring guns or dope to school, or have sex on school grounds, there is little moral education. That, the thought is, is best left to the family and the religious institutions they partake in, if any.

How could we fill the vacuum if we think we should? One worry, there are many, is the common assumption in America, but that is not a piece of philosophical necessity, that religions are the site of ethics, and religion does not belong in schools, and thus ethics doesn't either. What is true is that all ethical traditions, sacred ones and secular ones, are embedded in larger philosophical traditions, most of which are religious or spiritual, but there is no necessity.

In order to think wisely about moral education, about the content of character that a liberal society could aim to create in its public institutions or in private associations such as families and local communities, we need to reflect a bit on what kids are like to begin with.

Crooked Wood

One answer to the question of what the kids are like to begin with, comes from Xunzi, the third-century BCE Confucian, who along with Confucius and Mencius is one of the three greatest Confucian philosophers. Xunzi responds to what he takes to be Mencius's optimistic view that human nature is structured by seeds of virtue, and has moral excellence as its natural aim. According to Mencius, the four sprouts in human nature—compassion, deference, a sense of rightness and wrongness, and wisdom—are the beginnings of virtue, which will reliably become true, mature virtue in normal environments. The Mencian sprouts of virtue are like the genetic programs that in most ecologies yield beaks and wings in birds, or two arms and two legs in humans. The genetic programs almost always deliver the equipment that enables birds to fly and to fetch insects, worms, and fish, and that enables humans to walk and run to desirable things, and then to reach for, hold, and grasp these things. Likewise, the sprouts of virtue will, all else being equal, yield a *junzi*, a virtuous gentleperson.[5]

Over two millennia before Kant wrote that "out of the crooked timber of humanity no straight thing was ever made," Xunzi used the same metaphor to describe the extraordinarily difficult task that the moral community faces in shaping and disciplining the unruly charges that are our children. Each human is like a piece of gnarly undisciplined wood, which can be straightened by a skilled woodworker, but that in its nature resists straightening. In chapter 23 of the *Xunzi* with the title "Human Nature Is Bad," where 'bad' means something closer to unruly or hard-to-tame than bad in any moral sense, Xunzi writes:

> People's nature is bad. Their goodness is a matter of deliberate effort. Now people's nature is such that they are born with a fondness for profit in them. If they follow along with this, then struggle and contention will arise, and yielding and deference will perish therein. They are born with feelings of hate and dislike in them. If they follow along with these, then cruelty

and villainy will arise, and loyalty and trustworthiness will perish therein. They are born with desires of the eyes and ears, a fondness for beautiful sights and sounds. If they follow along with these, then lasciviousness and chaos will arise, and ritual and *yi*, proper form and order, will perish therein. Thus, if people follow along with their inborn dispositions, and obey their nature, they are sure to come to struggle and contention, turn to disrupting social divisions and order, and end up becoming violent. So, it is necessary to await the transforming influence of teachers and models and the guidance of ritual and *yi*, and only then will they come to yielding and deference, turn to proper form and order, and end up becoming controlled. Looking at it is this way, it is clear that people's nature is bad, and their goodness is a matter of deliberate effort.... [T]hus, crooked wood must await steaming and straightening on the shaping frame, and only then does it become straight. Blunt metal must await honing and grinding, and only then does it become sharp. (23)

Xunzi's philosophical psychology need not be read as contradicting the Mencian sprout view—close reading of the passage indicates that Xunzi sees each of the Mencian sprouts—so much as calling attention to the fact that whatever the beginnings or spontaneous features of human nature (*xing*) are, they are a normatively indeterminate or mixed lot. Some seeds can be extended in hypertrophic, unwholesome ways, for example, the "fondness for profit" can easily become ruthless selfishness, and the beginning of loyalty can develop into mindless tribalism and nationalism. Furthermore, the beginnings, seeds or sprouts, whatever they are, contain the germs for good plants—for example, *yi* for the sense of rightness—and for plants—for example, the fondness for beauty—that can be good if tamed and disciplined, as well as seeds for weeds—seeds for wanting more than my fair share—which cause trouble, take over the garden, strangle other plants, and invade other gardens.

Is Xunzi right that the moral project must work with materials that have the following natural features?

1. We are born with a "fondness for profit" that if allowed free rein or if encouraged or developed, will produce "struggle and contention," and at the same time it will cause the sprout of "yielding and deference," a Mencian sprout, to "perish."
2. We are born with "feelings of hate and dislike" that if allowed free rein or if encouraged or developed, will lead to "cruelty and villainy," and "loyalty and trustworthiness" (in the vicinity of Mencian sprouts) will "perish."
3. We are born with "desires of the eyes and ears, a fondness for beautiful sights and sounds" that if allowed free rein or if encouraged

or developed, will lead to "lasciviousness and chaos," and tendencies to "ritual and *yi*, proper form and order" (Mencian sprouts) will "perish."

4. Overall, our original, inborn nature is such that if we "follow along" with it, if we grow all aspects of it, we will be led to "struggle and contention"; we will create "social divisions" and we will be led to violence.

Assuming that the picture Xunzi gives of the child's first nature as a mixed bag from the moral point of view, is credible, what about his proposal for the way forward, for moral education? The child needs "to await the transforming influence of teachers and models" who teach discipline through ritual practice and education in righteousness. In this way the child, like crooked wood, awaits "steaming and straightening," or like bent metal awaits "honing and grinding." The content of the character of the child who becomes a *junzi* is, in the first instance, a deliberate creation of the moral community, which equips them with the requisite virtues of a good person, which include the capacities of the person themself to eventually exert the sort of "deliberate effort" required to keep the common disruptive tendencies under wise control. Possibly, after considerable practice in virtue, the child becomes a grownup who finds being a good person more or less natural. They come to enact moral excellence in something like the *wu-wei* manner that an accomplished athlete performs in their sport.[6]

The Moral Sense of Babies

We can now better assess a psychology like Xunzi's, thanks to two millennia of cross-cultural observation, as well as to experimental work in the mind sciences. In the twentieth century, Jean Piaget showed that naturalistic, empirically rigorous observation of children was possible, and the project he began is now flourishing. We live in a golden age of child psychology, and work on the moral development of children has been able to speak with more than anecdotal confidence about some of the core dispositions of children. In particular, we know much more about the first-nature settings for kindness and fairness, what Frans de Waal (2013) calls "the twin pillars of morality." The consensus picture is not one in which kids are devils or angels, but a bit of each, as well as malleable, open to straightening and development by way of modeling, imitation, direct instruction, and absorption of the way or ways of worldmaking that are encouraged in the dominant, local ecology, and eventually, perhaps most importantly, to becoming skilled at self-cultivation. But only if such skills are deliberately taught and consciously modeled.

Paul Bloom's *Just Babies: The Origins of Good and Evil* (2013b), is a terrific summary and analysis of the relevant findings, many of which Bloom and his wife Karen Wynn, are responsible for. Bloom writes:

Our Natural Endowments Include:
- A moral sense—some capacity to distinguish between kind and cruel actions
- Empathy and compassion—suffering at the pain of those around us and the wish to make this pain go away
- A rudimentary sense of fairness—a tendency to favor equal divisions of resources
- A rudimentary sense of justice—a desire to see good actions rewarded and bad actions punished. (5)[7]

Here are some compelling experimental findings: Some of these findings involve the foundations of the first pillar of kindness, sharing, possibly empathy and compassion; others involve the foundations of the second pillar in dispositions to fairness and equity. From the get-go, kids show signs of self-regarding emotions like pride, shame, and guilt, and other-regarding emotions like resentment and anger, and they take a certain amount of pleasure in exacting revenge.

1. As early as 1 year old, children prefer puppets in a show they have just watched who were nice, helpful, and cooperative to puppets who are mean, unhelpful, and uncooperative.
2. Children start to share, for example, crackers, a little bit, with family and friends at about 6 months. But often only if the other individual indicates a desire that they do so.
3. At around 2 years of age, children will voluntarily share crackers with unrelated individuals if it is not costly to them personally, that is, if there are plenty of crackers for them.
4. Both human toddlers and chimp toddlers will try spontaneously to help strangers who drop their keys or who are trying to open a door when their arms are full (Warenken and Tomasello 2006).
5. Before 2 years of age, children cannot control the impulse to touch a toy when the adult who has forbidden doing so leaves the room.
6. When caught touching the toy they were forbidden to touch, 60 percent of 16 month olds, but 100 percent of 18 month olds show signs of embarrassment, guilt, and fear.
7. By 16 months of age, but not at 10 months, children are highly attuned to equality of outcome and prefer puppets who are very fair, specifically that divide goods—for example, colored disks or stickers—evenly to other puppets. Similar bias has been shown in capuchin monkeys (Brosnan and de Waal 2003).

8. The equality of outcome bias is so strong that 6- to 8-year-olds will sometimes prefer to throw an extra good away, say, an extra sticker, rather than produce an unequal outcome in some distribution.

9. Children as young as 19 months do not think it odd if puppets distribute more of some good to another character who has done much more cooperative work, for example, pitched in more on cleaning up toys. So the equality bias yields some if the uneven payout tracks cooperation and effort.

In order to further explore children's views on fairness, three kinds of economic games have been adapted to children. The Dictator Game is simple. You have 2 pieces of candy (for adults, the good is money) and can offer one or none to an anonymous kid at your preschool, kindergarten, or school. What will you give away? The Ultimatum Game is trickier. It involves the task of distributing some good, for example, pieces of candy or stickers to an unknown other kid. The other child knows that someone (you) has, say, 10 stickers or 2 Skittles, and that individual can accept or reject your offer. If they reject it, no one—neither you nor they—get any of the stickers or candy. If they accept, you must give what you offer, and can keep the rest. What will you give away?

Public Goods Games or Third Party Punishment Games are still more complicated and involve games in which everyone benefits if all participate, but in which each individual will do better if they defect. The teacher tells the kids to put the toys away. Johnny suddenly needs to go to the bathroom. When he returns, all the toys have been put away. At what cost will the other kids, or some independent observer, punish a slacker like Johnny who doesn't pitch in? Does Johnny have to show a pattern of free riding to get his classmates or some third party, the teacher, mad, or does it come the first time he slacks off? Here are some results:

10. By the time children are 7 years old, about 50 percent give away one of two candies in Dictator compared with only 20 percent of 5- to 6-year-olds (Fehr et al. 2008).

11. In a variation of Dictator, where a child can deed a candy she does not possess and will not possess, she already has hers, at no cost other than deeding it, 80 percent of 7- to 8-year-olds will do so. But only 50 percent of younger kids do so, even though there is zero cost to them of so doing. It would simply be gratuitously nice.

12. In games where loss seems imminent, children between 4 and 7 will often spoil the game—for example, by upsetting the board—thus spiting the soon-to-be winner before they taste success.

13. In experiments that mimic some features of Public Goods, 4-year-olds are told stories about an uncooperative child who doesn't help his partner clean up. The 4-year-olds get that the partner who is

affected will be mad, but also think that friends of that kid—who are not directly affected—will be angry.

14. At 21 months, children will, if given the chance, offer a treat to nice puppets and punish, that is, take away treats from mean puppets.

15. At 5 months, infants prefer puppets that are nice overall, including to a mean character; but by 8 months they prefer the puppet who is mean to the bad guy over one who is nice to him. Bloom (2013b) writes, "So at some point after five months, babies begin to prefer punishers—when the punishment is just" (99).

16. In 2- to 6-year-olds, "most of what the children say to their parents about their brothers and sisters counted as tattling" (95).

17. It is rare for children to report good deeds of classmates to teachers, but very common to report norm violations.

18. Normally the child who is tattled on lies and says they did not do what it was truthfully claimed (based on the experimenter's observations) they in fact did.

19. Chinese babies prefer to look at Chinese faces. Caucasian babies prefer to look at Caucasian faces. Bloom puts it this way: "Not only do babies like familiar people, they also like familiar kinds of people" (105).

20. Babies like familiar voices, accents, and languages. When babies are raised among people who are different, these face and language preferences dissipate.

A quick inventory of 1–20 reveals the early development of capacities for empathy, compassion, mind reading, a sense of fairness, taking the perspective of another, and in-group favoritism as well as for pride, shame, guilt, embarrassment, anger, spite, revenge, and punishment. In almost all these cases, there is evidence that the relevant dispositions have seeds in the nature of the babies.[8] They also show what Xunzi surmised and would have predicted: A certain amount of fellow feeling, alongside a "fondness for profit," a strong strain of egoism, and strong affection for in-group members, as well as dispositions for coalitions that are easily recruited to create social divisions and seed distrust based on merely not looking like, or sounding like, my caretakers.[9]

There are three caveats about these findings, or perhaps they are simply reminders. First, the children studied are mostly WEIRD. Second, and relatedly, the children are not innocent of cultural formation. They range from 4- to 6-month-old babies, to toddlers, to 3- to 4-year-olds who are pre-preschool and pre-kindergarten, but not in most cases pre- one of the many varieties of alloparenting or day care, to 7- and 8-year-olds who are typically a few years into formal schooling. Children are carried on the chest, on the back, looking out, and looking in. And they are cared for in many different ways in different cultures.[10] The degree to which other adults—the father, grandparents, other women, older siblings and cousins, and in some cultures au pairs, nannies, and slaves—share in early nurturing is highly variable. There are natural and human-caused disasters that leave some children as street orphans or wards of the state. And then there are the children—child warriors in Somalia or the Congo, or girls captured and raped in internecine wars—who are victims of unimaginable trauma and permanent damage to their souls. Third, the studies report on similarities among kids and patterns in populations of children; but all these children are individuals with distinctive psychobiologies, temperaments, and personalities.

We need to be careful not to let generalizations about the ways that children are similar conceal the many ways they are different. In any population of individuals, there is bound to be phenotypic variation. In *The Philosophical Baby* (2009), Alison Gopnik writes about temperamental variation among children between "secure," "avoidant," and "anxious" varieties. Some of the variation comes from early experiences of parenting.[11] But some seems to come with the individual baby. The heart rate of newborns rises when they are presented with a novel object, say, a bright red octagon. About a third of newborns sustain the elevated heart rate longer than the other two-thirds of newborns. Later on, the children with the longer elevated heart rate to the novel object, self-report as shy, and their parents and teachers describe them as shy at much higher rates than the two-thirds of newborns who do not sustain the elevated heart rates as long (Kagan 1984).

It is an interesting question whether and how individual differences, whatever their cause, might make the moral project more or less difficult for different kinds of children. Do children with difficulty on impulse-control tasks, or those prone to seek instant gratification, or who are gregarious or shy face different challenges in learning to be good? Obviously, the child soldiers, some of whom have been required to assassinate loved ones, and the victims of gang rape may be unable to trust again, and just as sadly, to be trusted.[12]

Economic Games Across Cultures

I said we live in a golden age of child psychology. We also live in a golden age of experimental game theory. Before further commenting on what the results just summarized might mean for moral education and development, let me give a sense of some important findings from cultural anthropology and behavioral economics about typical adult behavior in games where goods need to be valued, priced, and exchanged.

By the the mid-1990s, consensus emerged that subjects in economic games such as Dictator, Ultimatum, and Public Goods, did not conform to a classical economic picture which said that, unbeknownst to the self, and in opposition to a certain ubiquitous and flattering self-image, each individual is, in fact, a completely self-interested, rational (but not entirely competent), economic calculator.

If each person is a rational egoist they ought always to try to maximize personal profit; but they don't. In Dictator, subjects reliably give about 50 percent to a stranger. In Ultimatum, recipients usually reject offers lower than 50 percent, so that no one gets anything. And in third-party Public Goods games, morally zealous bystanders are willing to pay money or give up valued goods (for kids, candy) to see a cheapskate or slacker punished. Furthermore, the amount of good stuff they are willing to give up in order to punish is proportional to the degree of free riding.[13]

Some say this shows that people are not rational, economic self-maximizers, because rational egoists would give nothing in Dictator and should not be willing to spend in Public Goods when they are not personally affected. Ultimatum is less clear, since it involves strategic prediction of the behavior of others. Others say the results just show the complexity of computing rational self-interest for gregarious social animals like us, who are, up to a point, team players, capable of conviviality. One might think such conviviality is part of our nature as gregarious social mammals. Aristotle says no one would choose to live without friends. Or one might think that a certain willingness to play nice is entirely instrumental. Getting certain goods sometimes requires using other people as means. In either case, decision-making would be constrained by a sense that I am a member of a family, clan, or school, as well as expectations that everyone will do their fare share in group projects, and that there will be future interactions with my teammates. Even if a particular experimental game is set up to hint that it is a one-off, and thus that I could behave as a sensible knave and get away with it, I might, based on everyday life, expect that will not be so, and that we will in fact meet again.[14]

In the mid-1990s the standard economic games began to be given to non-WEIRD people, mostly in the global south, and almost immediately differences in norms of fairness and punishment in these games were observed. Here are some examples (Henrich et al. 2007; Ensminger and Henrich 2014):

- The Hadza of northern Tanzania are full-time foragers and live in groups smaller than 50. The Hadza make low offers, 25 percent in Dictator and Ultimatum, which are also often rejected in Ultimatum. The Hadza will quickly avenge a personal slight in their community, but will not give much to punish free riders in Public Goods.
- The Au of New Guinea, a very poor group of forager-agriculturalists, with a bit of chicken and pig husbandry thrown in, live in groups of around 300. They make offers above 50 percent in both Dictator and Ultimatum, and in Ultimatum these generous offers are often rejected.

- The Tsimane', forager-horticulturalists of Bolivia, live in communities of a little over 300. Like the Hazda, they make low offers, 25 percent in both Dictator and Ultimatum, but they almost never reject any offer and never choose to punish free riders in the games; real life is another story.

The variation among groups such as these and many others that have been studied begs for explanation. Jean Ensminger and Joseph Henrich (2014) offer some plausible ones. For the Au of New Guinea, as for most people of Micronesia, generous gifts are a very big deal. The giver increases their prestige, but the recipient is on the hook for paying back in kind. For very poor people this is a burden. The explanation for why people from small-scale groups like the Hadza and Tsimane' do not spend to punish in Public Goods is because the role of being an anonymous third party is ecologically unfamiliar in societies where all transactions are up close and personal, largely face-to-face, and where reputation is easily tracked. In small communities, gossip and shunning can do the work that municipal fines do in larger societies composed of anonymous people (Skyrms 2004).

The consensus among anthropologists is that there is wide variation across cultural groups in standard economic games, and that this variance is explained not by first human nature, but by normative and structural features of different ecologies. Big difference makers are group size, market integration, and whether members of the group are members of a world religion or not. Ensminger and Henrich (2014, 131–33) summarize the results this way:

- Fair offers in economic games increase with market integration.
- Fair offers are higher for groups whose members are Muslims or Christians, rather than members of a local or tribal religion.
- Willingness to pay to punish increases as community size does.

Fair and Nice in Economic Games ≠ Fair and Good in Ordinary Life

The findings that North Americans are fair in economic games, and that fairness in economic games correlates with market integration, large population size, and membership in some world religion does not show that North Americans are fair in economic games because of these things. But suppose it is true that these three features are what are behind, in the causal sense, the results on these games. This would not at all show that North Americans are particularly fair overall, or highly attuned to equity overall, or that they are particularly good or nice outside of domains that demand fair economic exchanges. In fact, there is lots of evidence that, in real life, North Americans are not very attuned to fairness in the sense of actual economic equality inside American society. The compensation gap between top management and workers was about 20 to 1 in 1980. It is about 300 to 1 in 2015. And every day there are articles in the news about economic inequality. Today's headline in the *New York Times* (November 19, 2015) is this: "Half of New Yorkers Say They Are Barely or Not Getting By, Poll Shows." The article explains that "in the Bronx, 36 percent said there had been times in the past year when they did not have the money to buy enough food for their family; only one in five said they and their neighbors had good or excellent access to suitable jobs." Fifty-eight percent of the people in Manhattan, the richest borough, say "they are doing alright or thriving," but 30 percent say they are only barely getting by.

The fact that North American college students are fair in economic games might be explained by the fact that these are the norms they are taught are expected in everyday shopping and business transactions. There are entirely different rules for bartering, pricing, and negotiation at Walmart in New Jersey, namely, don't try to barter or negotiate, as opposed to at a souk in Tunisia, where bartering and negotiating are perfectly acceptable, even expected. North American college students are well socialized in the norms governing fair exchange as "fair exchange" is understood in their everyday ecologies.

The normative conformity on economic games coexists with deep veins of social Darwinist thinking in the blood and bones of Americans. Many students I teach think that there are "Masters of the Universe," most of whom work in Lower Manhattan, and they want to be among them. Consider, on the other side, that there is a vast amount of anthropological work that indicates greater economic equality in small societies with less market integration and more tribal religions than in WEIRD ones (Boehm 1999, 2012; Fry 2007). So, even if the Hadza and members of other small-scale societies share less on economic games, they share more of much less in real life.[15]

The key point is that in both the valuable research on little children and the research on both children and adults in the game theory experiments, there is a host of things in play at once. There is whatever the first-nature equipment of children is as members of the species *Homo sapiens*; whatever the individual nature, temperament, sex, and gender of each kid is; what antecedent structures are in place in the social and natural ecologies the child is born into, and how these ecological structures work to form character. All of these taken together will determine whether an economic game is read as an invitation to perform as people like us, be we Hazda of Tanzania or MBA students at Harvard Business School, deal with problems like these in everyday life, in our normal ecologies, or will explain how we would act in a situation like this, where the situation like this—an anonymous transaction between players in a market—might be the stuff of everyday life or entirely unfamiliar.

Philosophical Thought Experiments and Scientific Experiments

A fan of psychological and anthropological realism will want to know what these experimental findings about children and adults teach us overall, about children, adolescents, and adults socialized in different cultural ecologies. I am one of those fans, so I want to know this. Answers will help us think more clearly perhaps about moral education, about how, by whom, and by which institutions the thick content of character is to be provided, indeed how it is currently being provided assuming, what may not be true, that it is being provided. Do we possess now, in the second decade of the twenty-first century, something like a credible, empirically responsible, picture of human nature? I think the answer is yes. What is interesting is that the shape of this answer has been available for a very long time. We can see this if we put the experimental results in conversation with some classic philosophical thought experiments that claim to show what human nature is like deep-down-inside-beneath-the-clothes-of-culture. Consider these thought experiments from Plato, Hobbes, and Hume.

In *Republic*, Book II, Plato's brother Glaucon offers the myth of the Lydian shepherd as evidence for the view that morality is an imposition on the hearts and minds of individuals who want sex, money, and power, and are willing to murder to get these. Although the myth does not speak of the nature of your typical child, it is about someone who is an adolescent, a male adolescent, a particularly dangerous, possibly testosterone-poisoned, kind of interbeing.

Glaucon articulates what he calls "the received account"—it is not clear he ever endorses it—that abiding a moral order "is a mean or compromise, between the best of all, which is to do injustice and not be punished, and the worst of all, which is to suffer injustice without the power of retaliation."

He then says that we can confirm this for ourselves if we follow in our imagination the story of Gyges, the Lydian shepherd.

> Gyges was a shepherd in the service of the king of Lydia; there was a great storm, and an earthquake made an opening in the earth at the place where he was feeding his flock. Amazed at the sight, he descended into the opening, where, among other marvels, he beheld a hollow brazen horse, having doors, at which he stooping and looking in saw a dead body of stature, as appeared to him, more than human, and having nothing on but a gold ring; this he took from the finger of the dead and reascended. Now the shepherds met together, according to custom, that they might send their monthly report about the flocks to the king; into their assembly he came having the ring on his finger, and as he was sitting among them he chanced to turn the collet of the ring inside his hand, when instantly he became invisible to the rest of the company and they

began to speak of him as if he were no longer present. He was astonished at this, and again touching the ring he turned the collet outwards and reappeared; he made several trials of the ring, and always with the same result—when he turned the collet inwards he became invisible, when outwards he reappeared. Whereupon he contrived to be chosen one of the messengers who were sent to the court; where as soon as he arrived he seduced the queen, and with her help conspired against the king and slew him, and took the kingdom. Suppose now that there were two such magic rings, and the just put on one of them and the unjust the other; no man can be imagined to be of such an iron nature that he would stand fast in justice. No man would keep his hands off what was not his own when he could safely take what he liked out of the market, or go into houses and lie with anyone at his pleasure, or kill or release from prison whom he would, and in all respects be like a God among men. Then the actions of the just would be as the actions of the unjust; they would both come at last to the same point. And this we may truly affirm to be a great proof that a man is just, not willingly or because he thinks that justice is any good to him individually, but of necessity, for wherever any one thinks that he can safely be unjust, there he is unjust.[16]

Glaucon invites us to imagine two very similar shepherds, a just one and an unjust one who, prior to finding the ring, differ only in this way: Shepherd 1 is consciously aware of homicidal thoughts toward the king, as well as his desire to seduce and/or rape the queen, and he lusts to own the kingdom and possess all its riches. But he conceals this from others, who, we'll suppose, think his moral exterior matches his moral heart. Shepherd 2 has no such conscious thoughts. He is, as far as his own conscious thinking goes, of sweet and tame temperament. His insides and outsides are aligned as far as he consciously knows.

For the thought experiment to be confirmed as stated, we need to think that both shepherd 1 and shepherd 2 would immediately kill the king, seduce or, if necessary, rape the queen, and take the kingdom. We would need to think this because we would think that both shepherds have the same desires, the only difference being that shepherd 1 owns them consciously and shepherd 2 stuffs them. If one thinks that conscience is a thin, slightly protective, but easily dissolved veneer over antisocial desires, one might weaken the prediction to this: Shepherd 2 will eventually do what shepherd 1 does immediately. It will simply take a bit of time for him to see—he has been duped—that he no longer has prudential reason to be moral. If all reasons are prudential reasons, then he has no reasons at all. On the other hand, if one thinks that conscience can make certain things unattractive because they are wrong, and possibly teach that virtue is its own reward, then one might doubt that shepherd 2 would do what shepherd 1 would do ever.

What the thought experiment insists on are three kinds of disruptive motives in both just and unjust souls, for riches, for sex, and for power. It is fair to say that we see the beginnings of these desires for sensual pleasure, for good stuff, and for power in children.[17] And they each get a new jolt of energy in adolescence, at about the time one becomes eligible to be a shepherd, and to report to the king on the state of the flock.[18]

Ego's Three Poisons

Another famous philosophical thought experiment that receives partial confirmation from the human sciences comes from Thomas Hobbes. In chapter 13 of *Leviathan*, we are asked to imagine our situation as it was, perhaps, when the ice melted at the end of the Pleistocene. We, a small band of us, are huddled together in the cold and damp warily surveying each other, and some meager resources nearby, a small heap of edible mush. What shall we do next? How do I, or we, go on from here?

Hobbes imagines that if each one of us does what we want for ourselves, to eat all the mush, and perhaps also to have a quickie with the one over there, there will be a "war of each against each." "No arts; no letters; no society; and which is worst of all, continual fear, and danger of violent death: and the life of man, solitary, poor, nasty, brutish, and short."

If everyone sees that in the state of "war of each against each," no one gets anything that they want—not the mush, not the sex, nothing—we might agree (if we could figure out how to get everyone else on board as well) to a regimen of discipline and punishment under which we each have a chance to get by in what is neither the best way, which would be to have everything for ourselves, nor "the worst" way, which would involve dying a painful death in the stampede to the mush. Like the Lydian shepherd does, we make a compromise, agreeing to concede our rights to what we really want for the second-best outcome. Hobbes writes:

> So that in the nature of man, we find three principal causes of quarrel. First, competition; secondly, diffidence; thirdly, glory. The first maketh men invade for gain; the second for safety; and the third for reputation. The first use violence, to make themselves masters of other men's persons, wives, children and cattle; the second, to defend them; the third, for trifles, as a word, a smile, a different opinion, and any other sign of undervalue, either direct in their persons or by reflection in their kindred, their friends, their nation, their profession, or their name.

These three motives—competition, diffidence, and glory—are the sources of conflict (compare to the three poisons in Buddhism discussed in earlier chapters). First, people seek gain and thus compete over stuff—food, wealth, access to resources, including other people, their wives, and their children. The second motive, "diffidence," distrust and fear, arises because I recognize that you want at my stuff, perhaps to take my wife and enslave my children. I distrust and fear you because I know that this is what I want, and you are like me. Finally, even if I have enough food, sex, and help in the fields to harvest my bounty, I still want glory. I want you to recognize that I am something special. If you don't, I will want to crush you like a bug. For what? For a trifle.

There are two ways to read Hobbes's thought experiment.

I. 1. Everyone has equal satiable wants/desires/needs (for food, clothing, shelter, sex, money, glory, reputation; and against insecurity, living in a state of fear, danger, and the high likelihood of early and painful death).
   2. Everyone has (roughly) equal ability (to try) to get what they want.
   3. There is, at least, moderate scarcity.
   4. Therefore, there is a strong tendency (in the hearts and minds of everyone) for a war of each against each.

II. 1′. Everyone has equal insatiable wants/needs/desires, that is, there is some stuff that people want that they can never get enough of (it could be anything from the list, say, money or glory).
   2′. Everyone has (roughly) equal ability (to try) to get what they want.
   3′. Therefore, there is a strong tendency (in the hearts and minds of everyone) for a war of each against each.[19]

I. suggests that both actual war, as well as the tendency to the war of each against each, can be mitigated if the needs, desires, and wants of individuals can be satisfied, say, by there being enough food, clothing, and shelter, as well as, we'll suppose, sexual partners. According to II., there is no such thing as sufficiency of externalities, because at least some human desires cannot be satisfied for at least some people.

One criticism of both the Lydian shepherd thought experiment and Hobbes's state of nature thought experiment is that they prime us to think more individualistically about persons than is realistic, although to be fair, Glaucon does say that the shepherd with the magic ring will free his friends from prison. We are gregarious social animals and even if we are selfish, we are selfish for ourselves and our loved ones, possibly even for some wider group of teammates and compatriots. If our well-being depends on the labor of others and we are aware of this dependency, then we might not think it good or smart to off them and take their stuff. But taken together, the two thought experiments point to desires and motives that most will acknowledge are real: desires for food, clothing, shelter, sex, a certain security for life and limb, and some kind of social recognition.

What About Fellow Feeling?

Questions remain: Would the shepherd take more than his fair share if the society was egalitarian? We are not invited to consider that possibility. It would require changing the parameters of the thought experiment, so that there weren't the imbalances of status and power between the shepherd boy and the king. Would it make a difference? It might, based on the experiments that show that children, as well as capuchins and canines, have a strong equity bias. Then again, if human desires are such that we seek relative advantage, or especially if our desires are insatiable, then even in a situation of equality the desire to take more than one's fair share would be ever present. We need to know more about the sources of envy. Is envy diminished in egalitarian societies and enhanced in nonegalitarian ones? Do liberalism and capitalism, especially when taken together, create what might look like insatiability as opposed to what many think they do, namely, overfertilize tame, sensible desires and create ever new ones? I see you have more money than I do, and even though I have enough, I want more. My good-enough car looks shabby when I see a new model on TV, and I suddenly feel as if I need it. Karl Marx writes somewhat hyperbolically, "Under private property ... every person speculates on creating a *new* need in another, so as to drive him to a fresh sacrifice, to place him in a new dependence and to seduce him into a new mode of *gratification* and therefore economic ruin ([1844] 1964, 115).

David Hume provides a relevant thought experiment. Hume thought that different virtues—really the sets of virtues that make up the twin pillars of morality—have different bases in human nature. Justice is a cautious jealous virtue, invented entirely because it is useful practically and strategically, especially when it comes to dividing scarce resources. Whereas fellow feeling or benevolence, what we call kindness or compassion, is deeply rooted in human nature and fairly easy to cultivate. Hume writes:

> Let us suppose that nature has bestowed on the human race such profuse ABUNDANCE of all EXTERNAL conveniences, that, without any uncertainty in the event, without any care or industry on our part, every individual finds himself fully provided with whatever his most voracious appetites can want, or luxurious imagination wish or desire. His natural beauty, we shall suppose, surpasses all acquired ornaments: the perpetual clemency of the seasons renders useless all clothes or covering: the raw herbage affords him the most delicious fare; the clear fountain, the richest beverage. No laborious occupation required: no tillage: no navigation. Music, poetry, and contemplation form his sole business: conversation, mirth, and friendship his sole amusement. It seems evident that, in such a happy state, every other social virtue would flourish, and receive tenfold increase; but the cautious, jealous virtue of justice would

never once have been dreamed of. For what purpose make a partition of goods, where everyone has already more than enough? Why give rise to property, where there cannot possibly be any injury? Why call this object MINE, when upon the seizing of it by another, I need but stretch out my hand to possess myself of what is equally valuable? Justice, in that case, being totally useless, would be an idle ceremonial, and could never possibly have place in the catalogue of virtues. (*Enquiry* III,1)

Hume's Shangri La thought experiment involves several idealizations. We are more beautiful that we actually are, the weather is more perfect than it actually is, and most importantly, there is no external scarcity, all the stuff we want is abundant. You reach for my mango and eat it. This is not a problem, because there is another equally ripe one within easy reach. In Shangri La there are always more than enough Skittles and stickers, so no economic games have any costs. Unless, having fewer than you do of what is a "profuse abundance" for both of us, is conceived as a cost.

There are two obvious worries with Hume's thought experiment. First, not all things we want are easily replaceable like the mangoes in Shangri La. It is one thing if you take my mango (or my Skittles) since there is an equally desirable one right next to it that I can have. But if you want my partner, that is a different story. There isn't another just like her for me.[20] Second, if humans are prone either by mechanisms of envy to seek relative or comparative advantage or, what is related but different, if there are some desires that are insatiable, or some people who have some insatiable desires in certain domains of life, then all the music, merriment, and mirth will, at a minimum, be suffused with tension, as well as all the usual trifling, and sometimes with outright conflict. And in any case, there is the fact that there is no place on earth yet, or in any nearby possible world, where all citizens have been delivered from the normal vulnerabilities associated with some scarce necessities. That said, what Hume—like Mencius, Aristotle, Rousseau, and Darwin—does a better job of emphasizing than Glaucon or Hobbes, is the gregarious, prosocial side of persons. We are, I think, lovers of friendship and community, and not only because others are useful to us. Natural selection has taken care of making us fellow feelers who naturally love to be with others.

The encounter between several great philosophical thought experiments and recent experimental work reveals considerable agreement that we are mammals possessed of self-regarding and other-regarding tendencies. Read charitably, the great thought experimentalists I have discussed—Mencius, Xunzi, Plato, Hobbes, Hume—taken collectively, made pretty good surmises of what sort of human nature the moral community typically has to work with. We are each a different instance of crooked wood with great potential to be transformed into something better. The experimental work largely provides a needle point of detail to what we have known from the wisdom of the ages for a long time.

A Commerce of Mutual Light

It is time, as promised and in closing, to return to the topic of moral education with a better sense of human psychology thanks to the work we have reviewed in child psychology, economic game theory, cultural anthropology, and the wisdom of the ages. What could schools legitimately do to assist parents, private communal associations, and religious institutions with creating morally excellent characters from the crooked wood that constitutes humanity, if, that is, there is anything they could legitimately do in a liberal polity?

First a story: In 1966 I began college in New York City, and read Nathan Glazer and Daniel Patrick Moynihan's *Beyond the Melting Pot* (1963). The subtitle was *The Negroes, Puerto Ricans, Jews, Italians, and Irish of New York City*. The book was about what I took to be glorious news, namely, that America's greatest immigrant city had not become, as many expected, a thin gruel of bland and homogeneous customs and habits. The thought that this might happen was based for some on the expectation that the dominant WASP culture would demand conformity to their normative regime, and differences would be thinned out, possibly remaining mostly in the form of ethnic restaurants, and such memorial events as Saint Patrick's Day and Saint Anthony's Day celebrations. Others did not expect so much that the WASP normative order would dominate and drown out all the other distinct and flavorful ingredients of several great migrations, as that all the ingredients would produce some entirely new, but nonetheless homogeneous normative order, a broth of one flavor. Why? Because that is just what happens in melting pots or blenders.

But it didn't happen, and I continue to hope it won't happen. One reason I hope this, is the same as J. S. Mill's. In his 1848 *Principles of Political Economy*, Mill writes:

> But the economical advantages of commerce are surpassed in importance by its effects which are intellectual and moral. It is hardly possible to overrate the value, in the present low state of human improvement, of placing human beings in contact with persons dissimilar to themselves, and with modes of thought and action unlike those with which they are familiar ... it is indispensible to be perpetually comparing their own notions and customs with the experience and example of persons in different circumstances from themselves; and there is no nation which does not need to borrow from others, not merely particular arts or practices, but essential points of character in which its own type is inferior (Mill [1848] 1963, III, 17, 594).

Mill is speaking here mostly about business commerce as a resource for moral progress. Two centuries earlier, Gottfried Wilhelm Leibniz had seen the same prospect for moral growth in cross-cultural exchange. He thought that increasingly individualistic European culture had much to learn about goodness from the Chinese, about "essential points of character in which [the European] type is inferior." On November 12, 1689, Leibniz wrote to the Jesuit missionary Giovanni Laureati just before Laureati departed for China. Leibniz advised Laureati, "[I hope] you will remember the great business that has been given to you, promoting commerce between two such widely separated spheres. A commerce, I say, of doctrine and mutual light" (Perkins 2004, 125).

One objection, to those of us who relish variation and moral novelty and think it is a rich resource for moral critique and improvement, is to point out that we are the type who likes novelty. But there are many others who don't like novelty very much, and prefer normative conformity, reliability, and predictability instead. And furthermore, and most importantly, even if you allow adults to be moral experimentalists, you cannot raise good children if they are not imbued with moral confidence in their form of life, their way of worldmaking, in some set of moral ideals and exemplars that the relevant elders, typically the parents, set out as models for the kind of content of character they expect in them.[21] One certainly ought not encourage teenagers to be moral experimentalists. They are already way too inclined to test the boundaries and disrupt the moral order in thoughtless, gratuitous, and egoistic ways.

I think this is an interesting and important objection, perhaps it is an observation. Responding to it requires a certain amount of empirical information that I, as a philosopher, do not have. But in any case, I do not intend to advocate for teaching children that most things are up for discussion. I want only to defend something that I think is relatively innocuous, an obviously good idea, but not at all part of American moral education, especially K–12 public education. I think the idea avoids the objection that it is too confidence undermining, as well as the objections that it is a friend of some dangerous kind of relativism, and/or violates the separation of church and state by trying to impose a disguised, religiously endorsed moral order.

Here is the context for the proposal. Neoliberalism, the conjunct of the commitment to liberal democracy in the political sphere, and the commitment to more or less unfettered capitalism, is the dominant public normative order in America. Despite its dominance, it is not quite, not yet at least, the "inescapable framework" inside which we conduct all affairs of life. One reason is that almost all adults, and most children in multicultural, multiethnic, religiously diverse communities, are aware of different ways that different people conduct their "free and equal" lives. Not only is there diversity where many of us live, some of it moral diversity, but there are also some old habits of the heart that are recessive, but not totally forgotten or completely occluded from view, and that contain germs of moral sources worth rehabilitating, even if only sometimes and for certain purposes. For example, there are traditions of civic friendship that still animate town meetings in certain parts of New England. I was lucky enough to serve on Town Meeting in Wellesley, Massachusetts, in the early 1990s. There is the admirable solidarity of unionized workers in a few industries and states, and of activists in the ongoing projects of fighting anti-black racism and homophobia, and for humane treatment of displaced peoples. There is the esprit de corps, commitment, and conviction of firefighters and other first responders. There is the inspiring example of some healthcare workers and teachers who see themselves as having a vocation, not merely a job or a career.

One reason to worry that we may not have sufficient moral sources at our disposal at any given time, is because a moral ecology can sometimes change in a flash and without conscious planning or direction. Rapid change can lead to a situation where even inside a tradition there is deep forgetting, so deep that good old ideas are as hard to retrieve as good new ideas are hard to invent. Witness the difficulty of recovering and treating seriously ideas in our own tradition, like Epicurean and Stoic ones, which offer reasons for taking the satisfaction of desires less seriously, for not treating our personal aims and desires as urgent matters that the entire cosmos should make sure are satisfied right now. Or consider the difficulty many have reclaiming and taking seriously the old idea that we are stewards of nature, not just users of nature.

As recently as 1971, John Rawls argued that people in liberal democracies like the United States and Sweden believed in something like social democracy. Our considered view was one that favored maximal liberty and economic freedom, but only so long as those who are worst off, who suffer bad luck in life's circumstances because of the genetic lottery, economic location at birth, or because of race, gender, ethnicity, or country of origin, are taken care of first and also taken care of well.

But this is not the view embodied in our political institutions, not the political philosophy that has in fact revealed itself in America in the decades since *Theory of Justice* was published. The revealed view is one of rapacious capitalism, of individuals struggling in an extremely competitive atmosphere, who need to make sure they have a successful career so that they can take care of themselves and those near and dear. Of course, economic success is not the only end. In addition there is finding meaning, or, more usually, as Americans are inclined to say, finding happiness. But that, it is then said, is up to each individual. Except well, it isn't, or it isn't really; and thinking doesn't make it so.

Ethics and Religion in America

It is a common view, the view of the majority in America, that ethics typically come with religion, and not otherwise. This view is immensely consequential for how we think about moral education. Think about how radical it was for President Obama in his second inaugural address to mention "unbelievers" as part of our nation, and think how impossible it would be for Americans to elect a professed agnostic, let alone an atheist, to national office. This is because many worry that an agnostic or an atheist cannot be trusted; they lack strong moral sources. On the one hand, there is the view that we are a religious nation and that being morally good has to do with one's religion. Luckily, as far as religious diversity goes, the Abrahamic traditions generally agree about most major moral issues. So some moral agreement, and thus order, is guaranteed. But on the other hand, and partly because of the fact that ethics and religion are thought to be of a piece, there is the view that we need to keep ethics out of schools. Why? Because teaching anything ethically substantive would, given that ethics and religion are of a piece, involve bringing religion into the schools, and that is not allowed, given the separation of church and state. Moral and religious education are of a piece, and that piece is for the parents and the children to work out, possibly mediated by the church, mosque, or temple to which they belong (Appiah 2005; Brighouse and Swift 2014).

Put this ideology together with the very real confusion about what public schools are allowed to teach as far as virtues, values, and the circumstances of meaningful human lives go, and we get a situation like this: We are comfortable, it is fine and sensible, to hold out economic success as a central desirable end for a good human life. There is almost universal agreement that people ought to plan to work, develop skills that workers need, and then work. There is no agreement about what the schools are allowed to teach as far as the content of character goes. In fact, it is not even clear that liberal society should endorse teaching what King certainly hoped it would, namely, that racism is bad and that there is something deeply wrong with the fact that "One hundred years later [after emancipation] the Negro lives on a lonely island of poverty in the midst of a vast ocean of material prosperity. One hundred years later the Negro is still languished in the corners of American society and finds himself in exile in his own land. So we've come today to dramatize a shameful condition." Why might someone complain about teaching this? Because it has content. Our modus vivendi, some think, requires us to be neutral and not make value judgments in public institutions about what views or situations are "shameful."

There is something wrong here, probably several things. It seems to be a case where we have cut off the nose to spite the face. The idea of education as primarily career education, where universities sell themselves as laboratories for "innovation" and "entrepreneurship," and where politicians make fun of women's studies, black studies, and philosophy, actually the liberal arts and human sciences generally, as things that ought to be done on one's own time and one's own dime, reveals a problem, a serious imbalance. Why? Because most everyone thinks in their heart of hearts that what matters most, and also what they hope and expect to be remembered for when they are gone, is not for their bank account, their fancy cars, which elite schools they went to, the number of houses they own in Aspen and in the Hamptons, but the content of their character. What is to be done?

Soul Making

"Soul making," according to Kwame Anthony Appiah, is "the project of intervening in the process of interpretation through which each citizen develops an identity—and doing so with the aim of increasing her chances of living an ethically successful life" (2005, 164). Soul making is the project of giving character the sort of content that makes it possible to be a good person and live a good human life. There is wide agreement that soul making can be done privately by families and religious institutions, as well as by each individual themselves once they achieve some kind of wisdom and autonomy. The question is whether it can and should be done publicly in schools. Here are a few reasons to think some kind of soul making ought to be part of school curricula.

First, there is this fact: Economic success is the coin of the realm, it is culturally advertised as of singular importance, and schools are designed in large measure to produce reliable law-abiding citizens and workers, economically successful ones. But there is abundant evidence that economic success is not, in fact, the main way success in life is assessed either by the subject of a life or others. Success in life has to do with being a person of good, really excellent, character (Flanagan 2007; Haybron 2008).

If it is true that personal goodness is in fact judged as necessary for a good human life, then this ought to be taught to the youth. Keep your eye on the prize that is you; nothing less than the meaning and significance of your life—to yourself and to others—depends on the quality of your character. We allow a lot of spin in actual or imaginary eulogies (including by the self), but saying a person was good enough or decent is faint praise, really a judgment of a life that was acceptable, but not a success. We ought to aspire to something better, to excellence. The kids ought to be taught this, that excellence as a person is what, at the end of the day, matters most. Perhaps they should be taught to review how they are doing in that project each night before they sleep, after they have done their other, less important homework.

Still, we come back to the question of what content or contents of character are judged as excellent, and who has authority to inculcate them. Thinking optimistically, one can look for the zones of life where all the traditions represented in a plural community agree on some moral values, virtues, norms, and practices. Here, we might make progress if everyone in such a plural community agrees that one ought to be fair, just, kind, and compassionate, and that meanness and bullying are wrong. Values, virtues, and norms such as these have some substance, they are not will-o'-the-wisps. And thus we might gain agreement that the schools should teach these substantive values to the point that there is an unforced consensus about their shape and nature.

On the cup-is-half-empty side, one can point out that these virtues, and values, and norms will still need to be described fairly thinly, so as to avoid sectarian suspicions and disputes. If kindness is taught in Jesus's way or in the

Buddhist way or in the utilitarian way, we will be encouraging the youth to actively do things unto others to alleviate their suffering; whereas if it is taught in the Confucian way or in the Kantian way, the youth will be taught to refrain from doing anything to another that they would not want done to themselves.

This is true. But I see no reason why the kids cannot be exposed to such disagreements. Teaching about the different ways different people conceive and exercise very similar values and virtues attunes the young to charity in interpretation, to a type of loving attention, as well as to a proper humility, not thinking that one knows the right way to do things, and that other practices and ways of being are objectively weird or nonsensical.[22]

It may be enough if teachers have permission to teach what is the unforced consensus about the content of character among or across various traditions, so long as they also explain that different communities conceive priority relations among values differently. Then families, communal associations, religious institutions, and the children themselves can provide the details, the further filling out, as well as the trump rules as they see them.

There will be some forms of valuing, some virtues and norms, that can be acknowledged and discussed, but that will need to be marked as not part of the unforced consensus, lest even the most liberal elders object. *Ahimsa*, the Indic commitment to nonviolence, is an example. It follows too straightforwardly from *ahimsa* that we are morally reckless toward animals, which is almost certainly true, but not part of the unforced consensus in America.

The same goes for matters of the proper economy of the virtues and values, the relations among them. For the Buddhist, compassion is always trump. For the secular liberal, justice has pride of place; for the libertarian, it is freedom; and for a certain kind of religious person, it is the word of certain sacred texts. Clearly, the right answers to these disputes cannot be worked out in classrooms (it is unlikely that there are right, timeless answers to these questions). But these disputes can be taught about and discussed in a polity that prizes democratic reflection. We do ourselves a disservice and show disrespect for our children when we act as if they cannot be exposed to learning about the contours of human nature and difference without corrupting their hearts and minds or throwing them into some deadly relativistic or nihilistic identity disorder. We withhold from them resources for moral reason, imagination, and deliberation that might well serve them and future generations in the moral project.

In 1973 a teacher at Drake High School in North Dakota assigned Kurt Vonnegut's *Slaughterhouse-Five*. Parents complained and the head of the school board, Charles McCarthy, demanded that all thirty-two copies be burned in the school's furnace as a result of its "obscene language." Vonnegut then sent McCarthy this letter.

> If you were to bother to read my books, to behave as educated persons would, you would learn that they are not sexy, and do not argue in favor

of wildness of any kind. They beg that people be kinder and more responsible than they often are. It is true that some of the characters speak coarsely. That is because people speak coarsely in real life. Especially soldiers and hardworking men speak coarsely, and even our most sheltered children know that. And we all know, too, that those words really don't damage children much. They didn't damage us when we were young. It was evil deeds and lying that hurt us.

I think Vonnegut gets it just right, and his message applies to teaching young children about their own psychology, about the psychology of the adolescents and adults they will become, about common pitfalls in thinking about what is best, including best for oneself, and, finally, about religious and cultural difference.

Children get complex motivations. They understand that indifference can be banal and ordinary, and that meanness can be gratuitous. They themselves enact both, and have complex motivations toward the well-being of others. They also understand difference; they live in it. And they understand that adults can speak and act "coarsely." What children, just like adults, can use more of are models "that beg people be kinder and more responsible than they often are." And again, this is not just because the world can use more of such things, but because at the end of the day, these children, now grown, will judge the quality of their own lives, and will be judged by others, primarily on the quality of their character.

***

I'll end here. I have been wondering aloud, speculating some about modes of soul making that might be sensible and innocuous in schools, even under the watchful eye of the liberal state attuned, on the one hand, to catching out the teaching of anything that has sectarian content, and, on the other, anything that might make the kids come home as moral skeptics or relativists, who question parental or religious authority.

I do not know whether to be hopeful about schools doing more moral education as I imagine it. I can speak with somewhat greater confidence about the shape of normative moral philosophy at the college level. If ethics and moral psychology are to remain relevant they will need to be increasingly more anthropologically attuned and cross-cultural. The days when ethics could be conceived as a conversation about human excellence inside a single tradition that is a series of footnotes to Plato is long gone. There is no single tradition inside which that project can be carried out. We contain multiplicities. The good news is that the youth of today will be exposed to some of the beautiful varieties of moral possibility, and stand chances of not being trapped in their own upbringing. This is a good and hopeful thing. If we elders equip them with tools for honest, patient, critical imagination and tools for rational, patient self-cultivation, it could be a great thing. Time will tell.

Bibliographical Essay

11. Self-Variations: Philosophical Archaeologies

Most of the sources in psychology and anthropology for the dozen self-variations are cited with the specific self-variation in the text. I recommend those papers to anyone who wants to judge the evidence for themselves.

Like many philosophers, my interests in the nature of the self, modes of self-knowledge, and the construction and constitutions of selves are foundational, more or less continuous with my interest in the nature of consciousness and personal identity. William James's two chapters in the *Principles of Psychology* ([1890] 1981), volume 1, "The Stream of Thought" (IX) and "The Consciousness of Self" (X), are essential reading on both the self and consciousness. John Dewey's *Human Nature and Conduct* (1922) is a classic on communal self-construction. On the specific topic of personal identity, John Perry's *Personal Identity* (2008) is a fine collection of classic papers.

Charles Taylor's *Sources of the Self* (1989) stands alone as a monumental exploration and philosophical history of modern North Atlantic selves. Taylor's *A Secular Age* (2007) is a brilliant extension of that work in which he explains what we might mean when we say we are secular selves who live in a secular age, especially given that the majority of people, even in the North Atlantic, are religious. Robert H. Bellah's *Religion in Human Evolution from the Paleolithic to the Axial Age* (2011) and Ara Norenzayan's *Big Gods: How Religion Transformed Cooperation and Conflict* (2013) are two important books on the ways philosophical, religious, ethical, and self-conceptions coevolve with each other. Michael Sandel's *Liberalism and the Limits of Justice* (1982) remains a good source for getting a feel for the debate between a certain liberal, individualistic picture of the self, and a more communitarian one, as do several papers by Charles Taylor in his *Philosophical Papers* (1985), volume 1, especially "Self-Interpreting Animals" and "The Concept of a Person," and volume 2, especially "Atomism." Susan Moller Okin's *Justice, Gender, and the Family* (1989) is a classic on problems with the individualistic self from the perspective of feminist philosophy.

Anthropology is a treasure trove of excellent work on self-variation. I recommend Margaret Mead's controversial *Sex and Temperament in Three Primitive Societies* (1935); Marcel Mauss's "A Category of the Human Mind: The Notion of Person; the Notion of Self" (1938), and Clifford Geertz's, *Local Knowledge* (1983) and *The Interpretation of Cultures* (1973).

Some important and accessible work on the narrative self includes Alasdair MacIntyre's *After Virtue* (1981), Daniel C. Dennett's "Why Everyone Is a Novelist (1988)," and Jerome Bruner's *Making Stories* (2002). Galen Strawson's "Against Narrativity" (2004) challenges the narrative self view on both descriptive—it doesn't fit everyone—and normative grounds—it imposes an oppressive regimen of accountability on persons. For aficionados on the topic of self, Strawson's *Selves* (2009) and his *Locke on Personal Identity* (2011) repay close study.

The Buddhist no-self view figures heavily in this chapter. Two excellent sources on the meaning of no-self are Steven Collins's *Selfless Persons* (1982) and Mark Siderits's *Personal Identity and Buddhist Philosophy: Empty Persons* (2003). My *Bodhisattva's Brain* (2011) offers an interpretation of no-self that in my experience fits with what most contemporary East, South, and Southeast Asian Buddhists actually think when they speak of no-self, which also has the advantage of being something that many naturalistic Western philosophers could accept, unlike, for example, the extreme deconstructive view that Siderits and other Western analytic metaphysicians find in high church Mahayana Buddhism.

12. The Content of Character

In my last years of high school and first years of college I read some books that were formative, which sparked or reinforced my commitment to the value of diversity, as well as a deep interest in what Martin Luther King Jr. called "the content of character." I did not then and do not now think that plural value communities undermine the idea that there are moral excellences that survive their plural forms, and that we can encourage in each generation, forms of justice, respect, and love. I thank wise elders for exposing me to these books, and I am grateful to all the Irish, Italian, Jewish, Puerto Rican, and Black friends growing up who taught me a lot about identity, difference, and moral community.

In 1964 I read James Baldwin's *Another Country* (1962) on a trip with my Dad to Antigua in the British West Indies. I next read Martin Luther King Jr's *Why We Can't Wait* (1964) and Malcolm X's *The Autobiography of Malcolm X* (1965). In 1966, in a required freshman sociology class, we were assigned both William Whyte's *The Organization Man* (1956), which reinforced my strong sense that the military-industrial complex was as dangerous as President Dwight D. Eisenhower said it was just before he stepped down from office in

1960, and confirmed my sense of what I did not want to be when I grew up. Reading Glazer and Moynihan's *Beyond the Melting Pot* (1963) was a relief. I had never thought that diversity, most of which I knew from spending time with friends of different kinds, was once expected to blend away into a homogeneous mush, and I was deeply relieved to discover that it wasn't happening, at least not in New York City, where I lived. Other books that made me think about the plural ways of being human and the contents of character in tandem were Clyde Kluckhohn's *Mirror for Man* (1949), Herbert Marcuse's *One-Dimensional Man* (1964) and his earlier *Eros and Civilization* (1955), Karl Marx's *Economic and Philosophical Manuscripts of 1844*, Amiri Baraka's (aka LeRoi Jones) *The System of Dante's Hell* (1965), and Viktor Frankl's *Man's Search for Meaning* (1959).

I have only just started thinking about the importance of asking everyone, starting with the children, to aim really high morally for themselves and their community. When I was writing *The Really Hard Problem: Meaning in the Material World* (2007), I was struck by the large amount of empirical evidence from psychology, anthropology, and economics, that moral excellence is the best marker, first personally and third personally, for whether a life is a good one. Aristotle had said this, but the data supported it. I guess I had thought of the idea as mainly a kind of philosopher's wish for a world in which it was true that virtue was its own reward, despite the fact that this was not that world. But Viktor Frankl had put the idea in my head that it might be true sometimes in this world, when in *Man's Search for Meaning* (1959), he explored the effectiveness of deathbed psychodrama in helping people make good choices. When people, mostly patients in therapy, faced complicated existential choices, he would ask them to consider the choice not from the perspective of what they want now, looking forward, but from the point of view of the imagined end of life, looking back. In the deathbed exercise people make choices more aligned with goodness than when looking from the here and now to what is next and right in front of them. But then I started to see that there was actually lots of evidence across the human sciences that in fact it is true that most people do not really think that money, sex, drugs, rock 'n' roll, glory, and power bring happiness, but instead that things like goodness, love, and friendship do. So I came to think that this should be taught to the youth, continually reinforced, and that we ought to call on ourselves and each other to be as good as we can possibly be. Nothing less than the meaning, significance, and worth of life depends on being as excellent as we can be.

Mark Alfano's *Character as Moral Fiction* (2013) is a fine book that takes seriously the evidence that the crooked wood of humanity is hard to straighten, that perfect virtue is, in all likelihood, impossible for creatures like us, but that it is important nonetheless to attribute to each other virtues that we have partially (even ones we show only little signs of) so that we come to understand that working to develop them is a worthy aspiration. Linda Zagzebski favors very high standards for moral excellence, and, like me, is hopeful about realizing such excellence over generations. Watch for the publication of her wonderful 2015 Gifford Lectures, titled "Exemplarist Virtue Theory." Finally, I recommend two books by Kwame Anthony Appiah, *The Ethics of Identity* (2005) and *Cosmopolitanism* (2006), which are deeply personal, thoughtful, sensitive, and humble meditations on being oneself, and being and doing well in our new kind of cosmopolitan world. Appiah is as attuned as any philosopher I know to the rich resources that cosmopolitan worlds afford for moral imagination and moral improvement.

ACKNOWLEDGMENTS

This book began in my imagination a long time ago, while I was writing *Varieties of Moral Personality* (1991). Thus the people I need to thank go back to my earliest days of working in moral psychology in the 1980s. Larry Blum, Amélie Rorty, David Wong, Ruth Anna Putnam, Margaret Rhodes, Andreas Teuber, and Jennifer Radden were there at the beginning when we started the—still going after all these 30+ years—moral psychology group in Cambridge, Massachusetts, in 1984. I am deeply grateful to them and the other pilgrims. I think it fair to say we encouraged each other to do ethics and moral psychology in a new key, in a way that consciously conversed with psychology, anthropology, and the other human sciences, and that was actively engaged with issues of social justice, race, culture, and gender. Around the same time, in the mid-1980s I started to correspond with Galen Strawson about the nature of the self and self-variation. I am grateful to Galen for encouraging over the years my heterodox thinking about the possibilities for being different kinds of selves by his own heterodox thinking about the self.

Throughout the 1980s and 1990s, Alasdair MacIntyre encouraged my engaging non-Western sources. At first, I did so quietly and on the side, maintaining, for all everyone knew, a research agenda devoted to straight-arrow philosophy of mind, Western ethics, and moral psychology. In the 1980s and 1990s, Ifeanyi Menkiti, Kwasi Wiredu, and Anthony Appiah served as my first teachers on African philosophy. Akin Ogundiran has been my recent go-to person on African philosophy.

My study of comparative, cross-cultural philosophy was energized and focused at the turn of the new millennium, when I was invited to Dharamsala, India, to talk with the Dalai Lama and his team about destructive emotions.

In 2000 David B. Wong came from Brandeis to Duke, and in 2003 we taught a comparative philosophy course together. It was then that I started to study seriously Classical Chinese philosophy. Hagop Sarkissian, Dave's and my PhD student, now a distinguished professor, was also a great teacher in Chinese philosophy.

I found the Chinese philosophy community extremely welcoming. Along with David Wong, P. J. Ivanhoe, Kwong-loi Shun, Ted Slingerland, Roger Ames, Eric Hutton, Steve Angle, Chris Frazer, Chad Hansen, Hui Chieh Loy, Manyul Im, Sorhoon Tan, Tongdong Bai, Dan Robins, Amy Oberding, and Justin Tiwald were ever at the ready to patiently teach what I needed to know.

I am grateful to members of the Columbia University Comparative Philosophy Seminar in New York City, which I started to attend in 2005, for continuous inspiration and support over the years, especially Chris Kelley, Jonathan Gold, Chris Gowans, Mark Siderits, Marie Friquegnon, Raziel Abelson, and Tao Jing.

In 2012 P. J. Ivanhoe, to whom this book is dedicated, invited me to spend a term at the Center for East Asian and Comparative Philosophy (CEACOP) at City University Hong Kong, which he directs. I was supported by a generous grant from the Academy of Korean Studies and funded by the Korean Government (MEST) (AKS-2011-AAA-2102). The CEACOP is an outstanding community of scholars and I am grateful to Sungmoon Kim, Hsin-wen Lee, Eirik Harris, Richard Kim, Xueying Wang, Wenqing Zhao, Yan Hiu Yeng, and other colleagues there for their friendship and conversation during the autumn term, 2013. At CEACOP, I wrote most of my Aquinas Lecture, "Moral Sprouts and Natural Teleology: Contemporary Moral Psychology Meets Classical Chinese Philosophy," which I then gave at Marquette University in the spring of 2014. That lecture contains some of the main ideas in early chapters of this book. I was able to present some of my ideas about cross-cultural philosophy to audiences at Chinese University of Hong Kong, Lingnan University, and Hong Kong University.

In Hong Kong, P.J., Sungmoon Kim, and Richard Kim introduced me to some debates in Korean neo-Confucian philosophy about the moral emotions. I was gripped and set to thinking about how these debates would be discussed from the perspective of contemporary evolutionary biology and moral psychology. I spoke about those connections at Sungkyun University in Seoul, Korea, in the autumn of 2013. Myeong-seok Kim and Yougsun Back were immensely helpful interlocutors. A bit later, Jin Park, David H. Kim, Eric Nelson, A. Charles Muller, Don Baker, and Halla Kim invited me into some further discussions of Korean moral psychology, and introduced me to the debates among Buddhists and Confucians in Korea about human nature and the human good.

I am lucky to have three friends who are judicious scientists and also philosophically extremely sophisticated: Paul Bloom, Alison Gopnik, and Frans de Waal. I have had many opportunities over the years to benefit from their wise counsel on matters of human nature and moral development.

I thank Jonathan Haidt for welcoming my critically constructive perspective on his work over the years. Substantial differences between me and Haidt on moral modularity, dual-processing architecture of mind, and the power of reason and imagination were sharpened in a lively "Author Meets Critics" session in April 2012 at the American Philosophical Meetings in San Francisco, where I served as a critic, along with Allan Gibbard and Jeannette Kennett, of Haidt's *The Righteous Mind*.

These ideas, as well as ideas about the relevance of descriptive psychology and anthropology to normative ethics, were advanced at a small conference in Sicily in the summer of 2012, on the psychology and biology of morality, where Frans de Waal, Patricia Churchland, Philip Kitcher, Darcia Narváez, Steve Martin, and Simon Blackburn shared their wisdom.

Over the last fifteen years, I have set to traveling the world as an amateur anthropologist exposing myself to the ways of worldmaking I discuss here, which are still alive in the blood and bones of contemporary people. I thank all the anonymous informants on all six inhabited continents (as well as the crew and fellow passengers on the Russian research vessel I took to Antarctica) who spoke honestly and openly with me about how they see things and what matters. I learned a lot, including about myself, from all of you.

In the last three years I have spoken about various parts of the book as they were coming into final form. In 2012–13, I was the Indian Council for Philosophical Research (ICPR) Distinguished Annual Lecturer, and spoke on the virtues of doing world philosophy in New Delhi, Allahabad, Lucknow, and Kolkata. In 2014, I gave the 78th Aquinas Lecture at Marquette on Mencius and contemporary moral psychology. I developed and refined those chapters thanks to critical feedback from audiences at Marquette, Georgia State University, and Fordham University.

I tried the chapter on destructive emotions in Buddhist and Korean neo-Confucian moral psychology at the University of Nebraska–Omaha in 2014. The chapters on anger generated lively discussions at Heidelberg University, Germany, the University of Oregon, and Stanford University in 2014, and at the University of Kansas in the autumn of 2015.

I tried out some of my ideas on world philosophy and cross-cultural moral education at Cal State Fullerton in the summer of 2014, and at the Society for Ethics Across the Curriculum meetings in Greenville, South Carolina, in the autumn of 2015 and at Rutgers in the spring of 2016.

Davidson College in Davidson, North Carolina, hosted a two-day retreat on my work in the winter of 2015, where we talked about the chapters on how not to be trapped by one's upbringing, anger, and self-variation.

In May 2015, I spoke about the connection between a metaphysics of no-self and moral selflessness at City University Hong Kong. In June 2015, I gave the Leibniz Lectures on "The Geography of Morals" at Leibniz University, Hanover, Germany, where I also got to speak about Leibniz's enthusiasm for cross-cultural work, what he called a "commerce of light."

My final last-minute check on things occurred in December of 2015 at the National Indian Institute for Advanced Study (NIAS) in Bangalore, at a conference on "Consciousness, Cognition, and Culture." In Bangalore, friends and colleagues bolstered my confidence that there are indeed multiple ways that the self and its good are conceived, and that these offer opportunities for mutual learning and growth.

Over the course of the last three years, 2012–2015, I have had the privilege to be part of the "Contending Modernities Project" on Catholic-Muslim dialogue, sponsored by the Kroc Institute for Peace Studies at the University of Notre Dame, which has met in South Bend, Indiana, New York City, Doha, Qatar, and Rome. I am grateful to Scott Appleby and Ebrahim Moosa for welcoming me into this dedicated group of scholars and activists.

I cannot possibly name all the generous souls who have helped me think better, more clearly, and more deeply about the worth of comparative philosophy and the possibilities for moral improvement in alternative ways of worldmaking. But these folks stand out: Mark Alfano, Srinivas Aravamudan, Charlie Camosy, Amber Carpenter, Myisha Cherry, Stephen Clark, Cristian Coseru, Gregson Davis, Uljana Feest, Bronwyn Finnegan, Howard Gardner, Jay Garfield, Allan Gibbard, Charles Goodman, Chris Gowans, Sherine Hamdy, Damian Howard, Mark Johnson, Chris Kelley, Jennette Kennett, Meena Krishnamurthy, Kristján Kristjánsson, Béatrice Longuenesse, Bob McCauley, Deborah Mower, Shaun Nichols, Hanna Pickard, Grant Ramsey, Maura Ryan, Abdulahziz Sachedina, Mark Siderits, Michael Slote, Nancy Snow, Galen Strawson, Nina Strohminger, Evan Thompson, Robert Thurman, Mark Unno, Margaret Urban Walker, and R. Jay Wallace.

I am grateful to Duke University and the Center for Comparative Philosophy for supporting my work and allowing me a couple of leaves to do research and to write. Many colleagues at Duke besides David Wong have been encouraging: in Philosophy, Allen Buchanan, Jennifer Hawkins, Andrew Janiak, Gopal Sreenivasan; several PhD students are comparative enthusiasts, Alex DeForge, Jing Hu, Ewan Kingston, Seth Ligo, Daniel Stephens, and Sungwoo Um; Paul Griffiths and Stanley Hauerwas at Duke's Divinity School; Richard Jaffe, Hwansoo Kim, and Leela Prasad in Religion; my comrades in the "Humanities Faculty Collective," especially Nancy Armstrong and Toril Moi; and Sarah Beckwith, John Martin, Rob Mitchell, Thomas Pfau, and Heather Wallace in the Philosophy Arts and Literature (PAL) cabal.

I owe special thanks to Wenqing Zhao. I met Wenqing in Hong Kong in 2013 when she was finishing her dissertation. We started talking then about Confucianism, political philosophy, and feminism in China. Wenqing is a brilliant scholar and is now a postdoc at Duke's Center for Comparative Philosophy. She has become a treasured friend and collaborator.

In the autumn of 2015, I settled into residency at the National Humanities Center in Research Triangle Park, North Carolina, as Rockefeller Fellow for 2015–2016. The NHC is a scholar's paradise. I am grateful to its provision of a room of my own, and to the conviviality of my fellow scholars, especially Béatrice Longuenesse and Danny Walkowitz. I am thankful to Robert Newman and Elizabeth Mansfield, and the wonderful staff at NHC, for creating the ideal environment for thinking and writing. Karen Carroll deserves special thanks for serving as a most competent and conscientious copyeditor.

Thanks also to Peter Ohlin, my editor at Oxford University Press, for his wisdom, wit, and professionalism, and that of his colleagues, especially Emily Sacharin. Thanks also to the two anonymous readers for the press.

There are a few special friends who have taught me a lot about philosophy, life, and friendship: Pat Churchland, George Graham, John Horan, Nancy Snow, and Serife Tekin. Then there are the early morning boys at the coffee shop on 9th Street, especially Tony Johnson and, my brother from another mother, Carl Kenney. My wife, Lynn Ainsworth, has traveled the world with me in support of my vocation as philosophical anthropologist. At home she is my partner, my love, pretty much everything to me.

New Year's Day 2016
Durham, North Carolina

NOTES

Chapter 1

1. One doesn't need linguistic categories to do the work of organizing thought; economic practices and other social practices can do so by themselves. In *The Souls of Black Folk* (1903) W. E. B. Du Bois explains how the virtues of the Negro slave, open-heartedness, faithfulness, sincerity, submission, and humility, are also those of a good ox or dog.

2. Śāntideva (1997), the great eighth-century Indian Mahayana Buddhist poet and sage, recommends gratitude to those who provide opportunities to practice compassion and patience:

> Those who wish to cause me suffering
> Are like Buddhas bestowing waves of blessing.
> As they open the door for my not going to an
> unfortunate realm,
> Why should I be angry with them? (6.101)

In America, one hears this sort of idea expressed in a somewhat degraded way: "That asshole teaches me patience." There is work to be done.

3. Experimental philosophy has started to get into the study of cross-cultural differences. This is good. There are many such differences, and once we have an inventory at a certain time and place—for example, learning that Koreans rank respect for elders more highly than Americans do—we will want explanations for these differences. That will require excavation of historical and cultural resources. There is some cross-cultural work in experimental philosophy that looks, for example, at differences in moral judgments between cultures on trolley problems or even in differences in bilingual peoples' judgments on such problems when they are framed in the different languages they know. People seem to be more utilitarian when dilemmas are framed in their second language, especially when that language is English. I am interested in such work *if* it is supported by, and embedded in, deep understanding of the traditions it claims to compare; otherwise not. The reason is that moral differences are normally deep, embedded in complex forms of life, not superficial. *Parable*: Richard Shweder did important work in psychological anthropology in the 1990s. Teenagers in Orissa, India, think that a son getting a haircut and eating a chicken on the day his father died is very bad. Teenagers in Hyde Park, Chicago, think it is OK. So far we have a difference, but no understanding of the difference. Cultural understanding shows the difference to be complex but not a difference at a deep existential level. In both cultures there are webs of moral belief and significance that designate a parental death as monumentally important and that deem certain practices as impious and disrespectful. *Lesson*: It takes a hermeneutic, a theory of interpretation to frame and then understand local moral judgments and actions. And that requires some comprehension of a tradition, a form of life.

4. Some proponents inside moral and political philosophy of the cross-cultural or anthropological turn include Kwame Anthony Appiah, Kwasi Wiredu, Michele Moody-Adams, Elizabeth Anderson, Amartya Sen, Martha Nussbaum, Philip J. Ivanhoe, David B. Wong, Kwong Loi-Shun, Lawrence Becker, Judith Butler, Charles Mills, Carol Pateman, Chike Jeffers, Naomi Zack, James Maffie, Jonathan Lear, Tamler Sommers, and Justin E. H. Smith.

5. Consider: "Building bridges out of papier-mâché is wrong" and "One ought not build bridges out of papier-mâché." Both sentences are true inside the normal practice of engineering. Given that bridges are built to allow heavy objects (people, animals, carts, automobiles, etc.) to get across expanses of water, land, etc., they ought to be made of the right materials. Similarly, one might think insofar as morality is a system of hypothetical imperatives, where the antecedents are expressions of some facts about persons or the world, that the sentence "It is wrong to kill innocents" is true insofar as normally people like to feel safe, being murdered can be painful, loss of loved ones makes people sad, etc., and that therefore it is best to abide rules of not killing innocents.

Chapter 2

1. The point that there are no shared ecologies, in the sense of there being identical ecologies for any two organisms, is a conceptual point and a reminder. It is not intended to deny the scientific usefulness of the ordinary concept of an ecology to refer to something like an arena that provides a set of resources and has certain common features.

2. Scientists, mathematicians, and logicians, of course, gain propositional knowledge, "know-that," about each of these domains at much deeper levels than ordinary practical life requires.

3. John Rawls (1971, 1993, 1999), whose normative theory of justice Kohlberg claimed to find developmental evidence for, was himself emphasizing that his theory was a theory of political justice, not in the first instance, indeed perhaps not at all, a theory of personal morality. Consider: A theory of justice might entail that there ought to be a certain tax rate, and also mechanisms to enforce it. The taxes will be paid and the society might be just, but this could in theory happen without individuals having much of a personal commitment to justice.

4. The ideal speech community it is not just a community in which there is equal opportunity to speak but also a community in which, at least in theory, everyone has access to the same information—there are no rules of deference that run along lines of race, ethnicity, gender, and so on.

5. This is not a work in virtue theory. I favor virtue theories relative to the competition, and certainly as the best, among the contenders, for a normative theory that models well the normal acquisition, shape, structure, and dynamics of personal morality. I do not think virtue theory is adequate at the social and political levels, where structures like laws and tax codes need to be put in place to do what individual good people do not find easy to do on their own. Even as a model for individual morality, I am agnostic here as to whether all of moral psychology can be modeled according to character or virtue ethics. It depends, for one thing, on whether thinking and imagination are best assimilated to kinds of intellectual virtues.

6. It is an interesting question whether a moral conception should only promote realizable ideals. In *Varieties* (1991), I endorsed the principle of minimal psychological realism,

which says that a moral conception ought to be perceived as possible for creatures like us, which is not quite the same as saying is possible for creatures like us. Often a people endorses norms, values, virtues, ways of being and acting, which they hope future generations can realize, but which they know that they cannot fully realize for now in their individual or generational time. It is possible that some moral ideals are motivating while not even really being perceived as possible for creatures like us.

7. As for Piaget and Kohlberg, E. O. Wilson sees no mechanism to explain moral development and complains that thus far the theory is purely structural or formal, and not yet integrated with the rest of biology. He predicts that such theorizing, insofar as it reveals patterns or structures of moral development, will eventually be "incorporated into a broadened developmental biology and genetics (1975, 564), and suggests that where different people end up stage-wise may depend on selection at the genetic level as much as on cultural selection.

Chapter 3

1. In recent years, pretty much as I write, excellent, important, and widely discussed work at the intersection of ethics, neurobiology, evolutionary biology, primatology, psychology, and anthropology includes Frans de Waal (2006, 2009), Philip Kitcher (2011), Patricia Smith Churchland (2011), Sober and Wilson (1998), Boyd and Richerson (2005), Jonathan Haidt (2012), Joseph Henrich et al. (2007, 2010), Bowles and Gintis (2011), Paul Bloom (2013b), and Joshua Greene (2013). Walter Sinnott-Armstrong's five-volume series (2008–16) is a good source on some of the main areas of activity.

2. Myles Burnyeat (1980) coined the phrase "first nature."

3. There is controversy over who "invented" the idea of moral modularity. Some say Marc Hauser (2006); others say he "borrowed" the idea from John Mikhail (2011). That may be so, but neither invented it. Mencius did. One might distinguish between two kinds of modularists, monists and pluralists. Hauser and Mikhail are monists who follow Chomsky (and Rawls, who recommended the possible usefulness of thinking of the "justice as fairness" system along Chomskyean lines in 1971), and describe an organ for morality akin to the alleged language organ. The contemporary modularists I discuss call themselves social intuitionists or moral foundations theorists. They are pluralists and describe a set of independent modules, akin to Mencius's sprouts, that constitute the substrate of moral competence. As for who wins the naming contest, I wrote about both kinds of modularity theories, monist and pluralist, in *Varieties of Moral Personality* (1991). Howard Gardner's important theory of multiple intelligences (1983) was another early attempt to exploit the idea of modularity to improve the low quality of discussion of IQ. Gardner recommended that we think of intelligence as involving multiple, partly autonomous competences, for example, logical, linguistic, spatial, tactile-kinesthetic, and interpersonal and intrapersonal ones, which are subject to individual variation as well as differentially favored in different cultures. Gardner's pluralist view has implications for morality, since he thought that intrapersonal and interpersonal intelligence can be refined or not, and also that they can come apart. On most every view, self-knowing and the ability to sense what is going on with others matter to morality.

4. This last view is expressed in *Xunzi*. But Xunzi (314–217 BCE) lived after Mencius, and thus is not mentioned in *Mencius*.

5. It is an interesting and important question for all sprout or modular views whether and how *n* sprouts can yield more than *n* virtues.

6. Slingerland (2014) makes a persuasive argument that *wu-wei*, effortless negotiation of the social world, is a shared aim across otherwise different classical Chinese traditions. Ancient sage kings are revered because virtue and delicacy came to them easily, naturally. This *wu-wei* way of being-in-the-world can be regained, according to Confucians (see especially Xunzi), by practicing the ritual propriety and virtue modeled by noble ancestors or alternatively, according to Daoists, by aligning oneself, not with stale, ancient customs and rituals, but with the ways of nature, with the way a river or a stream naturally flows.

7. If having all four virtues well developed is not normal in the sense of "usual" (and it is not for Mencius who, like Confucius and every other classical Chinese philosopher, is nostalgic for a past Golden Age when virtue was normal in the sense of "usual") in the way having four limbs is, then we are owed an explanation of how and why the current environment fails to pull for the development of the four cardinal virtues in the same way we would need an explanation for odd numbers of limbs in terms of amputations, radiation poisoning, and the like (Flanagan 2008; Flanagan and Hu 2011). See 6A9 and 6A7 for some suggestions from Mencius for why sometimes the sprouts don't grow, or grow but die and whither.

8. The two senses of adaptation—adaptation[historical] and adaptation[current ecology]—are the usual way that philosophers of biology mark the distinction that psychologists make in terms of proper and actual domains (Peter Godfrey-Smith, 2009). Moral foundations theory (Haidt and Joseph 2008, 14) follows Sperber in dividing module triggers into proper and actual ones. They write, "Sperber (1994) refers to the set of objects that a module was 'designed' to detect as the *proper domain* for that module. He contrasts the proper domain with the *actual domain*, which is the set of all objects that in fact trigger the module."

9. Almost all natural teleologists, from Aristotle to Aquinas to Philippa Foot, think that there is something to this premise that says that we ought to allow, not interfere with, even to aid and abet, what nature sets us on course to develop, but that it is not solely because some equipment is natural that does the work, but rather that it is natural and in addition that it is suited to producing what is good in contemporary worlds.

10. Here we circle back to worries about the possibility of grounding the normative—familiar as early as Plato's "Euthyphro"—in a way that is not itself normative and/or otherwise question begging. The Euthyphro problem involves explaining why just because an über source, God or heaven or Mother Nature, endowed us with a certain set of moral beliefs or dispositions they are the right ones. If a moral belief or disposition was an adaptation in the past or even is an adaptation now, this means only that is conduces to fitness, to getting more of one's genes in the world down the road. But fitness has no very direct relation to goodness.

11. P. J. Ivanhoe writes (personal correspondence with the author), "The Qing Dynasty thinker Dai Zhen talked about those things that 'promote life' 遂生 by which he seemed to mean not only that it was fitness enhancing but happiness enhancing."

12. It may be, indeed it is almost certain, that considerations of flourishing or goodness or rightness sometimes require suppressing dispositions to fitness, for example, controlling reproduction by suppressing desire.

13. Ivanhoe (2000, 20–21; 2013, 25–28) emphasizes that almost all of Mencius's metaphors are agricultural rather than vegetative or botanical. The sprouts need and get

attention, otherwise they whither. In the parable of Ox mountain (6A8), Mencius makes the point that agriculture unaccompanied by tenderness and love of the land can destroy an ecology.

14. While proponents of moral foundations theory regularly call these five foundations "modules," they sometimes make a somewhat different, seemingly weaker claim: "All we insist upon is that the moral mind is partially structured in advance of experience so that five (or more) classes of social concerns are likely to become moralized during development" (Haidt and Joseph 2008, 381). This weaker claim is almost certainly true.

15. In a brilliant study of metaphors for morality in classical China, David Wong (2015) reminds us that "metaphors don't confirm themselves." To which we can add that one's preferences for one metaphor over another do not confirm them either.

16. One of the main topics of discussion in cognitive science over the last thirty years is about the relative roles of System 1, which is HOT, intuitive, and evolutionarily old, and System 2, which is slow(er) and involves deliberation, central-processing, thinking, sometimes vetoing the deliverances of System 1 (Kahneman 2011). All ancient philosophers in every tradition understood the basic architecture of mind as involving finding equilibrium among moods, emotions, passions, desires, and temperament on the one hand, and reason, deliberation, and conscious control on the other. *Caveat*: in principle, one could favor dual process theory without also advocating modularity. One might think that System 1 is a general-purpose system that takes care of its owner's safety and fitness, but not that it is divided into dedicated modules.

17. In some areas of mind science, modularity has been extremely useful. Neurologists see patients who have strokes or lesions that produce very specific kinds of functional knockouts, for example, the patient loses the ability to consciously see what is in one side of the visual field, or to see faces as faces, or the patient knows words but not syntax, or vice versa.

18. See P. S. Churchland (2011, 2013) for a rich discussion of the oxytocin-vasopressin caring system as an important basis for morality. But I think she may overrate the degree to which the care system can account for most of the core features of morality. P. S. Churchland is not a fan of moral or any other kind of modularity. Churchland (2011) and Christopher Suhler (Suhler and Churchland 2011) argue that if there really are modules inside the head, then there should be evidence that there are five or six neurobiologically dedicated processors involved. But there is no such evidence. In the absence of such evidence, it is not clear whether and how the modules explain moral psychology and moral behavior as opposed to merely providing a descriptive taxonomy for organizing zones of life and types of norms that arise in all or most ecologies for dealing with the problems of complex social life.

Chapter 4

1. Here are two examples from Haidt's role as public intellectual that also have nothing directly to do with "five modules": He is exercised about the lack of representation of conservative perspectives in social psychology; and he is exercised about a culture of victimhood among college students.

2. This leaves room for ethical and political critique of the extensions. Suppose one finds, as one will, that certain extensions of the original dispositions are brokered by "the rule of the stronger" to satisfy or accommodate only their interests. For example, I as leader

of the free world require deference from you my loyal underlings. If reasons at the norma-tive political level are supposed to be the kind of reasons that promote the good impersonally considered, then the fact that a "morality" promotes the good of a powerful interest group means that it lacks warrant. This is compatible with it, "the morality," enhancing the fitness (they have harems) or flourishing (they hold the money) of the power or numerical minority who is advantaged by it.

3. Quite a few neurophilosophers and cognitive scientists, M. Johnson (1993), P. M. Churchland (1995), Haidt (2001), Casebeer (2003), Casebeer and P. S. Churchland (2003), and P. S. Churchland (2011), think that virtue theory is best supported by, or is most consil-ient with, the empirical findings of psychology as well as by the functional architecture of mind as revealed by neuroscience. Moral psychological research does not seem to support the idea that humans are moral reasoning machines, often or consistently deploying the declarative rules of deontology or consequentialism. But there are formidable others, Peter Singer (2011) and Joshua Greene (2013), for example, who argue that consequentialism is favored by all the evidence (most of which is not psychological or biological), and that it is possible for rational creatures like us to live as consequentialists (which does not, happily for psychological realism's sake, require computing which among one's action opportunities at each moment will produce the greatest amount of well-being for the greatest number of sentient beings in the long run).

4. One might restrict 'morality' further to only the class of extensions of modules (in-cluding whatever interactions and hybridizations are possible) that also pass some kind of normative inspection, for example, actually produce some of the goods that a morality is supposed to produce.

5. Fodor is not trying nor does he believe it is possible to give a definition of modules in terms of necessary and sufficient conditions. It is not only that having each of these nine properties is not necessary for modularity but also that each of these admits of degrees. Some input systems will be more encapsulated than others both informationally and ana-tomically. Richard Nisbett suggests that the modularity hypothesis itself might be favored and appeal, in a confirmation bias sort of way to and because of a certain antecedent way of seeing and making the world. He writes (2004, 83): "Beginning in the late eighteenth and early nineteenth century, the West, and especially America, began to atomize, that is to say, *modularize* the worlds of manufacture and commerce." And he attributes the abil-ity to achieve modularization in commerce and industry to a certain antecedent way of worldmaking that involves the ability to carve reality into components, and that was also good for science. This suggests the possibility that seeing modules may be easier for people with certain kinds of analytic epistemic tendencies and that seeing their weaknesses may be easier for people attuned to relations rather than components. Modularization requires decontextualizing. If one favors emphasizing relations and holism, one will worry that modularity is ecologically unrealistic. To which there is this retort: Modularity is not eco-logically realistic, but it is helpful as a model for parsing different aspects of an otherwise intractable field of causal relations. One reason to be skeptical of Nisbett's surmise in the present case is that Mencius, the first moral modularity theorist, lived over two millennia before industrialization.

6. Gestalt psychologists, as well as phenomenologists like Merleau-Ponty and psychol-ogists who follow J. J. Gibson, have long argued that perception is for action, in which case the difference I am pointing to between perceptual modules and moral modules where

the former are more receptive than the latter, which are more action oriented, is at best a matter of degree. But this is a matter for another time. All I need for my purposes is that the moral modules or moral dispositions if activated are almost always emotionally weighty and action oriented.

7. By "doing something else," I have in mind cases where one can't stop salivating at the chocolate cake or wanting the drink – imagine the alcoholic in recovery. One can't stay in this particular situation and stop the feeling. The only option is to remove oneself from the situation, and this one can do, although it might be hard.

8. The requirement is not that all traits must be explained as adaptations as some say evolutionary psychology requires, but which I seriously doubt evolutionary psychology requires. It is weaker, to the effect that the explanation of the original equipment must be consistent with the theory of natural selection. Darwin himself allowed for other natural processes and principles besides natural selection, such as by-products, exaptations, spandrels, free riders, drift, random catastrophes, and so forth. I have argued (1995, 2000) that dream consciousness (as opposed to sleep itself) is not an adaptation but a spandrel. It just comes with selection for ordinary awake consciousness but it—the dreaming mentation part, as opposed to the resting part—serves no fitness-enhancing function. It just comes for free. It is possible that some virtuous and vicious tendencies are like this. Consider the way humans, even ones who don't care for dogs and cats or teenagers "ooh and aah" over puppies and kittens and newborns. Explanation: We were selected, as Mencius suggests in 2A6, to feel powerfully toward very young humans. Large heads and eyes relative to the body are a marker of a human newborn. You get puppy and kitten affection for free, by accident, as it were, on selection for a human baby care system that is attuned to large heads and eyes.

Chapter 5

1. This lacuna is a hot topic in political theory in Hong Kong, Taiwan, Korea, and even to a certain extent in China, in work on Confucianism and rights and Confucianism and democracy. See Sungmoon Kim (2014), Joseph Chan (2013), and Daniel Bell (2006).

2. Charles Goodman writes (personal correspondence): "Mencius very clearly reasons in accordance with in-group/out-group although he has no special sprout for it." See 3A5: "Does Yi Tzu truly believe . . . that a man loves his brother's son no more than his neighbor's new-born babe?" See also 4B29: "Now if a fellow-lodger is involved in a fight, it is right for you to rush to his aid with your hair hanging down and your cap untied. But it would be misguided to do so if it were only a fellow-villager. There is nothing wrong with bolting your door."

3. Van Norden (2007, 352) argues that the four Mencian sprouts govern four parts of life, where, for example, propriety (*li*) would not even match moral foundations theory's hierarchy/respect module since it is all about beauty. Benevolence, *ren*, would be the only good sprout match with the "five modules" compassion/care foundation. There is a general lesson here: The fact that we have terms that we use to name the Mencian sprouts, as well as the mature virtues of a *junzi*, does not mean that we have a good grasp on how, for example, fourth-century BCE *Ru* thinkers conceived of the sprout of *ren*, nor that we grasp what exactly realizing *ren* meant for them. The form, texture, and content of *ren* are not the same as benevolence in Hume, or *karuna* (compassion) in Buddhism, even at a time slice. It is

Confucian *ren*, specifically in terms of the *Mencius*, whatever the normative virtue designated as *ren* was for Mencius in fourth-century BCE China.

4. The "ploctypus" is an invention in Flanagan and Williams (2010). It is intended to express a common idea in population genetics about environmental sensitivity. Richard Lewontin (1974) describes many genotypic traits that are extremely sensitive to their environments for their phenotypic expression. So, even if a certain fruit fly genome reliably selects for a certain number of belly hairs at 72°F, the number of belly hairs can be dramatically different at other temperatures, even nearby ones. So, for any set of fruit flies where at 72°F, f1 has more belly hairs than f2, and so on for f3 > f4 > f5; it may be that at 70°F f5 > f4 > f3, etc. And at 68°F f1 > f3 > f5 > f2 >f4, and so on and so forth for every small ecological change. In general, for any theory, which depends heavily on sprouts, modules, or foundations to generate whatever it is that mature morality consists in, it will be good if the bottom level has either some sort of beginning for all the virtues or, that it allows hybridization so that some beginnings can merge to produce a novel competence. Another possibility is to allow that some moral learning is possible without much in the way of an underlying natural disposition to do whatever it requires one to do. Imagine the moral equivalent of a golf swing, which is quite unnatural, but can be learned and does the job. I think this class is large.

5. Graham et al. (2013) emphasize the "pragmatic validity" of moral foundations theory. This can be read as expressing an instrumentalist view of the modules rather than a conviction that they are psychological "reals." Consider the continents: How many are there really? Seven or five? Fivers join the Americas and Europe and Asia (Eurasia). How big does a land mass have to be to count as a continent rather than an island? Why Australia but not Madagascar? Remember when Pluto was a planet? Who decides such matters? Thanks to Kathryn Augusta Walworth Flanagan for the example.

6. The germ theory of disease helps explain why a person who is not naturally creeped out by rancid things or excrement might still want to avoid them. But imagine that someone who likes the idea of adult incest, and has a willing partner, wants reasons for why the disgust of morally zealous bystanders against it ought to be honored. The situation is somewhat different, since in the modern world it is hard to give convincing reasons that may have operated in the original evolutionary situation such as that heterosexual incest is genetically risky.

7. This matter of how many modules or domains or factors there are or need to be to adequately model morality is contested, as is where exactly the number of "things" are located, in the head or in the world. Kathryn Iurino and Gerard Saucier (2014) argue that Richard Shweder's (1991) three factor model works best to capture the cross-cultural evidence from almost thirty countries. Joshua Greene thinks the evidence supports two broad modes of moralizing composed of the first two modules, care/compassion and fairness/reciprocity, and separately the next three, loyalty/hierarchy, in-group/out-group, and purity/sanctity. He writes, "To provide strong evidence for a five-factor (or six- or n-factor) theory of morality, one would have to use a 'bottom-up' approach, testing the theory using test materials that were not designed with any particular theory in mind. . . . In Haidt's data, I see evidence for two continents, which may or may not have two or three interesting bulges (2013, 386)."

8. The fact that reason might have evolved to play a role other than truth-tracking does not in anyway entail that it cannot do so, or that it does not do so now. The pattern-recognition

abilities that allow us to do number theory and geometry did not evolve to do mathematics, but come for free on top of capacities that were designed for other purposes, for example, solving problems in moving through space, sorting objects, and recognizing useful sets and their members, separating the lions from the bunnies, the wheat from the chaff, and so on. This does not entail that we now do not do mathematics, prove theorems in it, and use those theorems in sciences that keep the bridges from collapsing, and the planes in the sky.

9. In conversation—it was in a hotel bar, so there is deniability—Allan Gibbard and Jeannette Kennett and Michael Lynch were part of this conversation, too—Haidt said that he thinks there might be a small band of people, a little tribe of philosophers for whom reason functions the way they say it can: to find truth, to logically assess the quality of evidence and arguments and to rationally persuade. But this function is very rare and next to impossible to inculcate in ordinary people.

10. Some neo-Confucians list five cardinal Confucian virtues, adding *xin* 信, which in this context means something like integrity or trustworthiness or faithfulness, or perhaps, wholehearted dedication. Zhu Xi (1130–1200) embraced the fivefold scheme of benevolence, righteousness, ritual propriety, wisdom, and trustworthiness or wholehearted dedication, but stressed *ren* "benevolence" as the preeminent and unifying virtue. The thought being that one will express all the other virtues properly if and only if one maintains benevolence or is benevolent. One wonders—this is the topic of the next chapter—whether we might need five sprouts to explain five virtues, or more generally if one is a dedicated sprout or module theorist whether one needs *n* sprouts or modules to explain how it is possible to have *n* virtues, whatever *n* is.

11. There is controversy among advocates of moral foundations theory about whether there is a sixth foundation or module. Haidt (2012) thinks there is a Liberty/Oppression foundation, which he uses to explain distinctive features of libertarian political psychology. Graham and others on the team are skeptical for now. The status of this sixth foundation doesn't matter for anything I say here. If there are moral modules, then the correct number could be Mencius's number four or the social intuitionists' number five or six, fewer or more.

12. Antonio Damasio (1994, 1999) and Joseph LeDoux (1996) have made an impact in mind science arguing that cognition is always rich with affective tone. Chinese philosophy never thought otherwise.

13. Many cultures keep "vital statistics" that officially mark events of great communal and economic importance. Cultural groups and local communities keep track of what Jennifer Johnson-Hanks (2006) calls "vital conjunctures." These include first communions, confirmations, bar mitzvahs and bas mitzvahs, school graduations, registering to vote, and so on.

Chapter 6

1. Korean neo-Confucianism is best understood as the complex outcome of mixing Huayan Buddhism with Mencius as interpreted by Zhu Xi 朱熹, the great twelfth-century commentator (see Van Norden 2008; Ivanhoe 2015a). Even as the diversity among kinds of Buddhism goes (Flanagan 2011)—there are only Buddhisms—Huayan is atypical, more Brahmanic (more Vedic or Hindu, we might say) than most varieties. Orthodox Vedic Brahmanism conceived of the soul, the *ātman* of a person, especially an upper-caste one, a

Brahmin, as reflecting perfectly in microcosm the divinity of Brahman (the creative source of all things). Most Buddhisms reject the idea of *ātman*, soul, self, for *anātman*, No-Self. This replacement of self (*ātman*) by No-Self (*anātman*) is often thought to be the main metaphysical move that levels persons, eliminates caste, and ends the self-aggrandizing puffery of the priestly classes. Huayan in China and Korea and unlike most Buddhisms accepted the Brahmanic picture of the microcosm-macrocosm mimicry, even identicality, of Brahman and *ātman*. But Huayan interpreted this relation to support the idea that each and every person, not just Brahmins, contained in themselves perfection, perfect principle, *li*, which, however, was hard to locate or see sometimes because it was mixed with *qi*, psychophysical energy.

2. Toegye (eventually Ugye takes his side) opens his debate with Kobong (whose team is joined eventually by Yulgok) by expressing (maybe) a version of *Outgrowth*. The four sprouts express pure Dao mind (Buddha nature). The seven emotions are expressions of our imperfect psychophysical nature, *qi*. He cites the authority of Zhu Xi, whose explanation, he says, is that "The Four Sprouts; these are expressions of *li*. The seven Emotions; these are expressions of *qi*." Toegye claims therefore that "Expressions of the Four Sprouts are pure principle and so wholly without moral flaw; expressions of the Seven Emotions include *qi* and so are a mixture of good and bad." Cases of unwarranted shame (or deference, and the like) are, as one would expect, an unwanted "outgrowth," due to the causal powers of *qi* not *li*. "As for people who feel shame and dislike about things which they should not feel shame and dislike about or who approve or disapprove of things they should not approve or disapprove of, in all these cases the cause is the turbidity of their *qi*."

3. Kobong arguably favors a version of *Ingrowth*. The four sprouts are not a separate, additional class of foundational dispositions in human nature, but simply the normative aspect of any of our (seven) regular emotions, namely, "the underlying veins beneath those expressions of the Seven Emotions that attain their complete and proper form." Twin observations are brought in support of his view that, first, the seven emotions can be expressed in ways that perfectly manifest moral principle as when one's grief or fear or anger is justified, and, on the flip side, every one of the Mencian sprouts can be expressed incorrectly. Kobong writes:

> Mengzi's joy, which was so great it would not allow him to sleep, was joy. Emperor Shun's punishment of the Four Criminals was anger. Kongzi's grieving to the point of being unsettled was grief. His feeling of delight when Minzi, Zilu, Zaiyou and Zigong attended upon him was delight. How could these not be expressions of principle in its original state? Moreover, if you look at the actions of ordinary people, you will also find that there are times when heavenly principle is expressed in full and proper measure.

Yulgok takes Kobong's side in favor of viewing the seven emotions as basic and incorporating the Mencian sprouts as their right or ideal form. Yulgok writes:

> The Four Sprouts cannot comprehend the Seven Emotions, but the Seven Emotions do comprehend the Four Sprouts. . . . The Seven Emotions are a comprehensive way of saying that among the movements of the human mind there are these seven. As for the Four Sprouts, this is a way of selecting out and referring to what is good within the Seven Emotions.

4. Many of the Buddhisms, especially Mahayana, settle on a metaphysical solution to the problem of poisons in our nature by making a move reminiscent of the *li-qi*

neo-Confucians, which, of course, makes sense since that metaphysic came from inter-actions with Buddhism. We humans possess the poisons at the level of our material (*qi*) realization, but our pure Buddha nature (*li*) is not affected by them. This fact makes possible the reclamation or reawakening or rediscovery of the perfection already within us, but obscured by the body.

5. An amazing debate occurs in the fourteenth century between Confucians and Buddhists about the pros and cons of each way of worldmaking, each form of life, in *The Culmination of the East Asian Confucian-Buddhist Debate in Korea*. See A. Charles Muller's wonderful translation (2015).

6. The Buddhist taxonomists who start with three poisons and then break them down, for example, anger, into many subtypes and offshoot types, are aware that some states are basic and sprout-like, and some are refined derivatives or, what is different, refined hybrids and refined amalgams. It is interesting that both virtues and vices can be refined, and that there can be "virtuosity" in the skill sense for both. There are standards of excellence among the vicious.

7. The history of science story here is fascinating. Mead did not, shall we say, react very well or honorably to Ekman's results. See Ekman's (1998) introduction and afterword to Darwin's *The Expression of Emotions in Man and Animals*.

8. See http://emotionresearcher.com/2015/08/the-great-expressions-debate-2/ for a terrific up-to-date primer on the debate about Ekman's view. There are many nuances: Faces can be suppressed; many emotions do not have faces, for example, jealousy and love; we read voice, body posture, movement, and context, as well as faces; emotions are not just expressive but also communicative (Flanagan 2009a).

9. Not all moral assessments are about mental states. Many moral assessments are about abstract matters, for example, equality is good, or actions and states of affairs, for example, murder is wrong.

10. Aristotle looks parochial when he speaks rhapsodically about the admirability of the "great souled" man, who is terrific—among other things because he is magnanimous, a Greek Bill Gates—and who knows and relishes knowing that he is terrific (a Greek Donald Trump). And Mencius looks parochial when he praises persons who, from a Western perspective, we would think are excessively deferential.

Chapter 7

1. Prominent anthropologists like Philippe, Descola (2005) and Eduardo Viveiros de Castro (2014) prefer speaking of "worlds" rather than "worldviews." Speaking of a "worldview" or Weltanschauung can make it seem that there is a determinate world, a way that world is from something like an objective point of view, and then various perspectives or interpretations of it. This may fit the astronomical case. But, especially in the sociomoral sphere, it is right to question the idea that there is any way that the world is prior to or independent of the coming-to-be of social practices that make those practices the ones they are. Normally, I speak of "ways of worldmaking" (Goodman, 1978), which captures the idea that there is ontological creativity and determination and not simply perspective taking on a single world, especially in the sociomoral spheres of life.

2. *Five Caveats*: First, holism does not entail that all the beliefs are related logically as axioms and theorems are in geometry. However, pointing out that beliefs are inconsistent

often works to destabilize belief since consistency is a widespread commitment. But even that is tricky. There are four or even five valued Indian logics, *catuskoti*, that say that propositions are true, false, both, or neither, which makes more logical space for disagreement than the rule that it is either p or not p. Logical relations aside, holism often simply means that around here we say x and then we say y. These two beliefs go together for us. In America it is common in some quarters to say, "Abortion is wrong" and also to say, "Abortion is not wrong in cases of rape and incest." These seem logically inconsistent but they are permitted, avowed, and said inside a certain moral framework. The second caveat is related. Holism can be narrow or wide lens. We could look at the moral perspective of individuals or groups or nation-states. Third, wholes are always in a process of dynamic adjustment. In part this is because of pressures between individuals and groups who see things somewhat differently even inside a form of life, as well as because of natural perturbations. It was common once in history and anthropology to refer to social groups "before contact" and "after contact," where the contact was with white Europeans. But nowadays everyone agrees that social groups most everywhere have almost always been in contact with other groups. There have always been forces of interpenetration and change, ecological and social. Fourth, wholes can change rapidly. Fifth, wholes can involve all manner of relations, admixtures, pidgins, creoles, hybrids, and intersectionalities, among homespun life-forms and alien ones (see Joel Robbins, *Becoming Sinners* [2004], for an anthropology of change in New Guinea that was both rapid and seemed to involve an odd overlay of a traditional taboo morality and Christian eschatology). After a week among the Achuar in Amazonian Ecuador someone told me that they were all Christians. I had read Descola's great book on the Achuar (1996), but I hadn't seen this coming, despite knowing that some missionaries had made their way to the rain forest in the 1980s. When I asked around among the Achuar, they acknowledged, neither reluctantly nor proudly, being Christians. But when I probed, it was clear that they were Christians only in a very weak sense. They wore their Christianity lightly on top of or alongside of their traditional beliefs. The spirit of the jungle, *arutum*, the life force behind everything, was the same as Jesus. But Jesus, as far as I could tell, was not, how shall I say, Jesus.

3. Isabel Wilkerson's *The Warmth of Other Suns* (2010) is the monumental story of multiple collisions, interpenetrations, moral pidgins, creoles, and smashdowns that occur during the great migration of six million descendants of southern slaves to America's North and West from 1910 to 1970.

4. There are many ways that all parties might express what it is that has gone wrong, what it is that is not for the best: There is too much violence; each group, including one's own, is overconfident about its way of seeing and doing things; there is inattention or careless listening to how other cultural groups conceive of things, and what they need and want; there is insufficient recognition of what the environment can support given current practices on all sides.

5. Ruth Chang (1997) attempts to regiment and operationalize talk of incommensurability among philosophers and recommends a more restricted use of the concept. She writes, "Weak incommensurability claims that there is no single unit by which all values [or items] can be measured. Strong incommensurability goes further; not only is there no single unit by which *all* values [or items] can be measured, but, between *any two* particular values [or items], there is no single unit by which they can be measured" (6).

6. If one thinks that every priceless thing is worth more than any priced thing, and if one thought that beauty is priceless, and that this piece of sand is beautiful, then one would

be committed to thinking that this grain of sand is worth more than all the money in the world. This will seem odd, even crazy, from a perspective that prices everything, but perfectly sensible from a perspective that doesn't. Thinking that the beauty of this grain of sand is worth more than all the money on earth is compatible with putting it down and taking the money. Thinking that the beauty of the grain of sand is priceless doesn't entail that I want to possess it.

7. One might want to say that the values were commensurable after all since they were measured or compared on the "mattering" scale. This is not an odd thought, and shows I think that any attempt to make the concepts of incommensurability and incomparability precise is fraught.

8. Quine worried about radical translation. The natives say 'gavagai' when we say 'rabbit.' So 'gavagai' means 'rabbit.' Not so fast, we intend 'rabbit' to refer to rabbits. But 'gavagai,' for all we know, might refer to 'undetached rabbit parts' or 'rabbit time slices.' If this is possible, then we might not ever get to the bottom of what the natives really mean. This means that there might be undetected ontological relativity even among peoples who have learned to speak respectfully to each other.

9. One hypothesis that is alive and well in some quarters of psychology is that there is a comparative consensus across every extant tradition that at some level of description all of these are virtues or good traits (Peterson and Seligman 2004): Justice, Humaneness, Temperance, Wisdom, Courage, Transcendence. If true, it is true at a very abstract level, since concepts like justice have very different content inside different normative conceptions.

10. Two points: (1) James Maffie (2012) writes of the sixteenth-century meeting of Franciscan missionaries and the Nahua (Aztec). The meeting was civil but involved wholesale failure to communicate perhaps because there was deep incommensurability. Not only were their worldviews different at the level of beliefs and norms, but they came with two different philosophical orientations, what Maffie calls "path-oriented" and "truth-oriented." The Franciscans were all on about transmitting the creedal truth of the Catholic religion, whereas the Aztec wanted to know how to get on along the "craggy cliff" of life. The game is different; the rules are different. This led to failure to communicate and produced what Maffie calls "double mistaken identity." (2) Some say that when there is radical alterity, incommensurability, fundamental disagreement, or inversion there can be no rational change of view. I doubt this. If two peoples can look and see how alien others are being, what they are doing, how they are conceiving things, then mutual understanding is possible, and the space of the other can be entertained and entered, if only, at first, in hazy ways. Once the move from mere entertaining of the other to entering his form of life begins, imagination, reflection, and comparison can start to do work that can displace, destabilize, adjust, and criticize both forms of life, or on the other side, increase confidence in the wisdom of one's own way of being or theirs. One could imagine a point even before conquest when there were some among both the Nahua and the Franciscans who started to detect the differences in basic philosophical orientation, metaphysics, and epistemology, and imagined ways into the other's way of thinking and being and began to actually understand the other, see what the other meant, was saying, and so on.

11. When and whether there is a "generally shared form of life" depends on the level of grain. A sport coat can look beige, indeed be beige from a distance, but be an alternating white and brown weave up close. In the twenty-first century one can speak of citizens of nation-states sharing a form of life, even though it will often be made up by a tapestry or

knit or network of different cultures, cultural groups, religions, and so on. Disputants over an issue like euthanasia in America will likely know and be conversant in a shared political and legal language. If they are of similar age, similar religious background, from the same region of the country, they might also be likely to weight certain values similarly. Choice and autonomy will be closer to the center of the web or weighted more heavily for some people than others, who might judge respect for all life and letting things happen in God's time as more central or weighty. The good news is that people often get what others are saying, doing, and meaning inside familiar moral language games if they have exposure to the way each other speaks, thinks, assesses moral matters. Often when people shake their heads at others as if they are aliens they are really just registering disagreement with how the other weights shared values or what trump rules they apply. When we meet with true alien forms of life, "peculiar" ones, communication is possible if we are willing to be patient and to pay respectful attention. If we are lucky, we might also see things we could copy and learn from, once we understand what the aliens are doing.

12. There are varieties of holism. Extreme holism is the view that once we fix a form of life or a language, every practice and every concept and utterance has a meaning and significance that is fixed by the entire web. One can't adjust one concept or belief without adjusting all others. Michelle M. Moody-Adams (1997, 45) thinks that the anthropologist Evans-Pritchard was an extreme holist. She writes:

> He insists that "all their [Zande] beliefs hang together, and were a Zande to give up faith in witchdoctorhood he would have to surrender equally his belief in witchcraft and oracles. . . . In this web of belief every strand depends on every other strand, and a Zande cannot get out of the meshes because this is the only world he knows. The web is not an external structure in which he is enclosed. It is the texture of his thought, and he cannot think his thought is wrong (Evans-Pritchard 1937, 194–95).

Moody-Adams rightly questions this general view. Webs are adjustable. Some beliefs are central and highly connected to many, possibly all other beliefs in a way of worldmaking, whereas others are peripheral, not well connected, and it is not costly to give them up. It may be that witchdoctorhood is at the center of the web for Zande in the way (some say) logic is for us. But not every belief is like that. Even among the Zande there are skeptics about witchdoctorhood. Furthermore, in the rare cases where there is a tight, internally consistent, and never-questioned web, once contact is made with outsiders there are novel resources for seeing things differently, adjusting concepts, and questioning some beliefs.

13. Mark Alfano deserves special thanks for helping me think about inversions, revaluations, and transvaluations. Alfano offers *Daybreak* ([1881] 1982) section 38, which is titled "Drives transformed by moral judgments," as compelling evidence that Nietzsche believed, or at least entertained, the radical view that not only have there been inversions in Western history—Nietzsche certainly believed that—but that basic human psychology is largely indeterminate in what it is directed at, how it feels, how it values whatever it is it values until it is given shape, structure, and content inside a particular form of life. Nietzsche writes:

> The same drive evolves into the painful feeling of *cowardice* under the impress of the reproach custom has imposed upon this drive: or into the pleasant feeling of *humility* if it happens that a custom such as the Christian has taken it to its heart and called it *good*. That is to say, it is attended by either a good or a bad conscience! In itself it has, *like every drive*, neither this moral character nor any moral character at all, nor even a definite attendant sensation of pleasure or displeasure: it acquires all this, as

its secondary nature, only when it enters into relations with drives already baptised good or evil or is noted as a quality of beings the people has already evaluated and determined in a moral sense.—Thus the older Greeks felt differently about *envy* from the way we do; Hesiod counted it among the effects of the *good*, beneficent Eris, and there was nothing offensive in attributing to the gods something of envy: which is comprehensible under a condition of things the soul of which was contest; contest, however, was evaluated and determined as good. The Greeks likewise differed from us in their evaluation of *hope*: they felt it to be blind and deceitful; Hesiod gave the strongest expression to this attitude in a fable whose sense is so strange no more recent commentator has understood it—for it runs counter to the modern spirit, which has learned from Christianity to believe in hope as a virtue. With the Greeks, on the other hand, to whom the gateway to knowledge of the future seemed not to be entirely closed and in countless cases where we content ourselves with hope elevated inquiry into the future into a religious duty, hope would, thanks to all these oracles and soothsayers, no doubt become somewhat degraded and sink to something evil and dangerous.—The Jews felt differently about *anger* from the way we do, and called it holy: thus they saw the gloomy majesty of the man with whom it showed itself associated at an elevation which a European is incapable of imagining; they modeled their angry holy Jehovah on their angry holy prophets. Measured against these, the great men of wrath among Europeans are as it were creations at second hand.

14. When I say "us," I mean North Americans. There is more than one "us" on the side of righteous anger. Confucianism has a place for righteous anger, but not perhaps Daoism.

15. Mozi (470–391 BCE) is something of a hero to me. I say he was the first pacifist, which is not quite right. Mozi was in fact something of a self-appointed diplomat during the Warring States period in China. When peace talks failed, Mozi supported, possibly led, mercenary forces that were willing to work for states that were unjustly invaded by others for gain. Mozi thought that offensive war was always wrong because it was always motivated by partiality (I want something for me or my people that I can't gain legitimately), and he argued for impartial concern (*jiān ài*) at the level of political morality.

16. The feigned anger of a parent or teacher is the possibility proof that the phenomenal feeling of anger and angry behavior sometimes come apart. The idea that there can be righteous indignation and moral outrage without the familiar angry feeling components is a different kind of case, which I think is also possible and invite the reader to consider.

17. During the civil rights movement in the 1960s Martin Luther King Jr. was on the righteous indignation side of the spectrum, whereas Malcolm X was more on the righteous anger side. They agreed that racism is outrageous and should be eliminated. Strategically, it was and still is an open question how to do so. On the question of whether even nonviolent civil disobedience adds fuel to the fire, King rightly thought it did. Thus, he had demonstrators sign commitment cards like this one from 1963:

I hereby pledge myself—my person and body—to the nonviolent movement. Therefore I will keep the following ten commandments:

1. Meditate daily on the teachings and life of Jesus.
2. Remember always that the nonviolent movement seeks justice and reconciliation—not victory.
3. Walk and talk in the manner of love, for God is love.

   4. Pray daily to be used by God in order that all men might be free.

   5. Sacrifice personal wishes in order that all men might be free.

   6. Observe with both friend and foe the ordinary rules of courtesy.

   7. Seek to perform regular service for others and for the world.

   8. Refrain from the violence of fist, tongue, or heart.

   9. Strive to be in good spiritual and bodily health.

   10. Follow the directions of the movement and of the captain on a demonstration.

I sign this pledge, having seriously considered what I do and with the determination and will to persevere.

Chapter 8

1. There is the expression "Don't get mad, get even," which contains the Stoic wisdom that anger gets involved in issues on "the outskirts of the case."

2. Nelson Mandela was released from the prison on Robbins Island in 1990. Between 1990 and 1993, when apartheid officially ended, as many as 50,000 blacks, about the same number of Americans who died in Vietnam, were killed in the mostly black-on-black civil war between the ANC and the Zulu-based Inkatha Freedom Party.

3. There are many reasons to think that everything from the situations that trigger anger, the way anger and its varieties seem, the norms that govern it, and the displays it causes are quite socially specific (Briggs 1970; Lutz 1988; Wierzbicka 2014). The way to work these matters out requires close attention to the semantics inside particular linguistic communities and subcommunities, something I am not equipped to do.

4. The big question for Buddhists is why deconstructing the self warrants altruism rather than egoism. I discuss this topic at length in *The Bodhisattva's Brain* (2011). Śāntideva offers one reason at 8.129, where he claims that it is an observable fact that egoists do not flourish, altruists do.

5. The first noble truth of Buddhism is *dukkha*, which is that the lives of sentient beings always involve suffering. There is death and disease, pain, not getting what one wants, not keeping what one has.

6. The details of what final nirvana consists in are contested. One view is that when full enlightenment is achieved for each and every sentient being then all sentient life is over, and the reason is that unenlightened sentient beings want things. Enlightened sentient beings have been released from desiring, wanting, attachments, and are (re)absorbed into the impersonal universe. Another view is that each sentient being is released and reabsorbed impersonally into the bosom of the universe when that being achieves enlightenment by seeing, among other things, that wanting things for oneself is the source of all suffering. Being reabsorbed impersonally may sound disturbing since it is familiar to us from what scientific naturalists think death is like. Eternal rest of that sort, where each one of us is once again nothing at all, as we were before our conception and birth, comes according to secular, scientific views, whether one achieves enlightenment or not. If one understands the ultimate Buddhist project as the end of sentient life as we know it, then we might find the prospect very disturbing. Samuel Scheffler (2013) argues that it is more disturbing for us to think of the species ending than of our own individual demise. It seems likely that different peoples have different attitudes toward individual death and species extinction and that these depend on background soteriologies and eschatologies and scientific theories.

Buddhist salvation takes a really long time, is collective, and then there is extinction. Abrahamic afterlives involve eternal bliss in heaven for good individuals. Neo-Darwinians think there is individual death and then eventually there will be species death, but not because everyone has become enlightened, just because species wear down and out, comets hit, deadly bugs arise. One final point: In my experience in South and Southeast Asia, many Buddhists believe nirvana is similar to Abrahamic heaven, and such views have many scriptural sources inside the Buddhisms.

7. There is a certain amount of trash talking among Buddhists. Mahayana Buddhists will say that Theravadans prize the arhat who seeks enlightenment on the mountaintop for himself alone, over the communal liberation that the bodhisattva aims at. Then again, Theravadans will claim that it involves less metaphysical extravagance, sometimes rejecting literal commitment to rebirth, which some, but not all, Mahayana sects believe.

8. One might claim that the temporal length of the project of becoming enlightened is really just a vivid metaphor for the extraordinary difficulty of the project, which conceived spatially might involve something like climbing a mountain 84,000 times higher that Mt. Everest, about the distance to the moon.

9. In the Pali canon, the earliest Buddhist scriptures compiled in the first century of the common era, anger is clearly marked as an unwholesome emotion. In *Yodhajiva sutta* (Bodhi 2003), a warrior asks the Buddha about the fate of soldiers who die in battle. The Buddha explains that they will not be reborn in heaven but in hell because they are filled with hate.

10. It might be better to say that anger is the worst of the unwholesome emotional states. Often Buddhists will say that the illusion of thinking that I am a permanent SELF is the biggest and deepest mistake. This mistake, we might say, is the worst epistemic mistake, whereas anger and greed, which are fed by ego, by selfishness, are emotional mistakes, affective mistakes, mistakes of the heart-mind fed by thinking that I am a permanent being, that I should get what I want, and keep it, that I matter in some way to the cosmos.

11. Many forms of cognitive behavioral therapy involve the idea that you should "Fake it 'til you make it."

12. Buddhism requires full compliance with the Rx. That is, one must work at all three: compassion and lovingkindness and patience. 'Patience,' as I use the word, is not exactly right for what the Buddhist intends. If I stand in line for ice cream I feel impatient, but not angry. If someone in front of me tests too many flavors, slowing the line down, I may feel frustrated or annoyed, but not angry. One reply is that the incompatible state of mind is something like forbearance (and some translations use this word), or alternatively that it is a combination of three states of mind, compassion, lovingkindness, and forbearance. Another reply is to say that anger comes in many forms and that impatience, annoyance, and frustration are types of anger, along with peevishness, sarcasm, disdain, and contempt; or to say that these might not be full-on anger but are kindling for it and need to be extinguished right away (6.71–74). Buddhism has its own Serenity Prayer for purposes of getting a grip on these beginnings, the fuel for the fire of anger. The serenity prayer says, "God grant me the serenity to accept the things I cannot change, the courage to change the things I can, and the wisdom to know the difference." Śāntideva writes, "Why be unhappy about something if it can be remedied? And what is the use of being unhappy about something if it cannot be remedied?" (6.10). Buddhist mindfulness practice involves many cognitive

reminders and skills such as this. I have heard the Dalai Lama joke that the Serenity Prayer must have been written by a Buddhist.

13. The four supreme virtues or states of mind in Buddhism are compassion, loving-kindness, sympathetic joy, and equanimity. These are illimitables, unsurpassables, virtues that there can never be enough of. Compassion (*karuna*) is the disposition to wish to alleviate suffering wherever and whenever it exists. Lovingkindness (*metta*) is the disposition to want to bring well-being where there is ill-being. Sympathetic or altruistic joy (*mudita*) is the disposition to feel happiness not envy for the successes of others, even in zero-sum games. Equanimity (*upekkha*) is a calm and serene state involving equalizing, even deflating the self so that my desires are experienced as no more (or less) worthy of satisfaction than those of any other being.

14. Many of the earlier verses of *The Bodhisattva's Way of Life* lead up to this powerful recommendation that we treat our enemies as if they were Buddhas offering us the greatest gift, practice for virtue with the continuous suggestion that we ought to treat all challenges in life, including the smallest physical discomforts and inconveniences, as opportunities to practice patience.

15. One might mount a concern, possibly an objection to the alleged natural attractiveness of the bodhisattva ideal in this way: Awakening *bodhicitta* and taking the bodhisattva vows are "naturally" attractive to Buddhists because they are normatively endorsed in communities that are Buddhist. Buddhists are not insensitive to this charge. Some will defer to the experience of expert meditators who tap into their Buddha nature, which allegedly is antecedent to all socialization, and they will claim to see or otherwise experience that the deepest desire is something like *bodhicitta*; the desire to alleviate suffering for all sentient beings. But here the worry repeats; adepts are studiously indoctrinated into the form of life that claims exactly this insight, and thus is a likely suspect for a strong confirmation bias. Another way to express the concern about the underlying epistemology is this way: Does the sort of meditation that reveals my "true nature" and mission uncover things as they really are, or does the meditation produce the hallucination that makes things seem a certain way?

16. Buddhists and Stoics are best described, using our terms, as determinists, or perhaps better, they do not entertain a concept of strong or libertarian free will.

17. The argument for the elimination of anger has multiple strands. Śāntideva even reminds us that when I suffer and want to strike out, I ought to consider that my own past karma is coming back to hit me like a boomerang: "Previously, I too caused just such pain to living beings. Therefore this is just what I deserve, I who have caused distress to other beings" (6.42).

18. One will sometimes hear Buddhists or neo-Confucians speak of loving Hitler on grounds that he could be your father, mother, or child. One response is that he could be my father, mother, or child, but in fact he isn't. He is Hitler. So drop the topic! But according to one extravagant form of Buddhism that shares with some kinds of Epicureanism the idea that the universe recycles every possible relation over an indefinite or infinite amount of time, Hitler will literally be my child, my mother, and so on, over and over again.

19. Many say that Buddhists shouldn't believe in any form of karmic survival either since the doctrine of No-Self denies that there is a self that is the same over the course of an ordinary human life, which entails that there is no self to survive across lives either. One way around this objection is for the Buddhist to argue that it is based on a flat-footed

misunderstanding of what they mean by *anātman* or no-self. Buddhism denies that there is an *ātman*, an unchanging self that constitutes an individual's essence, as well as nihilism or eliminativism, which say that individuals are nothing-at-all or lack altogether in continuity of consciousness. The mistake is to assimilate the doctrine of *anātman* to what we in the West would mean by saying that there is no self, as well as the contrast between what in the Indian tradition is meant by *ātman*, and what we mean by such terms as 'self' and 'soul' (Flanagan 2000a, 2011).

20. Again there is the objection that Buddhists shouldn't literally believe in rebirth, because their own doctrines of No-Self, Impermanence, Dependent Arising, and Emptiness undermine its very possibility. If I don't last across moments, days, or weeks, in what sense can *I* or *i* survive multiple incarnations? Why Buddhists believe in rebirth is then explained as a historical accretion from the larger mother Indic traditions, which could make sense of reincarnation because that more powerful tradition believed that sentient beings possess souls (*ātman*), which are indestructible. The whole web is thus unstable or inconsistent, but metaphysical and theological inconsistencies are hard to spot, and rarely cause trouble for the folk, or, alternatively, one might say that inconsistency is the hobgoblin of little minds.

21. Susan Brison, letter to the editor, *New York Times*, March 1, 2004. Insofar as Brison defends anger in her remarkable philosophical memoir (2002) as a response to terrible personal harm, it is forward-looking and healing anger, not the kind that is "greedy for revenge."

22. Envy is an angry feeling associated with competitive disadvantage. Others have more stuff, money, or fame than I do, and it infuriates me off. Seneca recommends that the polis minimize opportunities for experiencing envy by minimizing comparative disadvantage, especially in the education and social worlds of young boys. On this view, envy involves perception that I don't have some goods, that I am just as worthy as those who have the goods, and thus that I suffer not having those goods unjustly.

23. Some cognitive scientists think that there are perceptual or emotional universals that all people perceive in the same way, even if they lack words for them. On color, see Berlin and Kay (1969); on emotions, see Ekman and Davidson (1994). But skeptics abound (Wierzbicka 1999, 2014).

24. As in the Buddhist case, one might think of being peevish, clamorous, frantic, and surly as kinds of anger, perhaps low-grade varieties of anger, or as precursors of anger or kindling for anger, states that easily give rise to it. Either way they are dangerous. Seneca says, "It is always easier to banish dangerous passions than to rule them."

25. To say that anger or any other mental state involves System 2 is not to say it only involves System 2. Recall that the division of mind into two systems is a model and also that Daniel Kahneman (2011), the major contemporary proponent of dual process theory, says the systems are fictions. Peter Railton (2014) provides an utterly convincing argument for a picture of the moral mind as a highly interactive, continuously updating learning system, where Systems 1 and 2, now conceived as merely useful fictions, interact and cocreate feelings, thought, and action.

26. Objection: David B. Wong (personal communication) raises the interesting and important worry that if chess experts, race car drivers, sages, saints, and bodhisattvas operate with refined but nonetheless unconscious expertise, their skill set might still not be under conscious control at any given time. Reply: True, thus chess mistakes, car crashes, and sins. However, it is a feature of expertise that it kicks upstairs to consciousness problems that its

refined unconscious skill set is not equipped to deal with. So the chess player consciously puzzles over certain moves, and so on.

27. In Plato's *Republic*, Caephalus, the old man, says that he doesn't really know what morality is, but that it is easier to be moral when you are older. Some say that anger, like lust, afflicts young people, especially young men. Maybe. But one cannot put all the blame here on testosterone and other hormones. First, aggressiveness is not the same as anger. Second, there are many angry old people. Third, many of the elders, especially in politics, are seasoned at experiencing righteous anger and righteous indignation, and utilizing the energy and strength of young men to go fight in wars against "evil" others.

28. There are communities that do not get angry (or scared, etc.) in the ways we do, who have different norms of apt anger (Lutz 1988). Jean L. Briggs's book, promisingly titled *Never in Anger* (1970), describes a very small group of Eskimos, the *Utkuhikhalingmiut, Utku*, for short, for whom "Expressions of ill temper toward human beings (as distinct from dogs) are never considered justified in anyone over the age of three or four" (328). But these norms of anger are primarily in-group norms governing a thirty-person group of kin. The *Utku* are pretty constantly angry at and cruel toward their dogs, and think that white men are bad-tempered like dogs, possibly descended from them. Anna Wierzbicka (2014) makes an interesting and plausible argument that German colloquial counterparts to the English words 'fear' and 'anger' are *Angst* and *Wut* and that these do not at a fine level of analysis have the same semantics, phenomenology, psychology, or normative role.

29. In *Varieties of Moral Personality* (1991), I proposed a "Principle of Minimal Psychological Realism," which says that moral theory ought to be constrained by what the creatures to whom it is addressed perceive is possible. This is weaker than "is possible." Speaking for myself, I think that the Buddhist and Stoic arguments are worth taking very seriously, and that they, especially taken together, open up a possibility space that is radically underexplored.

30. Pierre Hadot (1995) writes wisely about "Philosophy as a way of life." This was certainly the way the Stoics and other Hellenistic philosophers conceived things, and Buddhism is built in the same mold, as a philosophy to be lived, abided, and enacted. The idea is that the work to extirpate anger is not remotely individual work, although that will be required at times. It is social work requiring work on the philosophical background and political and economic structures in order to create the conditions for the possibility of extirpation. That this way of life would eventually provide a distinctive ecological landscape makes what is now a rare outcome, more common.

31. One response to this line of argument is to argue that the nervous system is programmed to develop the basic emotions or innate modules even though the basic emotions or modules are not canalized, dedicated, or fully constructed at birth. Some say that something anger-like emerges at four to six months if one, especially the mother, restricts the baby's arm movements. Developing the basic emotions is like developing clear vision or like reaching puberty. By puberty you will get sexy people, as well as full-formed versions of all the basic and familiar emotions.

32. Both Jane Goodall (1986) and Frans de Waal (1982) have produced convincing evidence that chimpanzees are sometimes homicidal, and engage in organized violence to pay back past injuries. Such evidence that chimpanzees experience anger, act on it, and have no capacities to extirpate it, does not entail that humans don't have such capacities. That is, the existence of gratuitous, selfish, and moralistic aggression in nonhuman primates, which

cannot be controlled by them, is perfectly compatible with similar human tendencies that can be leveraged, controlled, by individuals and cultures.

33. It may be (it is an empirical question in psycholinguistics) that our concepts of retaliation, revenge, and payback involve essentially being angry. If so, then these are different concepts for Seneca and us. For him, there can be vengeful behavior without the subjective feeling or motivation that we might wrongly think must accompany it.

34. P. J. Ivanhoe suggests (personal correspondence) that "maybe one can pursue such ends not motivated by anger but still with what Bruce Lee called 'emotional content.'" In the opening scene of *Enter the Dragon* (1973):

LEE: [a student approaches Lee; both bow] Kick me.

[Student looks confused]

LEE: Kick me.

[Student attempts kick]

LEE: What was that? An exhibition? We need emotional content. Now try again!

[Student tries again]

LEE: I said "emotional content." Not anger! Now try again!

[Student tries again and succeeds]

LEE: That's it! How did it feel?

[Student thinks; Lee smacks his head]

LEE: Don't think. FEEEEEEEEL! It's like a finger pointing at the moon.

[Looks at student who is looking at the finger; smacks student again]

LEE: Do not concentrate on the finger or you will miss all of the heavenly glory!

[Student bows; Lee smacks him again]

LEE: Never take your eyes off your opponent . . . even when you're bowing!

[Student bows again this time keeping his eyes on Lee]

LEE: That's better.

[student walks away; opening credits begin]

35. David B. Wong (personal discussion) raises this question: If Seneca thinks we are plastic enough to extirpate anger altogether, then it would seem to follow that we are plastic enough to mold our natures so that we only express anger at the right time, in the right way, not too much or too little, as the Aristotelian containment theorist proposes we ought. Seneca says anger is easier to eliminate than moderate. His reason is that it is the nature of anger, once activated, to overreach. Compare: Alcoholics can abstain altogether from drugs and alcohol. But they can't use moderately or sensibly. A reply is that this is only true of alcoholics. Most people can use alcohol normally and responsibly. Seneca needs to be interpreted as thinking either that anger cannot be experienced and expressed responsibly by anyone or, more likely, that it is crazily addictive and impossible to contain for most people.

36. It is interesting that in his recommendations for the education of boys in *De Ira*, Seneca sounds very Aristotelian. Perhaps it is an accession to realism that one starts by moderating boys' expressions of anger and aggression. Only then can one expect the young men to be ready for the full regimen of therapeutic extirpation. The peaceful, communitarian Semai people of Malaysia have a saying that "there are more reasons to fear a dispute than a tiger." Tom Digby tells me (personal correspondence) that for Semai (living in Malaysia) "childrearing practices are virtually nonexistent—It's kind of a parenting anarchy situation, EXCEPT they discourage anger in their children, both—and this is crucial—girls and boys."

37. Normative permission is key. In a world in which anger is permissible, possibly virtuous, then anger is expected, and it will sometimes work. In a world where one is supposed to "fight fire with fire," and you do so, you will be judged normal in the anger department, as well as not a pushover. In a world in which anger is unacceptable, and you don't experience it, and don't normally respond angrily (which doesn't necessarily mean you can't stand up for yourself in this world), you might be injured by angry people in particular situations, but you will be reputed to be virtuous. The person who did you harm by anger will be judged as vicious. Different worlds, different contingencies of reinforcement, different normative guidance systems.

38. Marx thought that the promise of heavenly reward for the meek and humble was a transparent opiate.

Chapter 9

1. "I am angry and I am not angry" is a contradiction. "She is angry but I don't believe she is angry" is paradoxical (Moore's paradox) but not a contradiction. But "That is outrageous but I am not angry about it" is neither a contradiction nor a paradox.

2. When I refer to WEIRD anger it is shorthand for the folk norms about anger in America, first and foremost, then with diminishing confidence, on my part, in Canada, the North Atlantic, Oceana, and nations colonized by those nations.

3. Technically speaking, one could use a version of Gibbard's test in a Buddhist or Stoic world by interpreting the phrase "it makes sense to be angry about" to mean either "what in the olden days in this locale used to make the moral experts angry," or, better, something like "what it makes sense to judge as outrageous or as an outrage."

4. Most everyone thinks it is appropriate to extend some of the reactive attitudes, but not all of them, to nonhuman animals.

5. Sometimes P. F. Strawson, showing his Kantianism, speaks of the reactive attitudes as being activated when respect for my person fails to be acknowledged, or when my dignity is challenged. I doubt that our distant ancestors 250,000 years ago—or even two thousand years ago—conceived of themselves as suffering challenges to their dignity and self-respect. We, the WEIRD children of the Enlightenment, do sometimes, possibly often, experience affronts to our dignity as persons, and feel as if we are not treated with proper respect. Strawson can make room for this difference between the reactive attitudes of ancestral and modern persons. Although when it comes to the reactive attitudes Strawson is not a social constructionist—remember the reactive attitudes are original and natural—he is clear, in a way no one, to the best of my knowledge, has pointed out, that there are individual and cultural differences in everything from the intensity of the experience or display of each of the reactive attitudes to many of the conditions that activate the reactive attitudes.

6. Galen Strawson writes that some kind of guilt is a "chimpanzee thing . . . an ancient adaptive emotional reflex in social animals, encrusted, now, with all the fabulous complications and dreadful superstitions of human consciousness, but otherwise unchanged, an internal prod that evolved among our remote but already highly social ancestors" (2008, 215). He thinks, in a Nietzschean vein, that even if core guilt in chimps and in us evolved as a prod, it, but not perhaps nearby attitudes such as shame and remorse, has become oppressive and self-indulgent, and "adds nothing—nothing good— to moral being" (215).

7. Ecological landscapes exist at and can be described at multiple levels of grain. It may be that the landscapes of modern nation-states look very homogeneous from a wide-lens perspective, but that they are not. James C. Scott's *The Art of Not Being Governed* (2009) is a wonderful study of the stateless peoples of Zomia, an area of Southeast Asia encompassing highlands in Vietnam, Cambodia, Laos, Thailand, Burma, northeastern India, and several provinces in China. Scott describes an incredible array of forms of life among the peoples of Zomia. Because these stateless people are constantly interacting, while avoiding nation-state control, Scott speaks of the "indeterminacy of social forms in the hills" (269). It may well be, I think it is, that indeterminacy of social forms is more common than we might think. If Martians were to observe the ways the people in places like New York and London move from home to work and back, they would see shared norms, but if they were to get inside the hearts and minds of the citizens of these great cities they would see enormous diversity.

8. Eddy Nahmias and colleagues (2006) argue that most WEIRD people do not have the strong libertarian view of free will, but are compatibilists.

9. Galen Strawson thinks that the reactive attitudes come first "as a chimp thing," and do not presuppose in those forms any views whatsoever about responsibility, free will, punishment, and so on. He calls this "the emotional priority thesis" (2008, 2014). It says that the reactive attitudes do not depend on beliefs about agency, persons, or free will. However, these beliefs might be seeded by, or emerge from, those very emotions inside certain forms of living, perhaps as post facto rationalizations (2008, 219). Galen Strawson extends this point from the reactive attitudes to the dominant view about the self, which he says is a diachronic-narrative view. Nonhuman primates do not, and perhaps the original humans 250,000 years ago did not, experience themselves as diachronic-narrative persons with all the encrustations of free will and personal responsibility that we take for granted. Perhaps they were and seemed to themselves to be genuinely synchronic-episodic beings, all in the here and now. The view that persons are, and, what is different, ought to be diachronic-narrative critters is, Strawson-the-Younger thinks, a historical development inside a certain framework, a certain form of human social life. But it is not necessitated by our original nature, even our original nature as gregarious social animals that possess and use the reactive attitudes to coordinate social life.

10. Galen Strawson has in mind his "Luck Swallows Everything" (1998) as providing one of the "extremely powerful arguments" that shows that strong free will of this sort is incoherent, logically impossible.

11. After contemplating the Buddhists who engineer the dissolution of the delusions of self and free will, and we'll imagine of whatever else is crazy, Galen Strawson writes that "they are certainly inhuman, in some way. . . . I do not think we can really imagine what it might be like to be them" ([1986] 2010, 103).

Chapter 10

1. I am taking liberties with Wong's original argument, imagining that it extends to all the reactive attitudes. In fact, Wong focuses almost exclusively on feelings of deep sorrow and sadness that come when one loses a person one loves, not on anger. He can resist, and does in conversation, extending the argument to the conclusion that all the reactive attitudes, including anger, necessarily come with healthy attachments. So we both, in fact,

agree that this view is a serious contender: 4. Extirpation of some emotions/reactive attitudes and detachment with resilience. There are some emotions, for example, sorrow and sadness, that are perfectly acceptable, indeed that appropriately mark value and partly constitute certain human relations. There are other emotions, at least some members of the anger family, that may express an unhealthy egoism, harm the subject and the object, and so on, and be worth working to eliminate.

2. Some think that Buddhism is nowadays too accommodating, that the practice of skillful means to gain advocates is sometimes unprincipled and sells itself out. Buddhism is associated with happiness in the West (Dalai Lama and Cutler, 1998), but many say that classical Buddhism does not offer happiness, only mitigation of suffering. In the case of the Dalai Lama's interpretation of Buddhist teaching on anger, the worry would be that Śāntideva is categorically opposed to anger, but that is softened by the Dalai Lama to allow anger that we, his WEIRD audience, not he or orthodox Buddhists, judge as positive. The accommodation could be thought of as an accommodation to our practices or to these plus our views of persons (individual or corporate) as self-originators, which are also not Buddhist at all.

3. Michael K. Jerryson, *Buddhist Fury* (2011) and Michael K. Jerryson and Mark Juergensmeyer, eds., *Buddhist Warfare* (2010) are important books on how Buddhists throughout history, and even today in places like Myanmar (against the Rohingya) and Sri Lanka, have justified severe punishment, killing, war, and violence. Rupert Gethin (2004) and Emily McRae (2015) are good articles on the ethics of violence in early Buddhism and on Tantric practices for sublimating and metabolizing anger, respectively.

4. P. J. Ivanhoe writes (personal correspondence): "Maybe there is another view called something like '*Useful*.' When someone asks 'What did violence ever accomplish?' we can answer: 'Well, it got rid of an oppressive King and established a land of liberty, it saved the Union and freed the slaves, it defeated Fascism and Totalitarianism, hell, it's been damned useful.' One might say the same about anger. *Under certain circumstances it provides the motivation we need to fight.* Anger is a fallback, like a gun, it should be locked away and only taken out when there is no other choice, but then it has and can serve profound causes and well."

5. Emily McRae (2015) discusses the Wiesel story and says that only anger but not tears can properly mark the injustice. I don't see this. It would depend on what we are understood to be doing with various emotions and emotional expressions in various social ecologies.

6. Sherman (2005, 90) argues, based on testimony of ordinary soldiers, that some sort of "baseline resentment" of wrongs done by the enemy (Iraq invaded Kuwait; the Palestinians killed an Israeli youth; the Vietnamese fired on our ships in the Gulf of Tonkin) is part of the normal psychological structure of the modern soldier. But this fact need carry no normative weight. Even if all soldiers think they have right on their side, they can't all be correct, and furthermore the belief is easy to explain in terms of irrational features: confirmation bias, patriotism, fear, avarice, and brainwashing.

7. Seneca is clear that wearing the mask of anger, acting "as if" I am about to lose it, that there will be hell to pay, is sometimes necessary to produce certain effects. Parents and teachers of young children do this, as do coaches and platoon sergeants in the army.

8. It is worth emphasizing that anger might be said to be necessary to perceive injustice and/or to remedy injustice or both. I am questioning necessity at either and/or both locations. A very compassionate person would easily see the pain and suffering, the inhumanity,

in the Wiesel case. In a new article on anger, Nussbaum (2015) gives several examples that show how sorrow, compassion, and certain practical—"let's fix this"—attitudes can work where we might think only anger can. This is exactly my point about the Wiesel case, namely, that anger is not remotely necessary to restore humanity.

9. Lisa Tessman's *Burdened Virtues* (2005)—especially chapter 5, "The Burden of Political Resistance"—gives sensitive voice to the major arguments pro and con inside contemporary feminism for a role for righteous anger in politics. Margaret Urban Walker, *Moral Repair* (2006) is a deep work on the pragmatics and moral psychology of reparative justice. Walker explores the possibility of crimes that are unforgivable either because of their enormity or because the perpetrators will not take responsibility. The fact that an act is unforgivable does not mean that anger and resentment cannot be overcome. We might never forgive the psychopathic murderer, but we might adopt what Strawson calls "the objective attitude" and let go of the anger toward him.

10. There is a vast literature on how (and whether) truth and reconciliation worked (really, whether it is working) in South Africa and elsewhere. Nancy Nyquist Potter, ed. (2006) is a fine collection of papers on the philosophy, moral psychology, and psychiatry of the Truth and Reconciliation Commissions (TRC), specifically, and the collective healing process, generally. The very idea that truth and forgiveness might work in South Africa where anger and violence was normally the solution on offer, was made possible by a perfect philosophical storm: Desmond Tutu identified strands of that thought in Anglicanism; the Afrikaners saw a similar idea in the Dutch Reform tradition; Nelson Mandela, who was extremely angry for a very long time, saw it in the Hindu and Jain philosophy of *ahimsa*, nonviolence, that he had picked up from reading Gandhi; and most importantly, it was available in the indigenous philosophy of *Ubuntu*, according to which we are first and foremost communal beings, not atomistic individuals. According to *Ubuntu*, anger, rage, and violence do not injure a separate other; they harm parts of the whole of which I am a part.

11. Dawn Mikkelson's *Risking Light* (2014) is a powerful documentary that shows practices of forgiveness and healing among Cambodians who suffered atrocities under the Khmer Rouge, the "Stolen Generation" of Australian aboriginals, as well as individual victims of horrific harms in the United States. Mikkelson (personal correspondence) writes about the collision of moral perspectives, the difficulties of hermeneutical justice, and moral holism all at once:

> Based on my limited exposure to Buddhism through Kilong Ung and his family in Cambodia, [it seems] that anger is not a culturally supported emotion.... One thing I did find interesting was how many of our interviews of random people in Cambodia, including monks, seemed to point very strongly to Karma as the reason for Khmer Rouge genocide from both the victim and perpetrator perspective. I'm actually struggling with how to contextualize that footage in a succinct way, as without context and through a western lens, survivors of the Khmer Rouge often seem to allude to the idea that their plight during that time was due to a previous misdeed. This would really rub western audiences the wrong way and would look like victim-blaming. But also, because of this perspective, they don't seem to hold onto the anger toward perpetrators in the same way, because that was also the Khmer Rouge's Karma in play. Karma is also the reason to forgive, as without it you would keep building up bad Karma for yourself.

12. There is controversy among classical scholars about whether Seneca wrote prose works such as "On Anger," as well as the Senecan tragedies or whether there were two different Senecas. Gregory A. Staley (2010) thinks that they were one and the same. It doesn't matter for my point here, since the view about tragedy occurs inside the Stoic tradition.

13. Nussbaum (2015, 2016) has changed her mind about anger. Like Seneca, Śāntideva, and me, she thinks that if anger is intended to pass-pain it is normatively bad. She thinks this is anger's normal psychological profile. Nussbaum also explicitly rejects her earlier view discussed above that anger is psychologically inevitable and socially necessary to correct injustice. She writes, "it has often been thought (including by me, in many earlier writings) that anger provides an essential motivation to correct social injustice" (52). Nussbaum now thinks that if there is a kind of anger that is forward-looking and aims at amelioration it is OK, maybe good. She calls this last variety "transitional anger." Susan Brison's anger is clearly "transitional," as is what I call "righteous indignation."

14. The method of reflective equilibrium in ethics and political philosophy, which originates in Aristotle, and was honored as the method of ethics and political philosophy by John Rawls in the twentieth century, essentially acknowledges that the internalist predicament is our plight. The comparative philosopher accepts this, and emphasizes that superwide, cross-cultural, reflective equilibrium provides a better system of checks and balances, as well as greater imaginative resources, than narrow, parochial, culture-bound tests of reflective equilibrium. There are costs to superwide reflective equilibrium. It can undermine confidence when things are going well ("So what that some cultures in the Himalayan steppes do fine with multiple spouses, I am doing just fine with one, thank you very much!"). But superwide reflective equilibrium, essentially cross-cultural philosophy, can serve us well when we hit the wall and see no ways to solve some serious problem inside our form of life with the resources at our disposal. We might discover that solution strategies exist elsewhere in other actual or possible ways of being.

Chapter 11

1. In heterogeneous societies, ecologies that contain multiplicities, philosophers sometimes play the role of articulating and endorsing the dominant view. This is not always a good thing.

2. In *Sources of the Self* (1989), Charles Taylor attempts "to write a history of modern identity" in the North Atlantic. Taylor says that by concepts such as 'identity,' 'person,' and 'self' he intends "to designate the ensemble of (largely unarticulated) understandings of what it is to be a human agent: the senses of inwardness, freedom, individuality, and being in nature which are at home in the modern West." These "largely unarticulated" understandings "of what it is to be a human agent, a person, a self" that are "at home in the modern West" constitute the background, surround, framework, horizon—the penumbra—that carry a set of cultural understandings, a philosophy. Furthermore, "Selfhood and the good, or in another way, selfhood and morality, turn out to be inextricably intertwined themes" (3).

3. Understanding how the self is conceived among various peoples is a fairly reliable method for uncovering their "inescapable frameworks" and their "habits of the heart," their views about the proper form of sociomoral life, right action, best practices, good persons, good lives, and good communities (Bellah et al. 1985). In the other direction, getting a fix on

a moral code helps us see the shape and contours of the self. Charles Taylor writes, "a moral reaction is an assent to, an affirmation of, a given ontology of the human" (1989, 5).

4. Even if one thinks, let us suppose, that economics is the main determinant of social structure, one must allow that once a social structure, a form of life, a way of worldmaking has been fixed by, say, economic causes for economic reasons, it will be endowed with self-sustaining features. It might, as an ideology, get into the hearts and minds of a people—and thus cause them to resist quick change in response to new economic conditions. So suppose one thinks that the emphasis on order and harmony in classical Confucianism is due to the bad effects of constant war on the economy. One would also have to accept that classical Confucianism once articulated in the tradition of Confucius, Mencius, and Xunzi, then becomes a causal force going forward that might help or hinder future economic developments.

5. Here, I leave off the list of self-variations this one, which has been discussed a great deal in earlier chapters, and that will be discussed again in the final chapter, namely, *First Nature Selves*, what the basic motivational structure of humans is, if anything, deep-down-inside-beneath-the-clothes-of-culture. Different traditions conceive of human first nature in different ways, or perhaps it is better to say that they emphasize different aspects of first nature as promising for development or for suppression and rechanneling. The 14th Dalai Lama says that humans are innately good. Most Confucians take Mencius's idea that there are four positive sprouts in human nature very seriously. Neo-Confucianism, a child of Buddhism and Confucianism, claims that there is pure and perfect principle (*li*) in each person clouded only by body, *qi*, but awaiting recovery beneath it. Christians posit a fallen first nature, a core of egoism and dispositions to trespass. Aztec first nature is an unfolding, an interweaving, of cosmic pairs of order and disorder, balance and imbalance, being and nonbeing, and male and female that simultaneously constitute both each person who walks on a narrow, jagged, treacherous mountain path, and the mountain path itself (Maffie 2014, 525).

6. There is evidence from experimental philosophy that Chinese do not favor utilitarian judgments in trolley problems to the degree that North Americans do, that is, sacrificing one to save five (Ahlenius and Tännsjö 2012). This may mean that utilitarian selves are more likely to be approved of in contemporary North America than in China. Of course, there are also studies that show that drunken people PUSH in FOOTBRIDGE (Duke and Bègue 2015), as do psychopaths (Kahane et al. 2015).

7. It is not only that virtues are weighted differently in different traditions but also that virtues can be conceived as vices. For example, Gandhi thought many Westerners disliked Indians precisely for their virtues, simplicity, perseverance, patience, frugality, otherworldliness, and asceticism (1997, xxxv).

8. Some sociolinguists say that in North America, self-reference in hierarchical relations tracks lower status versus higher status more than it does egoism versus altruism. The underling writes the superior, "I wondered if I might speak to you later this afternoon?" The boss writes. "Yes, at 4 p.m."

9. In my experience, tell an educated American that zip code in early childhood is the best predictor of time in school versus time in jail, educational attainment, and money made in a lifetime, and there will be mumbling and denial.

10. It is an interesting question whether individuals or cultural groups who do not suffer from the self-serving bias are simply humble and modest or actually self-underestimating.

Suppose Jane knows that she is a very fast runner but is modest about her speed. Depending on how humility is valued, when and whether it is thought to veer too much toward low self-esteem, this would be judged as either a positive or negative moral quality. But suppose Jane doesn't realize how fast she is, even though the evidence is abundant. She underestimates her talent. In that case, no matter how attractive we find the quality, Jane has a mistaken belief.

11. These dozen self-variations are tantalizing. But they should be read with a certain amount of caution and skepticism. There are worries about sample size, overestimating difference, the appeal of exotica, appeals to stereotypes, confirmation bias, the lack of precision and, what is different, the polysemy of words like 'self,' 'identity,' 'self-conception,' and their suite.

12. Different cultures have different beliefs about whether we survive, what it consists in, what form "I" take, and whether and why it is a good thing (Obeyesekere 2002).

13. Familiar candidates for the glassy essence of THE SELF include my immaterial *res cogitans*, the transcendental unity of apperception, the Arch Ego, the noumenal "I," as well as various sorts of nonphysical and indestructible souls, familiar especially in the Abrahamic traditions. More pedestrian, deflated candidates for "the philosopher's self" include being an individual embodied member of the species *Homo sapiens*; whatever critter, or critter at a time slice, the word "I" points to, indexes, or names; some short-term representation in working memory that holds my sense of being myself, of who I am (phenomenal consciousness); a set of representations held in long-term autobiographical memory that grounds my historical sense of self-sameness (narrative consciousness); or the private personal stream of consciousness that is made possible by the evolution of animals with nervous systems that have direct connections to their own and only their own experiences. Cultural views about the nature of the philosopher's self—think of these as the folk versions of the esoteric, elitist views—deciding whether I am an indestructible soul, an ephemeral Buddhist *anātman*, or an unstable piece of perishable animal flesh—matter considerably to how people across the earth self-conceive.

14. Straightforward does not mean deductive. I am hungry, there is food on the other side of the river, and thus I ought to figure out a way to get to the other side of the river. It makes straightforward good sense. The conclusion is straightforward but not deductive, demonstrative, or a logical necessity. You cannot derive an 'ought' for an 'is.' It is naughty. No smart people—Buddhists are smart—claim deductive or demonstrative grounding for oughts, norms, and principles in ethics, etiquette, or epistemology.

15. Strictly speaking, there is no Buddhism, only Buddhisms, a plethora of related traditions that emerged, along with Jainism, on the Indian subcontinent in the fifth century BCE, as both a reaction to and a development of a host of indigenous threads that came eventually to be called Hinduism. The Buddhisms are now a dominant form of life throughout much of Southeast Asia, in Thailand, Cambodia, Vietnam, Myanmar, and Sri Lanka, as well as a significant form of life in parts of East Asia, in China, Korea, and Japan. And there are many Westerners who self-describe as Buddhists.

16. Despite the diversity among the Buddhisms, there is a common core, a common denominator. Buddhist sects agree that the "Four Noble Truths," the "Noble Eightfold Path," and the "Four Immeasurables" constitute a core philosophy.

17. Here is my baton pass to my friends who do experimental philosophy: I assume that contemporary Buddhists (real ones, not "Bourgeois Buddhists," http://www.huffingtonpost.

com/owen-flanagan-phd/do-american-buddhists-miss-the-point-of-buddhism_b_964188. html) are a good contrastive case to WEIRD folk on 1–12. The evidence in the psychological literature points to differences of the sort depicted in 1–12 in countries where nowadays a variety of traditions create the philosophical penumbra or penumbras, for example, Daoism, Confucianism, neo-Confucianism, admixtures of these with various Abrahamic religions, communism, and "you-name-it." But Buddhists are not singled out in the bulk of the work on 1–12. There is one exception, which will be published soon by Shaun Nichols and Nina Strohminger, and their colleagues. Early results show (personal communication) that (1) Tibetan lamas report much stronger No-Self beliefs than Christians or Hindus; (2) Tibetan lamas report a greater sense of impermanence than Christians or Hindus; (3) Tibetan lamas are much more likely to say they invoke 'No-Self' script to cope with death; (4) Tibetan lamas are much less generous on trade-off study, as compared to both Christians and Hindus; (5) Tibetan lamas report much greater fear on the "self-annihilation" factor of the Fear of Personal Death scale; (4) and (5) are very surprising if one thinks theory and practice align.

18. Max Weber (1930) thought that the Protestant ethic, which was the spirit of capitalism, was a gift of the Abrahamic traditions and its emphasis on individual salvation. MacIntyre (1966) provides an interpretation of recent secular ethics, in its Enlightenment and post-Enlightenment forms, as continuing to channel the very spiritual traditions it was seeking to leave behind. Kant's categorical imperative looks pretty much like the sublimated theology of a pietistic Lutheran trying not to speak as one. J. S. Mill says that the principle of utility is the same as the Golden Rule of Jesus of Nazareth. Even Sartre's existentialism preserves the sovereign individual, but now without any further normative guidance than what each individual can provide for themself.

19. Michel Foucault, Pierre Hadot, and Martha Nussbaum have each emphasized this way of thinking of philosophy, as involving *techniques de soi*, the therapy of desire, spiritual exercise, and self-fashioning. Hadot writes, "Philosophy then appears in its original aspect: not as a theoretical construct, but as a method for training to live and to look at the world in a new way. It is an attempt to transform mankind" (1995, 107).

20. Consensus is now that the historical Buddha died around 400 BCE (Prebish 2008). This is almost one hundred years later than most scholars believed a century ago, and makes him and Socrates contemporaries.

21. No-Self (*annata*; Sanskrit: *anātman*) is (technically or originally) not human or person (Pali: *puggala*; Sanskrit: *pugdala*) specific. In the first instance, it is the claim that no things have selves, *ipseity*; nothing is an independent thing. Nothing has an essence. Understood this way, and not in person-specific terms, one can see how this thesis (*anicca*) yields eventually the doctrine that all things are empty (Pali: *sunnata*; Sanskrit: *śūnyatā*).

22. One version of Buddhist reductionism, really eliminativism, says that the self completely dissolves ultimately (Siderits 2003). My self is not there at all, even now. Contrast that with the punctual self, the view that I am a series of self-stages that have some sort of psychophysical or phenomenal reality over certain short swaths of time (length to be determined). Buddhist reductionism denies this. Ultimately, there are not really even short-lived phenomenal states—the refreshing quality of a cool drink of water. There seem to be such states, but there aren't. So both horizontally and diachronically (No-Self), and vertically and synchronically (Emptiness), my self-hood (indeed, the self-hood of all relational and composite things) dissolves into something less substantial, something insubstantial, something

not really there at all. I offered a reply to Buddhist eliminativism in 2011. The gist of my re-sponse is this: It is easy to deconstruct the self conceptually by purely philosophical analysis so that it is analyzed into nothing, or analyzed into an infinite regress of concepts. But in reality, rather than in our concepts, there really are organisms that last awhile as the organ-isms they are. Some of these organisms are human selves, persons. They are impermanent. But they are something, not nothing at all, not totally empty. A self, a human self at any rate, is an impermanent creature that is normally and rightly identified in terms of continuity of consciousness and memory, which is normally made possible by a brain in a body in a world. The situation is akin to Zeno's paradoxes, which prove that there is no motion. But there is motion. In both cases, the paradoxical, puzzling views that there is no motion and that EMPTINESS is EMPTY are caused by allowing conceptual, purely logical analysis, to roam free from reality, free from the world.

23. Analytic philosophers in the West nowadays are disproportionately interested in one of the two major schools of Mahayana, *Madyamaka*, associated especially with Nāgārjuna, the greatest philosopher of Emptiness, and not insignificantly, the first named philosopher in the Buddhist tradition. The worldwide split is 60/40 Mahayana to Theravada. Somparn Prompta (2008) is an excellent introduction to contemporary Theravadan Thai. Three dif-ferences from *Madyamaka* stand out: (1) greater emphasis on self-perfection (the arhat ideal); (2) correspondingly less emphasis on saving the world (the bodhisattva ideal), in part because it is impractical; (3) an understanding of Emptiness and No-Self that is more directly psychological and moral than metaphysical, where saying one is no-self or empty (both of which are common in my experience in Thailand) are ways of saying that one has accepted such views as that one is impermanent and that neither the good of the universe nor my own personal good turn on my getting what I want. I am grateful to Professor Prompta and Professor Soraj Hongladarom, distinguished philosophers, for extremely helpful correspondence on this topic.

24. The view that there are no real essences is compatible with the view that science and philosophy try to corral what there is out-there, which is unruly and entirely nonconceptual and nonlinguistic, into categories that make it tractable by us.

25. Roger-Pol Droit (2003) explains how the original audience of Buddhism in Europe, especially Germany, in the nineteenth century found the nihilistic reading attractive.

26. Amber Carpenter (2014) is sensitive to the *metaphysics-lite* and *metaphysics-heavy* contrast among the Buddhisms.

27. It seems plausible that the dominant view of the self in secular precincts in the North Atlantic is neo-Lockean. Persons are individuals, perhaps animals, who have a certain con-tinuity and connectedness among their mental states, but that are not glued together as THE SELF that they are by an immutable essence such as a soul. Atheists, deists, agnostics, Darwinians, and skeptics can all be on board with a conception in this vicinity. Derek Parfit (1984) suggests that such a neo-Lockean view of the self as a psychologically continuous and connected process is close to the Buddhist view and ought to engender the thought that my connection to my future self (about whom I care) is no more substantial than it is to others in, say, my hometown right now. If I see reason to care about my future very old self, then I also have reason to care about others in my hometown right now (Flanagan 2011).

28. Oneness, as I use the term, is adopted from P. J. Ivanhoe (1998a, 1998b, 2015b), who uses it, in the first instance, to describe certain neo-Confucian metaphysical and moral views. See also Tien (2012) and Priest (2014) on moral and metaphysical oneness.

29. Paul Grice (1989) developed the idea that in different linguistic communities certain ideas are understood to be "implicatures" of other ideas. "Good son" means something different in contemporary America than in a classical Confucian culture. "Implicatures" are not logical implications; they are implications inside a form of life (part of "pragmatics"). I think this is a useful way to think of ethics in the broad sense. Ideas, feelings, and motivations go together because they are endorsed historically inside that form of life, they reach and maintain an equilibrium inside that form of life—quite possibly, if they are long-lived, because they do go well together—and they create the conditions for flourishing as conceived inside that form of life.

30. *Samadhi* meditation is calming meditation. *Vipassana* is insight meditation, insight into Impermanence, Dependent Origination, No-Self, and Emptiness. *Metta* is loving-kindness meditation, where one works at loving attention, being attuned to the weal and woe of other impermanent beings, and to cultivating the desire and skill to promote their well-being. It may be that the first two kinds of meditation might get one to see that one is No-Self, but that the third kind is required to put one in the mood, to inculcate or activate the desire to be unselfish. The *Metaphysics Lite* style of Buddhism might recommend that we go straight to *Metta* meditation, thinking that one can inculcate motivation to be compassionate without any insight whatsoever into esoteric truths like No-Self and Emptiness. A common thought is that *Metta* meditation taps into the preexisting sense that the wells of care and compassion (*bodhicitta*) in us, rather than the egoistic poisons, are our telos, our summum bonum. Human nature contains a host of natural desires, some self-centered, some compassionate and lovingkind. Somehow the latter desires are experienced or tagged from the start as good, right, as the ones that if we develop them, are the best. It is an interesting question whether (a) this is true empirically, and (b) whether and how we might explain it in terms of powerful selection pressures on humans to be cooperative that might have naturally tipped the balance in our mixed selfish and unselfish natures toward our cooperative, compassionate, altruistic side (Sober and Wilson 1998; Tomasello, 2009).

31. Schopenhauer gets this. Schopenhauer criticized Kant for thinking that pure practical reason can ground morality. At some point, the feeling of compassion is required. Schopenhauer was influenced by the Indic idea of Vedanta, where the thought is that the apparent boundaries between things are illusory (*maya*). Derek Parfit (1984) and Mark Johnston (2010) discuss whether a deconstructive view of the self or identity, which they rightly see as similar to certain Buddhist views, entails or bears any moral consequences—for example, favors, say, utilitarianism or Christian agape. The answer is that it gives reason to be motivated in either or both directions, but doesn't logically produce the motivation. David Wong reminds me that the skeptic will not be satisfied if the relation is only an "it makes sense" relation among certain metaphysical facts or even worse among certain metaphysical views, a certain set of sociocultural views about excellent people (bodhisattvas, for example), and a psychology that admits that at the start we are a mixed bag of egoism (the three poisons) and limited well of care and compassion (*bodhicitta*). This is true. Nothing will satisfy the skeptic.

32. Consider the Buddhist case: Enlightened Buddhists, arhats, and bodhisattvas, do not experience themselves as separate from other beings, which is, of course, compatible with ordinary Buddhists doing so. Or put another way: Arhats and bodhisattvas have, or are supposed to have, dotted-line boundaries with everyone, including strangers. Ordinary

Buddhists are also supposed to work toward this ideal, but are not expected to succeed at feeling themselves as one with all of humanity.

33. It isn't as if collectivist, porous selves are expansively porous and non-individualistic, and that nonporous selves are closed down, selfish, and self-absorbed. According to the PICTURE, porous selves are open, dependent, and porous to others inside their own normative community. But they do not view their fate as shared with out-group members, nor are they open to being cocreated by out-group members and influences. Individualistic, atomistic selves, on the other hand, according to the PICTURE, are no less open to out-group members and influences than to in-group ones. This fits several stereotypes, for example, that porous selfhood goes well with small-scale societies, and that liberal individualists are good citizens of the marketplace of ideas, as well as good boundary crossers. I do not think the connection is necessary. Buddhism and Jainism are universalist, explicitly attuned to the suffering of all sentient beings; whereas some members of Abrahamic faiths limit love of neighbor to a faith community, and some children of the secular enlightenment are nation state chauvinists.

34. See James Maffie (2014) on sixteenth-century precontact/preconquest Mexican metaphysics. The metaphysics embeds a process view of the self and metaphysic of morals that is aligned with the interdependent, porous, communal vision of things. This metaphysics still exists in many places in Mesoamerica, and is one reason that Latin American philosophy is so important in the exploration of the varieties of moral possibility.

35. *Caveat*: The empirical literature makes generalizations framed in terms of East Asians, South Asians, Southeast Asians, North Americans, and so on, when typically the samples are regional and based, say, on people from a city or a region. It is essential to recognize that these are generalizations, and that just as there is huge variation across states and regions of, for example, the United States or Brazil, so too is there variation in all these locales: different religions, different philosophical and linguistic communities, and multiple ways of worldmaking. The ecological perspective insists that at the end of the day we will need to examine all these matters in a fine-grained way, in terms of microecologies and microgeographies.

36. Aristotle thought something like this. If after I die, my children suffer, then I do, too. My life is objectively worse than it was at the time I died.

37. This will also be required for the non-WEIRD soul who sees the fences down among in-group members, but perceives high impermeable fences between in-groups and out-groups. Impermanence, Dependent Origination, No-Self, Emptiness, and Oneness suggest that thinking and acting as if there are such borders entails cognitive mistakes and engenders moral harm.

38. Two points: First, one might say that the doctrine of No-Self denies that there are real boundaries around selves and thus that, in terms of the deepest metaphysical facts, each actual living self is porous, actually empty at the very time, while alive, they think they are not empty (although impermanent, ever-changing). This metaphysically weighty view is out there. But one can also read the doctrine of No-Self in the metaphysically lite way as a recommendation to be less self-absorbed because everything including a subject of experience is impermanent, too. Second, there is still the important question of whether metaphysics and soteriologies that strongly emphasize interdependency and oneness do so widely and universally or only locally and chauvinistically, inside a small or large in-group, a family, clan, nation-state.

Chapter 12

1. Some philosophers distinguish the ethical project from the moral project along these lines: Ethics is broad inquiry and theorizing about how to live well, whereas the moral project involves what we owe each other, the zone of duties and obligations (Williams 1985; Scanlon 1998; Dworkin 2000; Appiah 2005). Philip Kitcher (2011) conceives of the ethical project in his book by that name as concerned with increasing altruism. I intend morality and the moral project to include both the narrow and wide projects.

2. Michael Walzer (1983) uses the idea of spheres in his work on justice, and something like it can be useful here. Walzer's idea is that justice means different things and requires different actions in different spheres, for example, in the family, on the one hand, and when hiring civil servants, on the other.

3. Tax policy often embeds prior philosophical debates and views about whether redistribution of wealth is just or not. In my experience, northern Europeans and Canadians take for granted in a way Americans do not, that tax law should be designed to mitigate luck.

4. In the case of inalienable or intrinsic rights, the agreement will be philosophically superficial but possibly, nonetheless, practically deep. Consequentialists might think that talk of inalienable rights is "nonsense on stilts," and Buddhists might think there are no intrinsic descriptive or normative features that attach to persons, while agreeing with the spirit of treating people as if they possess such things.

5. I don't actually buy this interpretation, since Mencius's metaphors are, as Ivanhoe (2000, 2002) says, typically agricultural rather than botanical.

6. If success at the moral project is analogous to being an accomplished athlete who overcomes certain natural instincts—say for how to pace oneself at the start of a marathon (the natural tendency is to start too fast), or to stay on the parallel bars (the natural tendency is to lean and thus fall), or to hit a golf ball (the natural tendency produces whiffs)—it is more like becoming a decathlete than like becoming proficient at just one sport. The reason is that morality does not confront one with only one kind of moral problem, but rather with many different kinds, really more than ten, so even a decathlon is not quite right. One other point: all great athletes will confront local conditions, a marathon to be run in unusual heat and humidity, or unusual competition, the opponent with the deep return of serve, which will require conscious deliberation and adjustments to their normal way of doing things. Confucius's autobiography occurs at 2.4 *Analects* and sums up the lifelong features of the moral project: "The Master says: At 15, I set my heart on learning. At 30, I know where I stand. At 40, I have no more doubts. At 50, I know the will of Heaven. At 60, my ears are attuned. At 70, I follow my heart's desire without crossing the line."

7. Bloom (2013b) adds, "We are by nature indifferent, even hostile to strangers; we are prone towards parochialism and bigotry. Some of our instinctive emotional responses, most notably disgust, spur us to do terrible things, including acts of genocide" (6). The good news is that "we have come to transcend the morality we are born with . . . our imagination, our compassion, and especially our intelligence give rise to moral insight and moral progress and make us more than just babies" (6).

8. One fertile area of research explores the similarities and differences in protomoral dispositions across species of nonhuman primates, capuchins, marmosets, bonobos, chimps, and great apes. Are they all aggressive when there is sexual competition? Not all and not always. Are they all patriarchal? No chimps are patriarchal, but bonobos are matriarchal. Do they ever go out of their way to share or only when encouraged? What about

turn-taking (De Waal 1982, 2009; Skerry, Sheskin, and Santos 2011; Tan and Hare 2013)? It depends on the species and the situation.

9. Bloom surveys several hypotheses that attempt to explain the development of racism (2013b, 105–28). The good news is that there is no credible hypothesis that claims direct selection for racism, rather they all explain why it is very easy to activate racism and every other variety of xenophobia in homogeneous communities, especially if there are conflicts among groups who look and speak differently.

10. David Lancy's *The Anthropology of Childhood: Cherubs, Chattel, Changelings* (2015) is a treasure trove of narratives about how children have been seen over world historical time and are still seen in many places. The view of children as cherubs, as precious angels, is rare, and reigns only in the twenty-first century among millennial elites. The idea of children as chattel, as replacements for elder workers who keep dying off, is very common. The view of children as changelings, sometimes angels and sometimes possessed of evil spirits, is compatible with the chattel view, and is activated especially when scapegoats for disasters are needed. Lancy's book and Whiting and Edwards's *Children of Different Worlds* (1988) provide good samplings of the multifarious ways babies are held and raised, how and where and with whom they sleep, and the multifarious ways they are socialized into a morality.

11. I do not discuss the topic of childrearing and caretaking remotely as much as it deserves. There are several noteworthy books that make it a zone of enormous salience for the moral project. Erin M. Cline's *Families of Virtue* (2015) argues for the "unique and irreplaceable role" of the family in the development of moral sensibilities, and contains a sensitive critical comparison of Confucian and Western modes of family life and the different ways certain virtues are conceived and taught in the family. Patricia Smith Churchland's *Braintrust* (2011) promotes the hypothesis "that morality originates in the neurobiology of attachment and bonding" (71). Churchland calls the oxytocin-vasopressin system "the neural platform" on which human morality is built. Oxytocin affects whether and how much caretakers care about offspring, how protective they are toward them, and so on. Touching, nursing, and sexual relations are partly produced by, and produce, changes in oxytocin levels, and by that mechanism create and fix ties that bind. Sarah Blaffer Hrdy's *Mothers and Others* (2009) is a fine ethology of the psychobiology and ethology of child-rearing. Darcia Narváez et al., eds., *Evolution, Early Experience and Human Development* (2012), is a valuable collection of articles on ancestral and contemporary parenting practices.

12. There is a lot of discussion in moral psychology about when children get the difference between conventional rules, these falling on the side of etiquette or manners, which are optional, and moral rules, which involve high-stakes matters as well as formal duties and obligations (Turiel 1983). But there are many cultures that do not read the moral terrain as so easily divided. In classical Confucianism, and in parts of East Asia today that are heavily indebted to Confucianism, what we would call manners is both moralized and aestheticized in virtues such as *li*, which encompasses not only how one behaves in ceremonial circumstances but also how one carries oneself and whether and how one reveals one's polite and respectful nature to others. Everything from how one moves one's hands when speaking, to whether one makes eye contact, and if one is supposed to not meet eye-to-eye, where one's eyes ought to be focused—up, down, sideways, and to which side. All these things are part of the inescapable normative framework. They are modeled as often as they are explicitly taught, which works because we are spectacularly good at learning by imitation (Hurley and Chater 2005; Flanagan 2008). In certain large households in Kenya, thirty

or forty members from an extended family dine together. In these communities, what we would call table manners are very big deals, matters of moral significance.

13. Work in experimental game theory tests individual decision-making, asking the subjects to make a choice about how much of some good they will offer to another (who is typically anonymous). One could do the same experiments with children and adults not by inviting the subject to make a choice, but by asking them what they should do, or what a good person would do, what Mary, mother of Jesus, or Buddha, or some local exemplar would do. One could ask what a bad person or a selfish person would offer? I'd expect that actual choices and ideal choices, "woulds" and "shoulds" would come apart in informative ways.

14. It is clear from all the studies that these economic games engage many emotions, from simple happiness at receiving a windfall to the positive feeling that comes from behaving fairly, to the satisfaction of spite, revenge, and punishment (Frank 1988).

15. Blake et al. (2015) is a fascinating study of seven societies—two WEIRD ones and five non-WEIRD—that investigates when kids between four and fifteen first show signs of aversion to a peer getting more that oneself (disadvantageous inequity, DI) and if and when they show aversion to getting more than one's fair share (advantageous inequity aversion, AI). All kids show DI at a young age. WEIRD kids, but not non-WEIRD kids (with one exception), show AI after ten or so. This makes sense because WEIRD cultures pull for norms that call on individuals to show that they can be trusted in economic transactions. Further research is needed to know whether the differences bespeak a difference in moral convictions and in the content of character, or simply indicate a smart strategy for gaining a good reputation in otherwise competitive, possibly winner-take-all—iterated economic games of the sort that results in the fifty-fifty split between New Yorkers who are thriving and those who are not, all of whom play fair.

16. The passage from *Republic* Book II continues:

> For all men believe in their hearts that injustice is far more profitable to the individual than justice, and he who argues as I have been supposing, will say that they are right. If you could imagine any one obtaining this power of becoming invisible, and never doing any wrong or touching what was another's, he would be thought by the lookers-on to be a most wretched idiot, although they would praise him to one another's faces, and keep up appearances with one another from a fear that they too might suffer injustice.

17. According to Paul Bloom (2013b), the tendency to violence peaks at two years. My own children, Ben and Kate, were perfect at that age.

18. I normally ask students to vote on whether the Lydian shepherd thought experiment gets things right, and I ask if they think there would be any gender differences in how a male and female shepherd would behave. They think it gets things right with some modification of the claim that the shepherd will immediately violate all norms, to distinguish between shepherds of the two types, the well-socialized type and the well-behaved but chomping-at-the-bit type. And they think the only gender difference would pertain to whether the women would try to seduce or rape the king, which the women say would depend on specific properties of the king.

19. This second argument for the war of each against each will work even if only some people have some insatiable desires. Such people will try to get what they want insatiably from those who are sated with the amount of, say, money, sex, and security they have. And those, the souls whose desires are moderate, will have to fight or be ready to do so.

20. In the late 1960s and early 1970s, we tried the philosophy that you should "love the one you're with." Even when everyone was cooperative and willing to do this, things didn't work out very well for most anyone.

21. The debate about how attuned one ought to make kids to the fact that morality contains optional spaces, where other good people do things differently, is an important and consequential one. See Bernard Williams (1985) and Richard Rorty (1989) for helpful reflections on this difficult question. I discuss the topic in *Self Expressions* (1996).

22. Appiah gives a nice example of how easily controversy can be generated. Imagine a teacher who allows weekly discussion of contemporary ethical issues, say, capital punishment and treatment of animals on factory farms. The teacher shows liberal restraint and never tells the kids what they think, say, that both are abominations. The teacher's only rule is that discussion is not over until every child has spoken. This might seem innocuous since it is purely methodological. But some Confucian parents might object on grounds that they think that kids should be taught to sit quietly and learn true beliefs from adults. The method itself undermines a value they want to inculcate in their children.

REFERENCES

Abramson, Kate. 2010. "A Sentimentalist's Defense of Contempt, Shame, and Disdain." In *The Oxford Handbook of Philosophy of Emotion*, edited by Peter Goldie, 189–213. Oxford: Oxford University Press.

Abu-Lughod, Lila. 2013. *Do Muslim Women Need Saving?* Cambridge, MA: Harvard University Press.

Adorno, Theodor W., and others. 1950. *The Authoritarian Personality*. Social Studies Series (American Jewish Committee). New York: Harper.

Ahlenius, Henrik, and Torbjörn Tännsjö. 2012. "Chinese and Westerners Respond Differently to the Trolley Dilemmas." *Journal of Cognition and Culture* 12 (3–4): 195–201.

Alfano, Mark. 2013. *Character as Moral Fiction*. New York: Cambridge University Press.

Annas, Julia. 1993. *The Morality of Happiness*. New York: Oxford University Press.

Annas, Julia. 2011. *Intelligent Virtue*. Oxford: Oxford University Press.

Anscombe, G. E. M. 1958. "Modern Moral Philosophy." *Philosophy* 33 (124): 1–19.

Appiah, Anthony. 2005. *The Ethics of Identity*. Princeton, NJ: Princeton University Press.

Appiah, Anthony. 2006. *Cosmopolitanism: Ethics in a World of Strangers*. Issues of Our Time. New York: W. W. Norton.

Appiah, Anthony. 2008. *Experiments in Ethics*. Cambridge, MA: Harvard University Press.

Appiah, Anthony. 2010. *The Honor Code: How Moral Revolutions Happen*. New York: W. W. Norton.

Aristotle. 1985. *Nicomachean Ethics*. Translated by T. Irwin. Indianapolis, IN: Hackett.

Baldwin, James. 1962. *Another Country*. New York: Dial Press.

Baraka, Amiri [LeRoi Jones]. 1965. *The System of Dante's Hell*. New York: Grove Press.

Barash, David P., and Judith Eve Lipton. 2011. *Payback: Why We Retaliate, Redirect Aggression, and Take Revenge*. New York: Oxford University Press.

Barkow, Jerome H., Leda Cosmides, and John Tooby. 1992. *The Adapted Mind: Evolutionary Psychology and the Generation of Culture*. New York: Oxford University Press.

Batson, C. Daniel. 2011. *Altruism in Humans*. New York: Oxford University Press.

Becker, Lawrence C. 1998. *A New Stoicism*. Princeton, NJ: Princeton University Press.

Bell, Daniel A. 2006. *Beyond Liberal Democracy: Political Thinking for an East Asian Context*. Princeton, NJ: Princeton University Press.

Bell, Macalester. 2013. *Hard Feelings: The Moral Psychology of Contempt*. New York: Oxford University Press.

Bellah, Robert N. 2011. *Religion in Human Evolution from the Paleolithic to the Axial Age*. Cambridge, MA: Belknap Press of Harvard University Press.

Bellah, Robert N., Richard Madsen, William M. Sullivan, Ann Swidler, and Steven M. Tipton. 1985. *Habits of the Heart: Individualism and Commitment in American Life*. Berkeley: University of California Press.

Berlin, Brent, and Paul Kay. 1969. *Basic Color Terms: Their Universality and Evolution*. Berkeley: University of California Press.

Blackburn, S. W. 1998. *Ruling Passions: A Theory of Practical Reasoning*. New York: Oxford University Press.

Blake, P. R., K. McAuliffe, J. Corbit, T. C. Callaghan, O. Barry, A. Bowie, L. Kleutsch, K. L. Kramer, E. Ross, H. Vongsachang, R. Wrangham, and F. Warneken. 2015. "The Ontogeny of Fairness in Seven Societies." *Nature* 528 (7581): 258–61.

Bloom, Paul. 2004. *Descartes' Baby: How the Science of Child Development Explains What Makes Us Human*. New York: Basic Books.

Bloom, Paul. 2013a. "The Baby in the Well." *New Yorker*, May 20.

Bloom, Paul. 2013b. *Just Babies: The Origins of Good and Evil*. New York: Random House.

Bloom, Paul. 2015. "Empathy: Overrated?" *Atlantic*, July 3. http://www.theatlantic.com/health/archive/2015/07/against-empathy-aspen-paul-bloom-richard-j-davidson/397694/.

Blum, Lawrence A. 1980. *Friendship, Altruism, and Morality*. International Library of Philosophy. London: Routledge & Kegan Paul.

Blum, Lawrence A. 1994. *Moral Perception and Particularity*. New York: Cambridge University Press.

Bodhi, Bhikkhu. 2003. *The Connected Discourses of the Buddha: A Translation of the Saṃyutta Nikāya*. Teachings of the Buddha. Somerville, MA: Wisdom Publications.

Boehm, Christopher. 1999. *Hierarchy in the Forest: The Evolution of Egalitarian Behavior*. Cambridge, MA: Harvard University Press.

Boehm, Christopher. 2012. *Moral Origins: The Evolution of Virtue, Altruism, and Shame*. New York: Basic Books.

Bowles, Samuel, and Herbert Gintis. 2011. *A Cooperative Species: Human Reciprocity and Its Evolution*. Princeton, NJ: Princeton University Press.

Boyd, Robert, and Peter J. Richerson. 1985. *Culture and the Evolutionary Process*. Chicago: University of Chicago Press.

Boyd, Robert, and Peter J. Richerson. 2005. *The Origin and Evolution of Cultures*. Oxford: Oxford University Press.

Brandon, Robert N. 1990. *Adaptation and Environment*. Princeton, NJ: Princeton University Press.

Brandt, Richard B. 1954. *Hopi Ethics: A Theoretical Analysis*. Chicago: University of Chicago Press.

Briggs, Jean L. 1970. *Never in Anger: Portrait of an Eskimo Family*. Cambridge, MA: Harvard University Press.

Brighouse, Harry, and Adam Swift. 2014. *Family Values: The Ethics of Parent-Child Relationships*. Princeton, NJ: Princeton University Press.

Brison, Susan J. 2002. *Aftermath: Violence and the Remaking of a Self*. Princeton, NJ: Princeton University Press.

Brosnan, Sarah F. 2006. "Nonhuman Species' Reactions to Inequity and Their Implications for Fairness." *Social Justice Research* 19 (2): 153–85.

Brosnan, Sarah F, and Frans B. M. de Waal. 2003. "Monkeys Reject Unequal Pay." *Nature* 425 (6955): 297–99.

Brown, Donald E. 1991. *Human Universals*. New York: McGraw-Hill.

Bruner, Jerome S. 2002. *Making Stories: Law, Literature, Life*. New York: Farrar, Straus, and Giroux.

Burnyeat, Myles F. 1980. "Aristotle on Learning to Be Good." In *Essays on Aristotle's Ethics*, edited by Amélie Oksenberg Rorty, 69–92. Major Thinkers Series. Berkeley: University of California Press.

Burton, Robert [Democritus Junior]. 1632. *The Anatomy of Melancholy: What it is, with all the kinds, causes, symptomes, prognostickes & severall cures of it; in three partitions, with their severall sections, members & subsections, philosophically, medicinally, historically, opened & cut up*. 4th ed. Oxford: Printed for Henry Cripps.

Carlson, Jon D., and Russell Arben Fox. 2014. *The State of Nature in Comparative Political Thought: Western and Non-Western Perspectives*. Global Encounters: Studies in Comparative Political Theory. Lanham, MD: Lexington Books.

Carpenter, Amber D. 2014. *Indian Buddhist Philosophy*. Ancient Philosophies. Durham, NC: Acumen.

Carrithers, Michael, Steven Collins, and Steven Lukes. 1985. *The Category of the Person: Anthropology, Philosophy, History*. Cambridge: Cambridge University Press.

Casebeer, William D. 2003. *Natural Ethical Facts: Evolution, Connectionism, and Moral Cognition*. Cambridge, MA: MIT Press.

Casebeer, William D., and Patricia S. Churchland. 2003. "The Neural Mechanisms of Moral Cognition: A Multiple-Aspect Approach to Moral Judgment and Decision-Making." *Biology and Philosophy* 18 (1): 169–94.

Chan, Joseph C. W. 2013. *Confucian Perfectionism: A Political Philosophy for Modern Times*. Princeton, NJ: Princeton University Press.

Chang, Ruth, ed. 1997. *Incommensurability, Incomparability, and Practical Reason*. Cambridge, MA: Harvard University Press.

Chang, Ruth. 2002. *Making Comparisons Count*. Studies in Ethics. New York: Routledge.

Churchland, Patricia Smith. 2011. *Braintrust: What Neuroscience Tells Us About Morality*. Princeton, NJ: Princeton University Press.

Churchland, Patricia Smith. 2013. *Touching a Nerve: The Self as Brain*. New York: W. W. Norton.

Churchland, Patricia Smith, V. S. Ramachandran, and Terrence J. Sejnowski. 1994. "A Critique of Pure Vision." In *Large-Scale Neuronal Theories of the Brain*, edited by Christof Koch and Joel L. Davis, 23–60. Computational Neuroscience. Cambridge, MA: MIT Press.

Churchland, Paul M. 1979. *Scientific Realism and the Plasticity of Mind*. Cambridge Studies in Philosophy. Cambridge: Cambridge University Press.

Churchland, Paul M. 1995. *The Engine of Reason, the Seat of the Soul: A Philosophical Journey into the Brain*. Cambridge, MA: MIT Press.

Clark, Candace. 1997. *Misery and Company: Sympathy in Everyday Life*. Chicago: University of Chicago Press.

Cline, Erin M. 2015. *Families of Virtue: Confucian and Western Views on Childhood Development*. New York: Columbia University Press.

Collins, Steven. 1982. *Selfless Persons: Imagery and Thought in Theravāda Buddhism*. Cambridge: Cambridge University Press.

Confucius. 2003. *Analects: With Selections from Traditional Commentaries*. Translated by Edward G. Slingerland. Indianapolis, IN: Hackett.

Conze, Edward. 1951. *Buddhism: Its Essence and Development*. New York: Philosophical Library.

Damasio, Antonio R. 1994. *Descartes' Error: Emotion, Reason, and the Human Brain*. New York: G. P. Putnam.

Damasio, Antonio R. 1999. *The Feeling of What Happens: Body and Emotion in the Making of Consciousness*. New York: Harcourt Brace.

Darwall, Stephen L. 2006. *The Second-Person Standpoint: Morality, Respect, and Accountability*. Cambridge, MA: Harvard University Press.

Darwall, Stephen L., Allan Gibbard, and Peter Railton. 1992. "Toward *Fin de Siècle* Ethics: Some Trends." *Philosophical Review* 101 (1): 115–89.

Darwin, Charles. (1872) 1998. *The Expression of the Emotions in Man and Animals*. With introduction, afterword, and commentaries by Paul Ekman. 3rd ed. New York: Oxford University Press.

Darwin, Charles. (1871) 2004. *The Descent of Man*. The Modern Library. New York: Random House.

Darwin, Charles. (1859) 2008. *The Origin of Species*. The Modern Library. New York: Random House.

de Beauvoir, Simone. (1949) 2010. *The Second Sex*. Translated by Constance Borde and Sheila Malovany-Chevallier, with an introduction by Judith Thurman. New York: Alfred A. Knopf.

de Waal, Frans B. M. 1982. *Chimpanzee Politics: Power and Sex Among Apes*. London: Jonathan Cape.

de Waal, Frans B. M. 1991. "Complementary Methods and Convergent Evidence in the Study of Primate Social Cognition." *Behaviour* 118: 297–320.

de Waal, Frans B. M. 1996. *Good Natured: The Origins of Right and Wrong in Humans and Other Animals*. Cambridge, MA: Harvard University Press.

de Waal, Frans B. M. 2005. *Our Inner Ape: A Leading Primatologist Explains Why We Are Who We Are*. New York: Riverhead Books.

de Waal, Frans B. M. 2006. *Primates and Philosophers: How Morality Evolved*. Edited by Stephen Macedo and Josiah Ober. University Center for Human Values Series. Princeton, NJ: Princeton University Press.

de Waal, Frans B. M. 2009. "The Tower of Morality." In *Primates and Philosophers: How Morality Evolved*, edited by Stephen Macedo and Josiah Ober, 161–82. Reprint, Princeton, NJ: Princeton University Press.

de Waal, Frans B. M. 2013. *The Bonobo and the Atheist: In Search of Humanism Among the Primates*. New York: W. W. Norton.

de Waal, Frans B. M., Patricia Smith Churchland, and Stefano Pargiani, eds. 2014. *Evolved Morality: The Biology and Philosophy of Human Conscience*. Leiden: Brill.

Dehaene, Stanislas. 2009. *Reading in the Brain: The Science and Evolution of a Human Invention*. New York: Viking.

Deloria, Ella Cara. 1988. *Waterlily*. Lincoln: University of Nebraska Press.

Deloria, Ella Cara. (1944) 1998. *Speaking of Indians*. Lincoln: University of Nebraska Press.

Dennett, Daniel C. 1988. "Why Everyone Is a Novelist." *Times Literary Supplement*, September 16–22.

Descola, Philippe. 1996. *The Spears of Twilight: Life and Death in the Amazon Jungle*. New York: New Press.

Descola, Philippe. 2005. *Par-delà nature et culture*. Bibliothèque des sciences humaines. [Paris]: Gallimard.

Descola, Philippe. 2013. *Beyond Nature and Culture*. Chicago: University of Chicago Press.

Dewey, John. 1922. *Human Nature and Conduct: An Introduction to Social Psychology*. New York: H. Holt.

Diamond, Jared M. 1997. *Guns, Germs, and Steel: The Fates of Human Societies*. New York: W. W. Norton.

Doris, John M. 2002. *Lack of Character: Personality and Moral Behavior*. Cambridge: Cambridge University Press.

Doris, John M. 2015. *Talking to Ourselves: Reflection, Ignorance, and Agency*. Oxford: Oxford University Press.

Douglas, Mary. 1966. *Purity and Danger*. London: Routledge & Kegan Paul.

Dretske, Fred I. 1981. *Knowledge and the Flow of Information*. Cambridge, MA: MIT Press.

Droit, Roger-Pol. 2003. *The Cult of Nothingness: The Philosophers and the Buddha*. Chapel Hill: University of North Carolina Press.

Du Bois, W. E. B. 1903. *The Souls of Black Folk: Essays and Sketches*. Chicago: A. C. McClurg.

Duke, Aaron, and Laurent Bègue. 2015. "The Drunk Utilitarian: Blood Alcohol Concentration Predicts Utilitarian Responses in Moral Dilemmas." *Cognition* 134: 121–27.

Dunbar, Robin. 1996. *Grooming, Gossip, and the Evolution of Language*. Cambridge, MA: Harvard University Press.

Dworkin, Ronald. 2000. *Sovereign Virtue: The Theory and Practice of Equality*. Cambridge, MA: Harvard University Press.

Edmonds, David. 2014. *Would You Kill the Fat Man?: The Trolley Problem and What Your Answer Tells Us About Right and Wrong*. Princeton, NJ: Princeton University Press.

Ekman, Paul. 1992. "Are There Basic Emotions?" *Psychological Review* 99 (3): 550–53.

Ekman, Paul, ed. 1998. Introduction and afterword to *The Expression of the Emotions in Man and Animals*, by Charles Darwin, xxi–xxxvi, 363–93. Edited by Paul Ekman. 3rd ed. New York: Oxford University Press.

Ekman, Paul, and Richard J. Davidson. 1994. *The Nature of Emotion: Fundamental Questions*. Series in Affective Science. New York: Oxford University Press.

Ekman, Paul, Wallace V. Friesen, and Phoebe Ellsworth. 1972. *Emotions in the Human Face*. New York: Pergamon.

Elsabbagh, Mayada, and Annette Karmiloff-Smith. 2006. "Modularity of Mind and Language." In *The Encyclopedia of Language and Linguistics*, 2nd ed., edited by Keith Brown, 8:218–24. Oxford: Elsevier.

Ensminger, Jean, and Joseph Patrick Henrich, eds. 2014. *Experimenting with Social Norms: Fairness and Punishment in Cross-Cultural Perspective*. New York: Russell Sage Foundation.

Evans-Pritchard, E. E. 1937. *Witchcraft, Oracles and Magic Among the Azande*. Oxford: Clarendon Press.

Everett, Daniel Leonard. 2009. *Don't Sleep, There Are Snakes: Life and Language in the Amazonian Jungle*. London: Profile Books.

Fanon, Frantz. 1952. *Peau noire, masques blancs*. Points. Paris: Éditions du Seuil.

Fanon, Frantz. 1963. *The Wretched of the Earth*. New York: Grove Press.

Fanon, Frantz. (1952) 2008. *Black Skin, White Masks*. Translated by Charles Lam Markmann. Forewords by Ziauddin Sardar and Homi K. Bhabha. Get Political 4. London: Pluto Press.

Fausto-Sterling, Anne. 1992. *Myths of Gender: Biological Theories About Women and Men*. 2nd ed. New York: Basic Books.

Fehr, Ernst, Helen Bernhard, and Bettina Rockenbach. 2008. "Egalitarianism in Young Children." *Nature* 454 (7208): 1079–83.

Fiske, Alan Page. 1991. *Structures of Social Life: The Four Elementary Forms of Human Relations*. New York: Free Press.

Fiske, Alan Page. 1992. "The Four Elementary Forms of Sociality: Framework for a Unified Theory of Social Relations." *Psychological Review* 99 (4): 689–723.

Fiske, Alan Page. 2004. "Four Modes of Constituting Relationships: Consubstantial Assimilation; Space, Magnitude, Time, and Force; Concrete Procedures; Abstract Symbolism." In *Relational Models Theory: A Contemporary Overview*, edited by Nick Haslam, 61–146. Mahwah, NJ: Lawrence Erlbaum Associates.

Flanagan, Owen. 1991. *Varieties of Moral Personality: Ethics and Psychological Realism*. Cambridge, MA: Harvard University Press.

Flanagan, Owen. 1992. *Consciousness Reconsidered*. Cambridge, MA: MIT Press.

Flanagan, Owen. 1996. *Self Expressions: Mind, Morals, and the Meaning of Life*. New York: Oxford University Press.

Flanagan, Owen. 2000a. "Destructive Emotions." *Consciousness and Emotion* 1 (2): 67–88.

Flanagan, Owen. 2000b. *Dreaming Souls: Sleep, Dreams, and the Evolution of the Conscious Mind*. Oxford: Oxford University Press.

Flanagan, Owen. 2002. *The Problem of the Soul: Two Visions of Mind and How to Reconcile Them*. New York: Basic Books.

Flanagan, Owen. 2007. *The Really Hard Problem: Meaning in a Material World*. Cambridge, MA: MIT Press.

Flanagan, Owen. 2008. "Moral Contagion and Logical Persuasion in the Mozi." *Journal of Chinese Philosophy* 35 (3): 473–91.

Flanagan, Owen. 2009a. "Emotional Expressions: Why Moralists Frown, Scowl and Smile." In *The Cambridge Companion to Darwin*, edited by Gregory Radick and Johnathan Hodges, 413–34. Cambridge: Cambridge University Press.

Flanagan, Owen. 2009b. "Moral Science? Still Metaphysical After All These Years." In *Personality, Identity, and Character: Explorations in Moral Psychology*, edited by Darcia Narváez and Daniel K. Lapsley, 52–78. New York: Cambridge University Press.

Flanagan, Owen. 2011. *The Bodhisattva's Brain: Buddhism Naturalized*. Cambridge, MA: MIT Press.

Flanagan, Owen, and Jonathan Adler. 1983. "Impartiality and Particularity." *Social Research* 50: 576–96.

Flanagan, Owen, Aaron Ancell, Stephen Martin, and Gordon Steenbergen. 2014. "Empiricism and Normative Ethics: What Do the Biology and the Psychology of Morality Have to Do with Ethics?" In *Evolved Morality: The Biology and Philosophy of Human Conscience*, edited by Frans B. M. de Waal, Patricia Smith Churchland, Telmo Pievani, and Stefano Parmigiani, 73–92. Leiden: Brill.

Flanagan, Owen, Valerie Gray Hardcastle, and Eddy Nahmias. 2001. "Is Human Intelligence an Adaptation?: Cautionary Observations from Philosophy of Biology." In *The Evolution of Intelligence*, edited by Robert J. Sternberg and James C. Kaufman, 199–222. Mahwah, NJ: Lawrence Erlbaum Associates.

Flanagan, Owen, and Kathryn Jackson. 1987. "Justice, Care, and Gender: The Kohlberg-Gilligan Debate Revisited." *Ethics* 97 (3): 622–37.

Flanagan, Owen, and Jing Hu. 2011. "Han Fei Zi's Philosophical Psychology: Human Nature, Scarcity, and the Neo-Darwinian Consensus." *Journal of Chinese Philosophy* 38 (2): 293–316.

Flanagan, Owen, Hagop Sarkissian, and David B. Wong. 2008. "Naturalizing Ethics." In *Moral Psychology*, vol. 1, *The Evolution of Morality*, edited by Walter Sinnott-Armstrong, 1–26. Cambridge, MA: MIT Press.

Flanagan, Owen, and Robert Anthony Williams. 2010. "What Does the Modularity of Morals Have to Do with Ethics? Four Moral Sprouts Plus or Minus a Few." *Topics in Cognitive Science* 2 (3): 430–53.

Fodor, Jerry A. 1983. *The Modularity of Mind: An Essay on Faculty Psychology*. Cambridge, MA: MIT Press.

Foot, Philippa. 1978. *Virtues and Vices and Other Essays in Moral Philosophy*. Berkeley: University of California Press.

Foot, Philippa. 2001. *Natural Goodness*. Oxford: Clarendon Press.

Foucault, Michel. 1972. *The Archaeology of Knowledge*. Translated by A. M. Sheridan Smith. World of Man. New York: Pantheon Books.

Foucault, Michel. 1978. *The History of Sexuality*. Vol. 3, *The Care of the Self*. Social Theory. New York: Pantheon Books.

Frank, Robert H. 1988. *Passions Within Reason: The Strategic Role of the Emotions*. New York: W. W. Norton.

Frankl, Viktor E. 1959. *Man's Search for Meaning: An Introduction to Logotherapy*. Boston, MA: Beacon Press.

Fricker, Miranda. 2007. *Epistemic Injustice: Power and the Ethics of Knowing*. Oxford: Oxford University Press.

Fry, Douglas P. 2007. *Beyond War: The Human Potential for Peace*. Oxford: Oxford University Press.

Gandhi, Mohandas. 1997. *'Hind Swaraj' and Other Writings*. Edited by Anthony J. Parel. Cambridge Texts in Modern Politics. Cambridge: Cambridge University Press.

Gardner, Howard. 1983. *Frames of Mind: The Theories of Multiple Intelligences*. New York: Basic Books.

Geertz, Clifford. 1973. *The Interpretation of Cultures: Selected Essays*. New York: Basic Books.

Geertz, Clifford. 1983. *Local Knowledge: Further Essays in Interpretive Anthropology*. New York: Basic Books.

Gethin, Rupert. 2004. "Can Killing a Living Being Ever Be an Act of Compassion?: The Analysis of the Act of Killing in the Abhidhamma and Pali Commentaries." *Journal of Buddhist Ethics* 11: 167–202.

Gibbard, Allan. 1989. "Communities of Judgment." *Social Philosophy and Policy* 7 (1): 175–89.

Gibbard, Allan. 1992. *Wise Choices, Apt Feelings: A Theory of Normative Judgment*. Oxford: Clarendon Press.

Gilens, Martin, and Benjamin I. Page. 2014. "Testing Theories of American Politics: Elites, Interest Groups, and Average Citizens." *Perspectives on Politics* 12 (3): 564–81.

Gilligan, Carol. 1982. *In a Different Voice*. Cambridge, MA: Harvard University Press.

Glazer, Nathan, and Daniel P. Moynihan. 1963. *Beyond the Melting Pot: The Negroes, Puerto Ricans, Jews, Italians, and Irish of New York City*. Publications of the Joint Center for Urban Studies of the Massachusetts Institute of Technology and Harvard University. Cambridge, MA: MIT Press.

Godfrey-Smith, Peter. 1994. "A Modern History Theory of Functions." *Noûs* 28 (3): 344–62.

Godfrey-Smith, Peter. 2009. *Darwinian Populations and Natural Selection*. New York: Oxford University Press.

Goldman, Alvin I. 1986. *Epistemology and Cognition.* Cambridge, MA: Harvard University Press.

Goldman, Alvin I. 1992. *Liaisons: Philosophy Meets the Cognitive and Social Sciences.* Cambridge, MA: MIT Press.

Goleman, Daniel. 2003. *Destructive Emotions: How Can We Overcome Them?: A Scientific Dialogue with the Dalai Lama.* New York: Bantam Books.

Goodall, Jane. 1986. *The Chimpanzees of Gombe: Patterns of Behavior.* Cambridge, MA: Belknap Press of Harvard University Press.

Goodman, Nelson. 1978. *Ways of Worldmaking.* Indianapolis, IN: Hackett.

Gopnik, Alison. 2009. *The Philosophical Baby: What Children's Minds Tell Us About Truth, Love and the Meaning of Life.* New York: Farrar, Strauss and Giroux.

Graham, Jesse. 2010. "Left Gut, Right Gut: Ideology and Automatic Moral Reactions." PhD diss., University of Virginia.

Graham, Jesse, Jonathan Haidt, Sena Koleva, Matt Motyl, Ravi Iyer, S. Wojcik, and Peter H. Ditto. 2013. "Moral Foundations Theory: The Pragmatic Validity of Moral Pluralism." *Advances in Experimental Social Psychology* 47: 55–130.

Greene, Joshua D. 2003. "From Neural 'Is' to Moral 'Ought': What Are the Moral Implications of Neuroscientific Moral Psychology?" *Nature Reviews Neuroscience* 4 (10): 847–50.

Greene, Joshua D. 2013. *Moral Tribes: Emotion, Reason and the Gap between Us and Them.* New York: Penguin.

Greene, Joshua D., and Jonathan Haidt. 2002. "How (and Where) Does Moral Judgment Work?" *Trends in Cognitive Sciences* 16 (12): 517–23.

Grice, H. P. 1989. *Studies in the Way of Words.* Cambridge, MA: Harvard University Press.

Griffiths, Paul. 1997. *What Emotions Really Are: The Problems of Psychological Categories.* Chicago: University of Chicago Press.

Habermas, Jürgen. 1984. *The Theory of Communicative Action.* Boston, MA: Beacon Press.

Hadot, Pierre. 1995. *Philosophy as a Way of Life: Spiritual Exercises from Socrates to Foucault.* Edited with an introduction by Arnold I. Davidson. Translated by Michael Chase. Malden, MA: Blackwell.

Haidt, Jonathan. 2001. "The Emotional Dog and Its Rational Tail: A Social Intuitionist Approach to Moral Judgment." *Psychological Review* 108: 814–34.

Haidt, Jonathan. 2006. *The Happiness Hypothesis: Finding Modern Truth in Ancient Wisdom.* New York: Basic Books.

Haidt, Jonathan. 2007. "The New Synthesis in Moral Psychology." *Science* 316 (5827): 998–1002.

Haidt, Jonathan. 2012. *The Righteous Mind: Why Good People Are Divided by Politics and Religion.* New York: Pantheon.

Haidt, Jonathan, and Fredrik Bjorklund. 2008. "Social Intuitionists Answer Six Questions About Moral Psychology." In *Moral Psychology*, vol. 2, *The Cognitive Science of Morality: Intuition and Diversity*, edited by Walter Sinnott-Armstrong, 181–217. Cambridge, MA: MIT Press.

Haidt, Jonathan, and Jesse Graham. 2007. "When Morality Opposes Justice: Conservatives Have Moral Intuitions That Liberals May Not Recognize." *Social Justice Research* 20 (1): 98–116.

Haidt, Jonathan, and Craig Joseph. 2004. "Intuitive Ethics: How Innately Prepared Intuitions Generate Culturally Variable Virtues." *Daedalus* 133 (4): 55–66.

Haidt, Jonathan, and Craig Joseph. 2008. "The Moral Mind: How 5 Sets of Innate Intuitions Guide the Development of Many Culture-Specific Virtues, and Perhaps Even Modules." In *The Innate Mind*, vol. 3, *Foundations and the Future*, edited by Peter Carruthers, Stephen Laurence, and Stephen P. Stich, 367–91. New York: Oxford University Press.

Haidt, Jonathan, Silvia Helena Koller, and Maria G. Dias. 1993. "Affect, Culture, and Morality, or Is It Wrong to Eat Your Dog?" *Journal of Personality and Social Psychology* 65 (4): 613–28.

Hampden-Turner, Charles, and Alfons Trompenaars. 1993. *The Seven Cultures of Capitalism: Value Systems for Creating Wealth in the United States, Japan, Germany, France, Britain, Sweden, and the Netherlands*. New York: Currency/Doubleday.

Han, Fei. 2003. *Han Feizi: Basic Writings*. Translated by Burton Watson. Translations from the Asian Classics. New York: Columbia University Press.

Harman, Gil. 2000. "The Nonexistence of Character Traits." *Proceedings of the Aristotelian Society* 100 (2): 223–26.

Hartshorne, Hugh, and Mark A. May. 1928–1930. *Studies in the Nature of Character*. Vol. 1, *Studies in Deceit*. Vol 2 (with J. B. Maller), *Studies in Service and Self-Control*. Vol. 3 (with F. K. Shuttleworth), *Studies in the Organization of Character*. New York: MacMillan.

Hassoun, Nicole, and David B. Wong. 2013. "Sustaining Cultures in the Face of Globalization." *Culture and Dialogue* 2 (2): 73–98.

Hatfield, Elaine, Richard L. Rapson, and Lise D. Martel. 2007. "Passionate Love and Sexual Desire." In *Handbook of Cultural Psychology*, edited by Shinobu Kitayama and Dov Cohen, 760–79. New York: Guilford Press.

Hauser, Marc D. 2006. *Moral Minds: How Nature Designed Our Universal Sense of Right and Wrong*. New York: Ecco.

Haybron, Daniel M. 2008. *The Pursuit of Unhappiness: The Elusive Psychology of Well-Being*. Oxford: Oxford University Press.

Henrich, Joseph, Robert Boyd, Samuel Bowles, Colin Camerer, Ernst Fehr, Herbert Gintis, Richard McElreath, Michael Alvard, Abigail Barr, and Jean Ensminger. 2007. "'Economic Man' in Cross-Cultural Perspective: Behavioral Experiments in 15 Small-Scale Societies." *Behavioral and Brain Sciences* 28 (6): 795–855.

Henrich, Joseph, Steven J. Heine, and Ara Norenzayan. 2010. "The Weirdest People in the World?" *Behavioral and Brain Sciences* 33 (2–3): 61–83.

Hobbes, Thomas. 1973. *Leviathan*. Everyman's Library. London: Dent.

Hoffman, Martin L. 2000. *Empathy and Moral Development: Implications for Caring and Justice*. Cambridge: Cambridge University Press.

Horkheimer, Max, and Theodor W. Adorno. (1947) 1972. *Dialectic of Enlightenment*. New York: Herder and Herder.

Hrdy, Sarah Blaffer. 2009. *Mothers and Others: The Evolutionary Origins of Mutual Understanding*. Cambridge, MA: Harvard University Press.

Hume, David. 1998. *An Enquiry Concerning the Principles of Morals: A Critical Edition*. Edited by Tom L. Beauchamp. The Clarendon Edition of the Works of David Hume. Oxford: Clarendon Press; New York: Oxford University Press.

Hurley, Susan, and Nick Chater, eds. 2005. *Perspectives on Imitation: From Neuroscience to Social Science*. Vol. 1, *Mechanisms of Imitation and Imitation in Animals*. Vol. 2, *Imitation, Human Development, and Culture*. Cambridge, MA: MIT Press.

Hursthouse, Rosalind. 1999. *On Virtue Ethics*. Oxford: Oxford University Press.

Hursthouse, Rosalind, Gavin Lawrence, and Warren Quinn, eds. 1995. *Virtues and Reasons: Philippa Foot and Moral Theory: Essays in Honour of Philippa Foot.* Oxford: Clarendon Press; New York: Oxford University Press.

Iurino, Kathryn, and Gerard Saucier. 2014. "Measurement Invariance of the Moral Foundations Questionnaire Across 27 Countries." Unpublished.

Ivanhoe, P. J. 1998a. "Early Confucianism and Environmental Ethics." In *Confucianism and Ecology: The Interrelation of Heaven, Earth, and Humans,* edited by Mary Evelyn Tucker and John Berthrong, 59–76. Cambridge, MA: Harvard University Press.

Ivanhoe, P. J. 1998b. "Nature, Awe, and the Sublime." *Midwest Studies in Philosophy* 21: 98–117.

Ivanhoe, P. J. 2000. *Confucian Moral Self Cultivation.* 2nd ed. Indianapolis, IN: Hackett.

Ivanhoe, P. J. 2002. *Ethics in the Confucian Tradition: The Thought of Mengzi and Wang Yangming.* 2nd ed. Indianapolis, IN: Hackett.

Ivanhoe, P. J. 2009. "Pluralism, Toleration, and Ethical Promiscuity." *Journal of Religious Ethics* 37 (2): 311–29.

Ivanhoe, P. J. 2013. *Confucian Reflections: Ancient Wisdom for Modern Times.* New York: Routledge.

Ivanhoe, P. J. 2015a. "The Historical Significance and Contemporary Relevance of the Four-Seven Debate." *Philosophy East and West* 65 (2): 401–29.

Ivanhoe, P. J. 2015b. "Senses and Values of Oneness." In *The Philosophical Challenge from China,* edited by Brian Burya, 231–51. Cambridge, MA: MIT Press.

Ivanhoe, P J., and Bryan W. Van Norden, eds. 2005. *Readings in Classical Chinese Philosophy.* 2nd ed. Indianapolis, IN: Hackett.

James, William. (1892) 1961. *Psychology: The Briefer Course.* New York: Harper.

James, William. (1890) 1981. *The Principles of Psychology.* 3 vols. *The Works of William James.* Edited by Frederick Burkhardt, Fredson Bowers, and Ignas K. Skrupskelis. Cambridge, MA: Harvard University Press.

Jeffers, Chike. 2013. *Listening to Ourselves: A Multilingual Anthology of African Philosophy.* SUNY Series in Living Indigenous Philosophies. Albany: State University of New York Press.

Jerryson, Michael K. 2011. *Buddhist Fury: Religion and Violence in Southern Thailand.* Oxford: Oxford University Press.

Jerryson, Michael K., and Mark Juergensmeyer, eds. 2010. *Buddhist Warfare.* Oxford: Oxford University Press.

Jin, X. 1987. "The 'Four-Seven Debate' and the School of Principle in Korea." *Philosophy East and West* 37 (4): 347–60.

Johnson, Mark. 1993. *Moral Imagination: Implications of Cognitive Science for Ethics.* Chicago: University of Chicago Press.

Johnson, Mark. 2014. *Morality for Humans: Ethical Understanding from the Perspective of Cognitive Science.* Chicago: University of Chicago Press.

Johnson-Hanks, Jennifer. 2006. *Uncertain Honor: Modern Motherhood in an African Crisis.* Chicago: University of Chicago Press.

Johnston, Mark. 2009. *Saving God: Religion After Idolatry.* Princeton, NJ: Princeton University Press.

Kagan, Jerome. 1984. *The Nature of the Child.* New York: Basic Books.

Kahane, Guy, Jim A. C. Everett, Brian D. Earp, Miguel Farias, and Julian Savulescu. 2015. "'Utilitarian' Judgments in Sacrificial Moral Dilemmas Do Not Reflect Impartial Concern for the Greater Good." *Cognition* 134: 193–209.

Kahneman, Daniel. 2011. *Thinking, Fast and Slow*. New York: Farrar, Straus and Giroux.

Kant, Immanuel. 2002. *Groundwork for the Metaphysics of Morals*. Translated by Arnulf Zweig. Edited by Thomas E. Hill and Arnulf Zweig. Oxford Philosophical Texts. Oxford: Oxford University Press.

Karmiloff-Smith, Annette. 1992. *Beyond Modularity: A Developmental Perspective on Cognitive Science*. Learning, Development, and Conceptual Change. Cambridge, MA: MIT Press.

Kim, Jaegwon. (1988) 1993. *Supervenience and Mind: Selected Philosophical Essays*. Cambridge Studies in Philosophy. Cambridge: Cambridge University Press.

Kim, Myeong-seok. 2010. "What Cèyǐn zhī xīn (Compassion/Familial Affection) Really Is." *Dao: A Journal of Comparative Philosophy* 9 (4): 407–25.

Kim, Richard T. 2015. "Human Nature and Animal Nature: The Horak Debate and Its Philosophical Significance." *International Philosophical Quarterly* 55 (4): 437–56.

Kim, Sungmoon. 2014. *Confucian Democracy in East Asia: Theory and Practice*. New York: Cambridge University Press.

King, Martin Luther, Jr. 1963. *Letter from Birmingham City Jail*. Philadelphia: American Friends Service Committee.

King, Martin Luther, Jr. 1964. *Why We Can't Wait*. New York: Harper & Row.

King, Martin Luther, Jr. 1985. *The "I Have a Dream" Speech as Delivered by Dr. Martin Luther King, Jr., August, 1963, Washington, D.C.* Produced and edited by Richard S. R. Johnson for the Center for Nonviolent Social Change. Atlanta, GA: The Center. Videocassette.

Kitayama, Shinobu, and Dov Cohen. 2007. *Handbook of Cultural Psychology*. New York: Guilford Press.

Kitcher, Philip. 1985. *Vaulting Ambition: Sociobiology and the Quest for Human Nature*. Cambridge, MA: MIT Press.

Kitcher, Philip. 2011. *The Ethical Project*. Cambridge, MA: Harvard University Press.

Kittay, Eva Feder. 1999. *Love's Labor: Essays on Women, Equality, and Dependency*. Thinking Gender. New York: Routledge.

Kittay, Eva Feder, and Ellen K. Feder, eds. 2002. *The Subject of Care: Feminist Perspectives on Dependency*. Feminist Constructions. Lanham, MD: Rowman & Littlefield.

Kittay, Eva Feder, and Diana T. Meyers. 1987. *Women and Moral Theory*. Totowa, NJ: Rowman & Littlefield.

Kluckhohn, Clyde. 1949. *Mirror for Man: The Relation of Anthropology to Modern Life*. New York: Whittlesey House.

Kohlberg, Lawrence. 1958. "The Development of Modes of Thinking and Choices in Years 10 to 16." PhD diss., University of Chicago.

Kohlberg, Lawrence. 1971. "From 'Is' to 'Ought': How to Commit the Naturalistic Fallacy and Get Away with It in the Study of Moral Development." In *Cognitive Development and Epistemology*, edited by Theodore Mischel, 153–235. New York: Academic Press.

Kohlberg, Lawrence. 1973. "The Claim to Adequacy of the Highest Stage of Moral Development." *Journal of Philosophy* 70 (18): 630–46.

Kohlberg, Lawrence. 1981. *Essays on Moral Development*. Vol. 1, *The Philosophy of Moral Development: Moral Stages and the Idea of Justice*. San Francisco, CA: Harper & Row.

Kohlberg, Lawrence. 1984. *Essays on Moral Development*. Vol. 2, *The Psychology of Moral Development: The Nature and Validity of Moral Stages*. San Francisco, CA: Harper & Row.

Kornblith, Hilary. 1985. *Naturalizing Epistemology*. Cambridge, MA: MIT Press.

Kuhn, Thomas S. 1957. *The Copernican Revolution: Planetary Astronomy in the Development of Western Thought*. Cambridge, MA: Harvard University Press.

Kuhn, Thomas S. 1970. *The Structure of Scientific Revolutions*. 2nd ed. International Encyclopedia of Unified Science, vol. 2, no 2. Chicago: University of Chicago Press.

Kwong-loi, Shun. 1997. *Mencius and Early Chinese Thought*. Stanford, CA: Stanford University Press.

Ladd, John. 1957. *The Structure of a Moral Code: A Philosophical Analysis of Ethical Discourse Applied to the Ethics of the Navaho Indians*. Cambridge, MA: Harvard University Press.

Lakatos, Imre. 1978. *Philosophical Papers*. Vol. 1, *The Methodology of Scientific Research Programmes*. Edited by John Worrall and Gregory Currie. Cambridge: Cambridge University Press.

Lakoff, George. 1987. *Women, Fire, and Dangerous Things: What Categories Reveal About the Mind*. Chicago: University of Chicago Press.

Lama, Dalai, XIV and Howard Cutler. 1998. *The Art of Happiness*. New York: Riverhead Books.

Lama, Dalai, XIV. 1999. *Healing Anger: The Power of Patience from a Buddhist Perspective*. Translated by Thupten Jinpa. Ithaca, NY: Snow Lion.

Lancy, David F. 2015. *The Anthropology of Childhood: Cherubs, Chattel, Changelings*. 2nd ed. Cambridge: Cambridge University Press, 2015.

Lear, Jonathan. 2008. *Radical Hope: Ethics in the Face of Cultural Devastation*. Cambridge, MA: Harvard University Press.

LeDoux, Joseph E. 1996. *The Emotional Brain: The Mysterious Underpinnings of Emotional Life*. New York: Simon & Schuster.

León Portilla, Miguel. 1966. *The Broken Spears: The Aztec Account of the Conquest of Mexico*. Translated by Lysander Kemp. Boston, MA: Beacon Press.

Levy, Robert I. 1973. *Tahitians: Mind and Experience in the Society Islands*. Chicago: University of Chicago Press.

Lewontin, R. C. 1974. "The Analysis of Variance and the Analysis of Causes." *International Journal of Epidemiology* 35 (3): 520–25.

Lukács, György. (1923) 1971. *History and Class Consciousness: Studies in Marxist Dialectics*. Cambridge, MA: MIT Press.

Lutz, Catherine. 1988. *Unnatural Emotions: Everyday Sentiments on a Micronesian Atoll and Their Challenge to Western Theory*. Chicago: University of Chicago Press.

MacIntyre, Alasdair C. 1953. *Marxism: An Interpretation*. London: SCM Press.

MacIntyre, Alasdair C. 1966. *A Short History of Ethics*. Fields of Philosophy. New York: Macmillan.

MacIntyre, Alasdair C. 1981. *After Virtue: A Study in Moral Theory*. Notre Dame, IN: University of Notre Dame Press.

MacIntyre, Alasdair C. 1984a. *After Virtue: A Study in Moral Theory*. 2nd ed. Notre Dame, IN: University of Notre Dame Press.

MacIntyre, Alasdair C. 1984b. *Is Patriotism a Virtue?* Lindley Lecture. [Lawrence]: Department of Philosophy, University of Kansas.

MacIntyre, Alasdair C. 1988. *Whose Justice? Which Rationality?* Notre Dame, IN: University of Notre Dame Press.

MacIntyre, Alasdair C. 1990. *Three Rival Versions of Moral Enquiry: Encyclopedia, Genealogy, and Tradition; Being Gifford Lectures Delivered in the University of Edinburgh in 1988*. Notre Dame, IN: University of Notre Dame Press.

MacIntyre, Alasdair C. 2013. "On Having Survived the Academic Moral Philosophy of the Twentieth Century." In *What Happened in and to Moral Philosophy in the Twentieth Century?: Philosophical Essays in Honor of Alasdair MacIntyre*, edited by Fran O'Rourke, 17–34. Notre Dame, IN: University of Notre Dame Press.

Maffie, James. 2012. "In *Huehue Tlamanitiliztli* and *la Verdad*: Nahua and European Philosophies in Fray Bernardino de Sahagun's *Coolquios y doctrina cristiana*." *Inter-American Journal of Philosophy* 3 (1): 1–33.

Maffie, James. 2014. *Aztec Philosophy: Understanding a World in Motion*. Boulder: University of Colorado Press.

Marcuse, Herbert. 1955. *Eros and Civilization: A Philosophical Inquiry into Freud*. Humanitas, Beacon Studies in Humanities. Boston, MA: Beacon Press.

Marcuse, Herbert. 1964. *One-Dimensional Man: Studies in the Ideology of Advanced Industrial Society*. Boston, MA: Beacon Press.

Markus, Hazel Rose, and Shinobu Kitayama. 1991. "Culture and the Self: Implications for Cognition, Emotion, and Motivation." *Psychological Review* 98 (2): 224–53.

Markus, Hazel Rose, and Shinobu Kitayama. 2010. "Cultures and Selves: A Cycle of Mutual Constitution." *Perspectives on Psychological Science* 5 (4): 420–30.

Marx, Karl. 1964. *Economic and Philosophic Manuscripts of 1844*. New York: International Publishers.

Mason, Michelle. 2003. "Contempt as a Moral Attitude." *Ethics* 113 (2): 234–72.

Mauss, Marcel. (1938) 1985. "A Category of the Human Mind: The Notion of Person; the Notion of Self," translated by W. D. Hall. In *The Category of the Person*, edited by Michael Carrithers, Steven Collins, and Steven Lukes, 1–25. Cambridge: Cambridge University Press.

McRae, Emily. 2015. "Metabolizing Anger: A Tantric Buddhist Solution to the Problem of Moral Anger." *Philosophy East and West* 65 (2): 466–84.

Mead, Margaret. 1935. *Sex and Temperament in Three Primitive Societies*. New York: W. Morrow.

Mikhail, John M. 2011. *Elements of Moral Cognition: Rawls' Linguistic Analogy and the Cognitive Science of Moral and Legal Judgment*. New York: Cambridge University Press.

Mikkelson, Dawn, dir. 2014. *Risking Light*. International episodic documentary web series, http://riskinglight.com/.

Mill, John Stuart, and John M. Robson. 1963. *Collected Works*. Toronto: University of Toronto Press.

Miller, Christian B. 2014. *Character and Moral Psychology*. Oxford: Oxford University Press.

Miller, Joan G. 1984. "Culture and the Development of Everyday Social Explanation." *Journal of Personality and Social Psychology* 46 (5): 961–78.

Mischel, Walter. 1968. *Personality and Assessment*. Wiley Series in Psychology. New York: Wiley.

Moody-Adams, Michele M. 1997. *Fieldwork in Familiar Places: Morality, Culture, and Philosophy*. Cambridge, MA: Harvard University Press.

Mozi. 2003. *Mozi: Basic Writings*. Translated by Burton Watson. Translations from the Asian Classics. New York: Columbia University Press.

Muller, A. Charles, trans. 2015. *Korea's Great Buddhist-Confucian Debate: The Treatises of Chong Tojon (Sambong) and Hamho Tuktong (Kihwa)*. Edited by Robert Buswell. Korean Classics Library: Philosophy and Religion. Honolulu: University of Hawai'i Press.

Murdoch, Iris. 1967. *The Sovereignty of Good over Other Concepts*. Leslie Stephen Lectures. London: Cambridge University Press.

Murphy, Jeffrie G., and Jean Hampton. 1988. *Forgiveness and Mercy*. Cambridge Studies in Philosophy and Law. Cambridge: Cambridge University Press.

Nahmias, Eddy, Stephen G. Morris, Thomas Nadelhoffer, and Jason Turner. 2006. "Is Incompatibilism Intuitive?" *Philosophy and Phenomenological Research* 73 (1): 28–53.

Ñāṇamoli, Bhikkhu, and Bhikkhu Bodhi, trans. 1995. *The Middle Length Discourses of the Buddha: A New Translation of the "Majjhima Nikāya."* Teachings of the Buddha. Somerville, MA: Wisdom Publications.

Narváez, Darcia, Jaak Panksepp, Allan N. Schore, and Tracy R. Gleason, eds. 2012. *Evolution, Early Experience and Human Development: From Research to Practice and Policy*. Oxford: Oxford University Press.

Nietzsche, Friedrich Wilhelm. (1881) 1982. *Daybreak: Thoughts on the Prejudices of Morality*. Translated by R. J. Hollingdale. With an introduction by Michael Tanner. Texts in German Philosophy. Cambridge: Cambridge University Press.

Nietzsche, Friedrich Wilhelm. 2005. *The Anti-Christ, Ecce Homo, Twilight of the Idols, and Other Writings*. Edited by Aaron Ridley and Judith Norman. Translated by Judith Norman. Cambridge Texts in the History of Philosophy. Cambridge: Cambridge University Press.

Nisbett, Richard. 2004. *The Geography of Thought: How Asians and Westerners Think Differently . . . and Why*. New York: Free Press.

Noddings, Nel. 1984. *Caring: A Feminist Approach to Ethics and Moral Education*. Berkeley: University of California Press.

Noë, Alva. 2004. *Action in Perception*. Cambridge, MA: MIT Press.

Norenzayan, Ara. 2013. *Big Gods: How Religion Transformed Cooperation and Conflict*. Princeton, NJ: Princeton University Press.

Nussbaum, Martha Craven. 1988. "Non-Relative Virtues: An Aristotelian Approach." *Midwest Studies in Philosophy* 13 (1): 32–53.

Nussbaum, Martha Craven. 1994. *The Therapy of Desire: Theory and Practice in Hellenistic Ethics*. Martin Classical Lectures. Princeton, NJ: Princeton University Press.

Nussbaum, Martha Craven. 1995. *Poetic Justice: The Literary Imagination and Public Life*. Boston, MA: Beacon Press.

Nussbaum, Martha Craven. 2012. *The New Religious Intolerance: Overcoming the Politics of Fear in an Anxious Age*. Cambridge, MA: Belknap Press of Harvard University Press.

Nussbaum, Martha Craven. 2015. "Transitional Anger." *Journal of the American Philosophical Association* 1 (1): 41–56.

Nussbaum, Martha Craven. 2016. *Anger and Forgiveness: Resentment, Generosity, Justice*. New York: Oxford University Press.

Obeyesekere, Gananath. 2002. *Imagining Karma: Ethical Transformation in Amerindian, Buddhist, and Greek Rebirth*. Comparative Studies in Religion and Society. Berkeley: University of California Press.

Okin, Susan Moller. 1989. *Justice, Gender, and the Family*. New York: Basic Books.

Parfit, Derek. 1984. *Reasons and Persons*. Oxford: Clarendon Press.

Park, Peter K. J. 2013. *Africa, Asia, and the History of Philosophy: Racism in the Formation of the Philosophical Canon, 1780–1830*. SUNY Series on Philosophy and Race. Albany: State University of New York Press.

Perkins, Franklin. 2004. *Leibniz and China: A Commerce of Light*. Cambridge: Cambridge University Press.

Perry, John. 2008. *Personal Identity*. 2nd ed. Berkeley: University of California Press.

Peterson, Christopher, and Martin E. P. Seligman. 2004. *Character Strengths and Virtues: A Handbook and Classification*. Washington, DC: American Psychological Association; New York: Oxford University Press.

Piaget, Jean. 1932. *The Moral Judgment of the Child*. Translated by Marjorie Gabain. International Library of Psychology, Philosophy, and Scientific Method. London: K. Paul, Trench, Trubner.

Piketty, Thomas. 2014. *Capital in the Twenty-First Century*. Translated by Arthur Goldhammer. Cambridge, MA: Belknap Press of Harvard University Press.

Plato. 1992. *Republic*. Translated by G. M. A. Grube. Revised by C. D. C. Reeve. Indianapolis, IN: Hackett.

Potter, Nancy Nyquist, ed. 2006. *Trauma, Truth and Reconciliation: Healing Damaged Relationships*. International Perspectives in Philosophy and Psychiatry. Oxford: Oxford University Press.

Povinelli, Elizabeth A. 2001. "Radical Worlds: The Anthropology of Incommensurability and Inconceivability." *Annual Review of Anthropology* 30: 319–34.

Prebish, Charles. 2008. "Cooking the Buddhist Books: The Implications of the New Dating of the Buddha for the History of Early Indian Buddhism." *Journal of Buddhist Ethics* 15: 1–21.

Preston, Stephanie D., and Frans B. M. de Waal. 2002. "Empathy: Its Ultimate and Proximate Bases." *Behavioral and Brain Sciences* 25: 1–72.

Priest, Graham. 2014. *One: On Being an Investigation into the Unity of Reality and of Its Parts, Including the Singular Object Which Is Nothingness*. Oxford: Oxford University Press.

Prinz, Jesse. 2011. "Against Empathy." *Spindel Supplement: Empathy and Ethics*. Special issue, *Southern Journal of Philosophy* 49: 214–33.

Prompta, Somparn 2008. *An Essay Concerning Buddhist Ethics*. Bangkok: Chulalongkorn University Press.

Putnam, Hilary. 1983. "Why Reason Can't Be Naturalized." In *Philosophical Papers*, vol. 3, *Reason and Realism*, 229–47. Cambridge: Cambridge University Press.

Quine, W. V. O. 1969. "Epistemology Naturalized." In *Ontological Relativity, and Other Essays*, 69–90. John Dewey Essays in Philosophy. New York: Columbia University Press.

Railton, Peter. 2014. "The Affective Dog and Its Rational Tale." *Ethics* 124: 813–59.

Rawls, John. 1971. *A Theory of Justice*. Cambridge, MA: Belknap Press of Harvard University Press.

Rawls, John. 1993. *Political Liberalism*. John Dewey Essays in Philosophy. New York: Columbia University Press.

Rawls, John. 1999. *Collected Papers*. Edited by Samuel Freeman. Cambridge, MA: Harvard University Press.

Richerson, Peter J., and Robert Boyd. 2005. *Not by Genes Alone: How Culture Transformed Human Evolution*. Chicago: University of Chicago Press.

Ricoeur, Paul. 1984. *Time and Narrative*. 3 vols. Chicago: University of Chicago Press.

Robbins, Joel. 2004. *Becoming Sinners: Christianity and Moral Torment in a Papua New Guinea Society*. Ethnographic Studies in Subjectivity. Berkeley: University of California Press.

Rorty, Richard. 1979. *Philosophy and the Mirror of Nature*. Princeton, NJ: Princeton University Press.

Rorty, Richard. 1989. *Contingency, Irony, and Solidarity*. Cambridge: Cambridge University Press.

Rorty, Richard. 1991. "On Ethnocentrism: A Reply to Clifford Geertz." In *Philosophical Papers*, vol. 1, *Objectivity, Relativism, and Truth*, 203–10. Cambridge: Cambridge University Press.

Rosenberg, Alexander. 2011. *The Atheist's Guide to Reality: Enjoying Life Without Illusions*. New York: W. W. Norton.

Ruddick, Sara. 1989. *Maternal Thinking: Toward a Politics of Peace*. Boston, MA: Beacon Press.

Sandel, Michael J. 1982. *Liberalism and the Limits of Justice*. Cambridge: Cambridge University Press.

Śāntideva. 1997. *The Way of the Bodhisattva: A Translation of the Bodhicharyāvatāra*. Translated by Padmakara Translation Group. Shambhala Dragon Editions. Boston: Shambhala. Distributed in the U.S. by Random House.

Sarkissian, Hagop. 2010. "Minor Tweaks, Major Payoffs: The Problems and Promise of Situationism in Moral Philosophy." *Philosopher's Imprint* 10 (9): 1–15.

Sartre, Jean-Paul. 2007. *Existentialism Is a Humanism = (L'Existentialisme est un humanisme); Including a Commentary on "The Stranger" (Explication de "L'Étranger")*. Translated by Carol Macomber; introduction by Annie Cohen-Solal; notes and preface by Elkaïm-Sartre; edited by John Kulka. New Haven, CT: Yale University Press.

Scanlon, Thomas. 1998. *What We Owe to Each Other*. Cambridge, MA: Belknap Press of Harvard University Press.

Scheffler, Samuel. 2013. *Death and the Afterlife*. Edited by Niko Kolodny. Berkeley Tanner Lectures. Oxford: Oxford University Press.

Schwartz, Shalom H., and Wolfgang Bilsky. 1990. "Toward a Theory of the Universal Content and Structure of Human Values with Confirmatory Factor Analysis." *Journal of Research in Personality* 38: 230–55.

Scott, James C. 2009. *The Art of Not Being Governed: An Anarchist History of Upland Southeast Asia*. Yale Agrarian Studies Series. New Haven, CT: Yale University Press.

Sellars, Wilfrid. 1963. "Philosophy and the Scientific Image of Man." In *Science, Perception, and Reality*, 35–78. New York: Humanities Press.

Seneca, Lucius Annaeus. 2010. *Anger, Mercy, Revenge*. Translated by Robert A. Kaster and Martha Craven Nussbaum. The Complete Works of Lucius Annaeus Seneca. Chicago: University of Chicago Press.

Sherman, Nancy. 2005. *Stoic Warriors: The Ancient Philosophy Behind the Military Mind*. New York: Oxford University Press.

Shweder, Richard A. 1990. "Cultural Psychology—What Is It?" In *Cultural Psychology*, edited by James W. Stigler, Richard A. Shweder, and Gilbert Herdt, 1–43. Cambridge: Cambridge University Press.

Shweder, Richard A. 1991. *Thinking Through Cultures: Expeditions in Cultural Psychology.* Cambridge, MA: Harvard University Press.

Shweder, Richard A., and Edmund J. Bourne. 1982. "Does the Concept of the Person Vary Cross-Culturally?" In *Culture Theory: Essays on Mind, Self, and Emotion,* edited by Richard A. Shweder and Robert Alan LeVine, 158–99. Cambridge: Cambridge University Press.

Shweder, Richard A., and Jonathan Haidt. 1993. "The Future of Moral Psychology: Truth, Intuition and the Pluralist Way." *Psychological Science* 4 (6): 360–65.

Shweder, Richard A., and Robert Alan LeVine, eds. 1984. *Culture Theory: Essays on Mind, Self, and Emotion.* Cambridge: Cambridge University Press.

Shweder, Richard A., Nancy C. Much, Manamohan Mahapatra, and Lawrence Park. 1997. "The 'Big Three' of Morality (Autonomy, Community, Divinity), and the 'Big Three' Explanations of Suffering." In *Morality and Health,* edited by Allan M. Brandt and Paul Rozin, 119–69. New York: Routledge.

Siderits, Mark. 2003. *Personal Identity and Buddhist Philosophy: Empty Persons.* Ashgate World Philosophies Series. Aldershot: Ashgate.

Sims, May. 2007. *Remastering Morals with Aristotle and Confucius.* Cambridge: Cambridge University Press.

Singer, Peter. 2011. *The Expanding Circle: Ethics, Evolution, and Moral Progress.* Princeton, NJ: Princeton University Press.

Singer, Tania, Ben Seymour, John P. O'Doherty, Klaas E. Stephan, Raymond J. Dolan, and Chris D. Frith. 2006. "Empathic Neural Responses Are Modulated by the Perceived Fairness of Others." *Nature* 439 (7075): 466–69.

Sinnott-Armstrong, Walter. 2008-2014. *Moral Psychology.* 4 vols. Cambridge, MA: MIT Press.

Skerry, A. E., M. Sheskin, and L. R. Santos. 2011. "Capuchin Monkeys Are Not Prosocial in an Instrumental Helping Task." *Animal Cognition* 14 (5): 647–54.

Skyrms, Brian. 2004. *The Stag Hunt and the Evolution of Social Structure.* Cambridge: Cambridge University Press.

Slingerland, Edward. 2011. "The Situationist Critique and Early Confucian Virtue Ethics." *Ethics* 121 (2): 390–419.

Slingerland, Edward. 2014. *Trying Not to Try: The Ancient Chinese Art and Modern Science of Spontaneity.* Victoria, BC: Crown.

Slingerland, Edward. 2015. Review of *Moral Sprouts and Natural Teleologies: 21st Century Moral Psychology Meets Classical Chinese Philosophy,* by Owen Flanagan. *Notre Dame Philosophical Reviews,* August 31.

Slote, Michael. 2007. *The Ethics of Care and Empathy.* London: Routledge.

Sober, Elliott. 1984. *The Nature of Selection.* Cambridge, MA: MIT Press.

Sober, Elliott, and David Sloan Wilson. 1998. *Unto Others: The Evolution and Psychology of Unselfish Behavior.* Cambridge, MA: Harvard University Press.

Sommers, Tamler. 2012. *Relative Justice: Cultural Diversity, Free Will, and Moral Responsibility.* Princeton, NJ: Princeton University Press.

Souief, Ahdat. 1999. *The Map of Love.* New York: Anchor Books.

Sperber, Dan. 1994. "The Modularity of Thought and the Epidemiology of Representations." In *Mapping the Mind: Domain Specificity in Cognition and Culture,* edited by Laurence A. Hirschfeld and Susan A. Gelman, 39–67. New York: Cambridge University Press.

Sperber, Dan. 2005. "Modularity and Relevance: How Can a Massively Modular Mind Be Flexible and Context-Sensitive?" In *The Innate Mind: Structure and Content*, edited by Peter Carruthers, Stephen Laurence, and Stephen P. Stich, 53–68. New York: Oxford University Press.

Srinivasan, Amia. 2014. "In Defence of Anger." http://www.bbc.co.uk/programmes/b04fc70p.

Staley, Gregory Allan. 2010. *Seneca and the Idea of Tragedy*. Oxford: Oxford University Press.

Strawson, Galen. 1998. "Luck Swallows Everything." *Times Literary Supplement*, June 26.

Strawson, Galen. 2004. "Against Narrativity." *Ratio*, n.s., 17 (4): 428–52.

Strawson, Galen. 2008. *Real Materialism and Other Essays*. Oxford: Clarendon Press; New York: Oxford University Press.

Strawson, Galen. 2009. *Selves: An Essay in Revisionary Metaphysics*. Oxford: Clarendon Press; Oxford: Oxford University Press.

Strawson, Galen. (1986) 2010. *Freedom and Belief*. Rev. ed. Oxford: Oxford University Press.

Strawson, Galen. 2011. *Locke on Personal Identity: Consciousness and Concernment*. Princeton Monographs in Philosophy. Princeton, NJ: Princeton University Press.

Strawson, Galen. 2014. "Freedom and the Self: Feeling and Belief." In *Oxford Studies in Agency and Responsibility*, vol. 2, *'Freedom and Resentment' at 50*, edited by David Shoemaker and Neal A. Tognazzini, 4–11. Oxford: Oxford University Press.

Strawson, Peter F. 1962. "Freedom and Resentment." *Proceedings of the British Academy* 48: 1–25.

Strominger, Nina. 2014. "Disgust Talked About." *Philosophy Compass*: 478–93.

Suhler, Christopher L., and Patricia Smith Churchland. 2011. "Can Innate, Modular 'Foundations' Explain Morality? Challenges for Haidt's Moral Foundations Theory." *Journal of Cognitive Neural Science* 23 (9): 2103–16.

Tan, Jingzhi, and Brian Hare. 2013. "Bonobos Share with Strangers." *PloS ONE* 8 (1): e51922.

Taylor, Charles. 1985. *Philosophical Papers*. Vol. 1, *Human Agency and Language*. Vol. 2, *Philosophy and the Human Sciences*. Cambridge: Cambridge University Press.

Taylor, Charles. 1989. *Sources of the Self: The Making of the Modern Identity*. Cambridge, MA: Harvard University Press.

Taylor, Charles. 1998. "Conditions of an Unforced Consensus on Human Rights." In *Dilemmas and Connections: Selected Essays*, 105–23. Cambridge MA: Harvard University Press.

Taylor, Charles. 2007. *A Secular Age*. Cambridge, MA: Belknap Press of Harvard University Press.

Taylor, Shelley E. 1989. *Positive Illusions: Creative Self-Deception and the Healthy Mind*. New York: Basic Books.

Taylor, Shelley E., and Jonathon D. Brown. 1994. "Positive Illusions and Well-Being Revisited: Separating Fact from Fiction." *Psychology Bulletin* 116 (1): 21–27.

Tessman, Lisa. 2005. *Burdened Virtues: Virtue Ethics for Liberatory Struggles*. Studies in Feminist Philosophy. New York: Oxford University Press.

Tien, David W. 2012. "Oneness and Self-Centeredness in the Moral Psychology of Wang Yangming." *Journal of Religious Ethics* 40 (1): 52–71.

Tomasello, Michael. 1999. *The Cultural Origins of Human Cognition*. Cambridge, MA: Harvard University Press.

Tomasello, Michael. 2009. *Why We Cooperate*. Cambridge, MA: MIT Press.

Tomasello, Michael. 2014. *A Natural History of Human Thinking*. Cambridge, MA: Harvard University Press.

Tooby, John, Leda Cosmides, and H. Clark Barrett. 2005. "Resolving the Debate on Innate Ideas: Learnability Constraints and the Evolved Interpenetration of Motivational and Conceptual Functions." In *The Innate Mind: Structure and Contents*, edited by Peter Carruthers, Stephen Laurence, and Stephen P. Stich, 305–37. New York: Oxford University Press.

Triandis, Harry C., Robert Bontempo, Marcelo J. Villareal, Masaaki Asai, and Nydia Lucca. 1988. "Individualism and Collectivism: Cross-Cultural Perspectives on Self-Ingroup Relationships." *Journal of Personality and Social Psychology* 54 (2): 323–38.

Tsai, Jeanne L. 2007. "Ideal Affect Cultural Causes and Behavioral Consequences." *Perspectives on Psychological Science* 2 (3): 242–59.

Tsai, Jeanne L., Jennifer Y. Louie, Eva E. Chen, and Yukiko Uchida. 2007a. "Learning What Feelings to Desire: Socialization of Ideal Affect Through Children's Storybooks." *Personality and Social Psychology Bulletin* 33 (1): 17–30.

Tsai, Jeanne L., Felicity F. Miao, and Emma Seppala. 2007b. "Good Feelings in Christianity and Buddhism: Religious Differences in Ideal Affect." *Personality and Social Psychology Bulletin* 33 (3): 409–21.

Tsai, Jeanne L., Felicity F. Miao, Emma Seppala, Helene H. Fung, and Dannii Y. Yeung. 2007c. "Influence and Adjustment Goals: Sources of Cultural Differences in Ideal Affect." *Journal of Personality and Social Psychology* 92 (6): 1102–17.

Tsai, Jeanne L., and Bokyung K. Park. 2014. "The Cultural Shaping of Happiness: The Role of Ideal Affect." In *Positive Emotion: Integrating the Light Sides and Dark Sides*, edited by Judith Tedlie Moskowitz and June Gruber, 345–62. New York: Oxford University Press.

Turiel, Elliot. 1983. *The Development of Social Knowledge: Morality and Convention*. Cambridge Studies in Social and Emotional Development. Cambridge: Cambridge University Press.

Van Le, Quan, Lynne A. Isbell, Jumpei Matsumoto, Minh Nguyen, Etsuro Hori, Rafael S. Maior, Carlos Tomaz, Anh Hai Tran, Taketoshi Ono, and Hisao Nishijo. 2013. "Pulvinar Neurons Reveal Neurobiological Evidence of Past Selection for Rapid Detection of Snakes." *PNAS (Proceedings of the National Academy of Sciences) of the United States of America* 110 (47): 19000–19005.

Van Norden, Bryan W. 2007. *Virtue Ethics and Consequentialism in Chinese Philosophy*. New York: Cambridge University Press.

Van Norden, Bryan W. 2008. *Mengzi: With Selections from Traditional Commentaries*. Indianapolis, IN: Hackett.

Viveiros de Castro, Eduardo. 2014. *Cannibal Metaphysics: For a Post-Stuctural Anthropology*. Translated and edited by Peter Skafish. Minneapolis, MN: Univocal.

Walker, Margaret Urban. 2006. *Moral Repair: Reconstructing Moral Relations After Wrongdoing*. Cambridge: Cambridge University Press.

Wallace, R. Jay. 1994. *Responsibility and the Moral Sentiments*. Cambridge, MA: Harvard University Press.

Walzer, Michael. 1983. *Spheres of Justice: A Defense of Pluralism and Equality*. New York: Basic Books.

Wambui, Betty. 2013. "Conversations: Women, Children, Goats, Land." Translated by Evan Mwangi. In *Listening to Ourselves: A Multilingual Anthology of African Philosophy*, edited by Chike Jeffers, 91–123. SUNY Series in Living Indigenous Philosophies. Albany: State University of New York Press.

Warenken, Felix, and Michale Tomasello. 2006. "Altruistic Helping in Human Infants and Young Chimpanzees." *Science* 311 (5765): 1301–3.

Weber, Max. 1930. *The Protestant Ethic and the Spirit of Capitalism*. New York: Scribner.

Whitehead, Alfred North. 1928. *Science and the Modern World: Lowell Lectures, 1925*. Cambridge: University Press.

Whitehead, Hal, and Luke Rendell. 2014. *The Cultural Lives of Whales and Dolphins*. Chicago: University of Chicago Press.

Whiting, Beatrice Blyth, Carolyn P. Edwards, and others. 1988. *Children of Different Worlds: The Formation of Social Behavior*. Cambridge, MA: Harvard University Press.

Whyte, William Hollingsworth. 1956. *The Organization Man*. New York: Simon & Schuster.

Wierzbicka, Anna. 1999. *Emotions Across Languages and Cultures: Diversity and Universals*. Studies in Emotion and Social Interaction, 2nd series. Cambridge: Cambridge University Press.

Wierzbicka, Anna. 2014. *Imprisoned in English: The Hazards of English as a Default Language*. Oxford: Oxford University Press.

Wikan, Unni. 1982. *Behind the Veil in Arabia: Women in Oman*. Baltimore: Johns Hopkins University Press.

Wilkerson, Isabel. 2010. *The Warmth of Other Suns: The Epic Story of America's Great Migration*. New York: Random House.

Williams, Bernard. 1981. "Moral Luck." In *Moral Luck*, 20–39. Cambridge: Cambridge University Press.

Williams, Bernard. 1985. *Ethics and the Limits of Philosophy*. Cambridge, MA: Harvard University Press.

Williams, Bernard. 1991. *Shame and Necessity*. Berkeley: University of California Press.

Wilson, Edward O. 1975. *Sociobiology: The New Synthesis*. Cambridge, MA: Belknap Press of Harvard University Press.

Wilson, Edward O. 1978. *On Human Nature*. Cambridge, MA: Harvard University Press.

Winch, Peter. 1958. *The Idea of a Social Science and Its Relation to Philosophy*. Studies in Philosophical Psychology. London: Routledge & Kegan Paul; Atlantic Highlands, NJ: Humanities Press.

Winch, Peter. 1964. "Understanding a Primitive Society." *American Philosophical Quarterly* 1 (4): 307–24.

Wong, David B. 1984. *Moral Relativity*. Berkeley: University of California Press.

Wong, David B. 1989. "Universalism Versus Love with Distinctions: An Ancient Debate Revived." *Journal of Chinese Philosophy* 16 (3–4): 251–72.

Wong, David B. 2006a. "The Meaning of Detachment in Daoism, Buddhism, and Stoicism." *Dao: A Journal of Comparative Philosophy* 5 (2): 207–19.

Wong, David B. 2006b. *Natural Moralities: A Defense of Pluralistic Relativism*. Princeton, NJ: Princeton University Press.

Wong, David B. 2015. "Early Confucian Philosophy and the Development of Compassion." *Dao: A Journal of Comparative Philosophy* 14 (2): 157–94.

X, Malcolm, with the assistance of Alex Haley. 1965. *The Autobiography of Malcolm X.* New York: Grove Press.

Xunzi. 2014. *Xunzi: The Complete Text.* Translated by Eric L. Hutton. Princeton, NJ: Princeton University Press.

Zhuangzi. 2009. *Zhuangzi: The Essential Writings with Selections from Traditional Commentaries.* Translated by Brook Ziporyn. Indianapolis, IN: Hackett.

INDEX